# Extreme Reactions

Focusing on the rising support for the populist right in Eastern Europe, this book examines how anger and resentment toward minorities is being utilized in politics. Bustikova details the process by which the acquisition of political power and demand for rights by ascendant minority groups precipitates a backlash of mobilization from the radical right. However, this book also argues that prejudice against minorities is not a sentiment exclusive to right-wing voters and is not the root cause of increasing support for the radical right. Rather, this study reveals, variation in how minorities are accommodated by the government explains the electoral successes and failures of radical right parties. By examining their capitalization on these feelings of discontent toward politically assertive minorities and with the governmental policies that yield to their demands, Bustikova exposes volatile, Zeitgeist-dependent conditions under which once fringe right-wing parties have risen to prominent but precarious positions of power.

LENKA BUSTIKOVA is Associate Professor of Political Science at Arizona State University. She serves as an editor of *East European Politics*. She received the 2015 Best Article Prize, awarded by the American Political Science Association's European Politics and Society Section, and the 2017 Best Paper Prize, awarded by the American Political Science Association's Comparative Democratization Section.

# Extreme Reactions

## Radical Right Mobilization in Eastern Europe

LENKA BUSTIKOVA
*Arizona State University*

CAMBRIDGE
UNIVERSITY PRESS

# CAMBRIDGE
## UNIVERSITY PRESS

University Printing House, Cambridge CB2 8BS, United Kingdom

One Liberty Plaza, 20th Floor, New York, NY 10006, USA

477 Williamstown Road, Port Melbourne, VIC 3207, Australia

314–321, 3rd Floor, Plot 3, Splendor Forum, Jasola District Centre, New Delhi – 110025, India

79 Anson Road, #06–04/06, Singapore 079906

Cambridge University Press is part of the University of Cambridge.

It furthers the University's mission by disseminating knowledge in the pursuit of education, learning, and research at the highest international levels of excellence.

www.cambridge.org
Information on this title: www.cambridge.org/9781108482653
DOI: 10.1017/9781108697248

© Lenka Bustikova 2020

First published 2020

A catalogue record for this publication is available from the British Library.

ISBN 978-1-108-48265-3 Hardback

Cambridge University Press has no responsibility for the persistence or accuracy of URLs for external or third-party internet websites referred to in this publication and does not guarantee that any content on such websites is, or will remain, accurate or appropriate.

*For David and Miriam*

# Contents

| | | |
|---|---|---|
| List of Figures | *page* ix | |
| List of Tables | xi | |
| Acknowledgments | xiii | |
| | | |
| 1 Introduction | 1 | |
| 1.1 The Argument | 5 | |
| 1.2 Democratization and Radical Right Mobilization | 8 | |
| 1.3 Outline of the Book | 14 | |
| | | |
| 2 A Theory of Radical Right Mobilization | 18 | |
| 2.1 Rival Explanations | 22 | |
| 2.1.1 Identity and Economy | 25 | |
| 2.1.2 Mainstream Parties | 33 | |
| 2.2 Sovereignty of the Dominant Group | 35 | |
| 2.2.1 Treacherous Mainstream Parties | 37 | |
| 2.2.2 Group Hierarchy and Demoted Groups | 43 | |
| 2.3 Minority Accommodation and Status Quo Shifts | 45 | |
| 2.4 Groups and Status Threats | 53 | |
| 2.5 Summary | 67 | |
| | | |
| 3 Radical Right Parties in Cross-National Perspective | 68 | |
| 3.1 Defining Radical Right Parties | 71 | |
| 3.2 Observable Implications of the Theory | 83 | |
| 3.3 Data Description and Estimation Strategy | 84 | |
| 3.4 The Statistical Model | 86 | |
| 3.5 Discussion of Empirical Results | 88 | |
| 3.6 Conclusion | 107 | |
| | | |
| 4 Mobilization against Hungarians in Slovakia | 109 | |
| 4.1 Hypotheses | 111 | |
| 4.2 Accommodation of the Hungarian Minority | 113 | |
| 4.3 Empirical Analysis and Data | 119 | |
| 4.3.1 Policy Hostility | 121 | |
| 4.3.2 Group Hostility | 128 | |
| 4.3.3 Economic and Sovereignty Threats | 130 | |

4.4 Radical Right Voters in Slovakia                      143
4.5 Identity Priming Experiment                          148
4.6 New Issues                                           153
4.7 Conclusion                                           157

5  Mobilization against Russians in Ukraine             159
   5.1 Accommodation of the Russian Minority            162
   5.2 Empirical Analysis                               175
       5.2.1 *Data Description*                         177
       5.2.2 *Policy Hostility*                         182
       5.2.3 *Group Hostility*                          185
       5.2.4 *Economic Threats*                         195
   5.3 Radical Right Voters in Ukraine                  197
   5.4 Conclusion                                       209

6  Conclusion                                           211

*Appendix*                                              222
*Bibliography*                                          255
*Index*                                                 293

# Figures

1.1 Votes for radical right parties per electoral cycle in
     post-communist democracies                                  *page* 4
2.1 Proportion of respondents from the dominant
     nationality feeling "very proud" to be the nationality
     specific to their country, 1990–2014                              26
2.2 Relationship between prejudice and electoral support
     for radical right parties                                         28
3.1 Violin plots of marginal effects based on censored
     regressions                                                       93
4.1 Spending on minority cultures in Slovakia,
     1995–2013                                                        116
4.2 Policy hostility: opposition to government transfers to
     the Hungarian minority in Slovakia                               127
4.3 Policy hostility: opposition to government transfers to
     the Roma minority in Slovakia                                    128
4.4 Group hostility: prejudice toward minorities by parties
     in Slovakia                                                      129
4.5 Economic threats: fear of worsening economic
     conditions in Slovakia                                           134
4.6 Economic threats by parties: fear of worsening
     personal economic conditions coupled with ethnicity in
     Slovakia                                                         136
4.7 Collective threats: fear of loss of sovereignty in
     Slovakia                                                         141
4.8 Predicted probability of voting for the radical right
     party in Slovakia                                                148
4.9 Identity priming experiment: government spending on
     Slovaks                                                          150

4.10 Identity priming experiment: government spending
     on Hungarians in Slovakia                                    151
5.1  Attitudes toward the official status of the Russian
     language in Ukraine, 1996–2014                               163
5.2  What form of coexistence should exist in the Ukraine
     for the Ukrainian and Russian languages?                    166
5.3  Policy hostility: support for government spending on
     Russians by Svoboda's voters, sympathizers and
     opponents                                                    184
5.4  Policy hostility by parties in Ukraine                       186
5.5  Attitudes toward Bandera and Stalin legacy by parties
     (May 2016)                                                   188
5.6  Number of Bandera monuments erected per year
     (1991–2013)                                                  189
5.7  Group hostility: prejudice toward Russians and Jews
     by parties in Ukraine                                        191
5.8  Group hostility: prejudice toward Russians by party
     blocs in Ukraine                                            193
5.9  Group hostility: prejudice toward Russians and Jews
     by parties in May 2016                                       194
5.10 Economic threat perception by parties in
     Ukraine                                                      196
5.11 Predicted probability of voting for the radical right
     party in Ukraine                                            207

# Tables

2.1 Ethnic structure in the post-communist world     *page* 61
2.2 Expectations of radical right party success based on the
    size of the ethnic minority group     64
3.1 Description of radical right and ethno-liberal
    parties     73
3.2 Combined vote shares of radical right parties since the
    founding elections     80
3.3 The electoral success of radical right parties in $t$ by
    a "coalition with one of the bilateral opposites" in
    $t - 1$     89
3.4 The electoral success of radical right parties in $t$ by
    coalition type in $t - 1$     89
3.5 Determinants of electoral support for radical right
    parties     90
3.6 Determinants of electoral support for radical right
    parties with institutional control variables     95
3.7 Determinants of electoral support for radical right
    parties: ideology     99
4.1 Expected change in a position on transfers that benefit
    groups after a nationality prime in Slovakia     112
4.2 Nationalities in Slovakia     117
4.3 Policy hostility by nationality in Slovakia (Spearman
    rank correlations)     122
4.4 The empirical determinants of policy hostility and
    group hostility in Slovakia     123
4.5 Determinants of policy hostility toward Slovaks
    (majority), Hungarians and Roma (minorities)     124
4.6 Group hostility toward Hungarians in Slovakia     131
4.7 Economic threats and sovereignty threats in
    Slovakia     138

4.8   Individual economic threats and collective
       sovereignty threats coupled with ethnicity in Slovakia
       (from Hungarians)                                                   140
4.9   Determinants of party vote in Slovakia                              144
4.10  Views on refugees by political parties in
       Slovakia (2016)                                                     155
5.1   Percentage of schoolchildren in elementary and
       secondary schools in Ukraine by main language of
       instruction                                                         165
5.2   Distribution of respondents who "strongly agreed"
       with the statement that "Russia threatens Ukrainian
       sovereignty" by parties (May 2016)                                  174
5.3   Voters and sympathizers of Svoboda party                            178
5.4   Regional distribution of Svoboda voters and
       sympathizers                                                        180
5.5   Respondents by nationality and language in
       Ukraine                                                             181
5.6   Svoboda sympathizers and opponents by
       nationality                                                         181
5.7   Svoboda sympathizers and opponents by
       language                                                            182
5.8   Determinants of support for Svoboda among voters,
       sympathizers and opponents in Ukraine: policy
       hostility                                                           198
5.9   Determinants of party vote in Ukraine (support for
       Svoboda by parties and party blocs: policy
       hostility)                                                          203

# Acknowledgments

This book has been a long time in the making. It started as my dissertation at Duke University in North Carolina when radical right mobilization in post-communist Eastern Europe was an anemic phenomenon. I recall a conversation with Herbert Kitschelt, as we returned from a conference at New York University organized by Michael Minkenberg, about whether such a fringe topic deserved sustained academic attention. The conversation was stimulated by a comment that Cas Mudde had raised at the conference. The radical right in Eastern Europe, he predicted, would always pale in comparison with Western Europe. Indeed, until today, the average vote share for radical right parties in Eastern Europe is lower than in the West. However, their impact on democratic institutions is arguably much larger, since they operate in under-institutionalized environments with weak norms governing public discourse and party competition. As the project has progressed, it is now abundantly obvious that identity politics is a political force to be reckoned with in *both* Eastern and Western European democracies.

It would not have been possible to write this book without the inspiration, encouragement and nudging from many individuals. John Aldrich, Judith Kelley, Herbert Kitschelt, Milada Vachudova and Jeremy Reiter were indispensable and incredibly helpful members of my dissertation committee at Duke University. As a graduate student, I tested the waters with my argument at various conferences, where Bonnie Meguid, David Art and Anna Grzymała-Busse were instrumental in moving the project forward. I received fantastic comments at my book conference from Anna Grzymała-Busse, Bonnie Meguid and Herbert Kitschelt as well as from colleagues at Arizona State University, especially Carolyn Warner, Michael Hechter, Sarah Shair-Rosenfield, Mark von Hagen and David Siroky. I also presented a portion of the manuscript at a workshop of the Nationalist and ethno-religious dynamics working group at the School of Politics and

Global Studies, where I received additional valuable feedback from
Yoshiko Herrera, Jeffrey Kopstein, William Mishler, Joshua Tucker,
A. Kadir Yildirim, Sean Kates, Magda Hinojosa, Miki Kittilson, Mark
Ramirez and Will H. Moore. Special thanks go to Carolyn Forbes from
the Center for the Study of Religion and Conflict for her kindness and
assistance since I arrived at ASU.

The Czech Institute of Sociology in Prague has graciously served as
my academic home in Europe. I thank Zdenka Mansfeldová, Simona
Pátková, Jindřich Krejčí, Máša Čermáková, Tomáš Kostelecký,
Zdenka Vajdová and Michal Illner for their unrelenting support and
for the opportunity to discuss ideas. Kai Arzheimer kindly provided me
with a temporary home at the University of Mainz in Germany and
facilitated a fellowship at the Zentrum für Interkulturelle Studien. In
Slovakia, I am indebted to Olga Gyarfášová, Marek Rybář and Zuzana
Kusá. In Ukraine, I am truly grateful to Yaroslav Hrytsak, Alina
Polyakova and especially Andreas Umland, and thankful for financial
support from IARO-IREX.

Many people have seen parts of this manuscript over the years and
offered welcome encouragement and feedback. My thanks go to
Nancy Bermeo, Pepper Culpepper, Jennifer Cyr, Rafaela Dancygier,
Sarah de Lange, Venelin Ganev, John Ishiyama, Cynthia Kaplan,
Paulette Kurzer, Amy Liu, Nikolay Marinov, Michael Minkenberg,
Connor O'Dwyer, Andrea Pirro, Grigore Pop-Eleches, Maria Popova,
Bartek Pytlas, Marek Rybář, Viktoriya Sereda, Ostap Sereda, Maria
Snegovaya and Sofia Tipaldou. At Cambridge University Press, John
Haslam unwearyingly answered my stream of questions.

Finally, this book would not have been completed without the love
of those closest to me. Special thanks go to my sisters, my father
Miloslav and my mother, Anna, for everything and especially for time
spent over the years with our daughter, Miriam; to Petra Guasti for her
friendship and frequent conversations about politics; and to my husband
David for inspiration and affection.

# 1 Introduction

[T]he newcomers are bent on improving their position and the established groups are bent on maintaining theirs. The newcomers resent, and often try to rise from, the inferior status attributed to them and the established try to preserve their superior status which the newcomers appear to threaten.

—Elias and Scotson, *The Established and the Outsiders*, 1994 [1965]

What motivates voters to support radical right parties? This book's core argument is that radical right voters are driven by their resentment against aspiring minority groups, and that radical right parties mobilize to curtail minority accommodation.

Consider the story of radical right mobilization against the Russian minority in Latvia, where Russian-speakers constitute more than a quarter of the population. In 2011, the electoral victory of a pro-Russian party, Harmony, emboldened Russian-speaking nationalists to compel the government to redress their grievances. Over a year-long campaign, pro-Russian movements and organizations gathered more than 180,000 signatures, forcing Latvia's authorities to call a referendum on granting official legal status as a state language to Russian. This escalation of minority demands reinvigorated an anemic Latvian far right, which mobilized around opposition to any concessions toward the Russian minority and united the conservative right with the far right to form a counter-coalition. On November 18, 2013, a torch-lit parade commemorating the ninety-fifth anniversary of Latvian independence attracted a large crowd of more than 12,500 people.[1] Organized by the far right and conservative youth movements in Latvia, the procession signaled a discernable surge in ethnic

---

[1] The size of the crowd was remarkable and roughly equivalent to the 2009 anti-government gathering of protesters and violent rioters against the 2008 economic downturn.

polarization, and a clear retort to the increasingly assertive Russian-speaking community. The protest emphasized Latvian independence and the Latvian language. Mobilization against the escalating demands of the Russian-speaking minority translated into a rejection of the language law and serious electoral gains for the Latvian radical right.[2]

Shifts in language rights often precede surges in radical right mobilization against encroachments on the dominant group's control over state affairs. Such radical right parties across Eastern Europe, which capitalize on popular discontent with politically assertive minorities and with public policies that cave to their demands, form the substance of this book. The core question is: Under which conditions do these parties at the fringe of the political spectrum rise to prominence and obtain seats in the parliament?

It is often assumed that economic malaise, institutional volatility and xenophobia lurk behind the rise of a family of parties variously referred to as the "far" right, the "extreme" right and the "radical" right. Economic malaise often leads to withdrawal from politics or to voting for redistributive center-left parties (Dolezalova et al. 2017; Grittersova et al. 2016), but not necessarily to political mobilization against minorities or radical right voting (Stockemer 2017). Institutional volatility, caused by the collapse of major parties, can actually rejuvenate the political system rather than send it on a downward spiral toward the extremes. Xenophobia is pervasive and socially accepted in many places covered in this study; thus, politicizing prejudice is not an innovative political strategy that would bring in new voters or differentiate radical right voters from the voters of many other parties.

This book proposes a new explanation for the rise and fall of radical right parties. In order to account for the electoral volatility of radical right parties, this study emphasizes the bilateral relationship between radical right parties and their "electoral enemies," the politically organized promoters of minority accommodation. It highlights the relational aspect of the dominant group's grievances (Abdelal et al. 2006; Brewer

---

[2] The National Alliance party – which serves as an umbrella for conservatives, economic liberals, the young nationalists from All for Latvia and the more established radical right party, For Fatherland and Freedom/Latvian National Independence Movement – has performed extremely well, both in the 2014 parliamentary elections and in the elections to the European Parliament, winning, respectively, 17 and 14 percent of the popular vote.

and Gardner 1996; Pratto et al. 2006). Groups are organized in social hierarchies (Goffman 1957; Koopmans 2005; Lipset 1960; Merton 1938) and the dominant group enjoys the privilege of governing the polity. Membership in the dominant group is mostly determined by nationality in Eastern Europe, where dominant groups are titular nationalities, and this is often affirmed constitutionally (Ramet 2007). While the concept of the dominant group mostly reflects majority–minority relations along ethnic lines, other attempts to change group-based social hierarchies (e.g., along lines of sexual orientation, religious confession or a historically defined non-native status) can trigger similar resentment among fringe members of the dominant group.[3]

The proposed theory therefore suggests that mobilization of the fringes of the dominant group is by opposition to the advancement of minorities, achieved via state-sanctioned policies and state-approved changes in narratives that relate to majority–minority relations.[4] The backlash that ensues when radical right parties mobilize against minority ascendance represents a reaction to the relative status enhancement of minorities, which engenders symbolic as well as objective humiliation for members of the dominant groups that face the prospect of diminished status. These shifts in the status quo between the dominant group and other groups are situational. This means that they reflect the context in which minority–majority hierarchies are entrenched, and also the erratic nature of the political demands issued by ethnic, religious and social minorities. Radicalized fringes of the dominant group view majority–minority relations as a zero-sum game. A negative shift diminishes their status as the major stakeholders in the state, since they view the ascendance of some groups as inevitably implying the descent of others. As long as minorities and their advocates do not mobilize politically, the radical right is generally quiescent.

The book assesses this theory of radical right mobilization in the new democracies across post-communist Europe, which offers an

---

[3] According to social dominance theory, the concept of the dominant group can also evolve around age, gender and other categories, such as religion or descent, that reflect power relations in various contexts (Sidanius and Pratto 2001).

[4] Social dominance theory suggests that these are attempts to erode the hierarchy using the hierarchy-attenuating institutions that serve to balance the impact of hierarchy-enhancing institutions (Pratto et al. 2006). However, it also expects the dominant group to be the most xenophobic one.

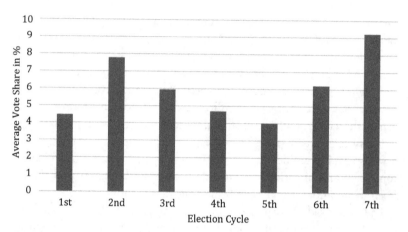

**Figure 1.1** Votes for radical right parties per electoral cycle in post-communist democracies.

important laboratory to study this phenomenon. When Eastern European countries shed their autocratic yokes after 1989/1991, they were ripe for far-right political movements to emerge and succeed. The left was discredited, at least in the European parts of the post-communist empire, which created an opening on the right. Moreover, the economic transition was painful for many. Yet when inflation, unemployment and insecurity skyrocketed, very few populists and demagogues emerged to capitalize on mass economic misery. Intolerance, xenophobia and homophobia were an everyday staple of communist societies, however suppressed by censorship and selectively contained by the police state. The newly democratizing societies were "free to hate" (Hockenos 1993), yet identity politics was surprisingly tame in the aftermath of the fall of the Berlin Wall across most of Eastern Europe, with the important exception of parts of the former Yugoslavia. The perfect storm of far-right mobilization after the collapse of communism never materialized in most places, until many years later; and in other countries, it has *still* not surfaced. For almost two decades, since the fall of the Berlin Wall, the average vote share for radical right parties was in the single digits (Figure 1.1) – quite lackluster when compared with Western European radical right parties (Kopecky and Mudde 2003; Mudde 2017, 2005a). Despite a permissive electoral environment, radical right parties in Eastern and Central Europe struggled to surpass the minimum electoral thresholds and obtain seats in parliaments.[5]

In general, we can identify two distinct waves of political mobilization of the far right in Eastern Europe. The initial wave, immediately after 1989, was quite mild, and reflected the enthusiasm of independence from Soviet interference. However, the mobilization that followed after the founding elections was a backlash against a system of governance based on political pluralism in which minorities organized and acquired political power. The second wave was more vicious and reflected two decades of experience with building political regimes based on diversity of views and interests. This created an aperture for minorities and their advocates to ascend to power and challenge the dominant group's grip on the state.

## 1.1 The Argument

The radical right is a highly variable political phenomenon – both over time within countries and across them – with important consequences for the quality of democracy (Arzheimer 2018). It therefore merits more systematic theorizing and rigorous comparative analysis, which this book aims to contribute.

The first task is to define some key terms. I define a radical right party as a single-issue party that occupies a niche, extreme position in the party system, and is either nationalistic and/or socially conservative.[6] A party that is nationalistic and socially liberal on gender issues, such as the Czech Communist Party, is not a radical right party. Parties are classified on the "second" (identity-related) dimension of party competition, regardless of their economic platforms. In fact, most radical right parties in Eastern Europe are left leaning and argue that governments should protect national economic interests and the dominant group.

---

[5] Figure 1.1 includes the following countries: Albania, Bulgaria, Croatia, Czech Republic, Estonia, Hungary, Latvia, Lithuania, Macedonia, Moldova, Montenegro, Poland, Romania, Serbia–Montenegro FRY, Slovakia, Slovenia, Ukraine. Figure 1.1 excludes the Croatian Party of Democratic Unity (HDZ), which is an outlier and a borderline case of a radical right party (at least in the 1990s when it was a post-war ruling party). Figures and tables that disaggregate vote shares for the radical right parties are in the Appendix.

[6] Niche parties include radical parties, green parties and territorial parties (Adams et al. 2006; Meguid 2005).

Radical right parties might supplement their appeals with populist, anti-establishment or anti-corruption rhetoric but these are not central features of their platforms. Selective anti-minority mobilization against politicized groups does not need to appeal to the "volonté générale" to aggravate voters. A direct connection between the populist leader and the electorate is not necessary to push back against minority rights. Moreover, radical right parties join governing coalitions and have been known to participate in graft, which erodes their anti-establishment appeals. Populism, anti-globalism and anti-elitism are ideologies compatible with radical right platforms, but do not in my view define them.[7]

The second issue is to clarify why the study of the radical right is important. First, the "new" radical right is the fastest growing party family in Europe (Golder 2016; Mudde 2007), and has adapted to the current circumstances and professionalized (Art 2011). In Western Europe starting in the late 1980s, and in Eastern Europe after 1989, the radical right has made a surprising comeback on the European political scene and cannot be ignored. Second, the radical right increasingly affects domestic policy decision-making, especially on minority issues and ethnic relations, in both the East and the West (de Lange 2012). Third, radical right parties have started to undermine the cohesion of the European integration process, and the process of radicalization has only accelerated after the fourth wave of European Union (EU) enlargement in 2004.

This book theorizes that the ire of radical right voters is not directed at *any* minorities, which would make it indiscriminate, but specifically at minorities (and their allies) that aspire to change the status quo by using the political process to their advantage. This resentment, embodied in the belief that certain minorities are undeserving of special rights that elevate their status, is distinct from xenophobia and overt

---

[7] The politics of exclusion and contestation is closely linked to populism. Populism is defined as the rule of "pure many" mobilized against the "corrupt few" (Mudde and Kaltwasser 2013). Being an elusive political category, it can be studied as a "thin" yet coherent ideology, rhetoric, ethos or "empty signifier" as well as a social movement or an expression of contentious politics. Following the will of the many is antithetical to democracy. Nadia Urbinati views populism as a disfigurement of democracy, since it reifies the popular will by suppressing the plurality of opinion and democratic procedures: "populism is a politics not of inclusion but primarily of exclusion" (Urbinati 2014: 147). By definition, the popular will of the people must be the will of the majority or the dominant group.

racism. Contrary to some conventional wisdom, I argue that radical right mobilization does not originate in the demons of xenophobia and group hostility, but rather stems from policy shifts that reflect political competition between majority- and minority-oriented parties and factions. Since resources are finite and prestige originates in hierarchies, any change in the status quo of minority–majority relations implies a loss, typically for the majority, and subsequently a grievance that can be politicized. Radical right parties are not interested in the annihilation or eradication of minorities, but rather in suppressing their desire to exercise greater political power, influence policy, obtain government resources and acquire positions of prominence. In short, the book's central claim is that *radical right support is fueled not by prejudice and xenophobia but by dissatisfaction with and resentment against ascending minority groups.*

Changes in language rights, as the book's opening story suggests, can signal an important shift in status. If a minority language becomes a regional language, in an area densely populated by a distinct ethno-linguistic group, this implies that minorities can officially communicate in their language with local state authorities, use their own names for villages and cities, and accrue more resources to educate their children in a language other than the one associated with the dominant nationality. Similarly, legislation that changes the status of an ethnic group to a "nationality" or "national minority" implies that the collective becomes eligible for more state funds. Such legislation signals that the group can mobilize, and/or that it has a political patron willing to advocate on its behalf. The shift simultaneously detracts from the status of the dominant group, which is now expected to treat the ascending minority more as an equal, and this mobilizes opposition against the change. Political groups associated with such shifts, and advocates of minorities that aim to change the status quo, invite the wrath of radical right party supporters.

Although it is intuitive to associate support for radical right parties with worsening economic conditions, rampant corruption or voter apathy and prejudice, the theory and evidence offered in this book suggest that none of these explanations withstands closer scrutiny. Instead, this book proposes that radical right support originates in policy hostility, defined as opposition to policies that change the status quo of ethnic relations. Radical right parties compete on a platform that seeks to counterbalance or roll back the political gains of minorities to the status quo ante.

## 1.2 Democratization and Radical Right Mobilization

The process of minority accommodation coincided with the process of democratization in post-communist Europe. Post-authoritarian democratic pluralism introduced new political rules of engagement, which empowered the dominant group to search for its national identity through a process of political competition, but also emboldened it to use the banner of the "people" in order to silence minority voices. By making demands and using the openness of the democratic process to their advantage, minority groups increased the salience of identity in the political process – but this did not always result in panic, especially when the dominant group was preoccupied with other critical issues, such as major economic and institutional reforms or international threats.

The principles of radical right politics proposed here are general, but the empirical scope of this book is limited to post-communist democracies. The post-communist context is unique in that the process of democratization preceded and ultimately facilitated the expansion of minority rights once autocratic regimes weakened and a plurality of voices entered the competitive political arena. This differs from more established contexts, such as in Western and Southern Europe, where the democratic opening occurred earlier and the struggle over minority rights was not associated with a concurrent regime change. What is nonetheless general is this: the ability of minorities to extract concessions by aptly using the toolkit of democratic procedures leads to resentment among members of the majority who begin to question the loyalty of the regime elites to the dominant group.

Another general principle is that radical right mobilization is inherently cyclical and sporadic. As minorities and their advocates are pushed back, the perceived urgency of reifying the dominant group and its leading position diminishes. But power-seeking minorities eventually regroup and offer their services to major parties in exchange for favors, and new demands arise. With time, new identities may emerge and new issues may enter the political arena. Minorities that have been silent in the past have incentives to adapt to national and global circumstances and to issue fresh demands.[8] Radical right mobilization mirrors such situational shifts, and thus any theory must incorporate these dynamics if it aims to predict the variable fortunes of radical right parties over time.

For example, in the span of just a few years, the radical right party Jobbik, which is now the second-largest party in Hungary, shifted its platform away from the one that was antagonistic toward Jews and toward a platform that mobilized against Islamic refugees from the Middle East. An opportunity arose, and the party seized it. Yet, in 2016, the party rejected a referendum on refugee quotas that would insulate Hungary and went on to declare its support for the Palestinian state and (conservative) Christian European values, while simultaneously drawing on support from rebellious youth movements and rock bands. Similarly, Jobbik's vitriolic incitement against Roma, which constitutes an important part of their anti-minority platform, has also fluctuated over the years from severe to rather mild. These quick, reactive shifts reflect the episodic nature of identity politics and the erratic salience of minority groups in domestic politics.

Radical right mobilization evolves around the exclusion of minority groups from access to power rather than around pocketbook economic issues. In this view, radical right mobilization represents a revolt against a political system that allows minorities to gain political power and advance minority causes. In a zero-sum setting, minority gains imply majority losses. Even though mainstream parties have delivered positive-sum payoffs in most European post-communist democracies over the past two decades,[9] parties also subscribed to ideas, such as minority protection and pluralism in the public domain, which have diluted the primacy of the dominant group.

Polities differ in how far they are willing to go to resolve the tension between "the people" and "the other" by curbing the pluralist dimension of representative democracy. In most cases, niche radical right parties endanger the political rise of minorities and minority rights, but do not threaten the system of representative democracy itself. That

---

[8] For example, sexual minorities take cues from nearby countries that have pioneered gay and lesbian rights, and realize that they can also take advantage of pluralism (O'Dwyer 2018).

[9] A few of these benefits include membership in the European Union, along with stability, access to markets and freedom of movement.

potential typically lies with large, radicalized mainstream parties, capable of thwarting electoral laws, institutions of oversight, independent courts and free media. The study of radical right parties thus reflects positively on the resilience of democratic institutions in managing majority–minority relationships and dealing with the challenges that arise when minorities become politicized.

While the ability of mainstream parties to fend for the dominant group shapes the radical right politics, so too do other seemingly unrelated issues that are strategically framed through the prism of encroachments on sovereignty. For example, corruption can morph into a betrayal in the eyes of the electorate, once it is framed as a sociotropic sovereignty issue (Klašnja et al. 2014; cf. Hanley and Sikk 2014). The shady sales of large state-owned lands and forests to foreign entities, corrupt large-scale privatizations of strategic assets to foreign firms and bribery in military procurement contracts that endanger national security are not just about personal enrichment and filling party coffers. These activities expose the lack of loyalty that mainstream parties have to the nation, its land, its historical industries and its status as a sovereign state. This framing compromises the mainstream parties' commitment to the dominant group and creates an opportunity for radical right parties to mobilize.

Younger and older democracies may react differently to such framing. Older democracies ought to be more resilient, having lived through decades of political contestation and having successfully absorbed (some) ascending minorities into the mainstream in the past through the democratic process. Resilience can also arise from a deeply internalized memory of overcoming past democratic breakdowns associated with violent, state-sponsored killing of minorities (e.g., Western Germany). Paradoxically, the absence of reflection over a deep historic trauma that has been overcome can leave some older democracies unprepared to deal with right-wing mobilization.

However, all else equal, younger democracies are generally more vulnerable to the corrosive effects of anti-minority mobilization. One danger stems from the parallel processes of building up democratic institutions and the state itself. Democratization allows minorities to ascend to power, which tempts politicians and voters – who want to ensure the supremacy of the dominant nationalities in state affairs – to select authoritarian shortcuts. Emboldened illiberal leaders then use the process of shutting out minorities from access to power channels as a smokescreen to restrict a plurality of opinion and eliminate political opponents.

Although many radical right movements today embrace the legacy of the fascist movements from the interwar period, their novelty lies in their adherence to the rules of electoral competition and – at least on the surface – their rejection of outright violence as a solution to internal political conflicts. Indeed, radical right parties benefit from the openness of electoral competition. Violence and cruelty delegitimize them in the eyes of the electorate and constrain their electoral appeals (Art 2011). Prestige derived from a dominant status is viable only if exercised over a subordinate group. It is in this Hegelian sense that the master depends on the slave for his status recognition (Hegel 1807). Radical right parties campaign not to physically eliminate the minority groups, but rather to reify power relations and their dominance in the state.

Radical right parties – in both Western and Eastern Europe – respond to the political successes of minorities and seek to counterbalance their political gains. Whereas radical right parties in Western Europe often target immigrants, this is less the case in Eastern Europe.[10] In general, the logic of the argument applies to all groups that mobilize on identity (e.g., religious groups, sexual minorities, immigrant groups), as long as these groups find advocates and allies willing to fight for their advancement, and this results in a (real or threatened) shift in the status quo.[11] On this count, any such politicized

---

[10] In Eastern Europe, radical right parties primarily mobilize against domestic ethnic minorities that have been settled for long periods of time, often centuries, and are sometimes physically indistinguishable from the dominant, titular nationalities (Rothschild and Wingfield 2000). The refugee crisis that peaked in 2016 introduced new "Western" topics into radical right mobilization as politicians rallied against non-European Muslim migrants and threats of terrorism.

[11] The ability of ethnic and social minority groups to form parties is sometimes hindered by their relatively small population size (especially when it comes to sexual minorities), but this does not mean that they cannot find political allies to represent their demands, which also opens the door for an electoral backlash. For instance, the Roma – an impoverished minority residing in many Eastern European countries – are well known for the inability to organize politically, but their interests can be defended by socially liberal parties. This is quite similar to the interests of immigrants and asylum seekers in Western Europe, whose rights and demands are debated among parties representing citizens with voting rights. Radical right mobilization is thus feasible even against minorities with limited

accommodation should provoke a political backlash that benefits radical right parties.

While ethnic parties are the ultimate political machines designed to address the grievances and ambitions of ethnic groups, not all minority groups have the same independent capacity for political mobilization. Small groups, such as sexual minorities and other groups that cannot overcome the hurdles of collective action, need to find patrons. Niche parties that advocate for socially liberal issues – diversity, openness and cosmopolitism – are natural political partners for marginalized groups, due to their ideological commitment to diversity. If socially liberal parties help such minorities, they signal that their pledges are real and not just rhetorical eyewash.

Support for social minorities also represents a break with the communist past and a nod toward Europe. In electoral competition, minority advocacy is at odds with the conservative and nationalist forces associated with the previous communist regime (Vachudova 2008b). Since social liberalism and openness to diversity are aligned with free liberal market positions and a pro-Western orientation in Eastern Europe (Kitschelt et al. 1999; Tavits 2005), pivoting toward the accommodation of minority rights signals a break with the authoritarian legacy and an endorsement of liberal European values.[12]

Similar to older Western democracies, radical right political parties in Eastern Europe greatly benefit from the openness of the electoral political arena (Givens 2005) by representing the radicalized expressions of mainstream ideas that are already present in democratic competition. Rather than calling for electoral authoritarianism, they advocate narrow visions of liberal democracy, where the voices of ethnic and social minorities are restricted. On this view, radical right

---

and weak political representation, provided that they possess the political backing of an ally.

[12] On the other hand, communism had many progressive elements. It experimented with new forms of ethnic identities, initiated secularization and empowered women in technical disciplines in the labor force (in a way that has still not been seen in the West). However, for the most part, communist regimes were socially conservative, prudish and hostile to diverse lifestyles and self-expression. The late communist era suppressed creativity in language, clothing, music, food and lifestyle. Cosmopolitan openness to diversity, including support for minority demands that are deviant from the mainstream status quo, resonated with the new post-authoritarian political landscape, especially among youth, socially liberal citizens and supporters of center-left political parties.

parties represent an essential, but still poorly understood, manifestation of democratic competition. In the East, responsiveness to the demands of minorities and democracy are bundled together, such that the backlash against establishment politicians and parties feeds off the intensity and depth of a thick, identity-based cleavage.[13] The ability of new liberal democracies to survive thus hinges on their ability to contain the backlash against the expansion of rights.[14] Despite the newfangled radical right in Eastern Europe, the authoritarian legacy of the interwar period is becoming an acceptable reference point, due to the elevated sense that liberal democracy is not compatible with a vision of societies ruled by dominant majorities.[15]

Radical right groups rally against the advancement of minorities on behalf of the dominant (often titular) group, and channel grievances associated with the ascension of minorities through the political process. The crucial element in these identity conflicts is that shifts in the status quo detract from the symbolic prestige and resources of the dominant group. Prestige and status are indivisible in the radical right worldview, and thus dominant status cannot be shared between groups. If the mainstream parties have compromised the dominant status of the group by striking deals with minorities and their advocates, some voters will perceive them as having betrayed the dominant group and will see radical right parties, which rarely if ever partake in such deals, as the last remaining fortification against minority advancement.

---

[13] Given the diversity in terms of ethnic heterogeneity, economic performance, cultural legacies and minority accommodation across East European countries, it is not surprising that radical right parties have had varied trajectories across the region. In some countries, such as Slovakia, Romania, Ukraine, Bulgaria, Estonia and Latvia, ethnicity and language create cleavages that clearly structure radical right politics. In more ethnically homogeneous countries, such as Hungary, Czech Republic and Poland, the ethnic cleavage is less pronounced and radical right politics is focused either on mobilization against Roma or on social and religious issues that map onto particular party systems.

[14] The major difference between Western and Eastern European democracies is that dissatisfaction with policies undertaken during the process of democratization, such as the expansion of ethnic and social minority rights, by politicians that are viewed as unaccountable, is increasingly linked to anti-democratic attitudes in the East (Minkenberg 2015). Although corrupt political practices are certainly present in Western Europe at the highest levels (Warner 2007), they are not associated with calls to modify democratic institutions to fit the "national needs."

[15] Cf. Carter et al. 2016.

Sovereignty is at the core of radical right mobilization. Conflicts over the ownership of the state are especially vitriolic when the status of the groups has been historically reversed and the new rulers feel insecure about their newly acquired dominance. Though some former dominant groups – such as Russians, Hungarians, Germans, Turks, Poles or Serbs – might be small minorities in their new states, they are a constant reminder to the now dominant group of its historical humiliation and subjugation. Conflict is not inevitable, however. Over long periods of time, the edges of contention can be blunted by institutions that address group grievances, by assimilation and by the replacement of older generations with new ones that are more accepting of minorities. Although there are long-term trends toward greater tolerance, this book shows that the radical right backlash against this trend can be observed in the short spasms of electoral cycles. While economic concerns can be negotiated and quarreling parties can find solutions that benefit both sides, compromises in the domain of identity and sovereignty signal betrayal. Some members of the dominant group may find it politically expedient to yield some of their sovereignty to minorities, but radical right groups regard it as treachery.

In sum, voting for radical right parties originates not in hatred against minorities, but rather in opposition to policies that accommodate their demands and elevate their status. The book's principal forecast follows from this – that changes in minority accommodation predict variation in electoral support for radical right parties. When radical right parties succeed, they actively promote policies that either reverse accommodation or create policies (e.g., language laws) that make future accommodation more difficult. Radical right parties are thus reactive, for they gain strength when accommodation increases, and lose strength when the status quo is preserved or accommodation recedes. The success of the radical right is, paradoxically, one of the main reasons for its failure.

## 1.3 Outline of the Book

Chapter 2 outlines alternative explanations, develops the proposed theory of radical right mobilization and derives empirical implications to be assessed and discussed in the subsequent chapters. The theory emphasizes the radical right's reactive nature and explains how the success of ethnic and socially liberal parties helps to explain temporal variation in the success and failure of radical right parties.

Chapter 3 tests this using an original time-series cross-national dataset covering all post-communist democratic elections after 1989. It assesses the project's core propositions about the electoral success of radical right parties at the cross-national level and over time. The results show that radical right parties tend to be more successful when ethnic and socially liberal parties (1) obtain policy-making powers via coalition participation, (2) express greater ideological extremism and (3) win a greater proportion of the popular vote.[16]

Chapter 3 also discusses the modifying effect of ethnic group size. The existence of an ethnic minority facilitates radical right mobilization, but mobilization is not proportional to the size of the minority groups. The mediating effect of group size, and the sequencing of the backlash, are discussed in the case study chapters: Chapter 4 (Slovakia) and Chapter 5 (Ukraine). Slovakia and Ukraine are both cases with contestation over minority issues,[17] but Slovakia is a country with multiple small minorities, whereas Ukraine has a large Russian minority. Slovakia and Ukraine were also selected to maximize variation on the dependent variable. Slovakia is a case of a success, where radical

---

[16] Chapter 3 faces data limitations. It controls for economic conditions in countries and finds almost no effects on radical right mobilization. Country-level data that capture discrimination against minorities in Eastern Europe (e.g., the Minorities at Risk dataset) show that discrimination is quite stable over time and does not map well onto electoral cycles. The level of discrimination is quite high across countries, although the data are not available for all groups, only for those that are viewed as at risk. As a result, the dataset is not suitable for a large-cross national analysis that spans more than two decades. Cross-national–level data that would capture group hostility against specific groups over two decades and many post-communist countries, and also indicate the ethnicity of the respondent and their vote choice, are not available. Reliable cross-national data on hate crimes, measured repeatedly and consistently over time, also do not exist.

[17] Ukraine offers a case of full contestation over minority issues, unlike other countries with Russian-speaking minorities. In the Baltics, "contemporary state institutions are entrusted to protect identities and interests of ethnic core nations, rather than all citizens" (Agarin 2016: 83). Only citizens of the pre-war republics and their descendants were entitled to automatic citizenship in Estonia and Latvia. Russian speakers with no citizenship rights cannot vote in national-level elections. Furthermore, proficiency in national languages excludes Russian speakers from political and administrative positions (Agarin 2016). For example, Latvia has more than thirty-three categories of employment barred for non-citizens (Hughes 2005).

right mobilization is a permanent feature of party politics, whereas Ukraine is a case of a failure for the radical right. I designed and implemented an original set of survey questions in both countries to test the theoretical implications of the theory at the individual level. The survey enables us to directly assess the effects of group hostility against *specific* groups that have (or do not have) political backing on voting, in addition to gauging the impact of economic anxieties coupled with ethnicity and attitudes toward targeted government spending on voting.[18]

The Slovak radical right is one of the most successful political forces in Europe today and has been extremely resilient since 1993. Studying it carefully allows us to track and examine the dynamics of accommodation over time with a small ethnic minority. Over the past two decades, the political scene in Slovakia has been quite stable in terms of the actors that anchor both political poles. This provides consistency over time in the analysis, since the actors are identifiable with transparent profiles and have established reputations. Moreover, the parties on the radical and ethnic side in Slovakia are both relatively large compared with many niche parties, and are therefore politically relevant for coalition formation. The political space in Slovakia has been characterized by a high degree of variation in the extent to which it is polarized on issues of national identity, and this variability enables us to illustrate the theory as a truly dynamic process of contestation.

---

[18] There are two challenges that one faces when using off-the-shelf cross-national surveys that lead to the design and implementation of original surveys. First, their comprehensive coverage of the whole post-communist region has little consistency over time. Second, given the fact that most radical right parties in Eastern Europe are weak, the statistical power to conduct any analysis has limitations. Surveys do not have enough respondents who voted for the radical right, which constrains inference. This leads many studies to be biased toward cases where parties are doing well in elections. But the cases of failure are equally puzzling and perhaps even more intriguing. To overcome these challenges, I implemented my own surveys in Slovakia and Ukraine to test what could not have been tested with publicly available data: the effects of group hostility against specific groups that have (or do not have) political backing on voting. The design of the survey in Ukraine anticipated that the pool of Svoboda (radical right party) voters would be small, so a question about "sympathizers" was included to track those who would hypothetically vote for a radical right party, if they had a second ballot. This strategy helped in understanding the determinants of support for the radical right even in a country where the far right has had relatively weak performance in elections.

The analysis of these dynamics in Slovakia sheds light on an important case of radical right and ethnic politics, while also helping us to understand adversarial political contestation in other countries that are increasingly confronted with issues of minority accommodation. Using an original survey with an embedded experiment and qualitative interviews with members of the main radical party and representatives of Hungarian ethnic parties, the results show that indignation over government transfers toward a politically backed minority (Hungarians) is a much stronger predictor of radical right voting in Slovakia than group hostility.

Chapter 5 examines the radical right in Ukraine. Unlike Slovakia, Ukraine has a large ethnic minority (Russians) that threatens the dominant nationality with an actual status reversal. Ukraine is also a country that has not finished nation building, and that has a vast pool of grievances associated with corruption, economic malaise and a fluid party system that generates new parties every electoral cycle. One might expect Ukraine to be a poster child for radical right mobilization. The radical right is very weak, however, and has struggled in elections since independence in 1991.

Drawing on original survey data and qualitative interviews with members of the main radical party, as well as supporters and opponents, the analysis shows that the logic of backlash is equally applicable in Ukraine, and sheds light on why some voters turn to radical right parties, even in such a different context. Indignation over governmental transfers toward a politically backed minority (Russians) is a stronger predictor of voting than group hostility (toward Russians). The chapter further analyzes the sequencing of political mobilization, and tracks the evolution of language policies in Ukraine along with their impact on the radicalization of the Ukrainian electorate.

Chapter 6 recounts the main argument, discusses the applicability of the book's main findings in other contexts and considers its primary policy implications for efforts to prevent democratic backsliding and to contain the influence of radical right ideology.

# 2 | A Theory of Radical Right Mobilization

For several decades, we have witnessed that political and intellectual class resigned its responsibility of protecting freedoms of their fellow citizens. Instead, they are focused on alleged group rights of minorities. Each so-called minority is preferred at the expensed of others. The principle of equality before the law is thus broken, members of "non-minorities" are discriminated against and deprived of basic civic freedoms.

—Declaration prepared for the *International Day of the Heterosexual White Man* in the Czech Parliament held on May 11, 2017. www.normalman.cz

Radical politics and the use of incendiary political appeals are enduring features of democratic party competition. They have been carefully examined in scholarship on the Western European extreme right, Latin American populism, racial politics in the United States and ethnic party competition in South Asia.[1] Radical right parties have a highly variable record of electoral success, posing a difficult puzzle for many theories of electoral behavior.[2] Their electoral success brings back memories of right-wing movements in Europe from the first half of the twentieth

---

[1] Radical right politics focused on efforts to exclude or halt the advancement of minorities emulates populism, since it reifies the popular will by restricting the plurality of opinion and by suppressing democratic procedures. Populism is often defined as the rule of the "pure many" mobilized against the "corrupt few" (for contextual adaptations, see Bustikova 2016b; Golder and Golder 2016). It is an ideology that pitches the people against the elite and calls for a greater congruence between the general will of the people and politics (Mudde and Kaltwasser 2011). Some have studied populism as a "thin" yet coherent ideology, a rhetoric, an ethos, an "empty signifier," while others see it as a social movement and an expression of contentious politics (Gidron and Bonikowski 2013). Following the will of the many, under the banner of radicalized fringes of the dominant group, can be antithetical to democracy. "Populism," on this count, "is a politics of exclusion" and can indicate a disfigurement of democracy (Urbinati 2014).

[2] I use the term "radical," rather than "extremist," to connote a party that does not challenge the democratic order of a given country, following Carter (2005).

century, which has induced the growing fear that such a dark period could again be on the European and possibly world horizon. Finally, radical right parties offer innovative appeals, and when voters become ideologically footloose, established parties pay close attention to their competitors and mimic them.[3]

Many democracies have been inundated with radical political parties, but the emergence, strength and survival of these parties varies tremendously across countries and elections. In certain countries, radical parties emerge, only to fade swiftly into oblivion, whereas in others such parties manage to survive across several electoral cycles with varied success. And elsewhere, noteworthy radical parties have never emerged at all. What explains this variation? Why are radical right parties stronger in some post-communist democracies than others, and what explains volatility within countries over time? How and why do radical right parties appeal to voters?

Throughout the 1990s, the study of the radical right parties in Eastern Europe was largely neglected, as most scholars focused on the success and failure of newly emerging mainstream political parties. Some attention was also paid to political extremism on the left, since the fate of the communist parties was seen as an important indicator of democratic consolidation.[4] After a decade of transition-oriented literature, the focus has slowly shifted to the study of extremism on the right, and the literature on radical right parties in Eastern Europe has since grown markedly and has become the subject of several significant studies.[5] Most of them have emphasized the idiosyncratic nature of

---

[3] The uncertainty reflects an era of "liquid modernity" (Bauman 2000).

[4] For scholarship on unreformed former communist parties, see Bozoki and Ishiyama 2002; Grzymala-Busse 2002; Ishiyama 1997.

[5] For scholarly contributions on this topic, see Alexseev 2006; Alonso and Ruiz-Rufino 2007; Anastasakis 2002; Art and Brown 2007; Beichelt 2003; Bútora 2007; Carpenter 1997; Dziewanowski 1996; Ekiert 2006; Enyedi and Erős 1999; Flesnic 2007; Gibson and Howard 2004; Gow and Carmichael 2000; Greskovits 2007; Grün 2002; Held 1996; Hockenos 1993; Ishiyama 2001; Kasekamp 2003; Kopecký and Mudde 2003; Krastev 2007; Kuzio 2002; Land 2001; Lang 2005; Lovatt 1999; Mareš 2006, 2003; Markowski et al. 2003; Merkl and Weinberg 2003, 1997; Michnik 2007; Minkenberg 2015, 2009, 2007, 2002; Minkenberg and Beichelt 2001; Mudde 2007, 2005a, 2005b, 2004, 2003, 2001, 2000; Mungiu-Pippidi 2007; Nissen 2004; Norris 2005; O'Dwyer and Schwartz 2010; Ost 2005; Polyakova 2015; Pop-Eleches 2010; Pupovac 2010; Ramet 2007, 1999; Rev 1994; Robotin 2002; Rosenberg 1996; Rupnik 2007; Schopflin 2007; Shafir 2008, 2007, 2002, 2000, 1997; Smolar 2007; Stefanova 2007; Stojarova and Emerson 2013; Szczerbiak 2007; Szocs 1998; Tamas 2007;

radical right mobilization, the importance of country specific factors or a unique sequence of domestic or international events that stimulated radical right mobilization.[6] Whereas we possess a reasonably solid understanding of why nationalism resurfaced after the collapse of communism to fill the ideological vacuum (Beissinger 2002; Brubaker 1997; Fish 1998), we have far less knowledge about why radical right parties come and go so erratically in the era of "normal," post-transition democratic politics.[7]

This book explores the survival, performance and dynamics of radical right politics during relatively stable and peaceful periods. It advances a theory of radical right mobilization grounded in a logic of electoral counter-mobilization that originates in resentment about adverse shifts in the minority–majority status quo. The core thesis is that radical right parties mobilize to keep minorities from advancing politically. The ire of radical right voters is not directed at all minorities, but at minorities (and their allies) that aspire to change the status quo in their favor through the political process. Radical right mobilization does not originate in the demons of xenophobia or group hostility, as is sometimes asserted, but rather in policy shifts that signal the social advancement of minorities.

The state is the ultimate sovereign that is charged with regulating the relationship between the dominant group and minorities, and providing the appropriate mix of accommodation, exclusion and repression. Radical right mobilization results from the sovereign's resentment

---

Temple 1996; Tismaneau 2007; Ucen 2007; Volovici 1994; Waldron-Moore 1999; Weaver 2007, 2006.

[6] These contributions have focused on a wide range of factors, including the agency of radical right actors (Minkenberg 2015), the interaction between the radical right parties, their mainstream competitors and ideology (Pirro 2015; Pupovac 2010; Pytlas 2016), attitudes toward democracy (Allen 2015), economic deprivation (Lewis 2009; Minkenberg 2002), the ideological roots of radical parties and the role of legacies in party competition (Held 1996; Hockenos 1993; Minkenberg 2009; Mudde 2005b; Ramet 1999), territorial disputes (Mareš 2009), European Union conditionality and Euroskepticism (Kopecký and Mudde 2003, 2002; Polyakova 2015; Vachudova 2008a) and the effect of mainstream party behavior and party system configurations in general (Mareš and Havlík 2016; Pop-Eleches 2010; Stojarová 2012).

[7] The reasons for radical right party emergence at times when communist federations disintegrated, and new states were born, almost certainly rely on a different causal logic, which is related to the contestation of political boundaries, the threat of civil wars and endowments from the previous regime (Jowitt 1992; Kitschelt 1995; Petersen 2002; Ramet 1999; Vachudova 2008b).

regarding its diminished status,[8] and represents a revolt against a political system that has allowed minorities to legitimately gain political power and thereby to advance their causes. Fringes of the dominant group resent both material and symbolic gains that minorities achieve, and demand a policy recalibration back to the status quo ante. Mainstream parties that allowed these adverse changes to transpire are viewed as "traitors" to their own people. For this reason, they are not seen as credible advocates for containing or reversing policy shifts that promote minorities.[9]

This book's theory of why radical right parties succeed and fail can be characterized as a sequence. First, there is a minority with the ability to mobilize and seek accommodation. Then, the minority should be large enough (but not too large, as I discuss later) – or must find allies – to enact change to the status quo. Third, the government extends protection or accommodation to the aspiring minority group as a result of its (or its allies') political mobilization. Finally, the fringes of the dominant group become alarmed, and the radical right emerges (or reemerges) to defend the majority group's dominance and to block or roll back minority accomodation.[10]

Radical right parties do not wish to eradicate minorities, but rather aim to suppress their desire to wield greater political power, influence policy, obtain governmental resources and acquire positions of prominence, including symbolic recognition. Exclusion or suppression is a reaction to the erosion of status and prestige that the dominant group possesses. Radical right support is not fueled by prejudice and xenophobia per se, which is usually much more prevalent in the general population than what the electoral results for radical right parties – mostly in single digits – would indicate. Instead, this book shows that frustration with ascending minority groups – perceived as threats to the status quo – motivates radical right voters and governs the success of radical right parties.

[8] The sovereign is the "people," here defined as a dominant group.

[9] Polities differ in how they define "the people" but also in how far they are willing to go to resolve the tension between "the people" and "the other" by curbing pluralism in representative democracies. In most cases, niche radical right parties endanger the ascent of minorities, but not the system of representative democracy itself. That honor belongs to large, mainstream parties, capable of thwarting electoral laws, institutions of oversight, independent courts and free media.

[10] See Elias and Scotson (1965) on the sociological dynamics between established groups and outsiders.

This chapter develops these arguments into a unified approach to the study of radical right mobilization. After first considering plausible rival explanations, three aspects of the theory are developed: (1) threats to the sovereignty of the dominant group, (2) shifts in the status quo and accommodation of minority groups and (3) threats of a status reversal related to minority group size. Since the erosion of the dominant group's power to govern as a sovereign is at the heart of radical right mobilization, the chapter first explores the conditions under which identity and sovereignty become salient. Next, it discusses status quo shifts in minority–majority relations and how they engender resentment and backlash. Finally, it specifies the conditions under which minority groups can mobilize and threaten the dominant group with status reversal. The chapter concludes by deriving seven testable hypotheses that inform the empirical chapters to follow.

## 2.1  Rival Explanations

Since Roger Eatwell's seminal essay (2003), it has become customary to differentiate explanations of radical right success as being driven by either demand-side or supply-side factors. On the one hand, demand-side explanations view voting for the radical right parties as a mirror that reflects the wishes of the electorate. Parties echo the demands of the voters and they surge alongside anxieties that reflect xenophobia, economic anxiety, ethnic competition, infatuation with charisma, and fears associated with crime, or any feasible combination of these factors. As these concerns fade in the eyes of the voters, demand for radical right parties evaporates and their electoral fortunes suffer (Golder 2016).

On the other hand, supply-side explanations focus on the strategic moves of the parties and assume that there is a relatively fixed pool of patriotic right-wing voters that can be mobilized, either by the mainstream or by the fringe parties. For example, in one supply-side theory, the presence of a Christian democratic party has been shown to weaken the radical right vote, since both draw support from the same pool of conservative voters, whom a more established party can electorally cannibalize, sapping support for the far right (Arzheimer and Carter 2006; Minkenberg 2015). Similarly, the radical right vote can be weakened if voters have the option of supporting a radicalized mainstream party that controls the state apparatus and can deliver on electoral promises with greater ease (Bustikova and Kitschelt 2009; Meguid 2008; Pytlas 2016).

Alternatively, electoral swings can be explained by new "opportunity structures" that create a favorable opening for innovative entrants (Kitschelt and McGann 1995) or by the commitment to professionalize the party apparatus (Art 2011). Since electoral support for the radical parties is rather volatile in both the West and the East (Arzheimer 2018), supply-side explanations would seem to have a comparative advantage in capturing the erratic nature of electoral support. However, a major weakness in the supply-side approach stems from its indifference to the underlying currents that shape party systems. Supply-side accounts discount the grievances that voters have accumulated over several electoral cycles and ignore historical reference points by which voters evaluate the performance of the mainstream parties.

These grievances and historical reference points help to explain why the breakthrough of radical right parties in Western Europe occurred in the 1980s, rather than at some other time. Adapted to democratic circumstances of the post–World War II era, the new far-right parties emerged after more than a decade of political and social change, reflecting new post-material values, greater gender parity, minority inclusiveness and social liberalism associated with broader societal cultural shifts. Ignazi famously labeled the eruption of radical right parties in Western Europe as a silent counter-revolution to this sweeping social change (Ignazi 1992). Similarly, Inglehart and Pippa (2016) noted that the emergence of democratically elected populist leaders and movements advocating ethnic exclusion coincided with a widening gap in values between those who embrace ethnic pluralism and those who are more wary of diversity. Generational shifts and value conflicts cannot account for the episodic bursts and busts of radical right mobilization, but they do help to identify cracks in party systems through which radical right parties might enter.

In linking the success of radical right parties to policy hostility against minority accommodation and attendant shifts in the status quo, this book challenges three common explanations of radical right voting: (1) cultural backlash, (2) economic anxiety and (3) proximate party competition.

Xenophobia is the core of the cultural backlash argument, but such group hostility is pervasive and targets both politicized and non-politicized minorities, such as Vietnamese and Chinese communities in Eastern Europe (Liu 2017a). Group hostility cannot account for the volatility of radical right voting from election to election. Radical right voting also does not follow from economic pains – there was no systematic cross-national spike in extremist voting during the economic transformation in the early 1990s or after the economic recession of 2008. However, economic grievances do matter when overlaid with ethnic minority accommodation. Opposition to governmental spending on *politicized* minorities is a strong predictor of radical right voting at the individual level, as subsequent chapters demonstrate clearly.

Third, the ability of radical right parties to steal votes from mainstream parties, their ideological "cousins," is not directly linked to their success. Rather than concentrating on the interplay between the radical right and the mainstream right, this book instead focuses on the interaction between two extremes: radical right parties and ethnoliberal parties. It shows that pressure from ethnic and socially liberal parties to shift the status quo provides a compelling account of the electoral volatility among radical right parties. Several other explanations have been advanced to explain the roots of parties and the divergence across countries in the East, but most fail to offer a unified theory that provides empirical traction over time and across a diverse set of cases.[11] For instance, differences in electoral formulas, thresholds and systems, which should intuitively be related to the success of niche parties, all appear peripheral to variation in the success and failure of radical right parties (Minkenberg 2015; Pirro 2015; Pytlas 2016).

In the course of developing its argument, this book builds on three key insights from recent scholarship on East European radical right. First, the analysis of the ideological core of the Eastern European radical right clearly suggests that nativism, and to some degree clericalism and irredentism, constitute its major ideational platforms (Pirro 2015). Economic grievances are therefore ancillary and need to be studied in the context of politicized minority issues. Moreover, both radicalized mainstream parties and radical right parties embrace left pro-redistributive positions, which suggests that economic grievances cannot differentiate the radical right and their radicalized ideological cousins from the mainstream (Bustikova 2018). Second, radical right parties are more blatantly racist than their Western counterparts (Minkenberg 2017). Due to the high levels of xenophobia in Eastern

---

[11] For recent overview essays on the radical right parties, see Golder 2016; Mudde 2016; Mudde and Kaltwasser 2018; Pytlas 2018; Rydgren 2018. Also Eatwell 2003; Kitschelt 2007, 2018; Mudde 2007; Norris 2005; Van der Brug and Fennema 2007.

Europe, mirrored in the rhetoric of parties, they should perform exceptionally well in elections. Yet the opposite is true: the radical right in
Western Europe is on average stronger (Mudde 2017). This indicates
that xenophobia cannot account both for the levels of support and for
volatility in radical right voting.

Third, analyzing the ideological core of populist radical right parties
in the East, Pirro (2015) concluded that nativism is their key ideational
component. However, he also discovered that mainstream parties –
"cousins" – react to the positions of radical right parties on specific
issue agendas and that the distinction between the mainstream and the
extreme is blurry. Similarly, using a different perspective, Pytlas (2016)
finds that radical right discourse in Eastern Europe easily travels
between the "niche" and the mainstream. His analysis of framing
contests shows that narrative shifts over the meaning behind issues are
common and that the spatial shifts of mainstream parties have no
discernible effect on the radical right parties (also Pirro 2015).

The implication of these seminal works is that the adoption of radical
ideas by the mainstream parties has an ambivalent effect on the electoral
fortunes of radical right parties. The rhetorical strategies of mainstream
"cousins" rarely influence the fate of the radical right parties in a
uniform manner. In order to uncover the sources of electoral volatility,
this book suggests that the interaction between two *opposing* poles of
the political spectrum – the ethnic and socially liberal parties and the
radical right parties – is the unit of analysis to investigate.

## 2.1.1 Identity and Economy

Two prominent explanations have dominated the study of radical right
voting: one focused on identity and the other more attentive to economics. Identity explanations for radical right voting patterns generally
focus on factors and processes surrounding the delineation of group
boundaries and the status of minorities (Rydgren 2018). Economic
explanations tend to highlight deprivation, ethnic competition over
scarce resources and the clash of material interests (Arzheimer 2009;
Kitschelt 2007; Mudde 2007; Rydgren 2008; Sniderman et al. 2004;
van der Brug and Fennema 2007). I will now explore identity and
economy, two demand-side explanations that suggest that party success
can be derived from the preferences of voters, and highlight their limitations as a way of introducing a different way of thinking about radical
right politics.

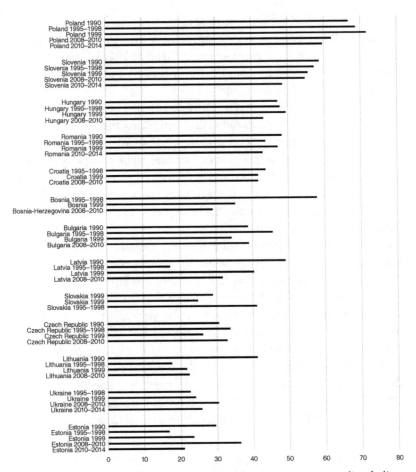

**Figure 2.1** Proportion of respondents from the dominant nationality feeling "very proud" to be the nationality specific to their country, 1990–2014.
*Source*: World Value Survey and European Value Survey

Identity-based explanations, which we might call pride and prejudice, have been proposed as the driving forces behind changes in the aggregate demand for radical right politics over time. Yet, as Figure 2.1 shows, national pride is relatively constant over time within countries.[12] There is some variation *across* countries from very proud nationalities, such as Poles and Slovenians, to places with less national

---

[12] This lists the responses of "very proud" from the members of the dominant nationalities. The members of the non-titular group are excluded. For a recent analysis of pride across countries and over time, see Wimmer 2017.

pride, such as Estonia and Ukraine. But this variation is *not* reflected in radical right mobilization either across countries or over time. For instance, Czechs are just about as proud as Slovaks, but the radical right mobilization in the Czech lands has been much more subdued. Since such pride also does not change much over time, it also follows that booms and busts of radical right mobilization cannot be derived from value orientations associated with national pride and patriotism. All else equal, very diverse polities are actually predisposed *against* radical right mobilization, since the dominant group is used to having a weaker grip on state affairs than in more homogeneous polities. By contrast, less diverse countries are more likely to have radical right parties because large majorities have become accustomed to being in charge and resent minority demands.

Prejudice is another common but not viable explanation. Intuitively, a surge in xenophobia should lurk behind any significant increase in the electoral success of radical right parties. If the radical right mobilization followed from the dominant group's degree of prejudice, it would be far more rampant and less erratic. As Figure 2.2 shows, however, there is no correspondence between shifts in xenophobic values and voting for the radical right parties (represented by black columns). It tracks vote shares and exclusionary attitudes associated with extremism over time, and demonstrates that between 2003 and 2017 vote shares do not follow from aggregate changes in attitudes (prejudice and welfare chauvinism).[13]

---

[13] The Demand for Extremism (DEREX) index is a composite index that measures the percentage of respondents in a given country who score highly on at least three out of four indices (prejudice and welfare chauvinism, right-wing value orientation, anti-establishment attitudes, and fear, distrust and pessimism) and are therefore most likely to support extreme right-wing politics. The prejudice and welfare chauvinism index measures the percentage of respondents who exhibit anti-minority/anti-immigrant attitudes, support restrictive immigration policies or exhibit socially exclusive leanings in general. The right-wing value orientation index measures the percentage of respondents who exhibit a powerful predilection for social order, adherence to traditional values, and who self-define as right-wing supporters. Indices are based on consecutive waves of the European Social Survey (2003, 2005, 2007, 2009, 2011, 2013, 2015, 2017). Source: Back by Popular Demand. Political Capital 2010, Budapest. http:// derexindex.eu. The European Social Survey consistently tracked attitudes during this time period. Earlier years are not available. The vote shares for Poland in 2015 represent the seats for Ruch Narodowy, a radical right party that run under the umbrella of Kukiz'15 political movement.

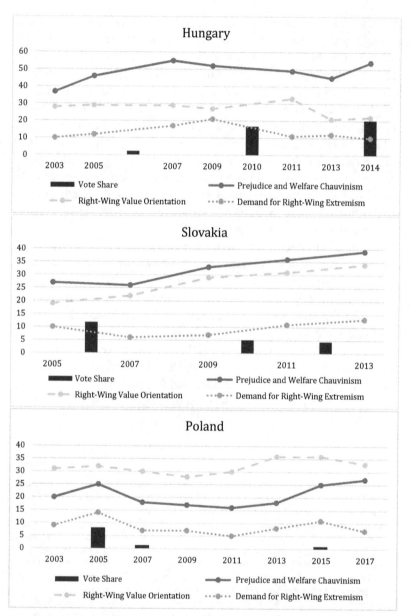

**Figure 2.2** Relationship between prejudice and electoral support for radical right parties.

*Sources*: European Social Survey and Derex Index (Political Capital). Vote shares: Electoral Commissions

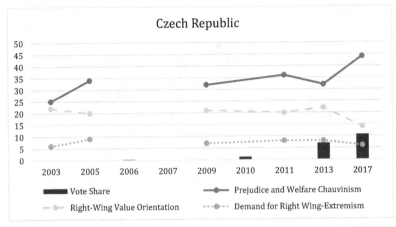

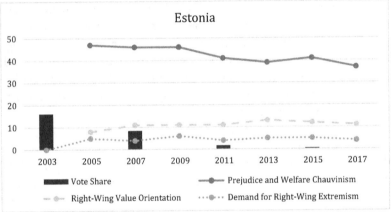

**Figure 2.2** (*cont.*)

In Hungary, for example, the large increase in voting for the radical right party, Jobbik, was *not* preceded by a surge in prejudice among voters. In neighboring Slovakia, the increase in prejudice over a ten-year period has been accompanied by a *decrease* in electoral support for the Slovak National Party. In Poland, Czech Republic and Estonia, the aggregate levels or prejudice are relatively stable over time and there is no clear relationship between radical right voting and prejudice. Although popular conceptions of the radical right emphasize xenophobia and group hostility toward minorities, the evidence is astonishingly mixed. Racism, at both the citizen and the

elite level, is so pervasive in Eastern Europe that appealing to xenophobic emotions does not constitute a unique strategy or a winning
formula for radical right parties (Bustikova 2015b; Bustikova and
Guasti 2017; Hockenos 1993; Mudde 2005a). Furthermore, group
hostility does not translate into party support – in other words, at the
macro-level, radical right parties are not stronger in countries with
more xenophobic attitudes (Krekó et al. 2010; Norris 2005).[14]
Similarly, at the micro-level, the evidence that radical right parties
exclusively draw supporters from hard-core xenophobes is also highly
suspect (Rydgren 2008).[15]

Cross-national differences in other factors, including party fragmentation, political accountability and legacies of interwar
radicalism, are also unable to explain why radical parties are stronger
or weaker in some countries, or to account for variation over time
within countries adequately, as the empirical analysis in Chapter 3
suggests. Although the economy in Latvia underwent extremely
troubling economic contractions, the economies in Poland and
Slovenia have remained prosperous – these differences in relative
economic deprivation have had no impact on radical right party
support (Minkenberg 2015).[16]

Economic anxieties, unemployment, and opposition to governmental redistribution have also been suggested as factors influencing
the success of radical right parties (Golder 2003; Swank and Betz
2003).[17] Adverse economic conditions can certainly create grievances that may later facilitate the rise of radical parties, and even

---

[14] On the effect of electoral institutions on radical right party success, see Carter
2002 and Givens 2005.
[15] Rydgren's study of six West European countries differentiates between
immigration skepticism and xenophobic attitudes and shows that
"xenophobic attitudes are a far less significant factor than immigration
skepticism for predicting who will vote for the new radical right" (Rydgren
2008: 1). Even if we were to concede that xenophobia drives the electoral success
of the radical right parties for some cross-section, it is hard to imagine that
xenophobic attitudes exhibit sufficient volatility across electoral cycles to
explain the variable support for radical right parties.
[16] Although the subject of this book is the radical *right* in Eastern Europe, the
predominant leaning of these parties, in economic terms, is toward the left
(Allen 2015; Bustikova and Kitschelt 2009).
[17] Others dispute the role of economic considerations and have focused on the
importance of identity issues, ideologies and party organizations that attract
radical right voters (Art 2011; Mudde 2007).

contribute to the survival of radical parties once they have emerged – yet grievances are generally too pervasive to explain variation in the emergence of radical parties across countries, and too static to explain cross-national volatility over time (Arzheimer 2009; Betz 1994; Kitschelt and McGann 1995; Mudde 2007; Oesch 2009). Economic considerations do figure into radical right voting, but mainly through welfare chauvinism and opposition to policies that facilitate economic improvement of minorities, a cornerstone for their political ascent in the state. Material conditions alone, decoupled from the context of majority–minority relations, and their symbolic implications, should not significantly influence the fate of radical right parties.

The socioeconomic profiles of voters also appear to play no significant role in determining vote choice for radical right parties (Bustikova and Kitschlet 2011).[18] One reason that makes finding the "quintessential" radical right voter in Eastern Europe challenging is the diffuse nature of economic risks spread across different segments of society because welfare protections were dismantled after 1989:

The deprivations caused by the retrenchment of encompassing, universalist quasi-socialist welfare states pretty comprehensively touched almost every group and stratum in society. If protest and alienation prompted by such policies does cue citizens to opt for radical right-wing parties, the supporters of such challengers should have diffuse socio-demographic characteristics. There is not a singular socioeconomic category which vulnerability would be so extraordinarily different from that of other categories to give it preponderance in the electorate of radical right wing parties. (Bustikova and Kitschelt 2009: 464)[19]

---

[18] Compare this with a study of radical right party Jobbik supporters who are often linked to the recent sharp economic downturn in Hungary. The study however shows that Jobbik supporters are not the "losers of the transition": the poor, unemployed, undereducated people. A significant proportion of Jobbik supporters (22 percent) are young and have a university or college education and are driven by cultural considerations rather than economic ones (Barlett et al. 2012; cf. Pirro 2016).

[19] Is it possible to find "the ultimate radical right voter" in Eastern Europe? Bustikova and Kitschelt (2011) found no economic or sectoral profiles. The study shows that the radical right voter in Eastern Europe, using available cross-national survey data, is male, but the effect is not strong and is generally either very young or very old. Radical right parties attract highly uneducated voters, measured as the number of years spent in school. Yet this finding is confounded by age since it applies to very old people with high school degrees or less

Yet the difuse nature of the risk does *not* imply that radical right voters are indifferent to the issue of redistribution. Quite the contrary, this book suggests that radical right voters care considerably about how state assets are divided and allocated, particularly when it concerns transfers between the majority and politically organized minorities.[20] It follows, if true, that radical right parties should succeed when they attract voters who oppose governmental spending on a politically organized minority and fail when they achieve their goals.[21]

What is distinct about the radical right voters, and what makes them different from parties that are ideologically similar to them, their mainstream competitors? In order to answer these questions, we need to analyze the relationship between group hostility and policy hostility. Government support and transfers to a politically organized minority shift the status quo in the majority–minority relationship. This state-sanctioned support ultimately leads to a backlash against

---

education. After controlling for age, the effect of education disappears in a cross-national analysis (Bustikova and Kitschelt 2011). At the cross-national level, Bustikova and Kitschelt found that anxieties associated with welfare state retrenchment contribute to radical right mobilization, as do patrimonial legacies of interwar regimes (Bustikova and Kitschelt 2009). Crude economic indicators are not related to radical right support. However, social policy reform retrenchment in universalistic welfare systems has a highly incendiary potential for political conflict and radical parties. Polarized patrimonial regimes are the most fertile breeding ground for the radical right due to the high levels of inequality and dissatisfaction resulting from a rapid dismantling of the welfare state (Bustikova and Kitschelt 2009).

[20] The alternative approach would suggest that radical right voters are more economically deprived or more prejudiced against minorities than voters of parties in their ideological neighborhood.

[21] The literature on West European radical right provides conflicting evidence on radical right voters' attitudes toward redistribution. Swank and Betz (2003) find that high levels of welfare state protection, which shield citizens in case of unemployment, reduce the appeal of extreme right parties. Golder adds high levels of immigration and the interaction between unemployment and immigration to the list of structural factors that benefit extreme right success (Golder 2003). The effect of unemployment on support for radical right parties in Western Europe is contested. Arzheimer finds mixed support for the joint effect of unemployment and immigration in Western Europe on votes for the extreme right and even questions the effect of unemployment on radical vote: "unemployment benefits can reduce support ... [only] in certain constellations" (Arzheimer 2009: 274).

political concessions. This is not due to economic deprivation, but rather because when the government demonstrates favoritism to minorities, the economic consequences of the government's actions become salient. Policy hostility escalates against deviations from welfare chauvinism, a preferential support for transfers that benefit the dominant ethnic group, long considered a cornerstone of radical right party support (Kitschelt and McGann 1995).

Building on this tradition by reconceptualizing welfare chauvinism in terms of policy hostility, the theory distinguishes between inward- and outward-oriented forms of welfare chauvinism. Policy hostility is defined as support for governmental transfers that exclusively benefit the majority (inward-oriented welfare chauvinism), or as opposition to governmental transfers that exclusively benefit minorities (outward-oriented welfare chauvinism). This distinction allows us to disentangle whether radical right supporters are distinct due to their support of the majority or rather due to their opposition to supporting a specific minority. It is commonly assumed that radical right support for governmental redistribution that benefits the ethnic majority automatically translates into an opposition to minority spending. But this need not be true. Indeed, the theory advanced here suggests that radical right voters are distinct in their opposition to governmental transfers toward politically organized minorities because those transfers erode the group hierarchy.

Typically, the concept of welfare chauvinism does not differentiate between minority groups. It simply posits that voters want (relatively) more resources for the dominant (ethnic) group. Yet, since the backlash mechanism is rooted in displeasure with the improved status of minorities via political channels, it is crucial to distinguish between opposition to transfers toward politicized groups and groups with only weak political sway. Radical right voters (compared with the voters of other parties) are neither more nor less hostile to minorities *without* political backing. It is only in the case of minorities with political backing, and privileges that have been afforded via political processes, that the theory expects radical right voters to mobilize.

## 2.1.2 Mainstream Parties

A different school of thought suggests that the electoral success of radical right parties does not originate from bottom-up pressures and electoral demands, but is instead "supplied" from the top down through conditions that create a more or less favorable environment for radical right parties to flourish.

In this vein, some have argued that a radical right party cannot thrive in the electoral space dominated by a strong radicalized mainstream party: its ideological cousin (Meguid 2005; Minkenberg 2015; Pirro 2015; Pytlas 2016; cf. Arzheimer and Carter 2006). Explanations of this kind focus on the role of policy convergence or divergence among mainstream parties in creating fertile ground for radical right parties (Kitschelt 1995; cf. Katz and Mair 1995). By focusing on the policy moves of the mainstream parties, many different predictions about the effect of policy convergence coexist in the literature, including at least three potentially contradictory claims: (1) the convergence of the mainstream parties opens up space for a radical right party to enter; (2) the polarization of mainstream parties facilitates outbidding, and consequently the entry of a radical right party; and (3) insufficient radicalization of the radical right's proximate competitor creates an opportunity for a radical right party (cf. Adams et al. 2006; Bale et al. 2010; Horowitz 1985; Kedar 2005; Kitschelt and McGann 1995; Meguid 2005).

One reason for this assortment of predictions is that many different mainstream party configurations and policy moves are compatible with a radical right party's success. For instance, the Czech Republicans emerged in the mid-1990s when mainstream parties were focused almost entirely on the economic transformation, and then disappeared well before mainstream politics assumed a more nationalist tone in the early 2000s, which led to a second wave of radical right parties. The Hungarian far-right Jobbik party coexists with its ideological cousin: Orbán's Fidesz. In Poland, however, the mainstream radicalized party – PiS (Law and Justice Party) – has thus far successfully prevented the electoral breakthrough of a strong new radical right party (after the decline of the League of Polish Families Party) and has even radicalized further after the 2015 elections.

The Hungarian Fidesz and Polish PiS blur boundaries between the radical right and the mainstream right. In Hungary, the radical right Jobbik coexists with Fidesz without any significant loss of electoral support. Moreover, regarding the refugees that reached the Hungarian boarder after the 2016 migration crisis, Fidesz advocates more extreme positions than Jobbik. But in Poland, the radicalized party PiS that also mobilized against the refugee threat faces anemic radical right competitors. Both are governing parties with broad agendas that evolved from moderate mainstream parties and radicalized over time in their efforts to weaken the democratic institutional framework in Hungary and later in Poland.

For proponents of supply-side theories, radical right party support varies largely as a result of mainstream party strategies, competition between proximate parties, perceptions of future coalition bargaining, internal party organizations, opportunity structures, electoral thresholds and party system features (Art 2011; Carter 2002; Givens 2005; Kedar 2005). While most East European countries fall under the broader umbrella of party systems with proportional representation, Hungary has a mixed electoral system that penalizes small parties. Yet Hungary has produced two radical right parties: MIÉP in 1990s and Jobbik in the 2000s. The rise of Jobbik, which acquired 12 percent of the seats in the Hungarian Parliament and became the third largest party in the 2010 elections, stunned Hungarian political experts at the time.

With the exception of Meguid (2005), who has reoriented the literature's emphasis on the role of mainstream *non-proximate* parties, the majority of party-oriented, supply-side accounts have tended to overlook or downplay the role of parties at the other ideological extreme.[22] This book brings these parties back in to the center of the political action, and continues the trend of moving away from the exclusive focus on nearby competitor parties in explaining the rise and fall of radical right parties (Meguid 2005). The theory recalibrates the study of the radical right to focus on the neglected role of bilateral opposite parties, which promote the accommodation of social and ethnic parties (Sartori 1976). To unpack this aspect of the theory further, the next section highlights three essential factors: sovereignty of the dominant group, accommodation of minorities and threats of status reversal.

## 2.2 Sovereignty of the Dominant Group

Like the magma in a dormant volcano, radical right party mobilization is often quiescent for extended periods of time before it explodes

---

[22] Sartori (1976) referred to these parties as "bilateral opposites."

erratically to unleash stifled gaseous grievances. This book views the radical right's "magma" as the historically entrenched hierarchy of groups that forms the state's agenda vis-à-vis minority group accommodation.[23] The trigger that unleashes the volcano's magma is a sudden adverse shift in the status quo that weakens the dominant group's sovereign control over the regulation of majority–minority relations and its status. This shift engenders resentment, which can be particularly severe if the mainstream parties are complicit in weakening the dominant group by facilitating the agenda of minority advocates. This resentment then translates into radical right mobilization. When minority advances have been rolled back or reversed, however, radical right mobilization wanes.

This theoretical framework bridges the supply-side and demand-side schools of radical right politics. From the supply-side perspective, the mobilization of minority groups and the resultant shifts in policies and representation account for swings in the electoral fortunes of radical right parties. In this respect, radical right mobilization is attuned to the accommodation of minorities and improvements in their status, and takes note of the extent to which mainstream and niche parties have served as minority allies (and, in the eyes of some, as "traitors"). As the minority group voices its demands and increases political pressure, the fringe members of the dominant group sound off the alarm, immediately increasing the political salience of identity and sovereignty issues. If this logic is a reasonable stylization of how radical right parties mobilize, then surges in support for radical right parties should follow from shifts that erode the balance between the dominant group and the ascending minority.

The demand side is also embedded in this account because it explains why shifts in the status quo resonate with voters and lead to political counter-mobilization. Fringe members of the dominant group defend a historically embedded, structural hierarchy between groups. Mainstream parties, as agents of the state, regulate minority accommodation. Changes in the status quo signal the ascendancy of the minority group and elevate their status vis-à-vis the dominant group. A relational shift that involves tangible goods, such as state resources

---

[23] Historical experiences with reversals of status hierarchies are often especially troubling in the eyes of the current electorate.

channeled toward minorities via a politicized process, is a strong validation of the minority group's power. However, symbolic erosion of the hierarchical order between the groups generates resentment as well. When the ascending group endangers the prestige of the established, the established fight back (Elias and Scotson 1965). When mainstream parties yield sovereignty, in order to respond to the dreams and demands of the minority, they may become discredited in the eyes of some voters. This creates an opportunity for radical right parties to present themselves as the true champions of the dominant group and its interests.

Radical right mobilization reflects the objective standing of the groups not in terms of their wealth and economic power but rather their perceived relative standing. Erosions of the status quo are perceived when minorities expand their symbolic and material resources by politicizing the state. By using the political process to extract their share from the budget, or to alter policies that involve allocations from the state and thereby erode symbolic prestige, they infringe upon the dominant group's sovereign control over the state. Radical right mobilization follows as a backlash from the fulfillment of minority demands through the political process. Let us now consider *how* mainstream parties, through their coalitions and accomodative policies, actually facilitate radical right mobilization.

### 2.2.1 Treacherous Mainstream Parties

Radical right parties occupy a niche near the extreme pole of the political spectrum and compete for votes with other, larger parties. In order to gain traction, voters have to opt out of supporting a mainstream patriotic party and flock to a more fringe, radical alternative that can address their concerns.[24] Voters who are concerned with the erosion of the dominant group's power, and view mainstream parties as having betrayed national interests, form the foundation of radical right mobilization.

Consider the question of acquiring agricultural land as an issue of national sovereignty. A cross-national study of East European voters

---

[24] On disappointed voters flocking towards anti-establishment parties, see Pop Eleches (2010).

has shown that radical right voters, across a wide range of countries, oppose selling land to foreigners (Bustikova and Kitschelt 2011). In Eastern Europe, the European Union granted a ten-year moratorium on the purchase of farmland by foreigners to all of the new members who signed the Treaty of Accession in 2003.[25] To comply with the European Union regulations, the ruling party Fidesz-KDPN in Hungary adopted a new Land Law on June 21, 2013, which removed the prohibition stipulated in the 1994 law that excluded foreigners from purchasing agricultural or forested land. Passing the law in the Hungarian Parliament on June 21, 2013, was highly contentious. The MPs from the radial right party Jobbik vehemently opposed it. Using the speaker's platform, Jobbik parliamentarians chanted "Traitors!" (*Hazaárulók!*) and called the new law an act of high treason.[26]

Radical right mobilization is a revolt of the fringes of the dominant group fueled by the view that the dominant group owns the state, and is not willing to share it or to let a third party interfere with its sovereign control over its policies. This possessive attitude toward the state and the nation is well expressed in the platform of the socially conservative, anti-establishment, far-right movement Kukiz'15 in Poland:

We love Poland. We are members of a great and brave Nation. We are the voice of the Nation who woke up and wants to regain control over its country. We know that everything that is best in our country results from patriotism, diligence and innovation of Poles. We do not allow the enormous potential and ambitions of the Poles to be wasted. Our strategy leads to the implementation of the basic constitutional principle that the supreme power in the Republic of Poland belongs to the Nation. These rules are enshrined in the Constitution, yet until now they were merly empty slogans. The power in Poland can not belong to the party oligarchy, nor can it belong to foreign governments, international corporations or foreign media. The power in our country belongs solely to the Nation![27]

The leader of the movement, former rock star turned politician Paweł Kukiz, finished third in the first round of the May 2015 Polish

---

[25] Source: European Commission 2016. Eight East European countries signed the Treaty of Accession in 2003: Czech Republic, Estonia, Latvia, Lithuania, Hungary, Poland, Slovenia and Slovakia.
[26] Source: Reuters 2013.
[27] Source: Kukiz'15 web page. Translated by the author.

presidential election. He criticized mainstream political parties for facilitating the rise of candidates from marginal identities into positions of power.[28] Kukiz'15 also attacked the Palikot Movement, an anti-clerical, socially liberal party, which assertively opened a political path forward for the candidacy of Anna Grodzka and Robert Biedroń, who became the first transsexual and the first openly gay members of the Polish Parliament. The progressive Palikot movement became the third largest party in the 2011 parliament. Their success, to quote Grodzka, signaled that "[t]oday, Poland is changing. I am the proof along with Robert Biedroń, a homosexual and the head of an anti-homophobia campaign."[29]

Four years later, anti-gay rock star and social activist Paweł Kukiz caused a political sensation when he finished third in the first round of the May 2015 Polish presidential election. He gained more than one-fifth of the vote (Szczerbiak 2017). Kukiz was a rebel candidate committed to the Catholic faith and its conservative teachings. His platform proposed radical changes to the Polish electoral system: the introduction of single-member constituencies, which would reflect the political will of a majority and therefore prevent the ascendance of non-traditional political candidates such as Grodzka and Biedroń.[30]

Mainstream parties can engage in different forms of "treachery." In addition to promoting non-traditional minority candidates and selling off agricultural land to foreign entities, other common kinds of treachery include providing tax havens for foreign firms to attract investment, or creating a legal framework that benefits political actors who selectively uphold the rule of law. Radical right parties embrace economic nationalism (Bustikova and Kitschelt 2009). In their eyes, when faced with the adversarial effects of the external markets, *their* state is obliged to tilt the balance in a way that benefits the interests of the sovereign group.[31]

---

[28] Kukiz criticized the mainstream political parties for having formed a cartel of political parties, a "partocracy," a system in which party oligarchs control the candidate lists and the process of candidate selection. Partocracy facilitates the rise of candidates from marginal identities into high political positions. In his view, partocracy undermines the sovereignty of the nation.

[29] Source: Huffington Post 2011.

[30] On social diversity, the number of parties and permissiveness of the electoral system, see Milazzo et al. 2018.

[31] On policy blurring of radical right parties, see Rovny 2013.

In Poland, the Law and Justice Party called Poland a "German–Russian" condominium when it was in the opposition, and claimed that Poland had been left in economic ruins by the liberal-conservative party, Civic Platform, which governed between 2007 and 2015. In general, it blamed the corrupt Civic Platform for mismanaging the economy by selling the country off to foreigners. In the election campaign, the Law and Justice party also invoked a wild conspiracy theory that the former Prime Minister Donald Tusk and ex-President Bronisław Komorowski, from Civic Platform, were "traitors" who conspired to kill President Lech Kaczyński in the 2010 Smolensk plane crash (Markowski 2018).

Being on the fringes gives radical right parties the luxury of retaining ideological purity. As a result, they can be more unhinged in pursuing aggressive rhetoric that targets minorities. By comparison, mainstream parties are more constrained in their ability to aggressively campaign against minorities and to compete with radical right parties. They also face the risk of factionalism if one bloc advocates much more extreme policies. Moreover, if minorities form parties or are backed by political advocates, mainstream parties may be in need of their support to build broad policy and governing coalitions.[32] This suggests that mainstream parties should generally be more wary of burning bridges with politically organized minority groups.

Since mainstream parties hold power, international actors also scrutinize them more aggressively than niche parties. Human rights organizations and institutions of the European Union exert pressure, leading parties to pursue less aggressive anti-minority positions in a way that they do not do with niche parties. For instance, in 2006, the club of European Socialists in the European Parliament temporarily suspended the Slovak mainstream party (SMER) due to its ties with the far right. Ten years later, the European Commission launched an investigation into whether the ruling Polish party (PiS) is overturning the rule of law with respect to independence of the judiciary and public media. After the rule of law in Poland further worsened in 2016, the European Commission activated the so-called Article 7 procedure in December

---

[32] On the volatility of the coalition formations, see Haughton and Deegan-Krause 2015.

2017. This was the first time it had ever been used.[33] Then, less than a year later, on September 12, 2018, it was used a second time to sanction Hungary, which was found to pose a systemic threat to the European Union's founding values.[34]

To a much greater extent than niche parties, mainstream parties engage in two-level games with their domestic constituents and international organizations. This means that mainstream parties are more easily tainted as collaborators because they participate in political projects that undermine national sovereignty, such as European Union accession, which allows the country to be scrutinized from abroad, or economic liberalization, which undermines the ability of states to freely manage their economies and subjects them to scrutiny by international monetary institutions. As such, mainstream parties are faced with external constraints that limit their portfolio of economic policies and state-building strategies. This eradicates differences between major parties and undermines their ability to position themselves as pioneers of niche positions. At the individual level, political opportunists from mainstream parties that use politics solely as a vehicle for personal enrichment further contribute to the perception of mainstream parties as "traitors."[35] This further diminishes the ability of the representatives of the nation-state to independently intervene in domestic affairs and compromises their credibility as champions of the dominant nationality and state sovereignty. Niche parties, such as radical right parties, have the luxury of not playing in the big league. They can therefore avoid culpability for large supra-national projects, and can focus on the ownership of the state by the dominant group as the nucleus of their platform.[36]

---

[33] Article 7 of the Nice Treaty states that the European Council can declare the existence of "a serious and persistent breach of fundamental rights." EU sanctions could potentially lead to a loss of EU voting rights.

[34] On the crisis of Polish democracy, see Kelemen and Ornstein 2016. Source: EURACTIV 2018.

[35] In more sinister circumstances, mainstream parties are locked in a collusive system of political patronage, which also puts the credibility of parties and politicians in question.

[36] Threats to the dominant status of the sovereign and the dynamic of minority accommodation shape the political salience over time, and explain the differential electoral success of radical right parties across electoral cycles. The benchmark against which the betrayal of the sovereign by the mainstream parties is evaluated is historical. For example, in Germany, the major German political parties are viewed as guardians of stability, inhibiting any repeat of the

Market reforms and a template laid out to join the European Union in the aftermath of the fall of the Berlin Wall were implemented in party systems with low levels of polarization (Fish 1998; Frye 2010; Kitschelt et al. 1999). The prospect of the European Union enlargement was viewed as beneficial to all (a positive-sum issue) and a pathway to extricate the new democracies from the control of the Soviet Union, thereby increasing their sovereignty. Radical right parties of the early 1990s were enthusiastic about returning to Europe (Bustikova and Kitschelt 2009).[37] In less than two decades, however, unification had a downstream effect that transformed it into a zero-sum issue. States ceded some sovereignty to obtain membership benefits. More importantly, new member states, by the act of joining, committed themselves to market liberalism, pluralism and the protection of minorities, and tied the hands of the dominant group. The shift toward greater minority sensitivity, in the view of some voters, came directly at the dominant group's expense.[38]

horrific interwar Nazi experience. The threat of the radical right parties in Germany is thus viewed through the lens of a collapsing fragile democracy. In Eastern Europe, sovereignty is often associated with right-wing autocracies. The mainstream parties in Eastern Europe after 1989 were mostly vigilant about parties linked to the left-wing autocratic communist regime (Bozoki and Ishiyama 2002; Grzymala-Busse 2002; Ishiyama 2009), and much less concerned about the interwar autocratic experience. Red communist dictatorships defeated or replaced brown pro-fascist regimes, in many cases. Liberal (or electoral) democracies, in turn, defeated communism. Since the anti-red narratives relate to the eras both before and after communism, radical right mobilization in Eastern Europe can be interpreted through the prism of lost (and then regained) national sovereignty, which makes legacies of brown autocracies even more relevant, appealing and tied to ethnic exclusion. Whereas economic issues allow for Pareto improvements, which benefit all groups, the domain of sovereignty is largely indivisible. Prestige associated with sovereign control cannot improve for both the majority and a minority at the same time, since hierarchies are by definition built on relative rankings and exclusion.

[37] Since the unification of Europe was viewed as bringing net gains, it was possible to mobilize civil society in support on a massive scale, and thereby to exert political pressure from below (Vachudova 2005; Vachudova and Hooghe 2009). Return of sovereignty to the dominant group, viewed through the prism of a security umbrella and a wealth magnet, was an issue of great importance across all party systems.

[38] The initial consensus that perceived the accession as beneficial for all had evaporated (Polyakova 2015). Party systems lost their centripetal glue, previously provided by the enthusiasm of new freedoms and by the benchmarks of the accession process that standardized policy agendas (Bustikova 2009b).

Mainstream parties can converge on an economic issue, which may be highly salient for the electorate, but a centrist position on identity issues implies that it lacks political importance (Spies and Franzmann 2011). The salience of identity issues is partly endogenous to the spatial positions of parties. An extreme position embraced by a minority group and its allies signals a shift in the status quo, which invariably alarms and radicalizes the dominant group. This shift in the status quo increases the salience of identity issues, for the process of accommodation naturally politicizes minority issues.

The mechanism behind this backlash argument is the spatial positioning of parties. Political parties take extreme positions only if they care about an issue dimension. As a result, the salience of issue dimensions is at least partly endogenous to spatial positioning. It is important to note that the reverse is not always the case, for parties may subscribe to some moderate positions (e.g., on issues that relate to economic reforms or trade policies), even though they think that the dimension is salient (Spies and Franzmann 2011). By highlighting a dimension through an extreme position, parties often provoke a backlash among those political actors that disagree.

The spatially extreme position of the advocates of minority rights mobilizes the radical segments of the dominant group. Their embrace of an extreme position spreads a sense of alarm among their opponents, helping them to overcome collective action problems in organizing and increasing the extent of polarization. Betrayal and treason can occur in different ways, but the minority group has to have the capacity to challenge the dominant group. This capacity is key to why group hierarchies matter for understanding radical right politics.

## 2.2.2 Group Hierarchy and Demoted Groups

The distinction between group hostility and policy hostility has important implications for understanding the structural conditions that enable the radical right to flourish.[39] The greatest potential for backlash is created when the accommodation of minorities is perceived as

---

After experiencing a loss, the resentment of the sovereign grew and radical right mobilization followed, contributing to the polarization of the political system.

[39] On policy hostility in immigrant–native conflict, see Dancygier 2010.

inconsistent with their historical position in the status hierarchy, or when it signals the desire of a demoted group to erode the hierarchy. The dominant group has especially good reason to be wary of the demoted group if it was an alien ruler in the not very distant past (Hechter 2013).[40] Demoted groups in Eastern Europe were created after the disintegration of empires in the wake of World War I and after the collapse of the Soviet Union. The mobilization of the demoted group – whether Russians, Hungarians or Turks – reminds the dominant group of its own past subjugation. If the demoted group is small, its demands are especially irritating, since they are inconsistent with its current size and reminiscent of the historical reversal of group hierarchies. Unlike the ambition of a large demoted group (e.g., Russians in Moldova or in Ukraine), the ambition of a small, demoted group does not typically pose an *existential* threat to the dominant group (e.g., Hungarians in Slovakia or Romania).

Therefore, what enables radical right parties to succeed is the threat posed by an aspirational minority. Radical right parties tend to do best when they target minorities that have been able to mobilize some political support, but do not have the capacity to reverse the group hierarchy (cf. Petersen 2002). If the aspirations of the minority are so threatening that their fulfillment would potentially reverse the status of the dominant group, voters tend to embrace large parties capable of withstanding the challenge because large, existential threats require large coalitions and competence in security issues. By contrast, an environment involving small threats is conducive to the rise of radical right niche parties, for they can unleash their exclusionary rhetoric without paying a substantial political price if they incite collective violence.

The size of the threat is of course related to the ethnic composition of countries. Group size signals the maximum scope of the minority's mobilizational potential. Historical evolution in the hierarchy of groups contextualizes the aspirations of the minority group, since the ambition of former rulers will draw the ire of the current sovereign.[41]

---

[40] For example, Hungarians formerly ruled over Slovaks, but are now a minority in an independent Slovakia. Similarly, Ukrainains, Estonians, Latvians, Kazakhs and Lithuanians, among others, were formerly ruled by Russians, but Russians are now a minority in all these countries.

[41] As a shortcut, group size speaks to the potential threat of aspirational minorities, although it does not indicate their degree of mobilization, which is ultimately more predictive of radical right success.

In countries with small minorities, the accommodation of minority demands results in the elevation of the minority's status. This change in the status quo irritates radical right voters, who vote to curb its further advancement. However, in countries with large minorities, change in the accommodation of a politically organized minority can drastically threaten the dominant nationality, and potentially lead to a complete status reversal where the rulers become the ruled.

Voters threatened with status reversal have good reason to fear the loss of their ethnic dominance, and thus to rally behind a large party that is more likely to win (and more capable of containing the formidable threat) than a niche radical right party. It follows that radical right parties will generally find it more difficult to attract voters faced with the prospect of an actual status reversal (i.e., in countries with a large minority population). Over time, the theory expects radical right parties will gain electorally when they satisfy the demand to rally against changes in minority accommodation, and predicts that such parties will suffer electoral defeats when policies designed to help minorities are reversed or blunted.

## 2.3 Minority Accommodation and Status Quo Shifts

To further develop the theory, it is now necessary to specify the conditions that contribute to shifts in the status quo and politicize minority–majority relations. The status elevation of a minority through governmental policies ("minority accommodation") generally unifies radical right voters, but two conditions must be satisfied for a radical right party to succeed. First, there must exist a bilateral opposite to the radical right party, such as an ethnic party or a party with a socially liberal agenda, benefiting social minorities like gays and lesbians, religious minorities or an ethnic underclass, such as Roma. Second, the success of the bilateral opposite party's demands must be salient. Conversely, the failure of radical right parties occurs when an electorally strong bilateral opposite is absent from the party system and when minority accommodation does not polarize the electorate.

In peaceful democratic settings, when competition between rival mainstream parties is intense, ethnic parties may be invited to help to form a governing coalition (Conrad and Golder 2010). Previous scholars have shown that, as a consequence, when mainstream parties need small ethnic parties to form coalitions, the political salience of ethnic cleavages in party competition increases (Kopstein and Wittenberg 2011, 2010; Wilkinson 2004). This dynamic benefits radical right parties, which react to the change in the status quo, and arise to counterbalance the strength of parties that advocate accommodating social and ethnic minorities in a manner that elevates the group's status.[42] The status elevation is a shift in the status quo, which happens when minority representatives are elected or appointed into public offices, when public office is used to benefit minorities, or when the state channels resources, typically in education or social welfare, to address minority issues. Status elevation can be also symbolic.

The electoral success of radical right parties is thus integrally tied to coalition politics. Although a large body of literature examines the dynamics of coalition formation (Adams et al. 2005; Conrad and Golder 2010; Laver 1998; Laver and Schofield 1990; Riker 1962; Volden and Carruba 2004), this research has almost completely overlooked the effect of coalition participation on issue salience.[43] Some scholars have shown that structural determinants and/or party movements affect issue salience, but party tactics and movements are themselves frequently driven by the need to form governing coalitions and by the distributive tensions built into such political alliances.

While supply-side theories see radical party success as most likely to ensue when identity issues are salient and when radical parties are perceived as "owning" identity issues, issue salience is typically treated as exogenous to the political system (Colomer and Puglisi 2005; Eatwell 2003; Lijphart 1984) or as an outcome of party strategies designed to secure a competitive advantage (Arzheimer 2010; Belanger and Meguid 2008; Laver and Schofield 1990). To explain shifts in salience, some scholars have chosen to focus on shocks such as immigration in-flow to the country (Olzak 1992), shifts in values induced by generational replacements (Inglehart and Welzel 2005),

---

[42] Radical parties contest funding schools or even universities with minority language instruction or policies aiming at a de facto bilingual administration of a country. Although the economic costs are marginal, they have implications for the status of groups and future employment opportunities. For example, the Estonian 1995 Law on Languages established language proficiency for public service jobs, which greatly disadvantaged Russian speakers (de Varennes 1999: 135).

[43] For an exception discussing group formation and issue salience, see Holyoke 2009.

or tectonic movements in the cleavage structure that bring cultural issues to the forefront of national politics (Bornschier 2010; Kriesi 1998; Lijphart 1968; Lipset and Rokkan 1967; Rohrschneider and Whitefield 2009).

Building on this research, the theory makes issue salience endogenous to the strength and the inclusion of ethnic and socially liberal parties in governing coalitions. To accommodate the demands of its smaller coalition partner, the moderate party must shift its position on identity issues closer to the more extreme policy views of its coalition partner (Kedar 2005). Moderate parties increase the salience of identity issues by promoting policies that offer non-core groups selective benefits and symbolic politics that shift the status quo (Kopstein and Wittenberg 2018; Wilkinson 2004).

Although structural approaches cannot by themselves explain the volatility of electoral success in succeeding elections, factors such as the presence of minority ethnic or social groups that demand accommodation from the majority serve as an important trigger for the success of radical parties. If represented by political parties, ethnic groups supporting the accommodation of minorities, and proponents of socially liberal policies, may be courted by moderate parties to form governing coalitions. The formation of coalitions with ethno-liberal parties increases the salience of identity issues because policies that privilege some groups over others magnify preexisting grievances, and fuel political resentment that benefits radical right parties.

The case of Slovakia illustrates this dynamic plainly. In 2002, the Hungarian ethnic party (MKP) in Slovakia was invited to join the governing coalition and used its power to promote minority schooling for the substantial Hungarian minority. After overcoming some internal discord, the radical right Slovak National Party (SNS) won almost 12 percent of the vote and a partnership in the 2006 governing coalition. The party used its influence to roll back the language law, which had expanded Hungarian language rights in Slovakia, and to strengthen the role of the (titular) Slovak language. At the same time, splits within the Hungarian ethnic party significantly blunted the political power of the Hungarian minority. This policy success, combined with discord in the opponent's camp, led to the demise of the SNS. Despite aggressively campaigning against Slovakia's participation in the very unpopular Greek bailout, SNS failed to secure a single seat in the 2012 elections. A referendum in 2015 seeking to expand the rights of gays and lesbians, which SNS strongly opposed, created a new lifeline for the party and expanded its portfolio of accommodative policies against which to mobilize.

Language is often a highly salient issue for minorities, since it determines whether their children will have the opportunity to be educated in the tongue of their parent(s) and thus to preserve and assert their identity (Liu 2014). Accommodation can involve allowing the use of minority languages in official settings, permitting cities to use bilingual signs, sanctioning the use of ethnic forms of female last names as well as acknowledging the rights of minorities to present their version of historical narratives.

Radical right parties rally their support from voters who would like to offset these perceived advantages being afforded to minorities. When radical right parties succeed, they actively promote policies that either reverse accommodation or create policies, such as language laws, that make future accommodation more difficult. When accommodation increases, the theory expects radical right parties to gain strength. Similarly, when the status quo is preserved or accommodation recedes, radical right parties tend to weaken. Instead of success breeding success, their success actually brings about their own failure.

As an illustration, consider what happened in Bulgaria, which did not produce a single radical right party until 2005 when the radical right party Ataka emerged seemingly "out of nowhere" and gained 8 percent of the vote.[44] In light of the theory, Ataka's sudden success is not surprising at all. In the 2001 election, "The Movement for Rights and Freedoms Party" (DPS) that represents Turkish interests was invited into a governing coalition and an ethnic Turkish minister became part of the cabinet (Ganev 1995; Popova 2016).[45] The coalition placed the DPS in control of the Ministry of Agriculture, which allowed it to block a proposal to trim state subsidies for tobacco

---

[44] There was a brief period of ethnic tensions, some violent, and accommodation in the early 1990s and attacks on Roma communities.

[45] Deutsche Presse-Agentur, July 20, 2001, cited in MAR 2008. On the incorporation of DPS in immediate post-1989 politics and the tacit alliance between DPS and the Bulgarian Socialist Party in early 1990s, see Petkova 2002; Spirova 2008: 489; Vachudova 2005; and Vassilev 2001: 53. On ethnic clientelism among ethnic parties representing the Turkish minority party in Bulgaria, and the Hungarian ethnic party in Romania, see Gavriliu 2010. The Turkish minority is about 9 percent.

cultivation, the occupational specialization of many Bulgarian Turks. DPS's growing influence in the Bulgarian political system led to a political backlash in the 2005 election. The newly founded Ataka declared "ethnic minorities with privileged access to policy-making" as their primary political target, and received 8 percent of the vote, and 21 out of 240 seats in the Bulgarian Parliament. This rise of the radical right in Bulgaria occurred at the same time when Bulgaria's economy was experiencing 7 percent growth and soon after Bulgaria had signed the EU accession treaty. This cuts against theories grounded in economic retrenchment, economic uncertainty and political instability at the same time that it lends further credence to the book's proposed theory.

An important empirical implication is that the formation of a governing coalition between a mainstream party and an accommodation-seeking party increases the probability of the radical right's success in the subsequent electoral cycle. The ruling coalition's accommodation of minority demands aggravates preexisting grievances, which strengthens radical right parties that promise to retract the politics of accommodation and to reverse the status quo shift. By identifying the electoral trigger that exacerbates identity-based grievances – the electoral success of bilateral opposite parties – along with a credible causal mechanism – resentment resulting from the change in the status quo – this book provides a theoretical framework to investigate the variable success of radical right parties over time within countries and not only across them.

Focusing on the political effect of bilateral opposite parties sheds light on a closely related issue in the study of radical right parties, namely, how mainstream parties should address the challenge of radical right parties. One theorized precondition for the rise of a niche party is the convergence of large mainstream parties on economic issues. Although the strategies of mainstream parties are important, I suggest that their influence operates primarily through their interaction with bilateral opposite parties, rather than through their convergence on economic issues. While convergence may open up a second dimension of party competition – identity – it is unclear whether and why extreme positions on identity should necessarily follow. Similarly, corrupt politicians can alienate and anger voters, and mainstream parties might converge on a "corrupt" focal point, but this need not cause radical right parties to emerge when simple protest parties with an anti-establishment appeal would suffice (Pop-Eleches 2010).[46] Given the volatility of their electoral success not only across countries, but also within them over time, any theory that has pretensions to predict must identify a similarly volatile trigger that would deepen or assuage identity-based grievances.[47] The theory advanced in this book therefore focuses on the largely neglected role of bilateral opposite parties in order to explain and predict when radical right parties succeed and fail in electoral competition.

Scholars fundamentally disagree about whether the most effective strategy to keep radical parties at bay is to radicalize (Bale 2003; Kitschelt with McGann 1995; Meguid 2005; cf. Bale 2003; Van der Brug et al. 2005) or to moderate (Arzheimer 2010; Capoccia 2001; Minkenberg 2002; cf. Carter 2005). Some studies have suggested that support for radical right parties decreases when the proximate mainstream party radicalizes on identity issues, since the mainstream party steals, and eventually molds, the extremist agenda. This effectively "squeezes out" the radical right (Meguid 2005; Pirro 2015; Pytlas 2016). Others submit that when a proximate mainstream party radicalizes, it facilitates the rise of radical parties, since the mainstream party legitimizes the extremist agenda and opens the door for the electoral breakthrough of radical challengers (Horowitz 1985; Krekó and Mayer 2015).

Predictions about the effect of a mainstream party "going rogue," and adopting some part of the agenda of a radical right party's challenger, hinge on key assumptions in directional and proximate models of voting. According to proximate voting models, when mainstream parties "go rogue," extreme parties should become extinct, unless large numbers of extremist voters are spatially concentrated in certain voting

---

[46] Niche parties include radical parties, green parties and territorial parties (Adams et al. 2006; Meguid 2005). The convergence approach cannot account for the variety of the extremist responses: convergence predicts the emergence of small parties with diverging policy preferences on the second dimension, but it is not clear why those need to be non-economic parties with extreme views on identity. Protest parties, niche parties or fiscally extremist parties can emerge as a reaction to convergence.

[47] Changes in levels of corruption and changes in the pace of convergence on economic issues, however, tend not to exhibit these dynamics to the degree that would be required to account for the temporal variability in the electoral success of radical right parties.

districts and centrist voters do not punish polarization. By contrast, the directional approach suggests that moderate voters will not punish a mainstream party when it moves toward the extreme policy position. Yet it also implies that radical right parties should disappear in the long run. In the proximity model, the median voter pulls parties toward the center, whereas in the directional model the mainstream party moves permanently away from the center to capture the extremist vote. But both imply that radical parties should disappear once parties have adjusted their strategies. Strategic, outcome-oriented, policy-balancing models (Abramson et al. 2010; Kedar 2005) suggest that voters may opt for the proximate competitors of their most preferred parties to pull policies in the desired direction. However, these models assume a high degree of voter sophistication, clarity of party platforms, and the identifiability of coalitions and future political alliances.

Meguid (2005, 2008) proposes that scholars shift the analytical focus away from the interaction between ideologically proximate parties and toward the "critical role of non-proximal parties in electoral competition." Meguid's core insight is that in order to split its main right-wing competitor, a mainstream left party may decide to move its position on an identity issue (e.g., immigration) to raise its salience.[48] If the mainstream right is confronted with a radical right party challenger, the mainstream left's move then forces the mainstream right to take a stance on immigration and to shift its policy position. The theoretical innovation of Meguid's argument lies in its insight that the radical right's success is partly determined by the movement of the mainstream left, which increases the salience of an identity issue, like immigration or religion, in order to create space for the radical right to break through and thus to weaken the mainstream right.

The theory developed here builds on this key insight and emphasizes non-proximate parties in two additional ways. It focuses on the role of extreme non-proximate, bilateral opposite parties (e.g., ethnic and socially liberal parties).[49] These parties are crucial because they most

---

[48] The mainstream left is proximal to the mainstream right and non-proximal to the radical right party. If the mainstream right adopts a tough stance on immigration, Meguid predicts that the radical right challenger will not be able to succeed.

[49] In some ways, this argument represents a return to an earlier literature on the origins of radical right parties in Western Europe, which recognized that the

substantially embrace policies that accommodate minorities, which radical right voters perceive as threatening and which radical right parties can exploit at election time. Following Kedar (2005), the theory presumes that a coalition between an extreme and a moderate party results in a mainstream party policy shift toward the extreme, which provides a platform and *casus belli* for the radical right to make political inroads.

Whether the moderate party embraces or distances itself from the program of the radical right does not have a direct effect on the radical right's electoral chances. Instead, I suggest that radical right voter resentment is not created directly by moderate parties, but rather by their accommodation of ethnic and socially liberal (ethno-liberal) parties, which triggers a shift in the status quo.[50] The theory emphasizes the importance of changes in the *salience* of identity issues, rather than changes in policy positions per se, to the electoral success of radical right parties. While some shifts in policy positions coincide with changes in identity issue salience, this is not always the case. Minorities can be accommodated without policy shifts. If an ethnic party joins a governing coalition, is allocated a government portfolio and uses it to distribute pork to its ethnic constituency, the mainstream coalition partner does not move an inch on a programmatic policy axis. Political parties that accommodate minorities modify issue salience, even when they do not entail policy shifts, and this in and of itself positively shapes the radical right's odds of success.

When politically organized minorities ascend to power and governments pursue pro-minority issues, non-economic issues gain salience. This implies that salience is a function of party system polarization. When mainstream parties satisfy the demands of minorities, political

---

sudden rise in radical right-wing politics in the 1980s was initially a form of backlash against the new political forces representing voters with post-material, socially liberal values and green parties (Ignazi 1992; Kitschelt with McGann 1995; von Beyme 1988). These initial insights have been largely lost in the ensuing debate, which has focused on the profile of radical right voters, the institutional and structural determinants of radical right support and on the dynamics of competition between the mainstream parties.

[50] The effect of mainstream party tactics depends critically on an omitted variable, namely, the presence of an ethnic or a socially liberal party and the extent to which the moderate mainstream party accommodates it. When an ethnic or socially liberal party is accommodated in a coalition, it fuels resentment. As a result, the moderate party is compelled to further embrace accommodation, which only intensifies umbrage and benefits the radical right party.

polarization increases and minority–majority issues spike in salience. As a result, accommodative mainstream parties do not react to salient issues that concern an already polarized electorate, a portion of which demands accommodation, but rather manufacture salience by making accommodation into a politically contested issue.

As a result, the party system becomes more polarized when ethnic and socially liberal parties advance in social and political status. Radical right parties form or remobilize to reverse gains already made by groups they oppose. In this sense, radical right parties are inherently reactionary in response to minority accommodation. Conversely, when the status quo is maintained and no major concessions to minority groups are granted, radical right-wing parties generally fail to emerge or, if they are already in power, tend to suffer electoral defeat in the next election.

Whereas earlier supply-side research has generally treated the radical right's electoral prospects as a function of either mainstream or proximate party strategies, this book argues that temporal variation in the success of radical right parties is triggered by the success of ethnic and socially liberal parties on the left and the complicity of mainstream parties in facilitating "adverse" shifts in the status quo. Radical right parties arise to push back against the electoral strength and policy impact of parties advocating accommodating policies toward ethnic and social minorities. This back-lash mechanism generates three empirical implications that are tested in subsequent chapters. Radical right parties should be more successful when bilateral opposite parties (1) obtain policy-making powers via coalition participation, (2) express greater ideological extremism and (3) win a greater proportion of the popular vote.

## 2.4 Groups and Status Threats

From the electoral perspective, the baseline threat of ethnic groups lies to a large extent in sheer numbers: their head count (Chandra 2005). It signals their full, even if hypothetical, mobilization potential. For a variety of reasons – such as economic voting (Tucker 2006), cross-cutting cleavages or in-group factionalism – this potential may never be realized. In general, as the size of the group increases, the potential threat of the group increases as well, due to the pool of ethnic votes that is available, but this straightforward effect can be dampened as a result of other factors.

In democracies with small (but peaceful) ethnic minorities, the legitimacy of the titular, dominant nationality is rarely contested. Even if the ethnic minority is politically organized, voices its grievances and achieves some measure of accommodation, it cannot attain dominance in a fully democratic setting.[51] The primacy of the status of the dominant nationality, supported by its sheer head count, in such countries is not in peril. Although a small minority does not have the capacity to overthrow the dominant group, it can erode its status. Relational changes in power balances mobilize the fringe members of the dominant group who resent shifts in the status quo and seek to reverse minority gains. Group size is crucial to understanding the mobilization capacity of minorities. It determines the potential magnitude of the threat and the subsequent reservoir of resentment resulting from status elevation. Group size influences cross-country differences in the success and failure of radical right parties, but it does not follow that the mobilization capacity of a group increases linearly with its size or that it is constant over time (Zuber and Szöcsik 2015).

Ethnic groups may suffer from factionalism and split their representation into two (Hungarians in Slovakia) or even three ethnic parties (Albanians in Macedonia), which weakens their bargaining power with the government and mainstream parties (Cunningham 2014). The mobilization capacity of an ethnic group can be also blunted when economic concerns trump identity issues, such as when Russians in Estonia and Latvia opt for mainstream parties that address general economic inequality (Kasekamp 2015a,b). This means that the mobilization capacity of relatively large groups – sometimes as large as 10–15 percent of the population – might be less than their head count would imply, since larger size does not automatically

---

[51] Politicized ethnicity, and the distinction between nationality and citizenship, is common across the region. This specific understanding of nationhood is reflected in the constitutions of East European countries. Almost all post-communist constitutions "make reference to either popular sovereignty or national sovereignty." Some even single out specific nationalities. For example, Article 2 of the Romanian Constitution claims: "national sovereignty shall reside within the Romanian people." The same is true of the constitutions of Croatia, Serbia, Slovenia and Slovakia (Ramet 2007). Article 11.4 of the 1991 Bulgarian constitution contains a provision banning political parties "formed on an ethnic basis." Art. 11.4: "There shall be no political parties on ethnic, racial or religious lines, nor parties which seek the violent seizure of state power."

translate into greater power (Bernauer and Bochsler 2011). Furthermore, overcoming the challenges of collective action increases in difficulty with group size.[52]

It is not uncommon for a numerically small group to fiercely challenge the status quo. For example, anti-Jewish and anti-Muslim sentiments might be mobilized, despite their numerically minor size due to the material and symbolic implications of their demands. Countermobilization ensues when minority advocates scrutinize the actions of the dominant group or if the allegiance of the minority group to the sovereign is in doubt. Similarly, gays and lesbians, small as a fraction of a general population, can swing the status quo, through a combination of privileged access to policy makers and with the backing of international organizations. Proposing laws that would allow them to adopt children is a highly controversial policy in Eastern Europe, which has triggered a strong negative reaction (Bustikova 2015a; Minkenberg 2015; O'Dwyer and Schwartz 2010).

Demands can generate a momentary backlash. For example, Slovakia witnessed a short, very temporary, surge of anti-Semitism before it separated from the Czech lands, due to the mobilization against a handful of Slovak intellectuals of Jewish heritage who advocated for the preservation of Czechoslovakia. After the federation of Czechs and Slovaks was dismantled, and Slovakia gained independence in 1993, the sentiment immediately receded (Bustikova and Guasti 2012). Likewise, the 2000 publication of Jan Gross's book *Neighbors* in Poland challenged the dominant narrative, claiming Polish complicity in communal violence against Jews, thereby undermining the sacred status of Poles as victims of Nazi aggression. This preceded the rise of the League of Polish Families, a radical right party. Similarly, the discussion to remove a pigsty from the location of a World War II Roma concentration camp in 2017 in Lety, Czech Republic, forced Czechs to acknowledge that Roma were victims and Czechs were complicit.[53] This politicized latent tension in Czech–Roma relations. Both

---

[52] Olson 1965. Liu (2017b) finds that minority language recognition is determined by group size and that democracies without a sizable ethnic majority are more likely to recognize minority demands.

[53] The discussion to remove the camp started in the mid-1990s and, eventually, polarized the debate about Lety, especially after 2013 when the United Nations Human Rights Committee asked the Czech Republic to shut down the pigsty. Source: Reflex 2018.

narratives rattled the moral superiority and dignity of the dominant group and challenged its historical portrayal of the period, in which the titular group perpetrated no acts of violence against minorities, and was not a passive enabler of the Nazi genocide.

A more recent example is the backlash against migrants from Syria and the Middle East. Resettlement quotas, however small, that the European Union proposed to accommodate refugees, mostly of Muslim faith, triggered a backlash in Eastern Europe. A key reason is that it challenged the right of dominant groups to control their own migration policies. The backlash was vicious, but temporary. After the European Union backpedaled, and decided to contain the crisis by relying on the refugee camps in Turkey, the salience of the issue receded.

Minority groups, and their allies, threaten the dominant group with their ability to shift the status quo. This can be a symbolic move, such as a high-profile commemoration of a memorial dedicated to minorities that implies, or even acknowledges, the involvement of the dominant group in past atrocities, thereby undermining its social prestige and dominance. A new memorial signals that the minority was able to engage in collective action and rally around a cause. It can also reveal the presence of powerful allies acting on its behalf. All of these speak to the group's mobilization capacity and its threat to the status quo. Minorities can also obtain more tangible benefits. If elected to parliaments or local councils on the ethnic minority ticket, they can directly affect policy-making and control the allocation of governmental resources.

As a result of electoral thresholds, typically between 3 and 7 percent, the sheer numerical size of minority groups is important. Policy advancements, such as the right of recognized minority groups to use their language in official matters, are tied to the requirement that the proportion of minorities residing in a certain locality is over 10, 15 or sometimes 20 percent. For these reasons, minority group advances are generally easier when the group is sizable enough that it can garner support for its cause. But all else being equal, the elevation of a small group is less threatening to the sovereign status of the dominant group than the advancement of a large group.

When minorities gain, some members of the dominant group become alarmed, and then rally behind political parties best positioned to put the breaks on minority empowerment. Voters from the dominant group seek champions of their cause. The best candidate is a party that has not been wheeling and dealing with other parties, and has not been tainted by its complicity in implementing policies that have compromised the dominant position of the titular nationality. In short, voters want a "pure" party. International human rights agreements that bind the hands of the dominant group, economic liberalization that allows foreigners to seize and control assets, and media laws that allow for voices at odds with the majority's narratives are processes that require cooperation from all mainstream parties. At the same time, such agreements and policies reduce the maneuvering space of the dominant group in many domains of public life, and diminish the credibility of mainstream parties as protectors of the sovereignty of the dominant group. The result is that radical right parties acquire an advantage when voters become alarmed and agitated by minority accommodation.

All democratic polities make choices about the degree of accommodation that will be afforded to minorities. In some countries, minorities can form parties, can be invited to join governing coalitions and can receive governmental portfolios. In other countries, minorities have no such right. Some governments channel resources toward areas where the minorities live (Hungarians in agrarian parts of Slovakia) or sectors in which minorities disproportionately work (e.g., Turks in tobacco farming in Bulgaria), whereas others do not or have disrupted state support (e.g., coal mining Russians in Eastern Ukraine, Roma as a low-skilled labor in the construction sector in the Czech Republic). These choices have (unintended) consequences for radical right parties, which thrive when they can appeal to voters that demand curbing or reversing the political inroads that minorities and their allies have recently achieved.

It is important to note that, for radical right voting, physical, dyadic adversarial *contact* between members of the majority and the minority is not needed. While geographic concentration facilities ethnic voting and the formation of ethnic parties, the spatial concentration of ethnic groups does not automatically translate into geographically concentrated radical right mobilization. Instead, analyses of the spatial distribution of radical right voting show that actually low-contact areas, such as Lviv in Ukraine, display the strongest support for the radical right. In Ukraine, the cradle of the radical right is in the (contemporary) ethnically homogeneous western part of the country. In the United Kingdom, ethnically homogenous localities supported Brexit in 2016 despite lacking dyadic contact with minorities. In Slovakia, the power base of radical right mobilization is located in central regions and not in regions with high ethnic concentration of Hungarians.[54]

Rather than contact theory, the argument proposed here is informed by the logic of (political) friends and foes, which does not necessitate physical promixity. Carl Schmitt was skeptical that the system of liberal pluralism can reconcile rifts between enemies through deliberation, and famously noted that "[t]he concept of the state presupposes the concept of the political" (Schmitt 1976 [1932]: 32). Schmitt viewed the state as the ultimate sovereign that defines the enemy. Backlash against minorities does not signal the collapse of parliamentary democracies, but it does demonstrate the limitations of political systems to negotiate differences between rivals. To denote rivals, Sartori introduced the concept of "bilateral opposites" – parties and actors on the opposite sides of the political spectrum – to characterize political foes that are suspicious of each other (Sartori 1976).

The dynamics of accommodation, resentment and backlash explain the odds of observing successful radical right parties within countries across elections. Differences in group size inform the tendency of radical right parties to form across countries. Contrary to studies that posit a linear relationship between the size of minorities and radical politics, however, this book posits a non-linear relationship. In more ethnically homogenous countries, galvanizing voters around accommodation, support and transfers for minorities provides few political payoffs to vote-maximizing parties. Such appeals should therefore be rare, and as a result radical right parties should be unlikely to emerge. In countries with a large minority, radical parties should also be unlikely to emerge, but for different reasons. Large groups can reverse hierarchies and therefore upsetting large groups is significantly more risky and politically costly than antagonizing small groups. Politicians are more likely to be circumspect about using exclusionary political appeals against large groups, for fear of instigating violence.[55]

---

[54] However, some evidence suggests that violent attacks coincide with radical right mobilization and voter support. Jobbik in Hungary draws votes from the capital city as well as from peripheral areas with high concentration of Roma who are attacked by far-right paramilitary guards. In the Czech Republic, (some) radical right support has been associated with areas of high Roma unemployment and ethnic clashes with skinheads.

[55] In Hungary, for example, Jobbik rejects any accusations that Jobbik party members committed any of the recent atrocities against Gypsies, and denies any explicit or implicit support for the perpetrators. "Our party does not

By contrast, radical right parties thrive in countries with small minorities. Providing seats and portfolios to a small minority group elevates its status, and thereby shifts the status quo. This provokes resentment among the majority that politicians can exploit to galvanize voters without much fear of paying a significant political cost or inciting large-scale conflict.[56]

Mobilization does not follow from census numbers. This view contradicts expectations from ethnic competition theories that associate larger minority groups and larger influxes of immigrants with increased political mobilization along ethnic lines (Olzak 1992: 35), and therefore assume a linear relationship between ethnic group size and radical politics. Studies of Western Europe have found no evidence of a relationship between the size of non-native groups and the electoral success of radical right parties at the cross-national level (Kitschelt with McGann 1995; Norris 2005; Stockemer 2015a). Instead, irrespective of their exact numerical size, scholars have highlighted the importance of policy hostility aimed at immigrant groups in instigating native–immigrant conflict (Dancygier 2010).[57]

Other scholars have emphasized instrumental reasons to explain why minorities are sometimes targeted or protected by state authorities and mainstream parties, also largely regardless of their numerical size. Violence was consciously averted in India when minorities were needed for political coalition formation (Wilkinson 2004). In war-torn Poland, Jews had a lower probability of being subjected to a pogrom if they were not viewed as an obstacle to the larger national project and were not expected to ask for special concessions after the

---

encourage or support any violence, should it come from anybody and in any way or form. However, we do not and will not tolerate the humiliation, threatening, robbing, and killing of innocent people trying to live a humble but honest life." Márton Gyöngyösi MP, Leader of the Foreign Affairs Committee of Jobbik Movement for a Better Hungary, May 28, 2011.

[56] Provided that large segments of minorities are not disenfranchised, as they were until recently in the Baltics.

[57] Kitschelt with McGann (1995) contest the notion that support for the radical right is driven by increasing numbers of immigrants in Western Europe. The literature linking immigration and support for the radical right, however, yields different results at the aggregate and subnational levels. While cross-national studies sometimes find a correlation between immigration levels and radical right vote shares (Givens 2005), studies of subnational regions just as often find no correlation (Kitschelt 2007) or find the effect mediated by economic considerations (Golder 2003).

war (Kopstein and Wittenberg 2018, 2011). In the American South, whites were less likely to flee the local Democratic Party in the late 1960s when black mobilization did not threaten their ability to exert political influence (Hood et al. 2012). A backlash against minorities in Western Europe might ensue once accommodative policies become widely viewed as too extensive.[58]

Table 2.1 displays the ethnic structure in post-communist democracies: the size of the largest minority and the size of the dominant nationality. If radical right party success was linearly increasing with the size of the minority, we should see countries such as Bosnia and Herzegovina, Estonia, Latvia, Macedonia, Montenegro and Ukraine, where the largest minority is at least 20 percent of the population, to have the strongest radical right parties. However, the evidence is more consistent with the framework proposed here that links strong parties with small minorities (e.g., Bulgaria, Romania and Slovakia; cf. Bustikova and Kitschelt 2009), and weak radical parties with large minorities (e.g., Macedonia, Moldova and Ukraine) and with ethnically homogenous countries (e.g., Albania, Czech Republic, Slovenia).

While ethnic parties are obvious candidates to campaign for targeted transfers and symbolic resources to ethnic minorities (Chandra 2005; Hechter 1987; Kitschelt and Wilkinson 2007; Kolev and Wang 2019; Kopstein and Wittenberg 2010, 2009), mainstream parties may also advocate material and non-material concessions to ethnic groups to lure them into forming a coalition.[59] The size of the minority influences the

---

[58] But according to Givens and Case (2014), more anti-racist legislation may also result.

[59] Exogenous changes in the country's economic conditions can have a large impact, since resource scarcity makes it more difficult for parties to justify both welfare retrenchment and minority accommodation. It follows that the electoral prospects for radical parties are remarkably bright when targeted redistribution combines with welfare retrenchment. The economic program of radical parties is often viewed as secondary. Oesch (2009), for example, finds that supporters of right-wing populists are motivated by identity politics rather than by economic grievances. Other scholars explored the economic program of radicals, and conclude that it usually combines welfare chauvinism targeted against immigrants with elements of neoliberal or centrist-right economic programs (Kitschelt with McGann 1995; Mudde 2007; Norris 2005; but cf. Sniderman et. al. 2004; Hainmueller and Hiscox 2007 find that anti-immigrant sentiments are mediated by education).

Table 2.1 Ethnic structure in the post-communist world

| Country | Third census | Largest minority | (%) | Dominant nationality | (%) | Second census | Largest minority % | Dominant nationality % | First census | Largest minority % | Dominant nationality % |
|---|---|---|---|---|---|---|---|---|---|---|---|
| Albania | 2011 | Greeks | 0.9 | Albanian | 82.6 | 1989 | 3 | 95 | None | – | – |
| Bosnia and Herzegovina | 2013 | Serbs | 30.8 | Bosniak | 50.1 | 2000 | 37.1 | 48 | 1991 | 31.2 | 43.5 |
| Bulgaria | 2011 | Turks | 8.8 | Bulgarian | 84.8 | 2001 | 9.4 | 83.9 | 1992 | 9.4 | 85.7 |
| Croatia | 2011 | Serbs | 4.4 | Croatian | 90.4 | 2001 | 4.5 | 89.6 | 1991 | 12.2 | 78.1 |
| Czech Republic | 2011 | Moravian | 5 | Czech | 64.3 | 2001 | 3.7 | 90.4 | 1991 | 13.2 | 81.2 |
| Estonia | 2015 | Russian | 25.1 | Estonian | 69.1 | 2000 | 25.6 | 67.9 | 1989 | 30.3 | 61.5 |
| Georgia | 2014 | Azeri | 6.3 | Georgian | 86.8 | 2002 | 6.5 | 83.8 | 1989 | 8.1 (Armenian) | 70.1 |
| Hungary | 2011 | Roma | 3.1 | Hungarian | 83.7 | 2001 | 1.9 | 92.3 | 1990 | 0.46 | 98.5 |
| Latvia | 2011 | Russian | 26.9 | Latvian | 62.1 | 2002 | 29.6 | 57.7 | 1989 | 34 | 52 |
| Lithuania | 2011 | Polish | 6.6 | Lithuanian | 84.2 | 2001 | 6.7 | 83.4 | 1989 | 9.4 | 79.6 |
| Macedonia | 2002 | Albanian | 25.2 | Macedonian | 64.2 | None | – | – | 1994 | 22.9 | 66.5 |
| Moldova | 2004 | Ukrainian | 8.3 | Moldovan / Romanian | 75.8 | 2004 | 8.4 | 78.2 | 1989 | 13.9 | 64.5 |
| Montenegro | 2011 | Serbian | 28.7 | Montenegrin | 45 | 2008 | 32 | 43 | 2003 | 32 | 43.2 |
| Poland | 2011 | Silesian | 1.1 | Polish | 96.9 | 2002 | 0.4 (German) | 96.7 | 1988 | – | – |
| Romania | 2011 | Hungarian | 6.5 | Romanian | 88.9 | 2008 | 6.7 | 91 | 1992 | 7.1 | 89.5 |

Table 2.1 (cont.)

| Country | Third census | Largest minority | (%) | Dominant nationality | (%) | Second census | Largest minority % | Dominant nationality % | First census | Largest minority % | Dominant nationality % |
|---|---|---|---|---|---|---|---|---|---|---|---|
| Russia | 2010 | Tatar | 3.7 | Russian | 77.7 | 2002 | 3.8 | 79.8 | 1989 | 3.8 | 81.5 |
| Serbia | 2011 | Hungarian | 3.5 | Serbian | 83.3 | 2002 | 3.9 | 82.9 | 1991 | 4.46 | 79.9 |
| Slovakia | 2011 | Hungarian | 8.5 | Slovak | 80.7 | 2001 | 9.7 | 85.8 | 1991 | 10.8 | 85.7 |
| Slovenia | 2002 | Serbian | 1.9 | Slovene | 83.1 | 2002 | 2.7 | 83.1 | 1991 | 2.8 | 88.3 |
| | | | | | | | (Croatian) | | | (Croats) | |
| Ukraine | 2001 | Russian | 17.3 | Ukrainian | 77.8 | 2001 | 22 | 77.8 | 1989 | 22.1 | 72.7 |

Source: Censuses in individual countries. Assembled by the author.

risk and the cost associated with pursuing accommodative policies.[60] When the minority group is small, accommodation is less costly and less risky.[61] When the minority is large and peaceful, the power of the titular nationality, the dominant group, *can* be contested, especially when a new country emerges from secession and a previously dominant nationality finds itself as a new minority – that is, when the ethnic group's position in the status hierarchy has been reversed (Beissinger 2002; Gellner 1983; Hechter 1987; Horowitz 1985; Laitin 1998; Olzak 1992; Petersen 2001). This applies to Russians in the Baltics, Central Asia, Moldova and Ukraine, as well as to Serbs in Bosnia and Herzegovina, Kosovo and Croatia, Germans in Czechoslovakia, and to many other formerly dominant groups that did not relocate after political borders had changed. A large and enfranchised ethnic minority can contest the dominant group by challenging the constitutional status of minorities and its language, as happened in Ukraine.

In countries with large ethnic groups, radical right parties are disadvantaged when the boundaries between issues of "minority accommodation" and "reversal" become blurred, and are therefore unlikely to be successful when they target voters concerned with a substantive threat to the majority's dominant status. By seeking status elevation,

---

[60] If the preference to cater to one's own ethnicity is innate, then redistribution is likely to be easier in ethnically homogeneous, immigrant-free societies (e.g., Alesina et al. 1999; Habyarimana et al. 2007; Soroka et al. 2006). Yet evidence that ethnic diversity undermines public goods provision (Alesina et al. 1999; Luttmer 2001; Roemer et al. 2007) is contradicted by evidence that immigration influx does not reduce expenditures on welfare states (Banting and Kymlicka 2006; Crepaz and Damron 2009). These incompatible results suggest that both high and low levels of government spending may co-vary with the presence of a minority (or immigrant) ethnic group. For an overview of different mechanisms of why ethnic diversity undermines public goods provision, see Habyarimana et al. 2007.

[61] Radical actors mobilize in states with relatively small minorities that represent small threats, not in multi-ethnic states with large ethnic groups, and in polities with established institutions and constitutions that determine majority–ethnic minority status, not in countries with unresolved ethnic boundaries. Radical right parties thrive in situations where ethnic boundaries are institutionalized and where the minority, often with the help of a large party representing mostly the dominant nationality, the majority, tries to negotiate concessions and benefits. Once boundaries are institutionalized, peaceful negotiations between groups move to the domain of policy and rights. The expansion of rights, without challenging the core ethnic boundaries, creates powerful grievances. For the most part, the radical right's fight against the accommodation of minorities is neither life threatening nor regime changing.

Table 2.2 *Expectations of radical right party success based on the size of the ethnic minority group*

| Structural precondition: ethno-cultural divisions | Countries | Expectations: radical right party success |
|---|---|---|
| Ethnically homogeneous | Albania, Czech Republic, Hungary, Poland, Slovenia | Moderate |
| Small ethnic minorities | Bulgaria, Croatia, Lithuania, Romania, Serbia, Slovakia | Strong |
| Large ethnic minorities | Estonia, Georgia, Macedonia, Moldova, Latvia, Ukraine | Weak |

a politically organized and large ethnic minority can threaten the titular nationality with status reversal, which leads radical right parties to lose their competitive edge. They lack the requisite credibility to contain a threat from a large group.

Table 2.2 summarizes these theoretical predictions regarding how ethnic structure relates to support for radical right parties across countries. In countries with small, politically organized minorities, radical right parties are most successful. In countries with large ethnic minorities, especially those with contested state building, titular nationalities build encompassing party coalitions to secure political dominance. This weakens the ability of radical right parties to carve out a niche against more broadly defined parties.[62] The failure

---

[62] Radical parties can mobilize around authoritarian ("grid") issues as well, but the redistributive impact of socially liberal policies is less profound. In countries where accommodation of gays and lesbians and abortion is politicized or where Roma find a political patron, radical right parties rally against socially liberal parties but their potential is weaker due to the absence of a strong ethnic party. In an ethnically homogenous country, galvanizing voters around redistribution toward ethnic minorities is more difficult, though not impossible. Radical parties can mobilize around social authoritarian issues as well, but the redistributive impact of socially liberal policies is less profound. Alternatively, a minority abroad (Albanians, Hungarians, Serbs, Russians) can substitute for the lack of an in-group against which to mobilize. For irredentism and influence of external actors in domestic minority rights, see Jenne 2007; Mareš 2009; and Saideman 2001. Radical parties can mobilize around social authoritarian issues as well, but the redistributive impact of socially liberal parties is less profound.

of radical right parties in countries with large minorities originates in threats to dominance of the titular nationality through status reversal.

Table 2.2 summarizes the theoretical expectations based solely on the size of the largest ethnic minority group. There are, of course, tensions arising from a trade-off between theoretical minimalism and case complexity. For example, Hungary is an anomalous case. Ethnic structure alone would predict a moderately strong radical right party, but currently Jobbik is quite strong.[63] Jobbik is unlikely to be "a flash in the pan party." On the other hand, the party has dramatically softened its positions in response to the radicalization of the mainstream party, Orbán's Fidesz. This flexibility stems from the fact that Hungary does not have a well-entrenched ethnic party or a strongly institutionalized ethnic cleavage that would anchor anti-minority mobilization. As a result, Jobbik can display considerable ideological flexibility and even moderation. Since 2016, Jobbik broke away from its extremist outbidding with the ruling Fidesz and moved to the center. The radical right party distanced itself from anti-Semitism and from paramilitary home guards. In November 2016, Jobbik blocked a law proposed by Fidesz to modify Hungary's constitution that would prevent refugees from coming into Hungary. The law required a two-thirds super-majority. Jobbik abstained and sunk the proposal. Jobbik also sided with the opposition, when it supported Central European University's fight to continue operating in Hungary lawfully. Central European University was founded by George Soros and is associated with pro-Western cosmopolitan liberalism, yet Jobbik came to its defense, or as the former leader Gábor Vona noted: "it is not about George Soros and the CEU but Viktor Orbán's Bolshevik agenda." In 2018, Jobbik contributed to the defeat of the Fidesz candidate in a small city of Hódmezővásárhely by supporting Péter Márki-Zay, a joint candidate backed by left parties (MSZP, DK). Jobbik, in alliance with other opposition parties, poses a long-term threat to the constitutional super-majority of Fidesz.

Deeply rooted political ethnic threats sustain radical right parties over time. If politicized minorities are not present, radical right parties are ideologically more malleable and less constrained in their strategic positioning vis-à-vis other parties. This ideological

---

[63] Jobbik vote shares since 2010 have oscillated between between 16 and 20 percent in three parliamentary elections.

flexibility stems from ethnic homogeneity. Parties can also discover new topics and mobilize on new "thin" issues, such as the perceived threat of immigration, Islam, abortion and LGBT rights. Ideological flexibility can help in the short run, but it will fade away, unless parties match new issues with established cleavages, such as religious divisions. For example, the new radical right party Slovak Brotherhood (ĽS-NS) led by Marian Kotleba capitalized on the anti-refugee hysteria in 2015/2016 but the anti-Muslim appeal eventually lost steam, partially because almost no refugees wished to live in Slovakia. Elusive enemies make for difficult targets and pose challenges for mobilization.

In sum, ethnic composition is a structural enabler of radical right mobilization, while the volatility of votes over time is due to minority accommodation. When the status elevation of a large minority changes the status quo, and threatens the dominant majority with status reversal (Petersen 2002), radical right parties are prone to fail because they do not have the strength to credibly fight a substantial threat from a large group.

This theoretical discussion implies the following set of testable propositions at both the election level and the individual level that are explored empirically in the next chapters:

1. Radical right mobilization follows after periods of political accommodation of minority demands, when the status quo of majority–minority relations has shifted.
2. Radical right mobilization follows after ethnic parties or parties that are advocates for minorities achieve positions of political power and increase their influence (including seats in the parliament, cabinet positions and participation in governing coalitions).
3. Radical right mobilization follows after major laws or policies that expand the rights of minorities are enacted.
4. Radical right mobilization is lowest in countries with large minorities that can reverse the hierarchy of the groups.
5. At the individual level, group hostility is not a unique characteristic of radical right voters.
6. At the individual level, policy hostility against politicized minorities is a unique characteristic of radical right voters. Policy hostility is defined as an opposition to governmental spending that benefits minorities.

7. At the individual level, fears of security threats that erode the dominant group are unique characteristics of radical right voters.

## 2.5 Summary

Shifts in the status quo that politicize resentment in minority–majority relations are crucial to radical right mobilization. Resentment springs from challenges to the dominance of the sovereign – that is, from the erosion in control that the dominant group exercises over the state. This helps to explain within-country variation over time in radical right party success, but countries also possess different baseline propensities for such parties to succeed. Group size plays a somewhat unintuitive role in producing radical right mobilization, since countries with large, threatening, ethnic minorities are predicted to have weaker radical right parties.

Accommodating the demands of a *small* minority engenders resentment among the majority, leading to a backlash that benefits radical right parties. Yet when the dominant group is faced with a threat of status reversal or a substantial security threat from a *large* minority, voters instead typically rally behind a large mainstream party, which tends to reduce the vote share for radical right parties.

The next chapters assess this framework at two levels. First, using an original dataset covering all post-communist elections, it examines the success and failure of radical right parties over elections and across countries. Second, using original surveys with embedded experiments in Slovakia and Ukraine, it analyzes the individual-level micro-foundations of voter support for radical right parties.

# 3 | Radical Right Parties in Cross-National Perspective

Naturally I also know how many Hungarian compatriots of ours ... how many people of Hungarian origin live in Israel and how many Israeli Jewish compatriots of ours live in Hungary. But I believe that the time has come, especially during such conflict, to consider making a list of Jews living in the country, especially those who are in the Hungarian Parliament and the Hungarian government, who, indeed, post a national security risk to Hungary.

—MP Márton Gyöngyösi, deputy head of Jobbik, debate
on the Israeli–Palestinian conflict in the Hungarian Parliament,
November 26, 2012

In April 2016, a young girl was brutally attacked, strangled and robbed on a train after she refused to give one euro to a seventeen-year-old Roma in Slovakia.[1] She survived, but soon after, the leader of the far-right party, led by Marian Kotleba, announced that the party would send voluntary patrol units to selected trains to protect passengers from "asocial elements who do not pay the fare." Since April, far-right bodyguards/vigilantes have not only been patrolling the trains but also distributing pamphlets calling for the creation of a voluntary "home guard" to establish law and order. The media mocked the patrols. However, since they usurped the authority of the police, the Slovak government passed a law in August 2016 outlawing them.[2] The cruelty of the assault sparked an outrage. The public perceived it as a sign that the Roma, which constitute between 2 and 8 percent of the population, no longer play by the rules and need to be reined in, rather than as the act of a lunatic or an

---

[1] Source: Pluska 2016. This chapter is derived from an article: "Revenge of the Radical Right," *Comparative Political Studies* 47 (12): 1738–1765 (Bustikova 2014).
[2] Source: iDnes 2016.

ideologue. Given the viciousness of the attack, the public criticized the police for its soft response.[3]

The controversy was unexpected insofar as it came after more than a decade of efforts and initiatives that the Slovak government pursued to implement more inclusive policies toward Roma and to redress their grievances. Less than five years before the incident, in 2013, the Slovak government revisited its strategy for Roma integration, which included a new anti-discrimination law aimed at creating a level playing field and equal opportunities for Roma (Lajčáková 2013). In part, this was a result of external pressures facing Slovakia. In 2011, the European Court of Human Rights embarrassed the Slovak state by sentencing the government to compensate three Roma women for forced sterilizations (Guasti et al. 2017). It also lost several cases for failure to protect Roma against violent attacks and was again required to compensate the victims.

At around the same time, the Roma community became more assertive.[4] In March 2012, a civil society activist, Peter Pollák, was the first Roma ever elected to the Slovak Parliament. In the 2012 election, Pollák found an ally in a small anti-establishment political movement: OL'aNO (Ordinary People and Independent Personalities), which explicitly states in its manifesto that it is committed to the equality of opportunity for all ethnic groups. The president of the mainstream party OL'aNO publicly supported Pollák as a Roma candidate and placed him on the top of the party electoral list. OL'aNO helped with fundraising efforts and a campaign strategy that targeted middle-class Roma and opened up access to mainstream media. In 2012, Pollák was one of the sixteen candidates elected to the parliament on the OL'aNO's ticket. In October 2012, based on the recommendation of Ministry of the Interior, he became a government plenipotentiary for Roma communities. The process of electing Pollák to a nation-wide office marked a significant success for those organizations, parties and individuals committed to the advancement of Roma in Slovakia.

---

[3] The perpetrator was not arrested immediately, because he was a first-time offender.

[4] See Jenne (2004) on the paradox of minority bargaining in the presence of external sponsors.

The effort to elect Pollák did not go unnoticed. The campaign billboard of the Slovak National Party (SNS), the more established of the two far-right parties in Slovakia, attacked the leader of OL'aNO, Igor Matovič, for "wanting to get gypsies [i.e., Roma] into the parliament!". The other radical right party, Kotleba's "People's Party – Our Slovakia," also rallied against Pollák.

The (anti) OL'aNO billboard was remarkable. For the first time since Slovakia became independent in 1993, Roma were attacked not for their social and economic issues but for their desire to attain political power, and their political allies were implicated for their efforts to help them. Traditionally, Roma have been attacked in electoral campaigns in Eastern Europe as lazy welfare "parasites," but not for their political aspirations.

Polláck's rise was thus extraordinarily significant. He replaced an ethnic Slovak on the government plenipotentiary for Roma communities, becoming the first Roma in the position in a nod toward more "native rule." He became an outspoken critic of police brutality against Roma and publicly supported a harsh sentence for an off-duty municipal police officer who killed three Roma in their home in the town of Hurbanovo. His statement that tough sentencing "will set an example" was drowned out by the outpouring of support for the officer from the public, which dismissed the Roma victims because of their past criminal records.[5] In 2015, Pollák called for a special investigation of police brutality in the district of Michalovce, where fifteen Roma were injured in a police raid. In 2016, he filed a motion with the prosecutor general to ban Kotleba's far-right party, and even called for a criminal investigation of its leaders and members.[6]

The outrage of far-right vigilantes on the Slovak trains should be understood as a reaction to a new context, exemplified by the attempted strangulation and robbery, in which the police has lost its ability to maintain social order. By 2016, the state had set a precedent of punishing police officers for excessive use of force, and law enforcement authorities were more legally constrained in addressing issues

---

[5] Sources: Pravda.sk, June 18, 2012; *Slovak Spectator*, June 17, 2012; Pluska.sk, April 4, 2015.
[6] Source: NewsNow 2016.

involving Roma. The newly elected Roma parliamentarian condemned police violence and publicly shamed the dominant majority. The vigilantes reacted to this change in the status quo in which a Roma representative rose to prominence and was strategically placed in a governmental advisory body responsible for minority rights protection. The vigilantes challenged not the Roma community but the institutions of the state that were perceived as no longer being capable of addressing Roma criminality. Similarly, the radical right parties sought to curb the increasing appetite of the Roma to meddle in the Slovak state's affairs, a role that the current political parties were demonstrably not interested in or willing to perform.[7] Most importantly, the conflict allowed for the ascension of a prominent Roma activist into politics and modified state policies toward the Roma minority. It demonstrates the reactive nature of radical right parties and the mobilization that ensues after minorities, with the help of their allies, change the status quo.

This chapter emphasizes the relational aspect of grievances tied to the improvements of the political standing of minorities and tests several observable implications of the theory presented earlier. The theory is tested with an original party and election-level dataset covering all post-communist democracies over the past twenty years. The results show how the rise and fall of radical right parties is shaped by the politics of minority accommodation, consistent with the theory.

## 3.1 Defining Radical Right Parties

Since identity policies exist on what is traditionally understood to be the right and the left, a useful party typology should place parties using their positions on identity issues.[8] My classification system for parties is built on the grid-group theoretical framework, first developed by anthropologist Mary Douglas (Douglas and Wildavsky 1982; Thompson et al. 1990). Two ideological dimensions define this

---

[7] Sources: National Democratic Institute 2012; State Department 2014.
[8] This chapter explores peacetime electoral dynamics, and does not seek to explain politics at the time of the collapse of the communist regimes (Bunce 1999).

typology – nationalism and sociocultural conservatism – and these dimensions correspond to two modes of social control: group and grid. A radical right party is defined as a party that scores high on social authoritarianism and nationalism (high grid and high group). Radical right parties are classified as being high on grid and high on group, or high on one of these two dimensions and "neutral" on the second dimension. Using this logic of party classification, radical right parties are either highly nationalistic or highly socially conservative.

If a party scores high on only one dimension and low on the other dimension, it is not classified as a radical right party. Some communist parties support social minorities and gender equality (low on grid), yet score high on nationalism (group).[9] This framework is therefore particularly helpful in deciding whether some of the former unreformed communist parties (red-brown parties) should qualify as radical right parties. For example, the Czech communist party is not coded as a radical right party because it scores very low on the grid dimension as a result of its advocacy for gender equality and access to abortion.

The "bilateral opposite" of a radical right party is an ethno-liberal party. Ethno-liberal parties are those that score low on both grid and group or low on one of these two dimensions and "neutral" on the second dimension. Small East European socially liberal parties embrace multiculturalism and the protection of minorities, and are often advocates of Roma rights. Even though multiculturalism is a universalistic position, it implies that social-liberal parties support policies that would elevate the Roma from poverty and reduce their social exclusion. Small socially liberal parties in Eastern Europe are both rare and recent.

A party that propagates nationalism on behalf of the titular nationality would qualify as a radical right party, whereas a party making cross-ethnic appeals and demanding minority rights would be coded as an ethno-liberal party. Small economically and socially liberal parties generally support policies of minority accommodation, as do ethnic

---

[9] Eastern European radical right parties support redistribution (Bustikova and Kitschelt 2009), whereas Western European radical right parties span the spectrum from the economic right to left (Mudde 2007). On red-brown parties, see Ishiyama 2009.

**Table 3.1** *Description of radical right and ethno-liberal parties*

| EL | M-PC-EL | M-PC-RR | RR |
|----|---------|---------|-----|
| | | | |

| *Ethno-liberal party* | | *Radical right party* | |
|---|---|---|---|

EL: ethno liberal party: party actively seeking ethnic and social minority accommodation (bilateral opposite) Grid-group typology: very low on group and/or very low on grid (or neutral on the second dimension)

M-PC-EL: moderate proximate competitor of the ethno-liberal party, party with moderately tolerant views on ethnic and social minority accommodation

M-PC-RR: moderate proximate competitor of the radical right party: party with moderately exclusionary views on ethnic and social minority accommodation (ideological cousin)

RR: radical right party: party actively opposing ethnic and social minority accommodation (bilateral opposite) Grid-group typology: very high on group and/or very high on grid (or neutral on the second dimension)

and some green parties. Some of the policies that ethno-liberal parties promote include minority autonomy in schooling, elevation of the minority language to the status of the official language, quotas for ethnic minorities in parliament, positive discrimination, preferential treatment of minorities in civil service hiring practices, state resources channeled to addresses minority grievances and preferential economic policies that disproportionately benefit minorities. Parties were classified using primarily three resources: expert surveys, party ideology and case studies.[10]

The grid-group typology generates four ideal types of parties in a two-dimensional grid-group space (for more discussion, see the Appendix). Schematically, the position of the parties on identity issues looks as shown in Table 3.1.

*Grid*: The policy positions of radical right parties are captured by authoritarian social and cultural conservatism. In its pure form, it has no ethnic basis. A political party scoring high on social authoritarianism dimension might campaign against accommodating gay and lesbian couples or against abortion. Similarly, a party that promotes law

[10] Additional material can be found in the Appendix.

and order, along with obedience to authority, religious or secular, would be classified as high on the grid dimension.

*Group*: The second dimension captures nationalism and is therefore associated with exclusionary appeals based on ethnicity. It conceptualizes identity in terms of "the ethnic other" and is grounded in a distinction between the in-group and the out-group. A party that propagates nationalism on behalf of the titular nationality would score high on the group dimension.

There are two types of radical right mobilization against minorities in Eastern Europe that roughly map onto the grid and group dimensions. The first (grid) is mostly found in ethnically homogenous countries and is characterized by mobilization based on socially conservative issues, against sexual minorities and targets ethnicities with limited ability and capacity to politically organize as well as small religious minorities.

Therefore, in the absence of a political minority with a considerable political muscle, lesser minorities and social groups are targeted. They constitute a fringe faction of the population and include gays and lesbians, Roma, Jews, Poles, Germans and Greeks. This category includes radical right parties in Albania, Czech Republic, Hungary, Lithuania, Poland and Slovenia. In more ethnically pluralistic societies, parties mobilize against constitutive, larger ethnic groups with a high degree of politicization. Radical right parties mobilize against ethnic parties or politically active minority groups to garner electoral support in Bulgaria, Croatia, Estonia, Latvia, Macedonia, Romania, Serbia, Slovakia and Ukraine.

The strongest radical right parties can be found in both categories. Perhaps the most successful and enduring radical right party is the Slovak National Party (SNS), which emerged in 1990s and has ever since dominated the fringe of the Slovak political spectrum. The SNS was present in seven out of nine pre-independence and post-independence parliaments. Since 1993, after Slovakia split from the Czechoslovak federation, SNS has served in half of the governments. This impact is highly unusual because most radical right parties in Eastern Europe are rather short lived and their electoral success is rather episodic and proceeds in bursts that rarely survive for more than two or three electoral cycles. On average, radical right parties are quite weak, rarely exceeding 7 percent of the popular vote in the electorate.

Weak electoral support for the radical right parties does not make for good headlines. The party that is currently most in the media spotlight is the Hungarian party Jobbik, due to its extreme rhetoric and its exceptional ability to attract over 15 percent of the popular vote in two consecutive national elections. Jobbik is also prominent in the media because of the Hungarian trajectory of democratic backsliding under the leadership of Jobbik's mainstream party cousin Fidesz, led by Viktor Orbán. Jobbik grew out of a student group organization and draws its support both from young, affluent and educated voters and from voters in economically depressed regions of Hungary. Although Jobbik is a political force to be reckoned with, one should keep in mind that two radical right parties, in Poland and Romania, were also in the limelight once before they disappeared into the oblivion. It is therefore plausible that a similar fate awaits Jobbik.

The anti-communist, anti-establishment Polish radical right party, League of Polish Families (LPR), won about 8 percent of the popular vote in the 2001 and 2005 elections. It was advocating socially conservative values and was supported by fringe elements in the Polish Catholic Church. It disintegrated after a strong opposition to the education minister, appointed by the LPR, and after a corruption scandal that involved regional savings banks. The scandal implicated the parties of the ruling coalition, including the LPR, and devastated their support. Similarly, the now defunct, but once prominent Greater Romanian Party peaked in the elections of 2000 and 2004 with double-digit popular support but imploded after the control of the founding father Corneliu Vadim Tudor weakened. These examples of prominent radical right parties gone bust illustrate the volatility of radical right party support and their episodic and meteoric nature.

The radical right in Eastern Europe is similar to its Western European cousins in its emphasis on mobilization against minorities. Until 2015, that mobilization was exclusively against minorities with electoral rights who have been settled in for centuries. The million-plus influx of refugees in Europe from Syria expanded the portfolio of minorities to rally against and, paradoxically, westernized the Eastern European radical right in its opposition to Islam and migrants with non-European backgrounds.[11] However, the radical right in Eastern

---

[11] Eastern Europe was home to refugees from Bosnia and Herzegovina who were of Muslim faith. Yet there was never rallying against refugees from former

Europe has three unique characteristics that distinguish it from its older Western European cousins. These unique characteristics are (1) left-leaning positions on the economy; (2) linkages between identity and political reforms, which leads to the association of minority policies with democratization and legitimizes state intervention on behalf of the dominant group; and (3) the coexistence of radical right parties with radicalized patriotic mainstream parties, which are often left leaning on the economy as well.

The grid and group dimension is based exclusively on definitions of identity-based group boundaries. The classification of parties is agnostic to the positions of the parties on economic issues and role of the state in managing the economy. While the reinforcement of group boundaries is essential for the ideological appeals of the radical right parties, economic appeals either are of a secondary nature or can be very flexible and dramatically change over time. The Italian Northern League party was known for its severely fiscally conservative positions, the Slovak National Party advocated for fiscal prudence in the 1990s, while the Bulgarian Ataka (Ganev 2017) or Greek Golden Dawn parties are feverishly anti-capitalist. The League of Polish Families had placed support for small businesses and local entrepreneurship prominently in its electoral manifesto, while the Hungarian Jobbik has been contemplating renationalization of private property in a stark contrast to its predecessor from the 1990s, MIÉP (Hungarian Justice and Life Party).

Radical right parties adapt their economic appeals to circumstances. After the fall of the Berlin Wall, radical right appeals were associated with calls for national independence, including disassociation from Soviet-style socialist economies. Anti-communism of the early 1990s was not compatible with a strong contestation of the role of free markets in economic exchange. This has changed over time as market liberalization undermined the grip of the newly independent states over their economies. With time, sovereignty became associated with the desire for the state to alleviate the pressures of competitive markets. Radical right parties embraced more pro-statist positions as tools to shield the dominant group. Once decoupled from the anti-communist

Yugoslavia comparable to mass demonstrations of summer 2015 against Islam that swept Eastern Europe and mobilized both mainstream and fringe parties against settlement policies for migrants.

cleavage, a variety of economic positions such as anti-market appeals, welfare chauvinism, entrepreneurship that benefits the dominant group and economic nationalism became compatible with radical right appeals.

In Eastern Europe, radical right parties are mostly left leaning, favoring state intervention and state correction of the markets either due to the external pressures of foreign competition or due to the domestic pressures over limited resources. The left and right dimension, on which parties are classified, therefore exclusively applies to identity and group boundaries, not to the issues of economic regulation and taxation. If the economic dimension was the primary tool of classification, most East European radical right parties would have to be placed in the center left or extreme left, with the acknowledgment of a high degree of uncertainty since parties maintain flexibility to blur and shift their economic appeals (Rovny 2013). Yet, despite the left leaning of the parties, it does not follow that the parties have a clear social base that links poverty to radical right voting (Bustikova and Kitschelt 2011; Tucker 2006). This is due to a variety of factors such as shallow anchoring of economic issues, the diffuse nature of economic risk that obscures the link between voting, income levels and occupational profiles (Bustikova and Kitschelt 2009), framing economic grievances as identity issues and linking them to erosions of group hierarchies due to the process of democratization. The empowerment of minorities after the electoral opening paradoxically emboldens the calls to bring the state "back in" to regulate the degree to which foreigners or the "others" ought to benefit from capitalism and calls for welfare protection to be put in place to alleviate inequalities. It ultimately legitimizes state intervention in markets, associated with the economic left.

The third common unique aspect of Eastern European radical right mobilization is the presence of radicalized nationalistic mainstream parties. The most prominent examples are Fidesz in Hungary, Law and Justice Party in Poland (PiS) and both major past and present social democratic parties of Prime Ministers Mečiar (HZDS) and Fico (SMER) in Slovakia. Although many Western European mainstream parties embrace tough policies on immigration and home-grown terrorist networks, Eastern European mainstream parties are, comparatively speaking, much more comfortable with their radical right cousins. Some blur the boundary between the far right and the mainstream right due to their radicalized rhetoric and policy agendas that diminish gender equality and ethnic inclusion. Radical right parties thus operate in a much more permissive environment, which is more tolerant of their exclusionary rhetoric and where they are incorporated into the governing coalitions. Moreover, radicalized mainstream parties are similarly left leaning and comfortable with using the state apparatus to intrude in the economy.[12] This configuration reinforces synergies between appeals that combine minority exclusion with economic protectionism at both the individual and state levels. It is important to keep in mind, however, that radical right parties have much more programmatic flexibility on the economic front as opposed to appeals based on identity boundaries and hierarchies that are core to their ideology.

In defining radical right parties, I have relied on three sources of information: (1) expert surveys, (2) ideology communicated through web pages of radical right parties including their Facebook and social media accounts, where available; and (3) comparison with classification in the scholarly literature on radical right parties. If parties were not listed in the surveys, the classification was determined by ideology and scholarly consensus. The list of parties that are contested as belonging or not belonging to the radical right party family and justification of controversial classification decisions is in the Appendix.

The position of the parties on group and grid was determined using three expert surveys: *Party Policy in Modern Democracies* (PPMD; Benoit and Laver 2006), the Chapel Hill Expert Survey (CH-H; Bakker et al. 2013) and the Democratic Accountability and Linkages Project (DALP; Kitschelt 2011). The group dimension is defined as the policy position of the party on "nationalism" (PPMD), "ethnic minorities" (CH-H) and "national identity" (DALP). The grid dimension is defined as the policy position of the party on "social" issues (PPMD), "social lifestyle" (CH-H) and "traditional authority, institutions and customs" (DALP). The expert estimates of party positions are in the Appendix as well as the full description of the questions from each of the three expert surveys and their respective scales.

---

[12] The Hungarian and Polish radicalized mainstream parties originated in anti-communist movements prior to the fall of the Berlin Wall in 1989.

The position of each party is relative to the position of other parties, since the experts evaluate all parties in a given party system. Radical right parties are those with the highest grid/group scores relative to other parties in the same country.

As Table 3.2 indicates, radical right parties in Croatia, Estonia, Latvia, Romania, Serbia, Slovakia and Slovenia have been steadily attracting some voter support since the early 1990s, although their electoral fortunes have fluctuated considerably across elections from 5 to 40 percent of the popular vote. Elsewhere radical parties emerged rapidly, only to disappear just as quickly, as in Albania, Macedonia and the Czech Republic, while in Moldova and Montenegro such parties hardly appeared at all. Table 3.2 shows how the strength of radical parties has varied considerably over time and across countries. (See Table A3.4 in the Appendix for more information on vote shares.) The list of parties is also shown in Table 3.2.

Radical right mobilization evolves around the bilateral relationship between the radical right parties and their "electoral enemies," the politically organized promoters of minority accommodation. Variation in minority political accommodation should predict change in electoral support for radical right parties. The case of Macedonia illustrates this logic. In 2001, a brief but violent armed conflict erupted between the ethnic Albanian militants and the Macedonian government, and was settled by the Ohrid Agreement, which improved the status of Albanians within Macedonia. The agreement elevated the Albanian language to an official status and established an Albanian speaking university in Tetovo. In the 2002 elections, the dominant party (VMRO-DPMNE) lost, and was replaced by a coalition called "Together for Macedonia Alliance," which ruled together with the largest Albanian ethnic political party (BDI), and created pro-Albanian legislation. In the 2006 election, an extremist, nationalist wing split from VMRO-DPMNE and targeted "minorities with privileges" (a euphemism for Albanians) and entered the parliament with 6 percent of the votes.

Moderate parties may court politically organized groups that support the accommodation of minorities and advocate socially liberal policies to form governing coalitions. When this ensues, radical right parties benefit from the resentment against political concessions to minorities. The electoral success of radical right parties is thus integrally tied to coalition politics.

Table 3.2 *Combined vote shares of radical right parties since the founding elections*

| | Elections | | | | | | |
|---|---|---|---|---|---|---|---|
| | 1st | 2nd | 3rd | 4th | 5th | 6th | 7th |
| Albania | 4.97 | 2.30 | 2.40 | 0.60 | 0.34 | | |
| Bulgaria | 1.13 | 0.54 | 0.18 | 0.07 | 8.14 | 9.36 | |
| Croatia | 50.00 | 47.51 | 31.85 | 6.37 | 3.50 | 3.00 | |
| Czech Republic | 5.98 | 8.01 | 3.09 | 1.08 | 0.17 | 1.14 | |
| Estonia | 11.50 | 16.10 | 8.40 | 1.70 | 0.40 | | |
| Hungary | 1.59 | 5.47 | 4.37 | 2.20 | 16.67 | | |
| Latvia | 11.99 | 14.37 | 5.39 | 6.94 | 7.67 | | |
| Lithuania | 4.01 | 2.77 | 0.28 | 1.75 | 0.63 | | |
| Macedonia | 0 | 0 | 6.10 | 0.24 | 2.51 | | |
| Moldova | 0 | 0 | 0 | 0 | 0 | 0 | |
| Montenegro | 0 | 0 | 0 | 0 | 0 | | |
| Poland | 2.85 | 5.63 | 7.87 | 8.00 | 1.30 | 0.07 | |
| Romania | 8.82 | 19.48 | 15.12 | 5.42 | 13.98 | | |
| Serbia Montenegro, FRY | 8.60 | 35.27 | 28.59 | 29.46 | 4.63 | | |
| Slovakia | 7.93 | 5.40 | 9.07 | 6.98 | 11.73 | 5.07 | 4.55 |
| Slovenia | 3.22 | 4.39 | 6.27 | 5.40 | 1.80 | | |
| Ukraine | 1.25 | 1.00 | 0 | 0.36 | 0.76 | 10.45 | |

Radical Right Parties

| | |
|---|---|
| Albania | PBK – BK – Balli Kombëtar (National Front Party) |
| | PBKD – Balli Kombëtar Demokrat (Democratic National Front Party) |
| Bulgaria | BNRP – Bălgarska nacionalna radikalna partija (Bulgarian National Radical Party) |
| | NSA – Nacionalen sayuz Ataka (National Union Attack, which includes BNRP [Attack Coalition]) |
| Croatia | HDZ – Hrvatska demokratska zajednica (Croatian Democratic Union) |
| | HSP – Hrvatska stranka prava (Croatian Party of Rights) |
| | HSP-ZDS – Hrvatska stranka prava – Zagorska demokratska stranka |
| | HSP-HKDU – Hrvatska stranka prava – Hrvatska Kršcanska Demokratska Unija |
| Czech Republic | SPR-RSČ – Sdružení pro republiku – Republikánská strana Československa (Sládek) |

**Table 3.2 (*cont.*)**

| Radical Right Parties | |
|---|---|
| | RMS – Republikáni Miroslava Sládka (Republicans of Miroslav Sládek) |
| | NS – Národní strana (National Party) |
| | NDS –Národně demokratická strana (National Democratic Party) |
| | DSS/DS – Dělnická strana/Dělnická strana sociální spravedlnosti (Workers' Party) |
| | Úsvit |
| | SPD – Svoboda a přímá demokracie Tomio Okamura |
| Estonia | ERSP – Eesti Rahvusliku Sõltumatuse Partei (Estonian National Independence Party) |
| | EK – Eesti Kodanik (Estonian Citizens) |
| | ERKL – Eesti Rahvuslaste Keskliit (Estonian Nationalists Central League) |
| | PE – Parem Eesti (Right Estonia) |
| | EIP – Eesti Iseseisvuspartei (Estonian Independence Party) |
| | Isamaa – Isamaa ja Res Publica Liit (Pro Patria and Res Publica Union) |
| Hungary | MIÉP – Magyar Igazság és Élet Pártja (Hungarian Justice and Life Party) |
| | MIÉP-Jobbik (MIÉP – Jobbik Magyarországért Mozgalom [Movement for a Better Hungary]) |
| | Jobbik – Jobbik Magyarországért Mozgalom (Movement for a Better Hungary) |
| Latvia | TB – Tēvzeme un Brīvībai (For Fatherland and Freedom) |
| | TB/LNNK – Apvienība Tēvzeme un Brīvībai/LNNK – Alliance for Homeland and Freedom |
| | LNNK – Latvijas Nacionālās Neatkarības Kustība (Latvian National Independence Movement) |
| Lithuania | LKDS/LTJS – Jaunoji Lietuva susivienijimas uz vieninga Lietuva (Young Lithuania – For United Lithuania) |
| | LNP-JL – Lietuviu Nacionaline Partija – "Jaunoji Lietuva" (Lithuanian National Party – Young Lithuania) |
| | LlaS – Lietuvos laisvės sąjunga (Lithuanian Liberty Union) |
| | LNDP – Lietuvos nacionaldemokratu partija (Lithuanian National Democratic Party) |
| Macedonia | VMRO-DPMNE - Vnatreška Makedonska Revolucionerna Organizacija – Demokratska Partija za Makedonsko Nacionalno Edinstvo (Democratic Party for Macedonian National Unity) |

**Table 3.2 (*cont.*)**

Radical Right Parties

| | |
|---|---|
| | VMRO-DP – Vnatreška Makedonska Revolucionerna Organizacija – Demokratska Partija |
| Poland | SN – Stronnictwo Narodowe (National Party) |
| | Party X – Partia X |
| | PWN-PSN – Polska Wspólnota Narodowa – Polskie Stronnictwo Narodowe (Polish National Commonwealth – Polish National Party) |
| | ROP – Ruch Odbudowy Polski (Movement for the Reconstruction of Poland) |
| | LPR – Liga Polskich Rodzin (League of Polish Families) |
| | LPR – Liga Prawicy Rzeczypospolitej (The League of the Right of the Republic |
| | [League of Polish Families (LPR) + Real Politics Union + Right of the Republic]) |
| Romania | PUNR – Partidul Unității Naționale a Românilor (Party of Romanian Unity) |
| | PRM – Partidul (Popular) România Mare (Party for Greater Romania) |
| | PNG – Partidul Noua Generație – Creștin Democrat (New Generation Party) |
| | PP-DD - Partidul Poporului – Dan Diaconescu (People's Party – Dan Diaconescu) |
| Serbia | SRS – Srpska radikalna stranka (Serbian Radical Party) |
| | NS – Nova Srbija (New Serbia) |
| | SPO – Srpski pokret obnove (Serbian Renewal Movement) |
| Slovakia | PSNS – Pravá Slovenská národná strana (Real Slovak National Party) |
| | SNS – Slovenská národná strana (Slovak National Party) |
| | ĽSNS – Kotleba – Ľudová strana Naše Slovensko (The People's Party – Our Slovakia) |
| Slovenia | SNS – Slovenska nacionalna stranka (Slovenian National Party) |
| Ukraine | KUN – Kongres Ukraiins'kikh Natsionalistiv (Congress of Ukrainian Nationalists) |
| | Rukh – Narodnyi Rukh Ukrajiny (The People's Movement of Ukraine) |
| | Svoboda (Freedom) |
| | Pravyi Sektor (Right Sector) |

## 3.2 Observable Implications of the Theory

The theory advanced here endogenizes issue salience, and argues that it is a function of the strength and the inclusion of ethno-liberal parties in governing coalitions, which polarize party systems. The salience of identity increases if the ethno-liberal party extracts policy concessions from its coalition partner or elevates minority representatives into positions of symbolic importance. Policies that privilege and elevate some groups over others magnify preexisting grievances, fuel resentment and create a political backlash that benefits radical right parties. The simple formation of a governing coalition between a mainstream party and an accommodation-seeking party should therefore increase the probability of the radical right's success in the subsequent electoral cycle.

If the theory developed here offers a useful framework for thinking about radical right parties, there should be evidentiary support for three observable implications. The first hypothesis, deduced from the proposition that radical right parties arise to counterbalance the electoral strength of the ethno-liberal parties,[13] suggests that strong radical right parties should arise after ethno-liberal parties have been successful (in terms of *vote shares*) in the prior election. The second implication is that radical right parties should become stronger after the ethno-liberal party has been included in a *governing coalition*, which permits small parties to influence policy. Obtaining a ministerial post permits the ethno-liberal parties to influence policies and to access state resources. The third observable implication is that radical right parties should succeed in proportion to the *ideological extremism* of the ethno-liberal party in the previous electoral cycle.[14] This chapter provides a systematic time-series analysis of these three theoretical implications in all post-communist democracies.

The theory generates three important observable empirical implications. These implications can be expressed as three hypotheses:

*Hypothesis 1*: When the vote share of an ethno-liberal party in an election held at time $t - 1$ increases, then the radical right party's vote share in elections at $t$ should also increase.

---

[13] Electoral strength is defined as the proportion of vote shares in the parliamentary elections.

[14] Ideological extremism refers to the absolute and relative degree of accommodation toward minorities sought by ethno-liberal parties.

*Hypothesis 2*: The inclusion of an ethno-liberal party in a governing coalition at time $t - 1$ increases the radical right party's vote share in elections at $t$.

*Hypothesis 3*: The inclusion of an ideologically extreme ethno-liberal party in a coalition in election $t - 1$ increases the radical right party's vote share in elections at $t$.

Using original party-level electoral data covering all post-communist democracies from 1990 to 2012, the results strongly support these hypotheses, and indicate that the rise and decline of radical right parties is shaped by the electoral fortunes of bilateral opposite parties and the accommodation of minority groups. In the next section, I introduce a new dataset and my estimation strategy. This is followed by a discussion of the statistical results and corroborative case study evidence, which follows in more detail in the next two chapters. The last section concludes with a discussion of the theory's external validity and its contribution to understanding the roots of radical right mobilization.

## 3.3 Data Description and Estimation Strategy

To investigate these hypotheses, I created an election-year and country dataset covering the period from the early 1990s to the present for all post-communist democracies.[15] The dataset is structured as a quasi-time series of ninety-three parliamentary elections in seventeen countries from 1991 to 2012 and the dependent variable is the natural log of the radical right party's combined vote share in elections held at time $t$.

To examine the backlash logic embedded in these hypotheses, I utilize three measures. The first measure, associated with Hypothesis 1, is the log of the ethno-liberal party's vote share in the previous electoral cycle. The second measure, to explore Hypothesis 2, accounts for the access of the ethno-liberal party to policy making and state resources using an indicator of its participation in the governing

---

[15] This excludes the first or initial elections and elections that were boycotted.

coalition during the previous cycle. Although the ethno-liberal parties must be strong enough to cross the electoral threshold in order to be considered for participation in a coalition, it is *not* the case that stronger ethno-liberal parties are more or less likely to be invited to join coalitions. For this reason, it is important to measure the strength of the ethno-liberal parties in terms of vote shares and their participation in governing coalitions independently. I also examine the effect of ethnic structure to test the claim that support for radical right parties is stronger in countries with smaller minorities.[16]

To investigate Hypothesis 3 – that radical right parties arise as a backlash to the ideological extremism of the ethno-liberal parties – I rely on the Manifesto Project (Volkens et al. 2010) for a measure of the proportion of quasi-sentences indicating the party positions on identity. In order to measure each party's ideological position on the identity dimension, I turn to the category referred to in the Manifesto Project as the "Fabric of Social Life."[17] It is comprised of three categories: national way of life, traditional morality and multiculturalism. The overall score is the sum of the positive evaluations minus the sum of the negative evaluations of three categories. A low score on the index, indicating high ideological intensity of the ethno-liberal party, is associated with tolerance, social liberalism and accommodation of minorities. A high score indicates the opposite.

To control for the incumbency effect on the radical right party's success, I include the natural log of the radical right party's vote share in the previous election as a lagged dependent variable. The second incumbency measure is an indicator of whether the radical right party was in the governing coalition in the previous electoral cycle. This is intended to control for advantageous access to state resources and the

---

[16] The size of the titular majority and the size of the minority are unrelated to vote shares for ethnic parties. Countries with larger minorities do not have stronger ethnic parties. Moreover, vote shares for ethnic parties fluctuate over time even though group size is relatively constant over time.

[17] The absolute ideological extremism of the ethno-liberal party is measured on the basis of the manifesto data and the score is based on positions expressed in the manifesto of the ethno-liberal party. The ideological extremism of the ethno-liberal party is indexed against its proximate competitor, a moderate, mainstream party that also supports the accommodation of minorities. The greater the distance between the two parties, the greater the relative ideological extremism of accommodation advocated by the ethno-liberal party.

gains in credibility that the radical right party earned during the previous electoral cycle.

Finally, since the dataset that I have created is structured as a pooled cross-national, quasi–time series, it is necessary to account for the fact that elections are nested over time within countries. To control for the time effects due to the fact that vote shares are measured in consecutive elections, I control for the years since the first, foundational election. I estimate a set of censored models with random effects to account for the hierarchical data structure.

## 3.4 The Statistical Model

Electoral success is measured as the vote share of the radical right party in a given country and election year.[18] To provide a sense of the distribution, the mean vote share for the radical right parties in ninety-three elections is 6.5 percent for the whole distribution and 7.7 percent for the non-censored part. The range is between 0.07 and 50 percent. In thirteen elections, the vote share of the radical right party was below 1 percent, and in fourteen elections no radical right party contested the elections at all.

I include *all* elections in the statistical analysis regardless of the absence or presence of the radical right parties on the ballot. This is done to avoid any potential bias from disregarding the "censored cases," defined as elections in which the radical right parties do not field any candidates. To include elections with zero vote shares, I use a latent variable model for censored outcomes (Golder 2003; Jackman and Volpert 1996; Swank and Betz 2003). The random effects model in non-linear panel data is widely preferred over the fixed effects model due to the inconsistency and bias of the maximum likelihood estimator.[19] I modify the model outlined in Greene (2008) and Henningsen (2011) and limit the censoring structure to the left side. This left-censored regression model for panel data with country specific effects can be written as follows:

---

[18] In the rare case that there are two radical right parties in one electoral system, it is measured as a cumulative vote share of all radical right parties.

[19] The maximum likelihood estimator in censored regression with fixed effects is widely understood to be biased and inconsistent when T, the length of the panel, is small and fixed. Since the random effect model is superior, there is no need to perform a Hausman test for fixed versus random effects.

$$y_{it}^* = x_{it}^T \beta + \varepsilon_{it} = x_{it}^T \beta + \mu_i + \nu_{it}$$
$$y_{it} = a \quad \text{if} \quad y_{it}^* \leq a,$$
$$y_i = y_{it}^* \quad \text{if} \quad y_{it}^* > a$$

The subscripts $i = 1, \ldots, N$ cover the countries, while subscripts $t = 1, \ldots, T_i$ indicate the time period, starting with 1 as the post-foundational election. $T_i$ is the number of years observed for the $i$th country; $\mu_i$ is a time-invariant country specific effect; and $\nu_{it}$ is the remaining disturbance. Assuming that the country-specific effects $\mu_i$ are independent of the covariates, we can estimate the parameters with a random effects model. Assuming further that specific country effects $\mu$ follow a normal distribution with mean 0 and variance $\sigma_\nu^2$, and $\mu$ and $\nu$ are independent, the likelihood contribution of a single country $i$ is given as follows:

$$L_i = \int_{-\infty}^{\infty} \left\{ \prod_{t=1}^{T_i} \left[ \Phi\left( \frac{a - x_{it}'\beta - \mu_i}{\sigma_\nu} \right) \right]^{I_{it}^a} \left[ \frac{1}{\sigma_\nu} \phi\left( \frac{y_{it} - x_{it}'\beta - \mu_i}{\sigma_\nu} \right) \right]^{(1 - I_{it}^a)} \right\} \phi\left( \frac{\mu_i}{\sigma_\mu} \right) d\mu_i$$

where $\phi(.)$ and $\Phi(.)$ denote the probability density unction and the cumulative distributive function, respectively, of the standard normal distribution, and $I_i^a$ is the indicator function with:

$$I_{it}^a = 0 \quad \text{if} \quad y_{it} > a$$
$$I_{it}^a = 1 \quad \text{if} \quad y_{it} = a.$$

An important assumption of the censored model is that the underlying process that causes the party to be absent from an election is identical to the process that explains the electoral support of parties that in fact entered the race. In addition to the fourteen elections in which no party was present on the ballot, there were twenty-six contested elections in which radical right parties received less than 2.5 percent of the vote, and thirty-nine contested elections in which parties received less than 5 percent of the vote.

Given that many countries impose a 5 percent electoral threshold, this large number of elections where radical right parties could not have been expected to win a seat in the legislature leads me to believe that it is not necessary to model the selection process in which no parties appear on the ballot separately. The theory should be able to explain cases in which parties do not contest the election as well as cases in which parties receive a negligible number of votes.

## 3.5 Discussion of Empirical Results

I first look descriptively at the electoral success of radical right parties. Using the total number of elections as the baseline, radical right parties succeeded (i.e., were able to win at least one seat) in 43 out of 93 elections. Of these 43 electoral successes, 37 were preceded by a "coalition with one of the bilateral opposites" (Table 3.3). The contrapositive is also informative: 37 out of 43 elections without a radical right party success at time $t$ were not preceded by a "coalition with one of the bilateral opposites" at $t - 1$. Table 3.4 further disaggregates coalitions into two groups – coalitions with ethno-liberal parties and coalitions with radical right parties – and shows that the results are robust. Using the total number of elections with "coalitions with one of the bilateral opposites" as the baseline, 37 of 50 elections with "coalitions with one of the bilateral opposites" in time $t$ resulted in the electoral success of the radical right party in the subsequent election. In 22 out of 33 elections, the electoral success of the radical right party was preceded by a governing coalition in which the ethno-liberal party obtained a portfolio. Radical right parties succeeded in two-thirds of elections when the ethno-liberal party controlled a governmental portfolio in the previous electoral cycle.

These descriptive statistics suggest a strong relationship between the government participation of an ethno-liberal party and the success of a radical right party and point to the plausibility of the backlash mechanism. The results also uncover a strong incumbency effect, showing that a radical right party held a portfolio in a government that preceded the electoral radical right's success in fifteen out of seventeen elections.

The case of Slovakia suggests the importance of holding a government portfolio for radical right mobilization. In 2002, the Hungarian ethnic party (MKP) was invited to join the governing coalition and used its power to promote minority schooling, including a new Hungarian-speaking Selye János University. MKP was also granted the portfolio for regional development and used it ruthlessly to channel resources to Hungarian districts. This remobilized the Slovak National Party (SNS), which was rife with internal discord and had been in decline. In the 2006 election, SNS reunited and secured almost 12 percent of the vote and a partnership in the governing coalition. This granted SNS the portfolio of the Ministry of Regional Development

Table 3.3 *The electoral success of radical right parties in t by a "coalition with one of the bilateral opposites" in t − 1*

|  | Coalition with B-L opposite in $t - 1$ | No coalition with B-L opposite in $t - 1$ | Totals |
|---|---|---|---|
| Electoral success of RR in $t$ | 37 | 6 | 43 |
| Electoral failure of RR in $t$ | 13 | 37 | 50 |
|  | 50 | 43 | 93 |

Electoral success of radical right party in $t$, (number of parliamentary seats >1)
Electoral failure of the radical right party in $t$, (no parliamentary seats gained in $t$)
Presence of a "coalition with one of the bilateral opposites" in previous elections $(t - 1)$
No "coalition with one of the bilateral opposites" in the previous electoral cycle $(t - 1)$

Table 3.4 *The electoral success of radical right parties in t by coalition type in t − 1*

|  | Ethno-liberal party in a coalition in $t - 1$ | Radical right party in a coalition in $t - 1$ | Totals |
|---|---|---|---|
| Electoral success of RR in $t$ | 22 | 15 | 37 |
| Electoral failure of RR in $t$ | 11 | 2 | 13 |
|  | 33 | 17 | 50 |

Electoral success of radical right party in $t$, (number of parliamentary seats >1)
Electoral failure (no parliamentary seats for radical right party in $t$)

and the ability to briskly shift resources away from Hungarian districts and toward predominantly Slovak districts.[20]

Turning to the multivariable statistical results, the electoral success of the ethno-liberal party in the previous electoral cycle increases the prospects for the radical right party in the subsequent electoral cycle, which is consistent with Hypothesis 1 (Table 3.5). Consistent with

[20] Source: Transparency International Slovakia, author's interviews in Slovakia, 2007 and 2008.

Table 3.5 Determinants of electoral support for radical right parties

| | (M1) | (M2) | (M3) | (M4) | (M5) | (M6) | (M7) | (M8) |
|---|---|---|---|---|---|---|---|---|
| Ethno-liberal party in coalition (t – 1) (1 = participated) | 0.522** (0.204) | 0.504** (0.204) | 0.520*** (0.197) | 0.553*** (0.195) | 0.499** (0.206) | 0.418** (0.209) | 0.519*** (0.201) | 0.472** (0.200) |
| Ethno-liberal party vote share (t – 1) | 0.249*** (0.087) | 0.230*** (0.082) | 0.246*** (0.084) | 0.263*** (0.090) | 0.268*** (0.087) | 0.191** (0.083) | 0.221*** (0.078) | 0.223*** (0.077) |
| Radical right party in coalition (t – 1) (1 = participated) | 0.665** (0.273) | 0.796*** (0.266) | 0.567** (0.265) | 0.616** (0.261) | 0.729*** (0.256) | 0.483* (0.282) | 0.535** (0.269) | 0.513* (0.273) |
| Radical right party vote share (t – 1) | 0.603*** (0.125) | 0.569*** (0.108) | 0.634*** (0.120) | 0.606*** (0.129) | 0.597*** (0.109) | 0.691*** (0.098) | 0.730*** (0.092) | 0.714*** (0.095) |
| Size of the titular majority | | 1.274** (0.527) | | | 1.180** (0.510) | | | 0.598 (0.541) |
| Economic volatility (election cycle) | | | 0.0579** (0.026) | 0.147*** (0.053) | 0.148** (0.060) | 0.0672** (0.029) | | 0.0474* (0.027) |
| EU membership (1 = member) | | | | 0.247 (0.248) | 0.122 (0.215) | | | |
| Interaction: EU * Econ. Volatility | | | | -0.116* (0.060) | -0.114* (0.060) | | | |
| Years since the first election | | | | | 0.00435 (0.017) | | | |
| Wealth – GDP/PC (t – 1) | | | | | | 0.0862 (0.176) | | |

| | (1) | (2) | (3) | (4) | (5) | (6) | (7) | (8) |
|---|---|---|---|---|---|---|---|---|
| Unemployment ($t-1$) | | | | | | -0.008 | | |
| | | | | | | (0.010) | | |
| Disproportionality | | | | | | | 0.026* | 0.014 |
| | | | | | | | (0.016) | (0.017) |
| Constant | -0.202 | -5.741** | -0.341* | -0.531** | -5.689** | -0.985 | -0.475* | -3.092 |
| | (0.192) | (2.312) | (0.197) | (0.235) | (2.232) | (1.575) | (0.244) | (2.323) |
| Sigma (u) | 0.234 | 0.129 | 0.211 | 0.259 | 0.138 | 2.72e-16 | 2.02e-16 | 2.19e-17 |
| | (0.177) | (0.217) | (0.176) | (0.171) | (0.204) | (0.182) | (0.176) | (0.152) |
| Sigma (e) | 0.662*** | 0.664*** | 0.645*** | 0.622*** | 0.630*** | 0.667*** | 0.644*** | 0.631*** |
| | (0.061) | (0.061) | (0.060) | (0.058) | (0.059) | (0.058) | (0.057) | (0.056) |
| Number of elections | 93 | 93 | 93 | 93 | 93 | 80 | 76 | 76 |
| Number of countries | 17 | 17 | 17 | 17 | 17 | 17 | 17 | 17 |
| Log likelihood | -91.93 | -88.61 | -89.54 | -87.75 | -84.84 | -76.52 | -71.04 | -68.88 |
| Chi-square | 107.5 | 143.5 | 118.7 | 114.7 | 157.5 | 157.2 | 163.1 | 168.7 |
| AIC | 197.9 | 193.2 | 195.1 | 195.5 | 193.7 | 173.0 | 158.1 | 157.8 |
| Censored observations | 14 | 14 | 14 | 14 | 14 | 12 | 11 | 11 |
| Uncensored observations | 79 | 79 | 79 | 79 | 79 | 68 | 65 | 65 |

Standard errors in parentheses; $* p < 0.10$, $** p < 0.05$, $*** p < 0.01$.

*Note:* Censored regression with random effects, DV: log of total vote shares for the radical right parties.

*Source:* Bustikova 2014.

Hypothesis 2, presence of an ethno-liberal party in a governing coalition also increases the electoral prospects of the radical right party in the next electoral cycle. Empirical evidence for Hypothesis 3 is discussed later in the text. The results, based on the relationship between the size of the titular majority and party support, indicate that the size of the minority is negatively related to the electoral prospect of the radical right parties, and that countries with smaller ethnic minorities are more likely to have more successful radical right parties.[21] Finally, I find evidence of a strong incumbency effect for radical right parties. The electoral strength of the radical right party in the previous cycle, and to a lesser extent its presence in the previous government, predicts the radical right party's electoral success in the subsequent electoral cycle.

To explore the marginal effects of the variables, I constructed a "violin plot" (Hintze and Nelson 1998). It combines the advantages of a boxplot, which indicate the average effect and the uncertainty, with a kernel density plot that more effectively shows the distribution of the variable's effect. Specifically, I constructed a box plot of the marginal effect under two high-probability scenarios and then added a rotated kernel density plot to each side of the box plot. The marginal effects are drawn from post-estimations using as the basis the censored regression Model 2 in Table 3.5.[22]

Figure 3.1 illustrates the marginal effect of two key variables. The top panel compares the expected vote share for the radical right at time $t$ when an ethno-liberal party was included in a coalition at time $t - 1$ (top right) versus when the ethno-liberal party was not included in a governing coalition (top left). The effect of being in a coalition increased the expected vote share for the radical right by a factor of roughly two, or double the share of votes. The bottom panel compares

---

[21] Minority size is based on the census in each country. While perceived group size may differ in some cases from actual group size, unfortunately the lack of data for the time period and countries analyzed here does not allow for testing this hypothesis.

[22] To examine the model's predictive performance on out-of-sample data, I used a cross-validation experiment to compare the Heckman and the censored approach, and found that the censored approach consistently performed better (Efron and Tibshirani 1993).

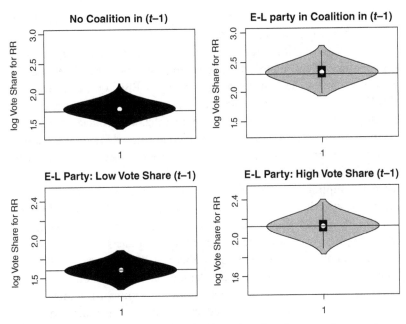

**Figure 3.1** Violin plots of marginal effects based on censored regressions.
*Note*: Based on censored regressions in Table 3.5, Model 2.
*Source*: Bustikova 2014

the expected vote share for the radical right at time $t$ (bottom left) when an ethno-liberal party received relatively few votes (25th percentile) at time $t - 1$ versus when an ethno-liberal party received a significant share of votes (75th percentile, bottom right). On average, the effect size is comparable to the coalition effect size. It roughly doubles the vote share for the radical right.

Spies and Franzmann (2011) show that party system polarization on cultural issues and the lack of polarization on economic issues jointly increase extremist voting. Whereas the presence of ethno-liberal parties polarizes the electorate and increases the salience on identity issues, parties can project positions on economic issues that are salient while also being centrist. Agreement among the major parties on the direction of market reforms signifies policy convergence (Frye 2002). At the same time, rapid economic policy changes will tend to increase the salience of economic issues. The analysis consistently shows that economic grievances, such as unemployment, are statistically unrelated to support for radical right parties (Table 3.5).[23]

To further explore the link between economic salience and support for radical right parties, I created a new measure of "economic volatility." It is based on the composite of six EBRD transition scores (EBRD 2013). A high score can be achieved by either swift reform developments or swift retraction from liberalization policies, relative to changes in previous years. The variable captures the average relative change in economic transition scores for each electoral cycle. The results in Models 3–6 (Table 3.5) show that high economic volatility increases support for radical right voting, controlling for unemployment and wealth. This suggests that indicators of volatility and policy uncertainty, often unrelated to objective grievances, are potentially stronger predictors of radical right voting than measures of economic deprivation and development (cf. Arzheimer 2009; Tucker 2006).

Since not all post-communist democracies are members of the European Union, and radical right parties are known for their Euro-sceptic views, I inspected the effect of EU membership on party strength. While the EU membership itself is unrelated to radical right support, it mediates the effect of economic volatility on radical right voting (Model 5 in Table 3.5). The interaction effect indicates that membership in the EU tempered the effect of economic volatility, which suggests that the promise of EU membership has had a calming effect on the accession countries (Kelley 2004a, b; Vachudova 2008a, b). By decreasing anxiety over the economic transition, entry into the EU slightly decreased support for the radical right.

To control for distinct features of the electoral system across countries, I use Gallagher's index of disproportionality, Rae's index of party system fractionalization and the Laakso-Taagepera measure of the effective number of parties. I found a modest effect for the effective number of electoral parties (Table 3.6) and disproportionality in the electoral system on radical right support (Model 7 in Table 3.6).

---

[23] I have tested for the interaction effect between the coalition presence of the ethno-liberal party and its vote share in the previous cycle and found the interaction insignificant. Myriad factors, including wealth, changes in wealth, changes in wealth indexed to 1990 levels of development, inflation, government expenditures, growth in government expenditures, welfare state development proxies, and both levels and changes in levels of these variables, all have no independent effect on the electoral strength of the radical right parties.

Table 3.6 *Determinants of electoral support for radical right parties with institutional control variables*

| | (M1) | (M2) | (M3) | (M4) | (M5) | (M6) | (M7) |
|---|---|---|---|---|---|---|---|
| Ethno-liberal party in coalition ($t - 1$) (1 = participated) | 0.463** (0.189) | 0.478** (0.187) | 0.520** (0.203) | 0.495** (0.205) | 0.573*** (0.177) | 0.581*** (0.178) | 0.484** (0.203) |
| Ethno-liberal party vote share ($t - 1$) | 0.222*** (0.078) | 0.223*** (0.078) | 0.167** (0.079) | 0.183** (0.081) | 0.231*** (0.074) | 0.228*** (0.074) | 0.227*** (0.079) |
| Radical right party in coalition ($t - 1$) (1 = participated) | 0.594** (0.256) | 0.778*** (0.261) | 0.551** (0.255) | 0.614** (0.267) | 0.534** (0.232) | 0.659*** (0.242) | 0.597** (0.273) |
| Radical right party vote share ($t - 1$) | 0.672*** (0.087) | 0.589*** (0.091) | 0.574*** (0.093) | 0.564*** (0.094) | 0.667*** (0.082) | 0.623*** (0.086) | 0.691*** (0.096) |
| Electoral threshold | −0.086 (0.099) | −0.015 (0.101) | | | | | 0.079 (0.104) |
| Size of the titular majority | | 1.206** (0.489) | | 0.513 (0.637) | | 0.746* (0.450) | 0.693 (0.558) |
| Effective number of parties (seats) | | | 0.027 (0.033) | 0.037 (0.035) | | | |
| Effective number of parties (votes) | | | | | 0.078* (0.043) | 0.084* (0.043) | |
| Disproportionality | | | | | | | 0.023 (0.017) |
| Constant | 0.177 (0.477) | −5.374** (2.301) | −0.0283 (0.240) | −2.357 (2.906) | −0.700*** (0.257) | −3.968** (2.005) | −3.815 (2.540) |

Table 3.6 (cont.)

| | (M1) | (M2) | (M3) | (M4) | (M5) | (M6) | (M7) |
|---|---|---|---|---|---|---|---|
| Sigma (u) | 0.213 | 0.126 (0.224) | 1.90e−17 | 3.34e−17 | 0.179 | 0.171 | 1.90e−16 |
| | (0.190) | | (0.121) | (0.120) | (0.147) | (0.148) | (0.166) |
| Sigma (e) | 0.688*** | 0.674*** | 0.616*** | 0.615*** | 0.602*** | 0.599*** | 0.640*** |
| | (0.056) | (0.054) | (0.056) | (0.056) | (0.052) | (0.051) | (0.057) |
| Number of elections | 93 | 93 | 68 | 68 | 83 | 83 | 76 |
| Number of countries | 17 | 17 | 15 | 15 | 17 | 17 | 17 |
| Log likelihood | −91.91 | −88.65 | −63.21 | −62.89 | −71.78 | −70.33 | −70.10 |
| Chi-square | 163.4 | 166.6 | 116.5 | 116.7 | 181.9 | 178.9 | 162.6 |
| AIC | 197.8 | 193.3 | 142.4 | 143.8 | 157.6 | 156.7 | 160.2 |
| Censored observations | 14 | 14 | 6 | 6 | 13 | 13 | 11 |
| Uncensored observations | 79 | 79 | 62 | 62 | 70 | 70 | 65 |

Note: Censored regression with random effects, DV: log of total vote shares for the radical right parties.
Robustness checks for the effect of electoral systems. Standard errors in parentheses.
* $p < 0.10$, ** $p < 0.05$, *** $p < 0.01$.
Source: Bustikova 2014.

Consistent with a controversial finding by Arzheimer and Carter (2006), support for radical right parties mildly increases as the disproportionality increases (cf. Givens 2005). The results from the censored regression model are unaffected by voter turnout, by urban/rural cleavage (Pop-Eleches 2010; Tavits 2005), by special rules that secure seats in parliament for ethnic minorities and by lower thresholds allowing ethnic parties to succeed in elections (Bernauer and Bochsler 2011). Cross-national differences in other factors – including economic grievances, fragmentation, political accountability, and a legacy of interwar radicalism – are also unable to explain why radical parties are stronger in some countries and at some times, but weaker in others.

To ensure the model properly accommodates the censored nature of the underlying data, I used Cragg's test to address the "corner solution model" specification (Greene 2008).[24] I also ran the mirror image of the model, predicting vote share for ethno-liberal parties by vote share and coalition presence of radical right parties in the previous electoral cycle, and found no effect of radical right vote share on support for ethno-liberal parties. I also tested for the robustness of ethno-liberal party coding by first excluding social liberal parties from the analysis and by recoding social liberal parties as mainstream parties. The results were robust to all of these modifications. I performed additional robustness checks by examining the effect of electoral system characteristics (Gallagher 2013) on support for radical right parties (Table 3.6). The results are remarkably robust to the inclusion of three indicators: (1) the electoral threshold, (2) the effective number of parties at the parliamentary level (seats) and (3) the effective number of parties at the electoral level (votes). The effective number of electoral parties (Models 5 and 6 in Table 3.6) shows a modestly significant and positive effect, which suggests that more diverse political systems produce stronger radical right parties. The electoral threshold and the

---

[24] I tested for the assumption that the censoring limit depends on the same distribution as the uncensored observations, which in our case is any vote share, even very small, for any radical right party that contested the election. I tested Cragg's corner solution model by using a two-equation system where the first equation estimates the probability of being above the censoring limit (the minimal number of vote shares) and the second is a truncated regression on the uncensored observation, all vote shares observed. The likelihood ratio test statistic was 15.6, which is an equivalent of the 0.05 critical value of chi-square with eight degrees of freedom. This led me not to reject the null hypothesis that the restricted model (e.g., censored regression) is true.

effective number of parliamentary parties do not exhibit statistically significant effects (Table 3.6).

I found a conditional support for Hypothesis 3, which predicted a positive relationship between the ideological intensity of the ethno-liberal party in the previous election and the success of the radical right parties (Table 3.7).[25] There is no relationship between the absolute ideological intensity of the ethno-liberal party in the previous election and future votes for a radical right party (Model 1 in Table 3.7).[26] It might be argued that this is hardly surprising, since the ideological intensity of the ethno-liberal party itself does not generate votes for the radical right party in the subsequent election without access to policy making and political power. Consistent with this interpretation, Hypothesis 3 is supported when the ideological intensity of the ethno-liberal party is considered jointly with the presence of the ethno-liberal party in the government.

The interaction of the ethno-liberal party coalition presence and its absolute ideological intensity is statistically significant in Model 2 (Table 3.7). The more accommodation sought by the ethno-liberal party that served in the governing coalition, the greater the electoral success of the radical right party in the following election. The effect of the ethno-liberal party's ideological intensity must be considered relative to the ideological intensity of the moderate proximate party. This is tested in Model 4 in Table 3.7, which includes an interaction between the presence of the ethno-liberal party in a governing coalition and its relative ideological intensity, defined as the ideological distance between the ethno-liberal party and its proximate moderate party competitor. Although the relative ideological intensity of the ethno-liberal party does not have an independent effect on the vote shares of the radical right party, its interaction with coalition presence points in the expected direction.

---

[25] I assume that higher proportions of the party manifestos (coded as quasi-sentences) that advocate multiculturalism and tolerance for minority views indicate more ideological intensity. There are a number of missing codings in the Manifesto Project, especially with regard to the evaluations of small ethno-liberal and small radical right parties, which reduces the sample size. Since missing manifestos are conflated with no radical right parties' contested elections, I decided against the implementation of the censored model.

[26] The same result is obtained for the relative ideological intensity of the ethno-liberal party.

Table 3.7 Determinants of electoral support for radical right parties: *ideology*

| | (M1) | (M2) | (M3) | (M4) | (M5) | (M6) |
|---|---|---|---|---|---|---|
| Ethno-liberal party in coalition ($t-1$) (1 = participated) | 0.740*** | 0.599*** | 0.628*** | 0.432* | 0.558** | 0.406* |
| | (0.224) | (0.222) | (0.211) | (0.224) | (0.235) | (0.234) |
| Ethno-liberal party vote share ($t-1$) | 0.172 | 0.219* | 0.203* | 0.243** | 0.228* | 0.248** |
| | (0.122) | (0.115) | (0.111) | (0.108) | (0.117) | (0.110) |
| Radical right party in coalition ($t-1$) (1 = participated) | 0.500 | 0.485 | 0.434 | 0.449 | 0.454 | 0.433 |
| | (0.373) | (0.310) | (0.315) | (0.301) | (0.317) | (0.307) |
| Radical right party vote share ($t-1$) | 0.666*** | 0.733*** | 0.741*** | 0.772*** | 0.737*** | 0.774*** |
| | (0.132) | (0.128) | (0.124) | (0.120) | (0.129) | (0.121) |
| Years since the first election | −0.025 | −0.034 | −0.035* | −0.050** | −0.024 | −0.043 |
| | (0.023) | (0.022) | (0.021) | (0.021) | (0.027) | (0.027) |
| Size of the titular majority | −0.294 | | | | | |
| | (0.805) | | | | | |
| Ethno-liberal party ideology, abs ($t-1$) | −0.025 | −0.002 | | | 0.004 | |
| | (0.026) | (0.026) | | | (0.028) | |
| *Interaction:* Ethno-liberal p. in coal. * Ethno-liberal party ideology, absolute | | −0.103* | | | −0.105* | |
| | | (0.054) | | | (0.055) | |
| Ethno-liberal party ideology, rel. ($t-1$) (distance from proximate competitor) | | | 0.021 | −0.008 | | −0.011 |
| | | | (0.025) | (0.028) | | (0.029) |

Table 3.7 (*cont.*)

| | (M1) | (M2) | (M3) | (M4) | (M5) | (M6) |
|---|---|---|---|---|---|---|
| *Interaction:* Ethno-liberal p. in coal. * | | | | 0.107** | | 0.107** |
| | | | | (0.053) | | (0.054) |
| Ethno-liberal party ideology, relative | | | | | 0.044 | |
| Economic volatility (election cycle) | | | | 0.064 | (0.099) | |
| | | | | (0.107) | | |
| Constant | 1.293 | −0.054 | −0.074 | 0.060 | −0.246 | −0.076 |
| | (3.635) | (0.424) | (0.414) | (0.401) | (0.536) | (0.508) |
| Sigma (e) | 0.66 | 0.66 | 0.60 | 0.57 | 0.67 | 0.59 |
| Number of elections | 39 | 39 | 38 | 38 | 39 | 38 |
| Number of countries | 13 | 13 | 13 | 13 | 13 | 13 |
| Chi-square | 65.68 | 76.55 | 81.08 | 93.01 | 75.32 | 90.72 |
| R^2 | 0.68 | 0.71 | 0.72 | 0.76 | 0.72 | 0.76 |

*Note:* Panel regression with random effects, DV: log of total vote shares for the radical right parties.

Standard errors in parentheses.

* $p < 0.10$, ** $p < 0.05$, *** $p < 0.010$.

*Source:* Bustikova 2014.

When an ethno-liberal party that seeks high levels of accommodation is included in a coalition, the radical right succeeded in the ensuing election.[27] Table 3.7 shows that the absolute and relative ideological intensity of the ethno-liberal parties matters only if the ethno-liberal parties obtain a platform to express their views and realize their preferences in coalition governments. I found no evidence that the positions of the mainstream parties themselves have any discernible effect on radical right party success. I also found no effect of ideological convergence of mainstream parties and no effect of the ideological distance between the mainstream right and radical right on radical right party success.[28] None of these robustness checks altered the core finding that the ethno-liberal party's coalition presence and its electoral success increase the vote shares for the radical right party in the following election. These results strongly suggest that the electoral success of radical right parties depends on polarization driven by non-proximate parties.

The bilateral opposite is crucial for radical right mobilization, as is the threat level represented by minority demands. The Hungarian minority in both Slovakia and Romania is mostly concerned with minority schooling for its children and college-age adults, the use of the Hungarian language in official settings, and governmental spending toward areas where Hungarians mostly live. Even if the Slovak or Romanian governments were to engage in a high degree of accommodation for their Hungarian minorities, this would never really call into question the dominance of the Slovak language in Slovakia or the Romanian language in Romania, nor would it undermine legitimacy of Slovaks and Romanians as the dominant nationalities.

---

[27] While most of the variables in Tables 3.5–3.7 are consistent across the models, the incumbency effect of the radical right parties' inclusion in the government is not confirmed by an analysis of the manifesto data. This might be due to the lower number of cases included in the analysis and multiple omissions of small parties due to missing data.

[28] I also did not uncover any effect of the radical right party's ideological intensity. The robustness checks included testing for ideological convergence of moderate parties (level and change), absolute ideological extremism of the radical right party (level and change), relative ideological extremism of the radical right party (level and change), ideological extremism of the ethno-liberal party's proximate competitor and ideological extremism of the radical right party's proximate competitor party.

Hungary exemplifies the importance of cosmopolitan socially liberal parties and their ability to find allies among the mainstream political players to achieve policy shifts. Like other Eastern European countries, Hungary has a Roma minority, which is estimated at 3 percent (or about 300,000) according to the 2011 census, but could be as high as 700,000 in a country of 10 million people according to the Council of Europe (2007).[29] Unlike other Eastern European countries, Hungary is unique across (both Eastern and Western) Europe for its high levels of Roma political inclusion – since the early 1990s, the Minority at Risk project has accorded Hungary the highest score for political protection of Roma in Eastern Europe (MAR 2008).[30]

In 1995, Hungary introduced an innovative minority self-government system, which allows minorities, including Roma, to establish elected bodies that represent their interests and serve as partners for the government at the local and national levels. In 2005, Hungary launched another new initiative called the "Decade of Roma Inclusion: 2005–2015," which was aimed at improving the socioeconomic standing and the social inclusion of Roma (Roma Decade 2005).[31] A small socially liberal political party called the Alliance of Free Democrats (SzDSz), which participated for two years in government before Jobbik rose to power, but dissolved in 2013, was the most vocal political advocate of Roma protection in Hungary, and was a magnet for the wrath of the Hungarian far right.[32] Intellectuals from SzDSz played an important role in founding an independent Roma organization, "Phralipe," after 1989 (Vermeersch 2006: 71), which advocated for the improvement of the Roma community's standing in Hungarian society. Aladár Horváth (from SzDSz) played a crucial role

---

[29] Roma are officially estimated to be 2–3 percent of the total Hungarian population, but unofficially their population proportion varies somewhere between 5 and 10 percent.

[30] The index has a four-point scale that is coded as follows: 0: no discrimination; 1: neglect/remedial policies, substantial under-representation in political office and/ or participation due to historical neglect or restrictions (explicit public policies are designed to protect or improve the group's political status); 2: neglect/no remedial policies; 3: social exclusion/neutral policy; 4: exclusion/repressive policy (a country that heavily discriminates against Roma, such as the Czech Republic, has repeatedly scored 3 on the index since 1990) (MAR 2008).

[31] Source: Polgár Foundation for Equal Opportunities 2008.

[32] One of its members, Viktória Mohácsi, was a leading activist in documenting discrimination, violence and hate crimes against Roma. In 2012, she asked for a political asylum in Canada due to fears for her personal safety.

in abolishing the distinction between ethnic and national minorities in the Minorities Act of 1992, which elevated the status of Roma from an ethnic minority to a national minority and significantly expanded their rights (Vermeersch 2006).

The Hungarian case illustrates mobilization against a small-scale threat and against a small bilateral opposite, which, in tandem with a mainstream socialist party, contributed to the expansion of Roma rights. In 1995, Hungary introduced the National Roma (Gypsy) Minority Self-Government, which gave Roma self-government and resources tied to a separate budget for their needs as well as access to political power at the local level.[33] The law on minority self-government proved very controversial, among both different Roma factions and the Hungarian majority.

Subsequently, the law has undergone a series of revisions (NDI/OSCE 2006).[34] The coalition government of the mainstream left socialist party (MSzP) and SzDSz (1994–1998) was responsible for a major shift in Hungarian policy toward Roma and recognized their broader special needs. It moved away from policies focused solely on Roma culture and language toward policies that provided Roma with subsidies and direct governmental transfers and increased their political power at the local level.

The socialist government of Péter Medgyessy followed in the footsteps and took a more deliberative approach by creating an expert council to solve Roma issues. The first sign of a severe backlash came in 2007 when Jobbik founded the Hungarian Guard to strengthen public order and to combat Roma as a public safety issue. Ferenc Gyurcsány, the prime minister from 2004 to 2009 who led a socialist-liberal coalition, further contributed to the polarization on

---

[33] In 442 communities, local Roma self-governments were formed after December 1994 elections, and complied with legal requirements (Human Rights Watch 1996: 124). The number of Roma minority self-governments that were created increased over time: 447 in 1994/1995, 771 in 1998, 999 in 2002, 1,118 in 2006 (NDI/OSCE 2006: 10). Other minorities such as Pols, Serbs and Slovenians formed self-governments as well. The budget of a minority self-government is approximately $3,000 per year at the local level and is not adjusted for size of the locality or minority (NDI/OSCE 2006: 6).

[34] The 2005 revision of the law stated that at least thirty voters must be registered in a given town in order for a new minority self-government to be created. Formation of regional self-governments was also allowed under the new amendments.

Roma issues. In a press conference in February 2009 he denounced state employees who would publicly speak about "cigánybűnözés" ("gypsy-crime"). Jobbik counteracted and called to combat "gypsy-crime" in their 2009 election campaign and ultimately became the third largest party in the 2010 election (Petsinis 2015; Varga 2014).[35]

Leaders of the socialist-liberal coalition became an immediate verbal target of Jobbik. For example, Mátyás Eörsi, a (former) high-profile member of the SzDSz and a prominent Hungarian politician, was singled out for his criticism of racism against Roma. Jobbik also questioned his loyalty to the Hungarian state due to his Jewish origin. Jobbik also capitalized on a backlash against a criticism of the police chief of the city of Miskolc who called out Roma-related crime and a lack of integration.

Miskolc, the fourth largest city in Hungary, has a large Roma minority of about 16,000, roughly 9–10 percent of its total population. In 1995, Roma took advantage of the Law on Minorities and formed minority self-government. Subsequently, they brought a lawsuit against the city's local council arguing that they cannot fulfill their duties because the city's local council was failing to provide them with adequate funds, earmarked by the central government. Roma claimed that withholding the funds was undermining their self-government functions mandated under the (new) law (Human Rights Watch 1996: 124). This contributed to the escalation of ethnic tensions in a city faced with economic decline and high rates of Roma poverty.

In 2009, the police chief of Miskolc, Albert Pásztor, criticized the high incidence of Roma crime in the city and declared that "coexistence with Roma compatriots does not work." Prime Minister Gyurcsány, of the mainstream left, immediately issued a harsh rejection of Pásztor's statement despite the overwhelming support Pásztor had across all political parties at the local level, including the socialists and liberals. Until 2010, the heavy-industry Miskolc voted for the socialists. Since the Pásztor controversy, the city has shifted its political

---

[35] There are other factors that led to the demise of the mainstream left socialist party, such as PM Gyurcsány's speech that was secretly recorded and then leaked. In the speech, he admitted that the socialist-liberal governmental coalition was "lying" to its citizens. The speech sparked massive protests in Hungary and eventually led to the resignation of Gyurcsány and the downfall of the socialist party.

support away from the left-leaning candidates and toward right-wing nationalistic Fidesz and radical right Jobbik.

An unprecedentedly large march against Roma crime called by Jobbik on October 17, 2012, attracted about 3,000 Jobbik supporters to Miskolc. Jobbik also swiftly reacted to allegations of fraud in the National Roma Self Government, after the right-wing Fidesz government started investigations into a serious of corruption scandals in August 2015. In reaction to the investigations, Jobbik's President Gábor Vona suggested taking back (Roma) properties, subjecting (Roma) leaders to a wealth gain audit and suspending (Roma) subsidies. In his own words: "What we are pouring taxpayers' money into is not even a barrel with a hole any more, but an abyss" (Jobbik Media Service 2015).

The political advocates of Roma rights demand the protection of Roma from violence, and promote their educational and economic opportunities. Any conceivable governmental policy that uplifts the Roma minority would in no way challenge the political, economic and cultural dominance of ethnic Hungarians in Hungary or the dominant nationalities in countries with high levels of anti-Roma mobilization, such as Bulgaria, Czech Republic, Slovakia and Romania. In countries with small ethnic minorities, since the status elevation of minorities does not threaten the majority status, polarized competition between the radical right party and its bilateral opposite ensues on the issue of minority accommodation. If the bilateral opposite is strong, and coalitional accommodation increases the salience of minority accommodation, then the radical right party becomes (and can remain) strong and viable, as it has in Slovakia and Romania.

There are of course alternative explanations that need to be addressed before accepting the theory advanced here. One might argue that radical right parties capitalize on security threats from abroad and far-right mobilization in a neighboring country, especially when co-ethnics are involved, but radical right parties ultimately benefit from domestic threats. This is best demonstrated in the Hungarian case.[36] Two of its radical right parties – MIÉP, which after the 2006 election never ever obtained a parliamentary seat and became marginalized, and Jobbik, which skyrocketed to prominence after

---

[36] On conflicting desires to appeal to Hungarians abroad by the Hungarian state, see Saideman 2001.

2010 elections – utilized grievances associated with the Treaty of Trianon that led to substantive territorial losses for Hungary after World War I. Yet the radical right in Slovakia and Romania, two countries that benefited from the territorial contraction of Hungary, is less concerned with the threat of Greater Hungary than with the lobbying efforts of Hungary in the European Council on behalf of Hungarian minorities in neighboring countries, and with the Hungarian government's policy of issuing dual passports for Hungarians living abroad.[37] The electoral prospects of radical right parties in Slovakia and Romania have also not been influenced by the rise of Hungarian Jobbik and the establishment of the Hungarian Guard (or its various subsequent offshoots after it was banned in 2008/2009). Jobbik was once openly affiliated with paramilitary groups that "hunt Gypsy [Roma] criminals" (McPhedran 2012; Stolz 2011), but, over time, the leadership has been more concerned with improving its image and has distanced itself from violence committed by the Hungarian Guard.[38]

Both Romanian and Slovak radical right parties peaked when the radical right in Hungary was very mild and before the far right in Hungary started forming violent paramilitary groups. On the other hand, the fact that Hungarians were once rulers and are now a small minority in neighboring countries benefits the radical right parties, since it is easier to rally voters who are irritated with a group that lost its historical standing and is now asking for accommodation from a subordinate social position.

Focusing on the political effect of bilateral opposite parties helps to address an important policy issue: How should mainstream parties address the challenge of radical right parties? Scholars fundamentally disagree about whether the most effective strategy to keep radical parties at bay is to radicalize or to moderate. Some have suggested that support for a radical right party decreases when the proximate mainstream party radicalizes on identity issues, steals the extremist issue and "squeezes out" the radical right. Others submit that when a

---

[37] Interviews with SMK (Hungarian ethnic party) representatives, Bratislava, 2008 and 2013.

[38] The conflicts between the paramilitary groups and Roma led to the death of Roma in at least a dozen cases. On analysis of Jobbik supporters based on Jobbik's Facebook fans and support for radical right ideology, see Barlett et al. 2012 and Krekó et al. 2015.

proximate mainstream party radicalizes, it facilitates the rise of radical parties, since the mainstream party legitimizes the extremist agenda and facilitates outbidding on the extreme pole of the political spectrum (Adams and Somer-Topcu 2009; Art 2011; Bale 2003; Capoccia 2001; Downs 2001; Ignazi 1992; Jenne 2007; Kelley 2004a; Mudde 2007). Although it is perhaps tempting to look for explanations of radical right party success in their immediate ideological neighborhood, these results indicate that such an approach may be misleading, for it risks attributing to the mainstream parties what should actually be imputed to the bilateral opposite parties. There is evidence to support the claim that *both* strategies can effectively shut radical right parties out of politics but may also make them martyrs of nationalist causes.

The theory and the analysis suggest that we should turn our attention to the study of non-proximate parties (Meguid 2005; Sartori 1976). Ethno-liberal parties are natural and credible representatives for highly accommodative policies toward ethnic and social minorities. When moderate parties bring them on board, the political pendulum swings in their direction, but the unintended consequence is an obvious political backlash against accommodation. Radical right parties are credible agents to carry forward this reactionary agenda and benefit electorally from the success of their ideological twins. The dynamic of political backlash against the accommodation of ethno-liberal parties is a real political force, and provides significant explanation for the rise and fall of the radical right across highly varied contexts.

## 3.6 Conclusion

This chapter derives three observable implications of the theory and tests them using an original dataset that covers every national election over the past twenty years in all post-communist democracies. The results offer strong support for the first two hypotheses and qualified support for the third one. The analysis shows that the electoral prospects of radical right parties improve with the electoral strength of their bilateral opposites, namely, the ethno-liberal parties. They also gain substantial strength when the ethno-liberal party serves in the government and when the ethno-liberal party is ideologically extreme. Although the literature has largely focused on the role of mainstream and proximate parties, this chapter shows that the radical right's ideological bilateral opposite – ethno-liberal parties – plays a crucial role. To a large extent, then, the rise and fall of radical right parties is a reactive political phenomenon, an electoral response to the political fortunes of their ideological twins. Parties advocating minority accommodation polarize party systems and empower radical right party appeals.

The argument advanced here represents a return to an earlier literature on the origins of radical right parties in Western Europe. Some of the first studies recognized that the sudden rise in radical right-wing politics in the 1980s was initially a form of a backlash against the new political forces representing voters with post-material, socially liberal values and green parties (Ignazi 1992; Kitschelt and McGann 1995; von Beyme 1988). Can this argument travel beyond Eastern Europe? While further analysis is needed to be more certain, the answer may lie in reassessing the well-established theory of consociationalism (Lijphart 1984). The political impact of power-sharing institutions might be mitigated by the size of the quarrelling groups. Netherlands initially avoided a large-scale conflict between its large segments of the society (Lijphart's "pillars") due to the accommodation, yet built-in mechanisms to placate minorities might have fueled radical right parties in countries such as Austria, Bosnia, Lebanon and Switzerland, where discontent has been generated by accommodation afforded to small minorities. In Eastern Europe, parties quarrel over language policies. Elsewhere, politicians argue over head-coverings and housing subsidies for ethnic minorities. The vehicles of accommodation differ across contexts, yet the argument that accommodation of minorities polarizes the electorate, increases the salience of non-economic issues and can create a political backlash may, alas, be universal.

# 4 | Mobilization against Hungarians in Slovakia

It was already in 1248 when one French bishop, after his visit of the Carpathian Valley, was surprised how could God give such beautiful country to such ugly people. He meant old Hungarians, because those were mongoloid types with crooked legs and even uglier horses.... Hungarians are a tumor on the body of the Slovak nation that needs to be immediately removed.[1]

—Ján Slota, former leader of the Slovak National Party

On February 14, 2013, the leader of the ethnic Hungarian party in Slovakia, József Berényi, installed a sign near a train station Okoč, in southern Slovakia, that displayed the Hungarian version of the village "Ekecs." He pledged that the party of ethnic Hungarians would install more signs, visible to travelers, on private properties, and, if possible, cement them in, so that they cannot be removed. The distinction between Slovak Okoč and Hungarian Ekecs might seem trivial to the outsiders, if it was not for the uncomfortable fact that the capital of the country, Bratislava, was historically a German–Hungarian city and belonged to the Hungarian kingdom. Before the creation of Czechoslovakia in 1918, the Slovaks were a minority in their current capital. To add insult to injury, all contemporary highway signs leading from Hungary to Slovakia refer to Bratislava using its Hungarian name: Poszony. The "village-level" provocation in Okoč was not unanswered. The leader of the Slovak National Party, Andrej Danko, called it "cheap theatre" and unfair given the fact that the Hungarian minority in Slovakia is "disproportionally accommodated."[2]

---

[1] In 2006, Ján Slota attacked Hungarians before the elections. Source: Sme. 2006.
[2] Source: SNS, February 15, 2013. A.Danko pre TASR.

The Slovak National Party (SNS), "the oldest party of all Slovaks," is one of the most successful radical right parties in Europe.[3] At its peak in 1990 and again in 2006, it amassed roughly 12 percent of the popular vote. At its lowest point, its support hovered around 5 percent in the elections of 1994 and 2012 (Gyárfášová and Mesežnikov 2015). Unlike many other radical right parties that have disappeared from the electoral arena within two to three electoral cycles, such as the League of Polish Families, Czech Republicans and the Hungarian Life and Justice Party, the SNS has maintained a presence since 1990 when it first emerged on the Slovak political scene.

The SNS party has significantly shaped the course of Slovak politics for more than twenty-five years and the relationship between the Slovak majority and Hungarian minority (Carpenter 1997; Deegan-Krause and Haughton 2009; Hanley and Sikk 2014; Haughton and Rybář 2008; Mesežnikov et al. 2008; Ucen 2007). SNS party representatives have served in five governing coalitions since the independence of Slovakia in 1992–1993. The Hungarian minority is concentrated mostly in the south, near the border with Hungary, as well as in the eastern parts of Slovakia. Whether the SNS was governing or not, the party has fought tirelessly against laws that expanded the language rights of the Hungarian minority. To some extent, however, the party dug its own grave – SNS's success in rolling back advances in minority rights undermined its raison d'être as a political party.

Disagreement with governmental support to a politically backed minority differentiates radical right voters from voters of other parties, and is the single strongest predictor of the radical right vote in Slovakia. While, on the surface, voting for the SNS might appear to reflect xenophobic preferences, this chapter shows that xenophobic attitudes and prejudice are pervasive among the voters of other parties. The distinctiveness of radical right voters lies in their opposition to the status elevation of politically backed minority groups. Slovakia has an electorally successful radical right party and a small ethnic minority and illustrates the logic of accommodation.

The radical right parties and the ethnic parties in Slovakia are both relatively large compared with some "niche parties" in other countries,

---

[3] Source: SNS self-description. www.sns.sk/o-nas-2/strucne-o-sns/. SNS tracks its origin to June 6, 1871. The electoral vote share percentages for SNS over time are 13.9, 7.93, 5.4, 9.2, 7.13, 11.73, 5.08, 4.55 and 8.64.

and so they are politically relevant for coalition formation. Second, the political space in Slovakia has been characterized by a high degree of variation in the extent to which it is polarized on issues of national identity, and this variability allows us to track a truly dynamic process of contestation. Finally, over the past three decades, the political scene in Slovakia has been quite stable in terms of the actors that anchor both political poles. This provides consistency over time in the analysis, since the actors are identifiable with transparent profiles and reputations that have been established over a relatively long time period.

The chapter has seven sections. After a brief discussion of the hypotheses and data, the following section discusses the evolution of minority accommodation in Slovakia and the context of the survey. The third, analytical section focuses on policy hostility and group hostility (xenophobia) toward minorities by party affiliation as well as on the role of economic and sovereignty threats. The section analyzes the relationship between attitudes toward governmental spending on minorities and support for the radical right parties. The fourth section examines radical right party voter profiles. The fifth section discusses the results of the identity-priming survey experiment. The sixth section briefly discusses new issues in Slovak politics. A final section concludes with a summary of the evidence and discusses implications for the theory.

The analysis indicates that support for radical right parties is driven neither by group hostility nor by economic deprivation. Economic considerations become salient for radical right voters when coupled with ethnicity and shifts in the status quo. Therefore, if radical right parties want to succeed electorally, they must attract voters who oppose the accommodation of politically organized minorities.

## 4.1 Hypotheses

I use an original household survey with an embedded experiment that I designed to examine the following hypotheses at the individual level. *Hypothesis 1*: Radical right voters are driven by policy threats. *Hypothesis 2*: Radical right voters are *not* distinct in their group hostility toward other minorities from voters of nearby mainstream parties, their ideological "cousins" (refutation of the prejudice proposition). *Hypothesis 3* tests economic grievances: radical right voters are not distinct in their positions on pocketbook or socio-tropic economic issues. To account for the role of sovereignty threats in nationalistic

Table 4.1 *Expected change in a position on transfers that benefit groups after a nationality prime in Slovakia*

| Parties/blocs | Slovaks (majority) | Hungarians (minority in a coalition) | Roma (minority) |
|---|---|---|---|
| Slovaks – Radical Right | 0 | 0 | 0 |
| Slovaks – right on identity | 0 | 0 | 0 |
| Slovaks – left on identity (coalition) | 0 | + | 0 |
| Hungarians – ethnic | – | + | 0 |

mobilization, *Hypothesis 4* expects that radical right voters worry about national sovereignty and are therefore distinct in their perception of collective (security) threats.

I also investigate conditions under which threat perceptions of voters of different parties increases. Table 4.1 summarizes theoretical expectations about the effect of priming on voter positions regarding governmental support for groups. Increased support for transfers is denoted as a plus; negative support is marked with a minus; and no change is indicated with a zero. Priming on national identity does not invoke threat to the dominant group. Because radical right mobilization is driven by changes in the status quo and not by nationalistic rhetoric that evolves around group hostility, radical right voters are not expected to shift their views. In addition, radical right voters are not expected to respond to nationalistic rhetorical triggers due to the ceiling effect.

Identity priming, an elevated sense of national identity among the dominant group, does not trigger fears that the state will be used to diminish the status of the dominant group. Therefore, I do not expect nationalistic priming to result in a change in an individual's position on transfers both for the radical right voters and for the voters of the mainstream right ("cousins").

Priming on national identity, however, simulates a threat among ethnic voters, since it reminds them of their minority status and of their subjugation to the dominant group. Similarly, the coalition partners of minorities are reminded of the vulnerability of their junior (ethnic) partner, as well. Minority voters and their allies are therefore expected to react to identity primes since it prompts fears related to the dependency of the minority on the capricious dominant group. Therefore, when faced with a priming threat, voters of ethnic parties as well as their coalition partners rally by increasing their support for transfers toward minorities whose political cooperation is needed. Voters of the coalition partners are expected to increase sympathy for transfers to the minority that is represented in a coalition, but not for a minority without any political weight (e.g., Roma). Therefore, ethnic voters and voters of parties that seek coalitions with ethnic minorities will change their position on transfers when experimentally primed on their respective national identity.

Data from an original survey of the adult population in Slovakia that I designed are used to test these hypotheses. The survey was conducted as a part of a representative omnibus survey in November 2009 by Focus, a survey organization based in Bratislava, Slovakia.[4] The survey queried 1,000 adult respondents using a sample with quotas for six variables (sex, age, education, nationality, size of community and region of residence) and was conducted two months after a controversial "push-back" language law was implemented in 2009. The questionnaire was administered as a face-to-face standardized interview. In order to understand the context of the survey, the next section discusses the politicization of minority rights in Slovakia.

## 4.2 Accommodation of the Hungarian Minority

Before proceeding to the analysis, it is important to discuss the political context in which the survey was fielded and the sequencing of minority accommodation in Slovakia and an ensuing political backlash. The Slovak National Party was reestablished immediately after the end of communism in the former Czechoslovakia. It made its first headlines in 1990 when its leader, Ján Slota, claimed that the legacy of the World War II–era pro-Nazi Slovak President, Jozef Tiso, should be reevaluated on the floor of the newly democratic

[4] Source: FOCUS, Centrum pre sociálnu a marketingovú analýzu, Bratislava, Slovakia. The questionnaire is reproduced in the Appendix. Funding for the survey was provided by the Department of Political Science, Duke University. The research design and some question wordings benefited greatly from the examples in Sniderman et al. (2004).

Czechoslovak Federal Parliament.[5] This was still before the split-up of Czechoslovakia. Since then, Slota's party has made revisionist claims about Slovak history, downplaying the legacy of the fascism and elevating the fact that the short-lived Tiso regime (1939–1945) was the first independent Slovak state.

The Slovak National Party emerged during the disintegration of Czechoslovakia as a vocal proponent of Slovak independence and Slovak nationalism. The Slovak leader, Vladimír Mečiar, negotiated the separation of the Czechoslovak federation over the summer of 1992 with the Czech leader, Václav Klaus, and Slovakia peacefully declared independence on January 1, 1993. After Slovakia became its own state (January 1, 1993), the focus of SNS attacks was redirected from issues of independence to minorities in Slovakia. In Slota's own words: "Hungarians are a tumor on the body of the Slovak nation that needs to be immediately removed."[6] The primary mobilizing factor behind the support for the Slovak National Party has been the successful political organization of the Hungarian minority and the accommodation of their demands in Slovakia.

SNS was immediately invited to join the first two post-independence governments, which is not surprising, since it was one of the parties that fought to break away from the Czechoslovak federation and thus embodied Slovak nationalism. In the 1992 election, immediately prior to independence, the SNS gained almost 8 percent of the popular vote and received five governing portfolios. Yet, as far as volatility is concerned, the more interesting questions are: What has sustained the SNS's electoral strength for almost three decades, and what accounts for variation in its electoral success over time?

After Slovakia's independence, SNS's electoral strength declined and the party barely crossed the 5 percent threshold in the 1994 election, since independence had been achieved and the initial "purpose" of the SNS disappeared. Fortunately for the SNS party, the Hungarian minority in Slovakia became more politically active and began making demands for minority accommodation in the middle of the 1990s. In

---

[5] President Tiso presided over an independent Slovakia that was separated from pre-war Czechoslovakia and was briefly an interwar ally of Nazi Germany.

[6] In Slovak: "Maďari sú nádor na tele slovenského národa, ktorý treba neodkladne odstrániť." Source: Hospodárske noviny 2012 and speech by József Berényi from the Hungarian party SMK–MKP, in the Slovak Parliament, April 8, 2008. Available at: http://dotankoch.sk/zaznamy/154118/madari.

particular, Hungarian activists demanded the expansion of minority language rights. Although Hungarian was recognized as a minority language under communism, the Slovak language was the only language allowed in official documents, and road and village signs were written exclusively in Slovak (Votruba 1998). In 1994, however, parliament passed a new law (Zákon Národnej rady Slovenskej republiky #54/1994), which listed 587 villages that could officially use both Slovak and non-Slovak names. The law stated that the name of the village could be displayed in the minority language if the population size of the minority group was above 20 percent.

In 1994, Hungarian activists scored a second major victory in their fight to allow for personal names to use Hungarian spelling.[7] The communist practice was to spell Hungarian last names with Slovak orthography. A new law (Zákon Národnej rady Slovenskej republiky #154/1994) enabled the official registration of names in Hungarian (and other minority languages) using that language's orthography. This meant that Hungarian women could register their last names without -ová or -á, which linguistically denote a female's last name in the Slovak language. This accommodative language policy was implemented during the interim Moravčík government in 1994, which relied on the support of Hungarian deputies. At the same time, there were new minority-friendly laws on birth registers, marriage certificates and the use of bilingual signs, consistent with the Council of Europe requirements (Daftary and Gal 2000).

Since 1990, the Hungarian minority has been represented in the Slovak Parliament and can be thought of as the bilateral opposite to the SNS. In the elections of 1990, 1992 and 1994, coalitions of Hungarian movements and parties received between 7 and 10 percent of the popular vote, but remained fragmented until 1998. The major event that led to the unification of all Hungarian parties and movements was an anti-coalition law, aimed at weakening movements and parties representing Hungarians. In order to cross the 5 percent threshold, the three Hungarian parties united and formed the Hungarian Coalition Party (SMK). When it ran for the first time in the 1998 elections, it received 9 percent of the popular vote, predominantly from

---

[7] Until 1994, the Linguistic Institute mandated the use of Slovakized suffixes for female last names (Votruba 1998; Zákon 1995).

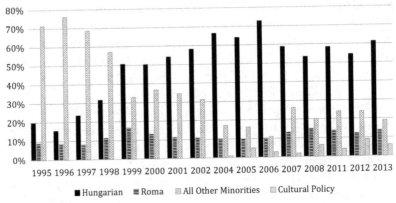

**Figure 4.1** Spending on minority cultures in Slovakia, 1995–2013 (as a proportion of budget, in %).

*Sources:* Data compiled by the author from a variety of sources. For 1995–2002: Spending on Minority Cultures, 1995–2002 (Ministry of Culture Budget for supporting minority cultures, in %), Report on the Implementation of the European Charter for Regional or Minority Languages in the Slovak Republic, Council of Europe, European Charter for Regional or Minority Languages, Strasbourg, 2003. Modified from: The provisions of funding for minority cultures in the 1995–2002 period from the special allocation under the Ministry of Culture budget chapter, p. 47, modified by the author. For 2004–2008: Spending on Minority Cultures, 2004–2008 (Ministry of Culture Budget for supporting minority cultures, in %), Third Report Submitted by the Slovak Republic Pursuant to Article 25, Paragraph 2 of the Framework Convention for the Protection of National Minorities, Council of Europe, Strasbourg, 2009, p. 20, modified by the author. For 2011–2013: Spending on Minority Cultures, 2011–2013 (chapter in the Budget of the Government of the Slovak Republic, in %), Fourth Report Submitted by the Slovak Republic Pursuant to Article 25, Paragraph 2 of the Framework Convention for the Protection of National Minorities, Council of Europe, Strasbourg, 2014, pp. 42–44, modified by the author

the Hungarian minority. This new political threat benefited the SNS, which saw electoral gains of approximately 3.5 percent.

Political power translates into economic gains. Figure 4.1 shows that the Hungarian minority is the largest recipient of governmental support for minority cultures since the late 1990s. Until late 1990s, the Hungarian minority was receiving much less in proportion to other minorities. Since the late 1990s, after the Hungarian minority stepped up its political game, they have been receiving at least 60 percent of the funds. Yet, as Table 4.2 show, the relative size of the Hungarian minority has been shrinking slightly in the last three decades. The spending figures reflect neither the demographic size of minorities nor changes in size over time.

Table 4.2 *Nationalities in Slovakia*

| Nationality | 1980(%) | 1991(%) | 2001(%) | 2011(%) |
|---|---|---|---|---|
| Slovak | 86.5 | 85.7 | 85.8 | 80.7 |
| Hungarian | 11.2 | 10.8 | 9.7 | 8.5 |
| Roma | | 1.4 | 1.7 | 2.0 |
| Other minorities | | 2.1 | 3.8 | 8.8 |

*Source:* Census of the Slovak Republic

EU-oriented parties won the elections in 1998, and the Hungarian Coalition Party (SMK) was invited to join the first and second Dzurinda's government in 1998–2002 and 2002–2006 (Vachudova 2005). Language policies aimed at accommodating the Hungarian minority immediately followed. The new law on minority languages, adopted in 1999, significantly expanded the rights of Hungarians (Zákon Národnej rady Slovenskej republiky #184/1999). The Hungarian deputies did not vote for the law, since it did not satisfy all of their (quite excessive) demands. The law did not expand the use of Hungarian in education, culture and media, but it allowed it in other official settings.[8] One of the major achievements of the law was a provision that granted equal status to minority languages in towns and villages where the minority population was greater than 20 percent. It allowed for issuing official bilingual documents, such as birth, death and wedding certificates. Minorities were granted the right to use their native tongue in all official transactions and documents with state government and local governments. Furthermore, the Slovak Hungarian Coalition Party was granted the portfolio for regional development in 2002, and used it ruthlessly to channel resources to Hungarian districts, adding insult to injury.[9] The Slovak state was showing a favorable face to the Hungarian minority.

Whereas some observers noted that the minority language law opened the door for Slovakia's admission to the European Union, the SNS argued that the law instead opened the door to the

---

[8] The Hungarian Coalition Party (SMK) was not pleased that the law did not go further and requested that the law protect the use of minority languages in education and media, but eventually compromised with Dzurinda (Kopanic 1999).

[9] Interviews, Transparency International, Bratislava, Slovakia, summer 2009.

"Madyarization" of southern Slovakia (Rafaj 2011).[10] The 1999 language law mobilized right-wing opposition to minority accommodation. SNS and mainstream populist party HZDS boycotted the vote. Moreover, before the law was passed, HZDS, SNS and Matica Slovenská (a cultural organization) collected 447,000 signatures that called for a referendum on the language bill. The proposed question was: "Do you agree that the Slovak language should be used exclusively in official contacts as it was before June 1, 1999?" Despite the fact that 350,000 signatures were needed to initiate a referendum, President Schuster blocked the referendum due to the prohibition of plebiscites on human rights issues (Daftary and Gal 2000: 32). It took ten years for SNS to overthrow the 1999 law.

If the logic of backslash is correct, the SNS should have gained substantially in the 2002 election, after the law was passed, in order to reverse the gains of the Hungarian minority. Yet the SNS was plagued with factionalism and internal rebellions against the controversial party's chairman, Ján Slota, and looked for a more "presentable" face of the party. This led to a split in the party and to the creation of a new radical right party, the PSNS (Gyárfášová and Mesežnikov 2015). The SNS and the new PSNS both contested the 2002 elections, but neither was able to independently surpass the electoral threshold to get a seat in parliament. After this electoral failure, however, they united again and contested the 2006 election to reverse the rising political power of the Hungarian ethnic minority.

In the 2006 election, the reunited SNS secured almost 12 percent of the vote along with a partnership in the governing coalition, which granted the SNS the portfolio of the Ministry of Regional Development and the ability to swiftly shift resources away from Hungarian districts and toward predominantly Slovak districts.[11] The SNS was invited to join the populist and nationalist Fico government (2006–2010), and in 2009 helped to pass a new language law, which severely restricted the use of minority languages (Smetanková 2012). The law declared that the Slovak language is an articulation of sovereignty (Smetanková 2012), and that Slovak must be used in all official settings, including

---

[10] Also: interview with Rafaj, Headquarters SNS, Bratislava, Slovakia, summer 2008.
[11] Source: Transparency International Slovakia, author's interviews in Slovakia, 2007 and 2008. The 2006 electoral gain of the SNS, following the period of minority accommodation, was the largest since the 1992 elections.

at the local government level.[12] The most controversial clause of the law was a fine of up to 5,000 euros for those who infringe on the provisions of the law.

Given the SNS's success in curbing the tide of minority accommodation, the backlash logic predicts that the electoral gains of the SNS should then decline in the next electoral cycle. Consistent with the theory, the SNS barely crossed the 5 percent threshold in 2010 election, and was not invited to form a coalition. Subsequently, in the early March 2012 elections, the SNS even failed to pass the threshold, which was partly due to the success of policies aimed at restricting the Hungarian minority's rights that the SNS implemented when in power. The SNS's weakness can also be attributed to the split in the SMK and the subsequent fragmentation of the ethnic Hungarian parties, which weakened the justification for the SNS as a wall against the demand of minorities.[13] According to the theory, the SNS should rise again once the Hungarian minority politically reunites and manages to reverse the controversial 2009 minority language law, a change that is certainly at the top of their agenda. Alternatively, if new issues that evolve around new group boundaries become politically contested, the radical right parties can shift their agendas and campaign against new forms of accommodation of, for example, gay couples or non-Christian refugees.[14]

## 4.3 Empirical Analysis and Data

I will now turn to the individual-level analysis to determine the nature of the radical right voter. The theory posits two forms of hostility against minorities: policy hostility and group hostility. Whereas prejudice and social distance against minority groups is at the core of group hostility, mobilization against laws and policies that benefit minorities and opposition to governmental support for minority

---

[12] It also urged the use of the Slovak language in other public situations such as during doctor visits.

[13] In 2009, the former leader of the Hungarian Coalition Party formed a new Hungarian party (Most-Híd).

[14] The referendum on same-sex marriage and adoption of children by same-sex couples in Slovakia in 2015, despite being eventually invalid, heightened the salience of traditional families and very effectively expanded the mobilizational potential of Slovak far-right groups beyond ethnicity. The recent refugee crisis was used in far-right mobilization as well.

groups constitute policy hostility. The theory expects radical right voters to exhibit a higher degree of policy hostility toward minorities when compared with voters of other parties, but not necessarily a higher degree of group hostility. To assess this distinction empirically, the survey included a measure of both group and policy hostility toward both Hungarian and Roma minorities (Hypotheses 1 and 2).

Whereas both Roma and Hungarians are targets of hostility, the Roma are far less politically organized. The Hungarian minority has been represented in parliament since 1993 and has participated in governing coalitions since Slovak independence. Although the European Union and neighboring Hungary actively monitor the situation of Hungarians in Slovakia, the principal advocates of Hungarian interests in Slovakia are ethnic Hungarian parties, which have also mobilized the EU pressure to achieve their political goals.[15] The main advocates of Roma rights are domestic NGOs and international organizations, which have urged several Slovak governments to redress the social and political exclusion of Roma since the early 1990s (Kelley 2004a; Vachudova 2005).[16] Rather than political parties, advocates for Roma rights are mostly non-political or foreign, whereas lobbyists for the Hungarian minority have a strong domestic political footing.

If voting for the radical right party was driven by general prejudice (cf. Rydgren 2008), we should expect radical right voters to display a high degree of group hostility toward both minority groups. More importantly, the degree of group hostility should differentiate radical right voters from other voters, especially their political "cousins." If voting for the radical right party is instead driven by policy hostility against a minority that has been politically accommodated, then we should expect radical right voters to display significantly more policy hostility toward the minority that has been able to extract political concessions from the majority.

[15] Interviews with Hungarian party (SMK) representatives in Bratislava, Slovakia, summer 2007–2008.
[16] The Roma's poverty, criminality and unemployment have been recognized as a relevant public policy issue worthy of governmental attention. Slovak governments have addressed the issue of Roma poverty and discrimination since the 1990s. In 2003, Slovakia established a special office to address the issue of Roma communities (Splnomocnenec vlády pre Rómske komunity; available at: www.romovia.vlada.gov.sk/1794/statut-splnomocnenca-vlady-slovenskej-republiky-pre-romske-komunity.php).

### 4.3.1 Policy Hostility

Policy hostility, operationalized as an opposition to governmental spending on groups, couples group boundaries and group hierarchies with economic considerations. Policy hostility is driven by irritation with the fact that state resources, guarded by the dominant group, are used to elevate a politically accommodated minority. In the words of SNS leader Andrej Danko on February 14, 2013: "the Hungarian minority has extra, above the standard, rights in Slovakia." Danko also highlighted the fact that (ethnic) politicians talk about fulfilling the rights of national minorities, but that they exclusively care about the Hungarian minority: "we do not get to hear [from the politicians of Hungarian parties] anything about the necessity to improve the conditions for the development of Ruthenian, Ukrainian, German, Polish, Croatian or Czech minorities."[17]

The purpose of the survey was to parse out attitudes toward inward-oriented and outward-oriented spending and whether the opposition to government spending on groups differs by nationalities and parties. The questions about governmental transfers toward different nationalities were framed so that the respondents were made aware of a trade-off between governmental transfers to different groups by explicitly positing a fixed pie of resources. The questions were prefaced by the following statement:

"In a current economic situation, it may be difficult for the government to cover all its expenses. When the resources are limited, and the government cannot raise taxes, some groups get more and some groups get less. In your view, as a citizen of the Slovak Republic, how should this situation affect Slovaks, Hungarians and Roma?" Then the respondents were asked: "Do you think that the government should spend a lot more, more, less or a lot less on [Slovaks/Hungarians/Roma]?"

These questions allow us to disentangle whether opposition to spending on minorities is universal across groups or whether it has its own unique characteristics, depending on the nature of the minority group. Since the questions separate the majority from minorities, it is also possible to parse out whether those who support more redistribution toward the Slovak majority also support less redistribution

---

[17] "Maďarská menšina má však na Slovensku nadštandardné práva," vyhlásil Danko. Source: SNS 2013. Translated by the author.

Table 4.3 *Policy hostility by nationality in Slovakia (Spearman rank correlations)*

| Policy hostility toward: | Hungarians | Slovaks | Roma |
|---|---|---|---|
| Hungarians | | | |
| Slovaks | −0.323 | | |
| Roma | 0.332 | −0.171 | |

*Note:* N = 861.

toward the minorities (Hungarians or Roma), which is the implicit assumption of welfare chauvinism.

The evidence from the survey suggests that the opposition toward minority transfers is independent from the approval of more redistribution toward the majority. Table 4.3 shows that the Spearman rank correlation between opposition to spending on Slovaks and on Hungarians is only −0.32. Therefore, less support for transfers to Hungarians does not translate into more support for transfers to the Slovak majority. There is also no relationship between attitudes toward transfers to minorities: less support for transfers to Hungarians does not translate into less support for Roma. These simple relationships suggest that attitudes toward spending on groups have to be examined separately and are driven by different mechanisms. The theory posits that radical right mobilization is rooted in the shifts in the status quo between the dominant group and the aspirational, ascending group. The trigger that activates radical right mobilization should be a change in spending on an accommodated minority, not *any* minority, and also not a decline in spending on the majority.

To investigate further that the origins of hostility differ by minorities, I investigate the determinants of policy hostility toward the majority (Slovaks) and minorities (Hungarians and Roma), and find that the determinants of support for governmental spending on Slovaks, Hungarians and Roma (and the effects of these attitudes on vote choice) are significantly different. Table 4.4 summarizes findings from Table 4.5 that show that the accommodated, aspirational minority is subject to a different mechanism that triggers policy hostility.

Economic anxiety is at the core of both prejudice and support for in-group, inward-oriented transfers for Slovaks and opposition to outward transfers to Roma. Support for transfers toward Slovaks and opposition to transfers toward Roma both originate in economic threats (Table 4.5).

Table 4.4 *The empirical determinants of policy hostility and group hostility in Slovakia*

| Grid (Authoritarian values) and Group (Nationality) → | Policy hostility | Opposition to transfers to the accommodated group |
|---|---|---|
| Economic anxiety → | Policy hostility | Support for inward-oriented transfers (toward the dominant group) |
| | Group hostility | Opposition to transfers toward the non-accommodated group Prejudice toward all minorities |

*Note:* Table 4.4 is based on empirical results from Table 4.5.

Yet economic anxiety, decoupled from ethnicity, is not at the core of policy hostility toward Hungarians. Later, the analysis of the identity experiment also shows that the aversion toward governmental support of Hungarians is not driven by economic considerations.

Table 4.5 illustrates that attitudes toward governmental spending on Hungarians are not driven by economic fears, whereas support for transfers to Slovaks and Roma is determined largely by economic factors. Economic pocketbook explanations – which suggest that the more the respondents are concerned with their personal and family finances, the more they oppose governmental transfers to Hungarians – are only weakly associated with attitudes toward governmental spending on Hungarians (Models 3 and 4 in Table 4.5). Authoritarian values predict opposition to government spending on Hungarians. National pride (pride in being a citizen of Slovakia) is a strong predictor of support for transfers to Slovaks, but is not a uniquely strong predictor of opposition to transfers to Hungarians.[18] In sum, attitudes toward transfers to the politically accommodated minority (Hungarians) are driven by authoritarian values and the respondent's nationality,[19]

---

[18] See the Appendix for the exact wording of the questions.
[19] Both are indicators of group (nationality) and grid (attitudes toward authority). Authoritarian values are indicators of the grid dimension.

Table 4.5 *Determinants of policy hostility toward Slovaks (majority), Hungarians and Roma (minorities)*

| | Policy hostility: majority (Slovaks) | | Policy hostility: minority (Hungarians) | | Policy hostility: minority (Roma) | |
|---|---|---|---|---|---|---|
| | M1 | M2 | M3 | M4 | M5 | M6 |
| Family financial situation (Two years ago) | -0.076 | | 0.176* | 0.140* | 0.022 | |
| | (0.072) | | (0.071) | (0.067) | (0.073) | |
| Personal financial situation (Two years from now) | -0.181** | -0.250*** | -0.054 | | -0.073 | |
| | (0.080) | (0.066) | (0.078) | | (0.081) | |
| National economy (Two years from now) | -0.050 | | 0.102 | | 0.251*** | 0.180** |
| | (0.072) | | (0.071) | | (0.072) | (0.057) |
| All families financial situation (Two years ago) | -0.005 | | -0.049 | | -0.075 | |
| | (0.087) | | (0.085) | | (0.089) | |
| Nationality (1 = Hungarian, 0 = else) | 0.899*** | 0.700*** | -2.055*** | -2.116*** | -0.342** | -0.345** |
| | (0.137) | (0.154) | (0.145) | (0.148) | (0.127) | (0.134) |
| Authoritarian values | | -0.109 | | -0.297** | | -0.125 |
| | | (0.104) | | (0.094) | | (0.098) |
| Self-esteem | | 0.222* | | -0.158 | | -0.068 |
| | | (0.103) | | (0.096) | | (0.102) |
| Household income | | -0.026 | | 0.011 | | 0.040 |
| | | (0.027) | | (0.022) | | (0.026) |
| National pride | | 0.201** | | | | |
| | | (0.065) | | | | |

| | | | | | | |
|---|---|---|---|---|---|---|
| Household size | | 0.095* | | | | −0.142** |
| | | (0.045) | | | | (0.043) |
| 1st cut point | −0.755 | 0.199 | −2.006 | −2.675 | −1.977 | −2.427 |
| 2nd cut point | 0.998 | 1.945 | −0.851 | −1.529 | −1.179 | −1.690 |
| 3rd cut point | 1.876 | 2.801 | 0.679 | 0.068 | −0.056 | −0.459 |
| Log likelihood | −675.5 | −589.05 | −746.5 | −727.6 | −730.1 | −653.6 |
| N | 774 | 672 | 752 | 742 | 799 | 730 |

*Note:* Cell entries are ordered probit coefficients with standard errors in parentheses.

Models 1–5 (M1, M2, M3, M4, M5) are robust to these controls: education, community size, gender, household size, occupation, age and national pride.

*** $p < 0.001$; ** $p < 0.01$; * $p < 0.01$.

whereas support for more transfers to the dominant ethnic majority (Slovaks) is driven by strong pocketbook concerns.

Economic pocketbook considerations are much more important determinants of attitudes toward governmental spending on the majority (Slovaks) and the unaccommodated minority (Roma). Support for greater transfers toward Slovaks and lesser for Roma sharply increases with respondents' expectation that their future personal financial situation will strongly deteriorate.[20] Since many Roma adults are unemployed and have more children than Slovaks and Hungarians, drawing on unemployment benefits and child allowances often invites criticisms of welfare parasitism.[21]

Now that we established that the determinants of opposition to governmental support for aspirational Hungarians are distinct from attitudes toward other groups, we want to find out if this specific attitude is related to radical right voting. Hypothesis 1 expects that radical right voters exhibit higher levels of policy hostility toward a politically organized minority, but not toward the minority group that is not organized.

Figure 4.2 displays support for governmental spending on Hungarians, the aspirational minority, by political bloc. The major parties are grouped into four political blocs: (1) voters of the radical right party – SNS voters are on the bottom; (2) mainstream right bloc ("cousins"): voters of the coalition partners of the radical right party; these include positions of the voters for SMER-SD and voters for ĽS-HZDS – second from the bottom; (3) mainstream left bloc: voters of the coalition partners of the Hungarian ethnic parties; positions of the voters for SDKU-DS and KDH are third from the bottom; and (4) voters of the ethnic Hungarian parties; positions of the voters for SMK and for Most-Híd are on the top.

---

[20] Household size has a similar effect: respondents with more children want more support for Slovaks and significantly less support for Roma.

[21] Roma draw on welfare support from the government. The government provides parents with allowances to cover a portion of expenses associated with child rearing. Roma, on average, have about twice as many children as Slovaks (or Hungarians) and child allowances are a crucial source of income for many Roma families (on Roma reproductive behavior, see Vano 2001).

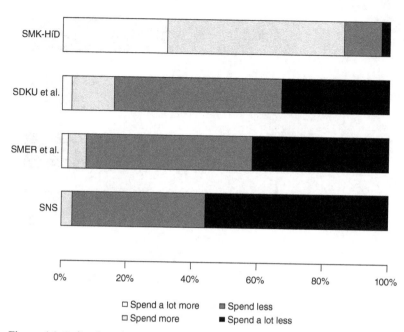

**Figure 4.2** Policy hostility: opposition to government transfers to the Hungarian minority in Slovakia.

Figure 4.2 shows that radical right voters (SNS) are much less inclined to support transferring governmental resources to the Hungarian minority. This extreme position on spending on Hungarians separates radical right voters both from the voters of the mainstream parties that form coalitions with the radical right party, their mainstream political "cousins" ($|t|$ = 2.4), and from the voters of mainstream parties that form coalitions with the Hungarian parties ($|t|$ = 4.0). This is consistent with Hypothesis 1: policy hostility directed specifically toward a minority group that was able to extract concessions from the majority and translate them into political power differentiates radical right voters from voters of other parties, including their cousins: voters for their proximate competitors.

Figure 4.3 displays attitudes toward governmental spending on Roma, a group that is minimally accommodated through the political process. It shows that radical right voters do not harbor policy hostility toward a non-accommodated group that is different from voters of other party blocs. Figure 4.3 also shows that attitudes toward transfers

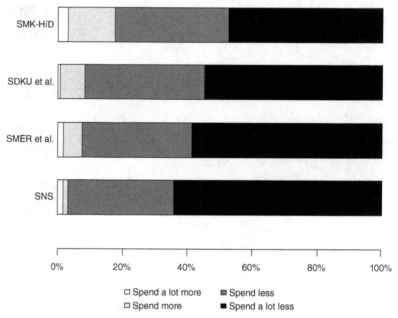

**Figure 4.3** Policy hostility: opposition to government transfers to the Roma minority in Slovakia.

benefiting Roma do not differentiate radical right voters from the voters of other major parties, especially their mainstream cousins. All voters reject government support for Roma.

### 4.3.2 Group Hostility

Hypothesis 2 predicts that group hostility (xenophobia) is not unique to radical right voters. I created a composite index of hostility as an additive index based on two questions to measure group hostility toward Hungarians and Roma.[22] Group hostility, a social distance measure, is an eight-item additive index. Two items are repeated for each of the two groups: Hungarians and Roma:

---

[22] The index of social distance is a composite index that combines two questions about having a member of the group as a neighbor and a life partner. The lowest value is two and the highest value is eight. I shifted the index for visual purposes. The span of the index is six.

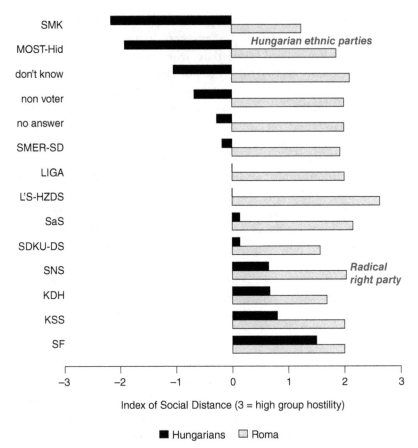

**Figure 4.4** Group hostility: prejudice toward minorities by parties in Slovakia. *Note:* Index of social distance toward Hungarians and Roma.

"To have [group name] as neighbor seems to me very attractive/somewhat attractive/somewhat unattractive/very unattractive."

"To have [group name] as a life partner seems to me very attractive/ somewhat attractive/somewhat unattractive/very unattractive."

Using group hostility (an index of social distance), Figure 4.4 shows that high levels of prejudicial hostility against Roma are constant across voters of all parties. Voters of the radical right party (SNS) are equally as hostile to Roma as voters of the Hungarian parties and voters for the major mainstream parties. Therefore, party affiliation does not allow us to differentiate group hostility toward Roma. This suggests that voting for the radical right party is not an expression of an indiscriminate group hostility and general prejudice specific to the radical right voting base.

Group hostility against Hungarians, however, does differ across political parties, but the radical right voters do not display the highest level of prejudice toward Hungarians when compared with voters of other parties. It is expected that voters of Hungarian ethnic parties will not display xenophobia to themselves. But among the parties that mostly represent the dominant (Slovak) group, the radical right voters do not stand out as harboring exceptionally extreme views (Figure 4.4).[23] This is consistent with the expectation that prejudice does not uniquely drive support for the radical right party.[24]

I explore group hostility toward Hungarians. Table 4.6 displays results of a regression analysis geared toward identifying the determinants of prejudice toward Hungarians, while controlling for socio-demographic and psychological factors. Group hostility is best predicted by the perception of economic and sovereignty threats from the Hungarian minority, after controlling for the respondent's nationality (Table 4.6).[25] These results imply that economic deprivation drives prejudice, as do fears of external threats, but prejudice is not unique to SNS voters.

### 4.3.3 Economic and Sovereignty Threats

In this section, I explore the role of economic and security threats in electoral support for the radical right (Hypotheses 3 and 4). I expect security threats to be salient for the voters of the radical right. I expect economic grievances to play a lesser role, unless they are coupled with considerations of ethnic hierarchies and blame that can be attributed to groups. The SNS memorandum adopted in 2012 speaks directly to sovereignty threats: "Enough of those governments who sell out our sovereignty and economic interests of Slovaks. Slovakia is currently in the state of total psychological, political and economic dependency and reliance. The economy strongly depends on foreign countries, small

---

[23] Voters of SF, KSS and KDH exhibit high levels of group hostility. SF is a marginal political party. KSS is a communist party. KDH is an influential Christian democratic party that served in pro-European governing coalitions. SF stands for a small party called Slobodné fórum that has rarely crossed the 5 percent threshold needed to enter the parliament. It is a splinter party from SDKU, the pro-democratic, pro-Western party.

[24] Group hostility does not predict vote choice for parties. See Appendix Table A4.1 and Table A4.2, which predicts group hostility in Slovakia using vote choice.

[25] Nationality is coded as a binary variable, where 1 = Hungarian nationality, 0 = all else, which is in most instances Slovak nationality.

Table 4.6 *Group hostility toward Hungarians in Slovakia*

| | M1 | M2 | M3 | M4 | M5 |
|---|---|---|---|---|---|
| Individual economic threat (Hungarians) | -0.709*** (0.138) | | -0.587*** (0.141) | -0.537*** (0.119) | -0.427** (0.134) |
| Collective sovereignty threat (Hungarians) | | -0.598*** (0.143) | -0.484** (0.148) | -0.334** (0.105) | -0.345** (0.116) |
| Collective sovereignty threat (Hungary) | -0.367** (0.118) | -0.233 (0.146) | -0.057 (0.150) | | |
| Collective sovereignty threat (EU) | -0.004 (0.120) | -0.119 (0.116) | 0.015 (0.118) | | |
| Nationality (1 = Hungarian) | | | | -1.61*** (0.219) | -1.88*** (0.266) |
| Authoritarian values | | | | | -0.117 (0.183) |
| Self-esteem | | | | | -0.115 (0.199) |
| Proud to be citizen of Slovakia | | | | | 0.080 (0.122) |
| Education | | | | | -0.003 (0.103) |
| Income | | | | | -0.015 (0.055) |

Table 4.6 (*cont.*)

|  | M1 | M2 | M3 | M4 | M5 |
|---|---|---|---|---|---|
| Community/city size |  |  |  |  | 0.024 |
|  |  |  |  |  | (0.051) |
| Gender |  |  |  |  | 0.064 |
|  |  |  |  |  | (0.169) |
| Household size |  |  |  |  | −0.153 |
|  |  |  |  |  | (0.085) |
| Not fully employed |  |  |  |  | −0.107 |
|  |  |  |  |  | (0.209) |
| Constant | 8.010*** | 7.433*** | 8.073*** | 7.601*** | 8.031*** |
|  | (0.401) | (0.366) | (0.395) | (0.314) | (0.685) |
| Adj. R^2 | 0.25 | 0.23 | 0.27 | 0.38 | 0.37 |
| N | 319 | 335 | 319 | 326 | 270 |

*Note:* Constants omitted. Cell entries are unstandardized OLS coefficients with standard errors in parentheses.

*** $p < 0.01$; ** $p < 0.05$.

and middle businesses are struggling. Food self-sufficiency is declining and the defense capability of Slovakia has decreased."[26]

Therefore, I evaluate two explanations: economic deprivation and issues of national sovereignty. Since I posit that radical right support is not rooted in generic economic insecurity, radical right voters should not be unique in their views on either their own financial situations or the financial situation of the whole country. But I do expect radical right voters to be distinct in their perceptions of collective security threats.

Figure 4.5 shows that that voters of the Slovak radical right party (SNS) do not perceive themselves as an economically deprived group when compared with voters for other parties. SNS voters do not have any specific occupational profiles and are not distinguished by any specific socio-demographic characteristics. Many of the radical right voters are men, but the effect of gender is not robust.[27] Radical right voters are also not distinct in their position on the economy (Figure 4.5). Economic propositions of radical right parties can be very inconsistent. Aside from economic nationalism, views change depending on the circumstances. Economic policies embraced by radical right parties might range from support for the free-market/deregulatory policies to help small businesses to economic interventionism that exclusively benefits local food providers. In the international arena, the radical right might happily accept EU funds to build local highways and, at the same time, oppose solidaristic policies of the eurozone to bail out Greece.

This economic pragmatism and policy flexibility is reflected in the voting base. When asked either about pocketbook economic threats or socio-tropic economic fears, the proportion of voters who fear a decline of current or future economic conditions is roughly the same across all parties. Interestingly, Hungarians in Slovakia, who are on average poorer and more vulnerable than Slovaks, are more concerned about the economy than radical right voters. In general, economic fears are very pervasive: over 60 percent of voters of all major parties think that the economic condition of most families in Slovakia is worse "now" when compared with the situation "two years prior."

---

[26] SNS Memorandum "Faithful to Slovakia." Programmatic memorandum of SNS approved on January 21, 2012, in Žilina. Available at: www.sns.sk/engine/assets/uploads/2010/03/Volebné-memorandum-2012.pdf. Translated by the author.

[27] There is, however, a regional base of SNS. Radical right voters are heavily recruited from the central region in Slovakia (Stredoslovenský kraj) near Žilina, home base of Ján Slota, the (former) SNS leader (Mesežnikov et al. 2008).

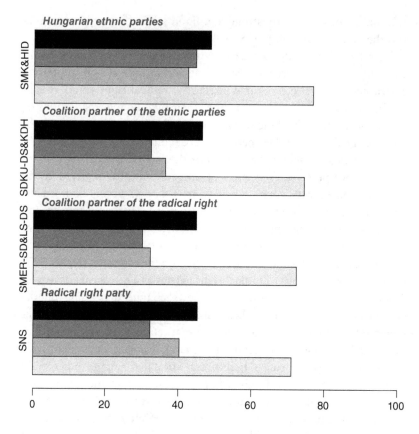

Figure 4.5 Economic threats: fear of worsening economic conditions in Slovakia.

Most voters of major parties fear that their economic conditions will worsen in the future, but there is no statistical difference on this issue among the parties and there is no significant difference between the voters of the two blocs of mainstream coalition competitors.[28] The SNS voters are equally fearful of their economic future, as are voters of

---

[28] ĽS-HZDS + SMER-SD (coalition partners of the SNS) and SDKU-DS + KDH (coalition partners of the Hungarian parties).

other parties. Radical right voters are neither distinctly economically deprived nor uniquely worried about the future of the national economy. This finding is consistent with our expectation that economic grievances, decoupled from their impact on group hierarchies, cannot account for radical right mobilization.

The effect of economic grievances changes, however, once we connect economic anxieties with ethnicity. When economic fears are coupled with ethnicity, SNS voters exhibit distinct tendencies that reflect ethnic competition over resources (Figure 4.6).[29] Figure 4.6 (black bars) shows that radical right voters are more likely to agree with the statement: "My economic condition will get worse due to Hungarians." SNS voters are less likely to give Hungarians a pass for their economic woes. The difference between the mean responses of the radical right voters and voters of their coalition partners (their political "cousins") on the issue of ethnic economic competition is statistically significant, whereas the difference between voters of two mainstream blocs is not.[30] In general, however, all voters, including the SNS voters, do not blame Hungarians for their economic conditions.

Hungarians pose no serious economic threat to Slovaks. Most voters of SNS reside in districts with *no* ethnic Hungarians. Despite the fact that radical right voters are not severely aggrieved by economic fears when compared with other voters, once economic issues are tied to ethnicity, SNS voters perceive Hungarians more as an economic threat. This indicates that the radical right party can carve its niche vis-à-vis its mainstream coalition partner by tying economic issues to ethnic relations and to its relative impact on the dominant group.

[29] The wording for the decoupled and coupled questions is the following. Decoupled: My economic conditions will get worse. Coupled: My economic conditions will get worse due to Hungarians.

[30] There is a considerable debate about whether it is permissible to treat individual Likert items as interval-level data, or whether they should be seen as ordered-categorical data. Some regard Likert items as ordinal data, and argue that one cannot safely assume equidistance between all possible responses, especially when there are only a few levels. In such cases, mean and standard deviation are not appropriate parameters to use in describing ordinal data. Rank, median and range – together with non-parametric tests – are usually more appropriate. Yet sometimes the wording of the response levels clearly implies symmetric responses. This suggests that treating such data as only ordinal omits information. If the respondent sees the question together with an actual scale, and especially if equidistance is strongly implied, the case for treating some Likert scales as interval-level data is strong, since the interval scale is a feature of the data and not of the labels (Clasen and Dormody 1994; Likert 1932; Nunnally 1978; Vigderhous 1977).

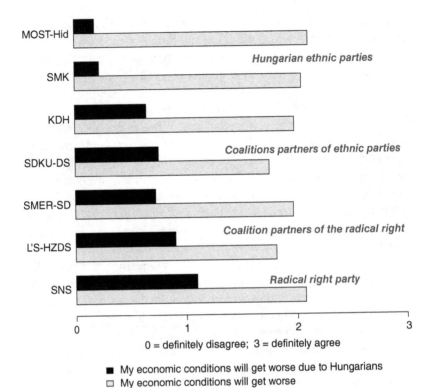

0 = definitely disagree;  3 = definitely agree

■ My economic conditions will get worse due to Hungarians
□ My economic conditions will get worse

**Figure 4.6** Economic threats by parties: fear of worsening personal economic conditions coupled with ethnicity in Slovakia.

The radical right wants to see the dominant group in charge of the state. Issues related to sovereignty and national safety are important. Identity threats are essential for radical right mobilization, and threats to national security endanger the grip of the dominant group over its own polity. Radical right voters should be distinct in their perception of collective security threats. In the survey, respondents were asked about multiple threats to Slovak sovereignty.[31]

Despite the fact that Slovakia and Hungary are both members of the European Union and NATO, nationalists on both sides of the border dispute the historical location of Slovakia on the map. Hungarian ultra-nationalists still reflect on the humiliation of the post–World War I Treaty of Trianon, which deprived Hungary of the territory that

---

[31] The threats are Hungarians, Hungary and the European Union. See the Appendix for question wording. On separatism, see Siroky and Cuffe (2015).

is now Slovakia. Slovak nationalists interpret the history of Slovak–Hungarian relations in the Austro-Habsburg Empire and afterward in terms of oppression, and view Hungary as posing a never-ending threat to the existence of the Slovak nation. The Hungarian minority, which has resided in Slovakia for centuries, is perceived as a disloyal fifth column of Hungary (Siroky and Hale 2017).

The perception that Slovak sovereignty is threatened may stem from three specific sources. The first is the European Union, which some see as unduly influential in determining the direction of domestic policy and international affairs. The second is Hungary, which some believe is not willing to put the Treaty of Trianon to rest, and may at any time challenge the right of the Slovak nation to self-determination. The third source is the Hungarian minority in Slovakia. It can be viewed as an embodiment of the interests that challenge the legitimacy of the Slovak state.

In order to evaluate the comparative importance of these threats, the survey included a question about threats to Slovak sovereignty.[32] Similarly to the questions on economic threats, one question was decoupled from ethnicity and one question was tied to the threat from Hungarians (Sniderman et al. 2004: 37). With regard to threats to Slovak sovereignty, one question did not specify the source of the threat, so as to decouple the threat from its potential sources, and the additional three questions linked sovereignty threats specifically to (1) Hungarians living in Slovakia (threat coupled with ethnicity), (2) the Hungarian state and (3) the European Union. The indicator of threat is thus "double-barreled": it simultaneously assesses the degree of perceived threat and how the respondents feel about Hungarians (as well as Hungary and the EU) as the source of that threat.

Table 4.7 presents Spearman rank correlation coefficients between the economic and security threat items. It displays correlations between decoupled and coupled threats. The respondents were randomly assigned to one of two groups. One was asked about general threats (decoupled). The second group was asked about threats originating from groups/actors (coupled threats).

---

[32] The question that addresses the threat to Slovak collective identity did not ask about the threat to Slovak culture because none of the minorities is viewed as a cultural threat. This is in contrast to the threat posed by ethnic minorities of Muslim faith, which Western European radical right parties view as culturally incompatible.

Table 4.7 *Economic threats and sovereignty threats in Slovakia*

| Threat | Threat: Decoupled | | Threat: Coupled | | | |
|---|---|---|---|---|---|---|
| | Individual economic | Collective sovereignty | Individual economic (Hungarians) | Collective sovereignty (Hungarians) | Collective sovereignty (Hungary) | Collective sovereignty (EU) |
| Individual economic | | | | | | |
| Collective sovereignty | 0.20 (468) | | | | | |
| Individual economic (Hungarians) | | | | | | |
| Collective sovereignty (Hungarians) | | | 0.60 (456) | | | |
| Collective sovereignty (Hungary) | | | 0.57 (456) | 0.79 (456) | | |
| Collective sovereignty (EU) | | | 0.47 (456) | 0.45 (456) | 0.42 (456) | |

*Note:* Cell entries are Spearman's rank correlations. Number of cases in parentheses.

The correlation between the decoupled threat items is only 0.20, which allows us to assess the impact of economic and sovereignty threats on voters independently. By comparison, threat judgments associated with Hungarians in Slovakia and with Hungary as a country are strongly related. The correlation between the threats posed to Slovak sovereignty by Hungarians and by Hungary is 0.79: those who fear Hungary (the country) as a threat to national sovereignty are similarly suspicious of the Hungarian minority in Slovakia. This confirms that, as a threat, Hungarians are viewed as a fifth column of Hungary.

There is also a strong correlation (0.60) between a perceived individual economic threat and perceived collective sovereignty threat due to Hungarians: those who view Hungarians as a threat to their economic well-being are also more likely to perceive them as a threat to Slovakia's sovereignty. Therefore, when threats are coupled with a reference to Hungarians, it becomes more difficult to untangle the impact of economic-driven and identity-based threats on voting. Coupled questions attribute threats.[33]

What are the sources of variation in threat perceptions? Table 4.7 shows determinants of economic and sovereignty threats that relate specifically to the Hungarian minority, and finds that the strongest predictor of threat perception is the nationality of the respondent. Yet economic anxieties play an important role in explaining both economic and sovereignty threats from Hungarians as well. The more respondents fear that their future financial situation will deteriorate, the more they perceive economic threat from Hungarians (Models 1 and 2 in Table 4.8).[34]

Although the personal characteristics of the respondent, such as low self-esteem and authoritarian values (Models 4 and 5 in Table 4.8), explain why some view Hungarians as a threat to collective sovereignty, it does not explain why some view Hungarians as an economic threat. It is noteworthy, however, that the respondent's economic insecurities explain both perceptions of threats to collective sovereignty and perceptions of economic threat from Hungarians. Economic anxieties therefore play a role in radical right mobilization but need to be filtered through the perceptions of group boundaries and minority group gains vis-à-vis the dominant group.

---

[33] This is fully consistent with findings in Sniderman et al. 2004.
[34] As a corollary, I also find that the lower the household income of the respondent, the higher the perception that Hungarians pose a threat to Slovak statehood (M4 and M5).

Table 4.8 *Individual economic threats and collective sovereignty threats coupled with ethnicity in Slovakia (from Hungarians)*

| | Individual economic threat (due to Hungarians) | | | Collective sovereignty threat (due to Hungarians) | |
|---|---|---|---|---|---|
| | M1 | M2 | M3 | M4 | M5 |
| Family financial situation (Two years ago) | −0.051 (0.099) | | | −0.062 (0.093) | |
| Personal financial situation (Two years from now) | −0.252* (0.111) | | −0.284** (0.092) | −0.077 (0.104) | |
| National economy (Two years from now) | 0.001 (0.097) | | | −0.089 (0.092) | |
| All families financial situation (Two years ago) | −0.151 (0.125) | | | 0.031 (0.114) | |
| Nationality (1 = Hungarian) | 1.466*** (0.240) | 1.088*** (0.223) | 1.356*** (0.261) | 1.660*** (0.215) | 1.380*** (0.212) |
| Authoritarian values | | 0.240 (0.228) | 0.186 (0.138) | | 0.296* (0.122) |
| Self-esteem | | 0.167 (0.130) | 0.179 (0.142) | | 0.339** (0.127) |
| Income | | −0.049 (0.031) | −0.045 (0.033) | | −0.099** (0.029) |
| 1st cut point | −2.880 | −1.438 | −2.072 | −1.645 | −0.679 |
| 2nd cut point | −1.983 | −0.579 | −1.193 | −0.712 | 0.194 |
| 3rd cut point | −0.788 | −0.518 | −0.047 | −0.370 | 1.233 |
| Log likelihood | −400.8 | −404.9 | −357.1 | −485.6 | −493.6 |
| N | 386 | 393 | 347 | 402 | 407 |

*Note:* Cell entries are ordered probit coefficients with standard errors in parentheses. Models 1–5 (M1, M2, M3, M4, M5) are robust to the following controls: education, community size, gender, household size, occupation, age and national pride.
*** $p < 0.001$; ** $p < 0.01$; * $p < 0.01$.

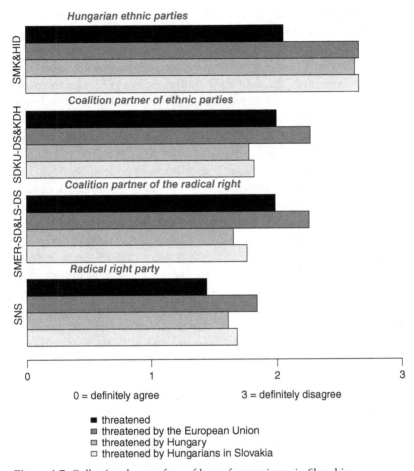

**Figure 4.7** Collective threats: fear of loss of sovereignty in Slovakia.

Finally, I turn to the security threat perception by parties. Figure 4.7 displays the degree of collective threat perception by the voters of the four political blocs and parties.[35] Voters of the radical right party exhibit the highest level of fear about the loss of sovereignty. This applies to all three specific threats – from the EU, from Hungary and

---

[35] The cut points in Table 4.8 are based on a latent continuous distribution of the attitudes that are empirically observed in one of four options in the survey. The algorithm automatically calculates the optional cut points.

from Hungarians living in Slovakia – along with general fear about collective threats to security.[36]

Figure 4.7 shows that SNS voters are different from other voters, especially when it comes to the *general* perception that Slovak sovereignty is threatened. This is in stark contrast to both of the mainstream blocs and the Hungarian ethnic parties who all exhibit the same levels of general sovereignty threats. The supporters of mainstream parties have very similar threat level perceptions, in terms of both general threats and threats specifically tied to the EU, Hungary and to the ethnic Hungarians in Slovakia. The bilateral opposites, the SNS and the Hungarian parties, polarize the party system. The ethnic parties are less fearful of the EU, Hungary and the Hungarian minority when compared with both the SNS voters and the mainstream blocs.

The difference between the collective threat perceptions of voters for the two mainstream competing political blocs ("ĽS-HZDS + SMER-SD" and "SDKU-DS + KDH") is not statistically significant, whereas the difference between the positions of voters for the mainstream parties and the positions of their respective allies (on the left and the right) is distinct (Figure 4.7).[37] Polarization on sovereignty issues is driven by the divergence of the bilateral opposites from their mainstream coalition partners and not by the divergence of the two mainstream parties (cf. Adams et al. 2006).

The radical right voters stand out as being exceptionally fearful about the threats that Slovakia is facing as an independent nation. Threats to sovereignty are legitimate concerns but they are not, at least at this very moment, life-threatening. The Hungarian military is weak and both Slovakia and Hungary are members of NATO and the EU. Hungary has not been threatening Slovakia with an invasion to retrieve lost historical territories to remedy the 1920 Treaty of

---

[36] Sensitivity to sovereignty threats suggests that radical right voters are sensitive to "law and order" issues such as threats to national security and, at the same time, are very concerned with the well-being of the nation.

[37] For example, voters for the Hungarian parties fear that the European Union poses a threat to Slovak sovereignty significantly *less* than voters of their mainstream political allies (SDKU + KDH). On the other side of the political spectrum, however, it is voters of the radical right party (SNS) who fear the European Union poses a threat to Slovak sovereignty significantly *more* than the voters of their mainstream political allies (ĽS-HZDS + SMER-SD). The t-value associated with the mean difference between the voters of the Hungarian parties and the voters of their coalition partners is about 3. The t-value associated with the mean difference between the voters of the radical right party (SNS) and the voters of their coalition partners (ĽS-HZDS + SMER-SD) is about 2.4.

Trianon. Security threats of this magnitude are rare and currently not present.

But this dynamic might change in the future. In 2017, the ruling Hungarian radicalized mainstream party Fidesz has officially called for the annulment of the so-called Beneš decrees that stripped Hungarians of citizenship and property after World War II. This led to deportations of Hungarians in 1947–1948 from Czechoslovakia. History books used in Hungarian public schools – especially after Orbán's reform that nationalized and centralized schools in 2012 – voice serious grievances over the Treaty of Trianon and the loss of "Upper Hungary," which de facto challenges the Slovak statehood. But as long as security threats are contained to the level of rhetoric, and voters do not need to run for protection to large mainstream parties, these findings are consistent with the expectation that fear of losing a "sovereign" state, due to the pressures from a multiplicity of actors, is an important ingredient of radical right mobilization.

## 4.4 Radical Right Voters in Slovakia

Who votes for SNS, the radical right party? In this section I turn to the individual-level profiles of voters. Proud Slovaks who oppose governmental support for Hungarians are the quintessential radical right voters.[38] Table 4.9 shows that the strongest predictor of radical right party vote is an opposition to transfers to Hungarians (Models 3 and 4), which is consistent with theoretical expectations. Opposition to spending, policy hostility, is noted in the table as "policy hostility: Hungarians." By contrast, opposition to transfers to non-ascending Roma does not predict support for the radical right and neither does support for more transfers to Slovaks. This is consistent with the expectations that support for radical right parties originates in opposition toward aspirational groups.

National pride matters as well, yet it would be misguided to attribute the radical right voters' indignation at transfers toward Hungarians to extreme patriotic pride. It is rather a consequence of dissatisfaction with the fact that the state might be used to enhance the aspirations of a minority. The survey included a question about national pride that neither stated nor implied any competition over resources. Radical

---

[38] I uncovered a modest effect of gender: radical right voters tend to be men. This is consistent with the fact that many studies of the radical right parties report that men are more likely to support radical right parties (Givens 2005; Immerzeel et al. 2015; Kitschelt 2007; Mudde 2007).

Table 4.9 Determinants of party vote in Slovakia

| Parties | | Spending on: majority (Slovaks) | | Spending on: minority (Hungarians) | | Spending on: minority (Roma) | |
|---|---|---|---|---|---|---|---|
| | | M1 | M2 | M3 | M4 | M5 | M6 |
| Radical right party (SNS) | Policy hostility (1 = spend much more on [nationality]) | -0.458 (0.266) | -0.480 (0.268) | 0.705** (0.242) | 0.694** (0.244) | 0.109 (0.224) | 0.133 (0.225) |
| | Nationality (1 = Hungarian, 0 = else) | -13.698 (564.36) | -13.817 (568.32) | -12.987 (520.09) | -20.833 (249.83) | -13.731 (477.57) | -17.688 (327.2) |
| | National pride (1 = very proud) | -0.499* (0.215) | -0.476* (0.217) | -0.612** (0.215) | -0.591** (0.216) | -0.621** (0.216) | -0.603** (0.217) |
| | Sex (1 = man) | 0.667* (0.292) | 0.690* (0.294) | 0.686* (0.291) | 0.711* (0.294) | 0.725* (0.288) | 0.738* (0.290) |
| | Occupational profile (0 = independent, 1 = dependent) | | 0.404 (0.375) | | 0.445 (0.377) | | 0.441 (0.374) |
| | Income | | 0.053 (0.075) | | 0.047 (0.075) | | 0.069 (0.073) |
| Coalition partners of the radical right party (SMER-SD & L'S-HZDZ) | Policy hostility (1 = spend much more on [nationality]) | 0.219 (0.137) | 0.194 (0.137) | 0.233 (0.130) | 0.175 (0.134) | -0.099 (0.121) | -0.094 (0.124) |
| | Nationality (1 = Hungarian, 0 = else) | -1.375* (0.560) | -1.385* (0.560) | -1.082* (0.576) | -1.162* (0.578) | -1.342** (0.499) | -1.390** (0.501) |

| | (1) | (2) | (3) | (4) | (5) | (6) |
|---|---|---|---|---|---|---|
| National pride (1 = very proud) | −0.521*** | −0.516*** | −0.492*** | −0.479*** | −0.510*** | −0.496*** |
| | (0.122) | (0.122) | (0.124) | (0.128) | (0.120) | (0.124) |
| Sex (1 = man) | 0.184 | 0.209 | 0.154 | 0.190 | 0.161 | 0.184 |
| | (0.165) | (0.165) | (0.170) | (0.176) | (0.163) | (0.169) |
| Occupational profile (0 = independent, 1 = dependent) | | 0.792** | | 0.797** | | 0.800** |
| | | (0.234) | | (0.242) | | (0.235) |
| Income | | 0.034 | | 0.033 | | 0.046 |
| | | (0.045) | | (0.045) | | (0.043) |
| **Coalition of partners of the Hungarian parties (SDKU-DS & KDH)** | | | | | | |
| Policy hostility (1 = spend much more on [nationality]) | 0.253 | 0.231 | −0.153 | −0.195 | −0.194 | −0.174 |
| | (0.165) | (0.168) | (0.149) | (0.153) | (0.140) | (0.144) |
| Nationality (1 = Hungarian, 0 = else) | −0.591 | −0.633 | −0.712 | −0.827 | −0.617 | −0.676 |
| | (0.518) | (0.519) | (0.540) | (0.543) | (0.468) | (0.469) |
| National pride (1 = very proud) | −0.237 | −0.223 | −0.205 | −0.176 | −0.265 | −0.224 |
| | (0.144) | (0.148) | (0.146) | (0.150) | (0.141) | (0.144) |
| Sex (1 = man) | 0.004 | 0.089 | −0.003 | 0.076 | −0.031 | −0.067 |
| | (0.202) | (0.207) | (0.206) | (0.211) | (0.197) | (0.202) |
| Occupational profile (0 = independent, 1 = dependent) | | 0.343 | | 0.331 | | 0.232 |
| | | (0.263) | | (0.268) | | (0.254) |
| Income | | 0.046 | | 0.039 | | 0.049 |
| | | (0.053) | | (0.054) | | (0.051) |
| **Hungarian parties (SMK & Most-Hid)** | | | | | | |
| Policy hostility (1 = spend much more on [nationality]) | 0.295 | 0.229 | −1.334*** | −1.417*** | −0.397 | −0.416* |
| | (0.165) | (0.168) | (0.149) | (0.153) | (0.140) | (0.144) |

Table 4.9 (*cont.*)

| Parties | Spending on: majority (Slovaks) | | Spending on: minority (Hungarians) | | Spending on: minority (Roma) | |
|---|---|---|---|---|---|---|
| | M1 | M2 | M3 | M4 | M5 | M6 |
| Nationality | 3.296*** | 3.308*** | 2.175*** | 2.000*** | 3.276*** | 3.203*** |
| (1 = Hungarian, 0 = else) | (0.359) | (0.371) | (0.405) | (0.427) | (0.335) | (0.343) |
| National pride | 0.493* | 0.494* | 0.538* | 0.621* | 0.561* | 0.589* |
| (1 = very proud) | (0.216) | (0.222) | (0.244) | (0.258) | (0.214) | (0.223) |
| Sex | −0.237 | −0.182 | −0.221 | −0.110 | −0.301 | −0.218 |
| (1 = man) | (0.330) | (0.336) | (0.351) | (0.362) | (0.321) | (0.328) |
| Occupational profile | | 0.522 | | 0.559 | | 0.588 |
| (0 = independent, 1 = dependent) | | (0.472) | | (0.530) | | (0.476) |
| Income | | −0.179* | | −0.212* | | −0.195* |
| | | (0.087) | | (0.096) | | (0.085) |
| Log likelihood | −1,129.13 | −1,081.97 | −1,061.87 | −1,014.29 | −1,169.08 | −1,115.11 |
| N | 896 | 861 | 859 | 824 | 926 | 887 |

*Note:* Dependent variable: Vote choice for a political party. Cell entries are multinomial logit coefficients with standard errors in parentheses. The base outcome is voters for all other parties combined and non-voters. Constants are omitted from the table. Detailed coding of the occupational decision is in the Appendix. Results are robust to a series of controls, such as education, community size, household size and age, as well as authoritarian values.

*** $p < 0.001$; ** $p < 0.01$; * $p < 0.01$.

right party voters and voters of coalition partners ("cousins") are indeed more patriotic when compared with the voters of Hungarian ethnic parties and voters of their coalition partners. However, when compared with each other, radical right voters and their "cousins" are the same: both are patriots.

Although national pride is an important determinant of support for the radical right party, patriotism is not its exclusive trait. In fact, national pride exerts even more influence on voting for the *mainstream* proximate competitor of the radical right party. Voters with high levels of national pride are more likely to vote for the political "cousin" than for the radical right. The effect of national pride on the vote for coalition partners of the radical right party is very robust. But opposition to transfers to Hungarians is the single strongest predictor of radical right party voting (Table 4.9). Importantly, policy hostility toward Hungarians has no effect on the vote for mainstream coalition partners of the radical right party. *What separates voters of radical right parties from their mainstream cousins is not patriotism, but opposition to transfers to Hungarians.*

To examine the substantive effect of policy hostility, Figure 4.8 displays the predicted probabilities of voting for the radical right party for voters with varying degrees of policy hostility. The simulation is based on a scenario where the respondent is a proud Slovak male.[39] The results indicate that a proud Slovak male who supports "a lot more transfers" toward Hungarians has a 2 percent predicted probability of voting for the radical right party, whereas the predicted probability of voting for the radical right for that same proud Slovak male who now "strongly opposes transfers" toward Hungarians increases to 14 percent. This is a very strong substantive effect. It also highlights the fact that what polarizes politics is not quarreling over national identity, but aversion to aspirations of non-dominant groups: the pull for minority accommodation on the one side of the political spectrum, and the pushback against it from the other side.

---

[39] National pride variable was set at answer "rather proud," which is the modal category for all respondents. The question reads: "Please tell me if you feel very proud, rather proud, rather not proud, not at all proud that you are a citizen of Slovakia?" (2 = rather proud).

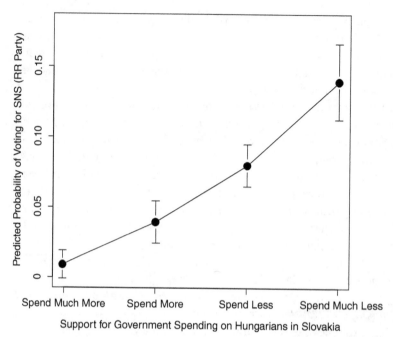

**Figure 4.8** Predicted probability of voting for the radical right party in Slovakia. Positive effect of policy hostility toward Hungarians.
*Note*: Simulations are based on Model 3 in Table 4.9.

## 4.5 Identity Priming Experiment

When do voters feel threatened by nationalistic rhetoric and under which conditions are respondents willing to change their positions on transfers? To further examine the sources of political polarization, I conducted an identity priming experiment in the survey. I have already established that radical right voters support lower levels of spending on Hungarians, while voters of the Hungarian parties support more. If nationality is invoked, who becomes sensitive to being primed and who feels threatened if reminded of the ethnic underpinnings of the state?

In the experiment, respondents were randomly assigned to one of two experimental conditions: in the first, their respective national identity was primed, and in the second their individual identities were primed. In the experimental condition when the respondent is primed on their personal identity the questions begin with the following introduction: "People differ in many ways and each human being is unique.

One person likes music, another likes to go for a walk, and still another likes to go out. Everyone is different."

In the condition when the identification is with their own nation, the questions begin with the following introduction: "People belong to different types of groups. One of the most important and essential of these groups is the nation you belong to. In your case you belong to the nationality [the administrator of the survey fills in the respondent's nationality]. Each nation is different."

After the national prime/individual prime introduction, all respondents were asked the following question: "In the current economic situation, it may be difficult for the government to cover all its expenses. When the resources are limited, and the government cannot raise taxes, some groups get more and some groups get less. In your view, as a citizen of the Slovak Republic, how should this situation affect Slovaks, Hungarians and Roma?"

(1) "Do you think that the government should spend much more, more, less or much less on Slovaks?"
(2) "Do you think that the government should spend much more, more, less or much less on Hungarians?"
(3) "Do you think that the government should spend much more, more, less or much less on Roma?"[40]

Figures 4.9 and 4.10 compare reactions to priming by parties and party blocs. Figure 4.9 displays changes in support for spending on the majority due to priming on nationality. Figure 4.10 displays changes in support for the Hungarian minority due to the prime. The bottoms of the figures show that radical right voters do not change views (SNS [Pe-P: personal prime], [Nat-P: identity prime]) on governmental spending neither toward the Slovak majority (Figure 4.9) nor toward the minority (Figure 4.10). Views of radical right voters on transfers are the same across both of the experimental conditions.[41]

National priming, however, increases anxiety among ethnic voters as well as among voters whose parties support minorities (due to the necessity of forming governing coalitions). Recall that the survey was done during the period of great contestation of the language

---

[40] Responses take the form of a modified Likert scale.
[41] This finding is similar to that of Sniderman et al. (2004: 44), who find a ceiling effect on the experimental treatment among those who strongly oppose immigration.

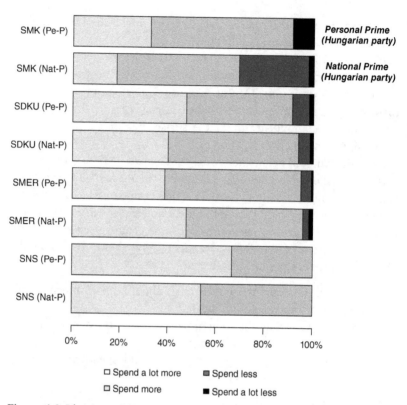

**Figure 4.9** Identity priming experiment: government spending on Slovaks. *Note*: Pe-P stands for the personal prime experimental condition. Nat-P stands for the nationalistic/identity prime experimental condition. SMK stands for combined preferences of SMK and Híd, Hungarian ethnic parties.

law. Minority voters and their coalition partners rally behind the governmental support for minorities, when national identities are evoked.

The evidence displayed in Figures 4.9 and 4.10 illustrates these findings. Figure 4.9 shows that, when primed on their Hungarian identity, voters for the ethnic Hungarian parties demand smaller transfers to the Slovak majority. The difference between the two experimental conditions is statistically significant ($|t| = 2.6$). While 32 percent of voters for the Hungarian parties support much more spending on Slovaks in the individual prime experimental condition, the number drops to 18 percent in the national prime experimental condition, which represents a statistically significant decrease. This reflects

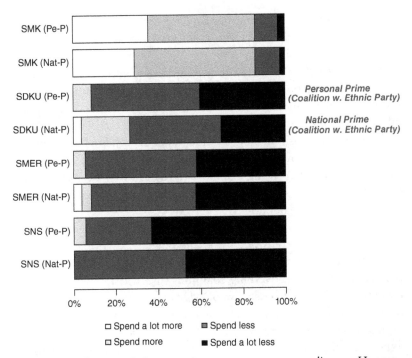

**Figure 4.10** Identity priming experiment: government spending on Hungarians in Slovakia.

*Note*: Pe-P stands for the personal prime experimental condition. Nat-P stands for the nationalistic/identity prime experimental condition. SDKU is a mainstream coalition partner of the Hungarian ethnic party.

anxieties of ethnic voters when reminded of their nationality in the context of a state that operates on fixed resources.

The experiment assesses whether respondents change their attitudes on spending on groups when mobilized on national identity. It also identifies voters who can be mobilized by raising the salience of national identity.[42] In contrast to the voters of ethnic minority parties, nationalistic mobilization does not trigger a sense of policy threat among radical right voters. They are in charge of their own state. In addition, the ceiling effect reinforces the fact that radical right voters do not shift toward greater opposition toward transfers, which they already strongly oppose. Radical right voters do not change their

---

[42] The priming experiment is modeled after Sniderman et al. (2004: 44–47).

position on transfers when primed on their national identity. Irritation with aspiring, ascending minorities, not love of a nation, is the source of radical right mobilization.

While policy hostility does not increase with identity salience among radical right voters, nationalist priming invokes fear among ethnic voters since it reminds them that they are merely tenants in the house inhabited by the dominant group. Ethnic party voters therefore react and change their position on governmental policy when experimentally primed on (their own) identity of a national minority. If priming triggers awareness of being a minority, voters of ethnic parties seek to protect themselves against threat of nationalism by changing views on governmental spending.

Despite the fact that the coalition partner of the Hungarian party (the mainstream party SDKU) does not openly advocate for ethnic minority rights, it has incorporated at least one of the Hungarian parties in three of its governing coalitions since 1991.[43] When primed on national identity, mainstream SDKU voters of the coalition partner of the ethnic Hungarian parties demand an *increase* in transfers for the Hungarian minority (Figure 4.7). The difference between the two experimental conditions is statistically significant ($|t| > 2$). Compared with the 9 percent that supported "much more" or just "more" spending on Hungarians in the individual experimental condition, the number jumps by a factor of three, to 27 percent, in the national prime experimental condition. The SDKU voters become more generous toward minorities.

Therefore, when primed on national identity, voters of the coalition partner of the Hungarian party side with the demands of the Hungarian minority in line with the practice and policies of the mainstream SDKU. Recall earlier evidence from the group hostility index showing that SDKU voters do not have warm and fuzzy feelings toward Hungarians. According to Figure 4.4 (group hostility) they are not less prejudiced toward Hungarians when compared with political "cousins" of the radical right parties (voters of other mainstream parties). Their willingness to support even more governmental transfers toward Hungarians in the national prime experimental condition suggests that their generosity is driven not by affection but by political considerations. Regardless of personal views, voters of the coalition

[43] Governments in 1998–2002, 2002–2006 and 2010–2012.

partners of the ethnic parties are willing to support Hungarians, since this is the price to be paid for political partnership.

Contrast the coalition partner voters' generosity toward Hungarians with their total lack of generosity toward the Roma (Figure 4.3). Although many Roma children are raised in extreme poverty, and mainstream parties recognize the need to improve their dismal condition, the Roma issue does not polarize large segments of the electorate. Despite the pariah status of Roma in Slovak society, all respondents, including voters for the Hungarian parties, strongly oppose any government support to Roma. Not surprisingly, the experimental conditions yield consistent indifference to the Romas' plight: voters did not increase or decrease their generosity toward Roma in the national prime experimental condition, regardless of party affiliation.[44]

The mainstream SDKU party stands for minority rights, but it does so primarily for the Hungarian minority. Contrary to Roma, the Hungarian minority is almost at economic parity with the Slovaks. Although it needs assistance much less than do Roma, it has considerably more political leverage, which allows it to extract economic and cultural concessions from its mainstream coalition partners. *The policy hostility of the radical right party originates precisely in these concessions.* The hostility is not directed toward Hungarians or Roma as ethnic groups, but rather toward concessions that satisfy political ambitions and enable minorities to ascend.

## 4.6 New Issues

The 2016 refugee crisis and demands of new groups brought new issues to Slovak politics. Marian Kotleba, a former computer science high school teacher, is a leader of a new People's Party – Our Slovakia party (ĽSNS: Ľudová strana – Naše Slovensko). The party rose to prominence in 2013 when Kotleba surprisingly won the governorship in the region of Banská Bystrica. Three years later, in 2016, ĽSNS won 14 seats in a 150-seat parliament with 8 percent of the vote. As a new governor, Kotleba removed the flag of the European Union from his office and abided by his promise to wean Slovakia off the developmental aid from the European Union. Therefore, he refused to participate

---

[44] The results from the identity priming experiment that concerned Roma are not represented graphically but simply reported by the author.

in financing modernization of fourteen high schools. Under his leadership, the development of the region was halted (Poláčková 2018) and Kotleba's inability to fix roads, combined with blunt nepotism, led to his electoral defeat (Bárdy 2015). He was voted out in 2017.[45]

Kotleba represents a new wave of radical right mobilization that opportunistically expands the portfolio of enemies. In 2016, Kotleba's party mobilized on the refugee threat warning that Slovakia will be flooded by "hordes of Muslim immigrants." He also ramped up mobilization against the Roma community, the gay and lesbian community and the Jews. Kotleba resuscitated dormant anti-Semitism in Slovakia (Bustikova and Guasti 2012). ĽSNS is an anti-system party. It is also more extreme than the Slovak National Party, which has been tamed by participating in multiple governing collations. Kotleba's political projects are viewed as a political threat to Slovak democracy (Kluknavská and Smolík 2016). In 2006, the Slovak Supreme Court dissolved the Slovak Brotherhood (Slovenská pospolitosť – Národná strana), the predecessor of ĽSNS. The Slovak Brotherhood openly pledged allegiance to the murderous Hlinka Guard that operated in wartime Slovakia by organizing marches and torchlit parades in paramilitary uniforms. Since then, Kotleba ditched his neo-Nazi outfit and modified his targets.

The electoral success of ĽSNS can be attributed to the appeal of an anti-establishment, highly vitriolic xenophobic rhetoric at the time of the refugee crisis. The electoral profile of Kotleba's supporters is difficult to carve out. ĽSNS voters are loyal to Kotleba, young and recruited from previous non-voters (Gyárfášová 2018). An analysis of 2016 elections at the district level shows that Kotleba's party performed well in ethnically *homogenous* regions with few Hungarians and Roma.[46] This is compatible with the theory proposed here that suggests that xenophobic appeals, matched with prevalence of group hostility among the public, do not map onto the electoral results.

---

[45] Marian Kotleba lost his position as the governor of the Banská Bystrica region. The party (ĽSNS) obtained only two seats (leaders Kotleba and Uhrík) out of 416 seats in the regional assemblies. The party lost 25,000 votes. In general, the 2017 regional elections in Slovakia were a defeat for both the populist left and the two radical right parties (SNS, however, was more successful than ĽSNS).

[46] This is in a stark contrast to the 2012 elections, in which Kotleba's party did very poorly and their appeal was associated with districts with Roma tensions (Kluknavská and Smolík 2016; Maškarinec and Bláha 2016).

**Table 4.10** *Views on refugees by political parties in Slovakia (2016)*

| Political party | Attitudes (10 = threat) |
|---|---|
| People's Party Our Slovakia (Kotleba) (radical right–extremist) | 9.37 (1.03) |
| Slovak National Party (SNS) (radical right) | 8.59 (1.55) |
| MOST-HÍD (Hungarian ethnic party) | 8.53 (1.65) |
| SMER-SD (large mainstream party, SNS coalition partner) | 8.51 (1.78) |
| Average response | 8.41 (1.84) |
| OĽANO–NOVA (conservative) | 8.14 (2.08) |
| Freedom and Solidarity (liberal/conservative) | 7.87 (2.01) |
| We Are Family (small populist party) | 7.65 (2.23) |

*Note*: Standard deviations in parentheses.
Question on refugees: A benefit or a threat for EU countries? (0 = benefit, 10 = threat)
Source: Gyárfášová 2018: 125; CSES/ISSP 2016.

A broad public views migrants who seek refuge in the member states of the European Union extremely unfavorably. Table 4.10 shows that in 2016, at the peak of the European migration crisis, the overall attitude toward refugees was extremely negative. On a scale where ten represents the most hostile view of the refugees, supporters of Kotleba's party hold the most extreme position.[47] However, their views are closely in sync with supporters of the radical right party SNS, the supporters of the Hungarian ethnic party and the voters of the largest Slovak party, SMER-SD. On average, all Slovak citizens view refugees as a high-level security threat. According to a representative public opinion poll conducted in April 2017, 82 percent of respondents

---

[47] The CSES/ISSP/Role of Government in Slovakia survey is from 2016. It has 38 respondents (out of 1,150) who declared that they sympathize with the platform of ĽSNS. The survey focuses on the refugee threat to European countries.

resolutely rejected the idea to allow refugees to settle in Slovakia (CVVM 2017). This implies that as the refugee crisis fades away, hysterical anti-refugee mobilization will lose salience and ĽSNS will have to adapt to changing circumstances.

The reactive logic of radical right mobilization applies to Kotleba's party as well. After a gay pride parade of 1,000 participants in the capital city of Bratislava on July 30, 2016, Kotleba called for an anti-protest against the "perverts." In 2015, Kotleba supported a (failed) same-sex marriage referendum ban. Later, his party drafted several laws that would protect "traditional" families. In 2018, ĽSNS proposed a law to restrict abortion, to extend maternity leave to three years and to increase child support conditional on "the desire of parents to work" (ĽS – Naše Slovensko 2018). None of these laws was implemented but they mark the transition in Slovak politics away from the traditional Slovak–Hungarian cleavage toward social and gender issues. It also politicized the Slovak Catholic Church since eighteen Catholic priests signed a petition to back the quest of the extremist party ĽSNS to restrict abortion (Topky 2018).

ĽSNS has a wide portfolio of enemies. Aside from a vitriolic mobilization against Roma, the party is also exploiting the traditional Hungarian cleavage. Stepping on the toes of the Slovak National Party, ĽSNS proposed an absurd law that would stop the so-called discrimination of Slovak children in districts ruled by Hungarians. Their law proposal suggested to bypass the local authorities in southern Slovakia and to sponsor Slovak schools for as little as five Slovak-speaking children who cannot find a school within a six-kilometer radius from their home (L'S – Naše Slovensko 2018). Since the party has a zero coalition potential, the law never passed.

The Slovak National Party (SNS) is irritated by Kotleba and is actively trying to eliminate ĽSNS from the political scene. In the summer of 2018, when visiting Israel, the leader of SNS, Andrej Danko, declared war on ĽSNS. Danko suggested restricting immunity of the members of the parliament who engage in anti-Semitic rhetoric. Danko's law was proposed in October 2018 (Národná rada 2018) and created an immediate controversy. Opponents argued that the law proposal restricts freedom of speech and equates an opposition to Israeli policies with anti-Semitism (Sme 2018). Sensing a threat, Kotleba drafted a counter-law that would equally protect Slovaks. The ĽSNS counter-proposal used Danko's proposal as a template and replaced "Jew" with "Slovak" and "Israel" with "the Slovak Republic" (L'S – Naše Slovensko 2018). Danko immediately rejected Kotleba's draft.

It is yet to be seen how this controversial proposal plays out. In 2013, Kotleba called the war expulsion of Jews an "optimal solution" and revealed the extremist nature of his platform. In 2017, the Slovak Prosecutor-General filed a motion to dissolve L'SNS on the grounds that, as an extremist, fascist party, it violates the Slovak constitution and Slovak laws. Therefore, L'SNS might be outlawed before the next cycle of parliamentary elections or it might be back in the parliament, perhaps repackaged under a new name. Kotleba will be, however, always associated with the changing nature of Slovak identity politics, accelerated by an unprecedented migration threat from non-European Muslim countries.

## 4.7 Conclusion

Forming coalitions with ethnic parties implies some degree of accommodation and shifts of the mainstream party's position away from the center (Kedar 2005). As minorities strive to advance, they demand resources, symbolic recognition and honor from the representatives of the dominant group. As their aspirations are being fulfilled, the radical right parties become alarmed and the political system polarizes. The divergence, however, is driven not by large party blocs distancing their views from each other but by the pressures of the "extreme" poles that diverge from their mainstream coalition partners. Accommodation comes at a price. Indignation over – and disagreement with – governmental transfers toward a politically backed minority is the single strongest predictor of the radical right vote. Radical right voters in Slovakia are proud of their nation, though what makes them distinct is not their nationalistic pride but their selective hostility against a politically backed minority and anxieties about security threats to their country. The individual-level analysis has shown that radical right voters are not distinctly xenophobic and not particularly poor, but that economic considerations become important to them when economic anxieties are viewed through the prism of ethnicity and group hierarchies.

Radical right mobilization is often associated with a heightened sense of nationalism and surges in patriotism and pride. Yet one has to ask: Why would a dominant group, comfortably in charge of its own state, bother with identity politics? A dominant group should not need to assert its dominance, unless the circumstances are changing and the ascending group is eroding the group hierarchy. It is the aspirations of the minority, and the "complicity" of some members of the dominant group, that, initially, change the issue salience and have the power to sway political views and polarize polities.

The experimental national prime condition simulated a scenario in which nationality issues are brought to voters' attention and made salient. Who responds to these situational triggers? Radical right voters do not react to identity primes. The experimental condition, by highlighting the ethnic nature of a state, elicited a sense of urgency among the minority and their allies. The shift in views occurred after nationality was evoked among the ethnic voters and voters of pro-minority mainstream parties.

Legitimization of minority demands then awakens the radical right supporters and mobilizes them to push back. The explanation examined here derives theoretical predictions from the backlash mechanism and can account for the seemingly puzzling empirical evidence that radical right parties can coexist and flourish alongside both moderate and nationalistic proximate competitors (cf. Bale 2003; Bustikova and Kitschelt 2009; Kitschelt and McGann 1995; Vachudova 2008b; Pop-Eleches 2010). The evidence confirms the crucial role of minority accommodation in accounting for variation in individual-level support for radical right parties, but also shows that nationalism itself is indeterminate. Political competition may be inundated with nationalism, but that need not translate into success for the radical right party. Political favoritism toward minorities coupled with economic anxieties viewed through the prism of majority–minority relations, and the resultant political backlash, provides a crucial mechanism that transforms garden-variety nationalism into a force for radical right party success.

# 5 | Mobilization against Russians in Ukraine

[Any] Russian bears responsibility for the crime of Russification, for the coercive replacement of the Ukrainian language with Russian, for the forced decision of many Ukrainians to abandon their language and culture.

—Oleh Tyahnybok, Leader of the Svoboda (Freedom) Party, Ukraine, 2006[1]

What is the fate of radical right parties in democracies with unfinished nation building, where large ethnic groups have coexisted for centuries?[2] The mechanism of backlash against an aspiring group that uses political channels to change the status quo should apply equally in an environment of under-institutionalized party systems. Chapter 4 on Slovakia demonstrated that the radical right party can be successful in the presence of a small but politically organized ethnic minority. It explored a situation when the radical right party and its bilateral opposite compete on the issue of minority accommodation and over the "status elevation" of a minority group.

The weakness of the radical right in Ukraine illustrates a puzzling case of an electoral failure of radical right parties in polities plagued by economic insecurity, vast corruption, fluid party systems and unfinished state and nation building. In Ukraine, the status of the dominant group is not clear due to the presence of a large (Russian) minority, a former ruler in some parts of the country. And yet, despite the messiness of the underlying conditions, when political forces backing Russian minority rights peacefully mobilized, the radical right seized the moment. Naturally, in countries with large minorities, a large and a politically organized ethnic minority has the ability to threaten the dominant nationality with a "status reversal." This presents unique

---

[1] Cited in Rudakov (2006).
[2] This chapter benefited from help and comments from Andreas Umland and Mark von Hagen.

challenges to radical right parties. If the security threat is imminent and credible, a small party is in no position to address it. Therefore, large-scale, looming threats benefit powerful mainstream parties if they are viewed as having the expertise and political power to avert the reversal.

Whereas Chapter 4 explored the micro-level determinants of the radical right party's success in Slovakia, this chapter provides a micro-level assessment of the electoral support for the radical right party in Ukraine, a country where Russians comprise between 17 and 20 percent of the population, but where there has not been a nationally successful radical right party since the adoption of the country's Declaration of Independence in 1991, with one remarkable exception in 2012.

The Euromaidan events of late 2013 catapulted the previously marginal radical right party, the All-Ukrainian Union Svoboda (the "Freedom Party"), to short-lived prominence. Representatives of the Svoboda party have occupied cabinet posts in the interim government, which has increased anxiety among pro-Russia leaders and citizens. After the annexation of Crimea by Russia and the outbreak of the conflict in Donbas, in the October 2014 elections, Svoboda lost half of its previous support, failed to cross the 5 percent threshold and obtained no seats in the parliament on the nationwide lists and only six seats on the constituency list. It is yet to be seen whether this represents a temporary setback or a more permanent electoral failure.[3] Regardless of the results of the most recent parliamentary elections, in 2012, at its apex, Svoboda amassed over 10 percent of votes in a national election, which is an impressive electoral result for any radical right party across Eastern Europe.

Scholars have attributed Svoboda's 2012 achievement in the parliamentary elections to a complex set of factors, including dissatisfaction with the major parties, protest voting against President Yanukovych, resonance of anti-establishment appeals with the voters,

---

[3] In the October 25, 2015, local elections, Svoboda performed above expectations and gained traction not only in its traditional stronghold in the West, but in Central Ukraine as well. The turnout in the local elections was between 41 and 51 percent. Svoboda won city elections in Ternopil (31%), and was third in Lviv city (12.5%). It obtained 14 percent of the vote in the Lviv region and 20 percent in Ternopil region. It performed very well in the city of Kyiv (11%) and Kyiv region (8%). Source: Central Electoral Commission of Ukraine 2015, also Dubovyk 2015.

disappointment with economic and political corruption, xenophobia, economic downturn and the reemergence of pre-war legacies (Cantorovich 2013; Kuzio 2007; Likhachev 2013; Moser 2013; Polyakova 2014; Shekhovtsov 2011, 2015; Umland 2013; Umland and Shekhovtsov 2013).[4] All of these factors were undoubtedly valid by creating a perfect storm.

At the center of the storm, however, were anxieties associated with the 2012 language law. The controversy that surrounded the adoption of the language law (2010–2012) was a situation when the demands of the Russian minority created a powerful backlash between Ukrainian nationalists. The radical right party succeeded in the 2012 parliamentary elections due to the high level of polarization on the language issue and the fact that Svoboda's mainstream competitor (led by the former Prime Minister Tymoshenko) was fragile and unpopular.[5] Svoboda could credibly channel the anger associated with the expansion of minority rights for ethnic Russians and Russian speakers in a situation when the mainstream party, more capable of reversing the threat of status reversal, was weakened.

Using an original micro-level survey designed by the author, this chapter analyzes the profile of voters for the radical right party, Svoboda, and compares them with voters of other parties. The survey was conducted before the national electoral breakthrough of Svoboda in 2012, during the time of heightened contestation over the rights of the Russian minority. The chapter provides context to understand the radical right in Ukraine and unpacks the relationship between status reversal, attitudes toward minority accommodation, and electoral prospects for the radical right in Ukraine.

---

[4] The Svoboda party has been characterized as an ethno-centric and anti-Semitic party: "Svoboda is a racist party promoting explicitly ethnocentric and anti-Semitic ideas. Its main programmatic points are Russo- and xenophobia as well as, more recently, a strict anti-immigration stance. It is an outspoken advocate of an uncritical heroization of the Organization of Ukrainian Nationalists – an interwar and World War II ultra-nationalist party tainted by its temporary collaboration with the Third Reich, as well as its members' participation in genocidal actions against Poles and Jews, in western Ukraine, during German occupation. Although Svoboda emphasizes the European character of the Ukrainian people, it is an anti-Western, anti-liberal, and anti-EU grouping" (Umland 2010: 1).

[5] Yulia Tymoshenko was imprisoned from 2011 to 2014 on charges of embezzlement. Furthermore, in 2011 blocs of political parties were not allowed to participate, which prevented Tymoshenko's party from filing in some districts.

## 5.1 Accommodation of the Russian Minority

In 2009, a representative survey showed that 41 percent of Ukrainians believed that the Ukrainian language should be the only state language and that more than half of Ukrainian respondents did not even consider the language issue to be critical (*Kyiv Post* 2009). When Ukraine joined the Council of Europe in 1995, it was required to sign the European Charter for Regional or Minority Languages (Fedotov 2015). Ukraine signed the charter in 1996, but it did not enter into force until 2006 due to problems with ratification. The spirit of the charter was to protect endangered languages. However, the Russian language was already widely used by both ethnic Ukrainians and ethnic Russians. The charter provided an opportunity to strengthen the position of the Russian language in areas where it had already achieved (spoken) dominance. Unintentionally, it became "the most important instrument for the promotion of the Russian [language] in Ukraine" (Moser 2013: 71), and enabled its suporters to advocate for it to be granted official status as a second state language.

This policy ultimately benefited ethnic Russians and created a backlash among Ukrainian nationalists. Figure 5.1 depicts attitudes toward granting the Russian language an official status. Until roughly 2010, most Ukrainians were sanguine about the possibility, but after the aggressive push for Russian language rights, public opinion has shifted and polarized. This sudden shift corresponds to the backlash against aggressive policies pursued by Russophile Azarov government appointed by Viktor Yanukovych in 2010, which enabled the subsequent nation-wide success of the radical right party Svoboda in 2012.

Russian speakers have been losing ground in Ukraine since Ukraine declared independence in 1991. Article 10 of the Ukrainian Constitution states that Ukrainian is the state language, but the constitution also guarantees and explicitly protects Russian and other languages of national minorities (e.g., Tatar, Hungarian, Polish). In 1991, the number of students in primary and secondary schools studying Ukrainian and Russian was roughly equal (Olszański 2012: 24).[6] However, schooling in the Russian language was more prevalent in the south and the east, reflecting deep historical cleavages.

---

[6] In 1991, 97.6 percent of children in the (Western) Ternopil district studied in Ukrainian compared with only 3.3 percent in the Donetsk district (source: Olszański 2012, from Eberhardt 1994: 247).

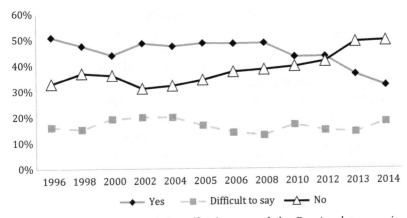

**Figure 5.1** Attitudes toward the official status of the Russian language in Ukraine, 1996–2014.

*Note*: Responses to "other" and "N/A" are not included. Question: Do you think it is necessary that the Russian language is awarded an official status in the Ukraine?

*Source*: Representative surveys by the Institute of Sociology, National Academy of Sciences, Ukraine; Results of National Surveys 1992–2014, "Ukrainian Society: Monitoring Social Change," p. 65

Already in 1787, only three years after the establishment of Lviv University, the Ukrainian language obtained the status of a regional language in territories of Galicia, which historically belonged to Austria-Hungary. The southeastern territories in Ukraine under the Russian empire had a different experience. In 1863, Russia prohibited publication of all Ukrainian-language books (with some minor exceptions), claiming that "a separate Little Russian [Ukrainian] language has never existed, does not exist and cannot exist" (Peterson 2014). Despite these historical cleavages (Darden 2014; Peisakhin 2013), schooling in the Ukrainian language was quickly becoming the primary language of instruction in post-1991 Ukraine.

In 1991, 45 percent of schools had Ukrainian as their primary language of instruction and 54 percent had Russian (Malinkovich 2005). By 1999, 67.4 percent children were taught in Ukrainian, and by 2005, 78 percent of pupils were instructed in Ukrainian, and only 21 percent in Russian (Bilaniuk and Melnyk 2008: 353). By 2010, the number of children instructed in Ukrainian increased to 82.1 percent, while the number of Russian-speaking schools dramatically declined, and almost entirely disappeared in western and central Ukraine (Solchanyk 2011).

Table 5.1 depicts a clear trend in regional polarization over schooling. By 2006, the main language of instruction for all elementary and secondary schools in western and central Ukraine was Ukrainian. In the western regions, which include Ternopil, Lviv and Ivan-Frankivsk, the strongholds of Ukrainian nationalism, there was no observable shift in schooling – the Ukrainian language in Galicia and beyond was already deeply embedded. Some shift occurred in central Ukraine, but the most dramatic change occurred in the south and the east. By 2006, there were only three areas where the Russian language still predominated in school instruction: the Autonomous Republic of Crimea and the two (now separatist) regions of Donetsk and Luhansk (cf. Giuliano 2015).

In most of the other Russophile regions, the dominance of Russian instruction was fully reversed in just over a decade (Table 5.1). The everyday usage of Russian did not follow these seismic shifts in schooling, but the writing was on the wall in the south and the east. In 1992, almost 37 percent Ukrainians were speaking mostly Ukrainian at home, and the number increased to 42 percent in 2011, but so did the usage of Russian as a main language spoken at home (from 29 to 35 percent). This signaled increased polarization on language, which was reflected in a decline in the number of those who spoke both languages at home (from 32 percent in 1992 to 22.1 percent in 2010; Solchanyk 2011).

Figure 5.2 depicts the increasing language polarization of the Ukrainian society. While the language cleavage was immediately observable in the schooling of small children, the use of the Russian language at home did not immediately decline as quickly, highlighting Ukraine's public and then private linguistic bifurcation and polarization.[7] Despite the fact that the daily spoken usage of Russian was not under threat, the progression of Ukrainian language schooling created anxieties among Russophiles.

The European Charter for Minority Languages created an opportunity to reverse this trend by adopting policies that would give

---

[7] Figure A5.1 in the Appendix shows shifts in language usage at home and language polarization.

Table 5.1 *Percentage of schoolchildren in elementary and secondary education schools in Ukraine by main language of instruction*

| | 1995–1996 | | 2000–2001 | | 2005–2006 | |
|---|---|---|---|---|---|---|
| | Ukrainian | Russian | Ukrainian | Russian | Ukrainian | Russian |
| **Ukraine** (all regions) | 58 | 41 | 70 | 29 | 78 | 21 |

Southeast Oblasts (regions) and Autonomous Republic (AR)

| | | | | | | |
|---|---|---|---|---|---|---|
| AR Crimea | 0.1 | 99.5 | 0.9 | 97 | 5 | 93 |
| Sevastopol city | 0 | 99.9 | 2 | 98 | 2 | 98 |
| Donetsk | 6 | 94 | 14 | 86 | 29 | 71 |
| Luhansk | 9 | 91 | 17 | 83 | 34 | 66 |
| Dnipropetrovsk | 46 | 54 | 68 | 32 | 78 | 22 |
| Zaporizhia | 31 | 69 | 45 | 55 | 60 | 40 |
| Kharkiv | 37 | 63 | 55 | 45 | 71 | 29 |
| Mykolaiv | 56 | 44 | 74 | 26 | 87 | 13 |
| Odesa | 32 | 66 | 47 | 51 | 65 | 33 |
| Kherson | 60 | 40 | 76 | 24 | 83 | 17 |

Central Regions

| | | | | | | |
|---|---|---|---|---|---|---|
| Vinnytsia | 91 | 9 | 98 | 2 | 99 | 1 |
| Kyiv | 92 | 8 | 97 | 3 | 99 | 1 |
| Kyiv city | 70 | 30 | 93 | 7 | 96 | 4 |
| Kirovohrad | 75 | 25 | 89 | 11 | 96 | 4 |
| Poltava | 83 | 17 | 93 | 7 | 97 | 3 |
| Cherkasy | 86 | 14 | 96 | 4 | 98 | 2 |
| Chernihiv | 81 | 19 | 94 | 6 | 99 | 1 |
| Sumy | 63 | 37 | 83 | 17 | 93 | 7 |
| Zhytomyr | 86 | 14 | 96 | 4 | 99 | 1 |

Western Regions

| | | | | | | |
|---|---|---|---|---|---|---|
| Volyn | 98 | 2 | 99 | 1 | 99.7 | 0.3 |
| Rivne | 99 | 1 | 99.7 | 0.3 | 99.9 | 0.1 |
| Khmelnytskyi | 92 | 8 | 98 | 2 | 99.3 | 0.4 |
| Ternopil | 99 | 1 | 99.7 | 0.3 | 99.8 | 0.2 |
| Lviv | 96 | 4 | 98 | 2 | 99 | 1 |
| Ivano-Frankivsk | 98 | 2 | 99 | 1 | 99.7 | 0.2 |
| Chernivtsi | 78 | 5 | 81 | 2 | 81 | 0.7 |
| Zakarpatia | 84 | 4 | 86 | 2 | 86 | 1 |

*Note*: Percentage of schoolchildren in elementary and secondary education schools in Ukraine, by main language of instruction (Ukrainian or Russian), in the 1995–1996, 2000–2001, and 2005–2006 academic years (Ministry of Statistics of Ukraine, 2006). *Source*: Bilaniuk and Melnyk 2008: 353 (cf. Malinkovich 2005).

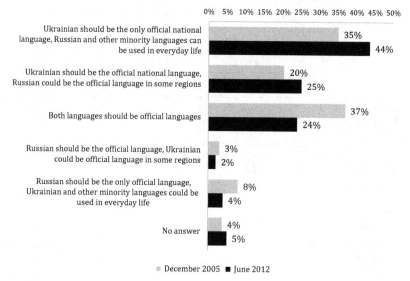

**Figure 5.2** What form of coexistence should exist in Ukraine for the Ukrainian and Russian languages?
*Source*: Razumkov Center 2012

Russophile parents more choices over schooling options. It was also an opportunity to create barriers to the further spread of the Ukrainian language. The status of the Russian language was never legally clear, but the controversial Charter for Minority Languages proved to be useful as a justification for challenging the status of the Ukrainian language, mostly at the local level.

In 2006, after the charter was finally approved after a long series of challenges, the regional councils of Donetsk and Luhansk, along with ten additional city/regional councils, voted for resolutions granting the Russian language an official regional status. This led to yet more protracted legal battles (Bilaniuk and Melnyk 2008: 350; Fedotov 2015: 15) and sparked the anger of the Congress of Ukrainian Nationalists (KUN, the nationalist predecessor of Svoboda), which called on the government to defend the Ukrainian nation and language (Umland and Shekhovtsov 2013).

The language issue escalated with the ascendance to power in 2010 of President Viktor Yanukovych, the former governor of Donetsk and an opponent of the leaders of the Orange Revolution. His Party of Regions ran on the platform of "one nation – two languages" (Olszański 2012).[8] President Yanukovych never delivered on his promise of language parity, but his administration aggressively promoted the use of the Russian language. He appointed a highly controversial historian, the Russian nationalist Dmytro Tabachnyk, to be the Minister of Education. This was viewed as "a spit in the face" to the residents of Galicia, a western region known for its Ukrainian nationalism and the widespread use of the Ukrainian language.[9] The period between 2010 and 2012 entailed vicious fighting over the language law (On Principles of the State Language Policy) in Ukraine, and led in 2012 to the adoption of a controversial language law in the parliament. A violent brawl even erupted during the debate between the MPs. After the law was passed, protests, marches and hunger strikes arose in central and western Ukraine, while the eastern regions of Luhansk, Donetsk and Crimean Simferopol celebrated. By 2012, public opinion had shifted – almost 37 percent supported giving Russian the status of the official language in 2005, and only 24 percent supported language parity in 2012 (Figure 5.2). At the same time, support for Ukrainian as the only language increased (Figure 5.2).

As the leaders of the Orange Revolution (2004/5), Yulia Tymoshenko and Viktor Yushchenko, were bickering and accusing each other of betraying their political principles, and as the Party of Regions was gaining strength, the radical right Svoboda party broke through in local elections in core Galician districts in 2010. Svoboda's success was helped by the fact that Yulia Tymoshenko's party, Svoboda's ideological "cousin," could not register for elections in some districts due to the changes in the electoral law. In 2012, after obtaining more than 10 percent of the popular vote, Svoboda obtained seats in the parliament – the first time since first 1991 that an independently run radical right party attained representation in the Ukrainian Parliament.

The Party of Regions, Lytvyn bloc and the Communist Party of Ukraine led by Petro Symonenko proposed the controversial draft of the Language Law in September 2010, two years before the general elections. On the surface, the law promoted the establishment of regional languages, which would greatly benefit Russian speakers, but it opened the way for establishing the Russian language as a second

---

[8] President Kuchma, who was elected in 1994, promised that Russian will gain the status of an official language, but after the election he backpedaled on his promises (Shulman 2005).
[9] Interviews in Lviv, Ukraine, summers of 2011, 2014 and 2016.

official language. Symonenko's Communist party, a (smaller) ally of the Party of Regions that was more extreme in its policy views, can be thought of as a bilateral opposite to Svoboda on language issues.[10] In 2012, Symonenko stated clearly that "out of all the political parties ... we [the Communist party] were consistently ... defending the idea that is essential to solve ... the question of Russian as a second state language" (Symonenko 2012). The protracted fight over the language law resonated strongly in western Ukraine and polarized the political scene.

After the fall of Yulia Tymoshenko, the Communist Party of Symonenko participated in the first caretaker government under Mykola Azarov (2010–2012), who led a three-party coalition under the leadership of the Party of Regions, and started working on a new language law. As opposed to the Party of Regions, the Communist Party voter base was less centrist, more ethnic Russian and geographically rooted in Crimea and the Donbas region in the east. The party's platform has evolved over time from Soviet to ethnic nationalism. Although the party has been vocal about the rights of ethnic minorities, it has always been adversarial to the rights of Crimean Tatars, and has always been mainly interested in promoting the Russian language, not the language rights of other minorities. Prime Minister Azarov filled his cabinet with Russophiles.[11] In July 2011, the Lviv regional council sent an appeal to President Yanukovych complaining that Azarov, as well as other prominent members of his administration, were violating the constitution because they were not using the Ukrainian language when conducting their duties in the office (Ukrainian News 2011). In 2012, when the law was passed, after scheming in the parliament, Azarov declared that the new law was a "reaction to the Russian language oppression" (Poliglotti4.eu 2012). The law polarized native Russian and native Ukrainian speakers. For most native Ukrainian speakers the law was unacceptable and 46 percent were very strongly opposed to it.[12]

[10] The Communist party, which has been outlawed in 2014/2015 in the post-Maidan pushback, has drawn on Soviet nostalgia and the electoral support of ethnic Russians in the eastern regions.

[11] According to Moser (2013: 118), however, Azarov began learning Ukrainian in 2010.

[12] Figure A5.2 in the Appendix shows attitudes toward the use of regional languages in the 2012 language law.

The law enjoyed overwhelming support among native Russian speakers. In less than a few years, an issue that was dormant soared to national prominence. The Party of Regions, with its even more extreme allies, decided to push the law through at any cost rather than adopt a more consensual approach, which infuriated Ukrainian patriots, especially in Galicia, which had spearheaded the fight for Ukrainian language, culture and dominance in the new state.

It is no surprise that among the first protesters against passing the language law in 2012 was the Lviv City Council, which was controlled by Svoboda. It declared the language law to be invalid on the territory of the Lviv region (Kyiv Post 2012a), questioned the legality of the law due to procedural violations and contested its constitutionality. Iryna Farion, Lviv's Regional Council deputy from Svoboda and a well-known advocate for the Ukrainian language, initiated the protest.[13] Two Galician regions joined the protest as well – the Ivano-Frankivsk City Council refused to recognize the law and the Ternopil Regional Council declared the law invalid and asked the constitutional court to annul it (Kyiv Post 2012b). Two prominent universities that are widely viewed as promoting Ukrainian culture and language, Kyiv Mohyla Academy and Lviv's Ukrainian Catholic University, criticized the constitutionality of the law and cited violations of voting procedures (Moser 2013: 354).

The battles over the expansion of the usage of the Russian language, which started in 2006 with the adoption of the European Charter for Minority Languages and led to unilateral declarations of Russian being the official language at the local level in the southeast, mobilized the radical elements among Ukrainian patriots as never before since independence in 1991.

Considering the electoral weakness of the Communist Party (Svoboda's bilateral opposite) and its lack of ideological extremism vis-à-vis the Party of Regions, one would not expect a strong radical right party to arise. Although Symonenko's Communist Party wanted Russian to be the second official language in Ukraine, and accused Ukrainian nationalists of fascism, electoral support for the Communist Party in 2006 and 2007 was only around 4 percent of

---

[13] Iryna Farion stirred a controversy during her visit to a kindergarten in Lviv on International Mother Language/Native Language Day (February 21, 2010) because she scolded five-year-old children for referring to themselves with Russian-sounding first names.

the popular vote.[14] The position of the Party of Regions on the status of the Russian language as a second official language was similar to the position of the Communist Party, yet the Party of Regions did not propose any law, despite its campaign promises, to elevate the status of Russian to a second official language. Yanukovych delegated the authority to determine the status of the Russian language to local authorities, and allowed the use of documentation in Russian, if the number of Russian speakers exceeded 10 percent in a region (Masalkova 2010).[15]

Although many fringe radical right parties have emerged in Ukraine since the early 1990s – for example, KUN (Konhres Ukrayinskykh natsionalistiv), UNA (Ukrainska natsionalna asambleya), OUN (Orhanizatsiya Ukrayinskykh natsionalistiv) and recently Pravyi Sektor – their electoral support has rarely exceeded 3 percent of the popular vote (Birch 2000; D'Anieri and Kuzio 2007; Kubicek 1999; Kuzio 1997; Shekhovtsov 2011; Solchanyk 1999; Umland and Shekhovtsov 2010; Wilson 1997).[16] In March 2009, however, Svoboda obtained 35 percent of the popular vote in the Western Ukrainian Ternopil regional council election (Shekhovtsov 2011).[17]

[14] Everything else equal, the theory predicts that a weak bilateral opposite leads to a weak radical right party. The Communist party, however, participated in the first Russophile Azarov government (2010–2012). The Communist party had strong support before 2006 but it was operating in a different institutional environment, which hindered the chances of a radical right party, a niche contender, to enter. After independence, Ukraine adopted a presidential system and shifted to a presidential-parliamentary form of government in 1996. Between 1997 and 2002 Ukraine had a semi-proportional electoral law (single member districts combined with proportional representation) with a 4 percent threshold. After 2002, Ukraine adopted a proportional system with a 3 percent threshold, which was lifted to 5 percent for elections in 2012 (Christensen et al. 2005). Therefore, for the 2012 election, the electoral system was a mixed semi-proportional system (single member districts and nationwide proportional system with a higher threshold).

[15] The language cleavage is salient in Latvia as well, as discussed earlier. In a 2012 referendum, Latvians rejected Russian as a second language (Herszenhorn 2012).

[16] Other electoral blocs and movements that embraced radical right ideology were the National Front (Natsionalnyi Front), Fewer Words bloc (Menshe sliv) and Social-National Assembly with its recently established paramilitary wing, the Azov battalion.

[17] The extremist Congress of Ukrainian Nationalists (KUN), one of many Svoboda's ideological predecessors, ran under the platform of Yushchenko's "Our Ukraine" (Kuzio 1997). Between 2002 and 2006, once elected to Verkhovna Rada for the Lviv district, Andriy Shkil (UNA leader) joined the Yulia Tymoshenko bloc faction (UNA-UNSO 2009; Verchovnaya Rada 2009).

Ternopil, in Western Ukraine, was part of the second Polish republic during World War II and is the site of the Huta Pieniacka village massacre of 500–1,000 ethnic Poles in 1944. Polish scholars have linked members of the patriotic Ukrainian Insurgent Army to the massacre. In 1989, a controversial monument to the massacre was built, then destroyed and then rebuilt in 2005. The Svoboda party vehemently opposed the monument and has been vocal in its opposition to Polish-Ukrainian reconciliation since 2003 (Olszański 2011).[18] In 2007, a new monument was unveiled in the presence of the Polish consul in Lviv. Svoboda's leader, Oleh Tyahnybok, sent a note of protest. On February 28, 2009, Ukrainian President Viktor Yushchenko and Polish President Lech Kaczyński met to commemorate the sixty-fifth anniversary of the massacre. Less than a month later, in March 2009, Svoboda made its first major inroads into Ukrainian politics in the Ternopil regional election.[19] Although Svoboda failed to gain national appeal in the presidential election in 2010, it has emerged as a serious political force in Western Ukraine.[20]

[18] Currently, however, Poland is one the strongest supporters of Ukraine's territorial integrity in the European Union.

[19] The pattern was similar in Poland and the Czech Republic before the first outbreak of a radical right party. The Polish Institute of National Remembrance, for example, challenged the historical narrative of the Jedwabne pogrom in 1941. It was long assumed that the murder of Jews was an act committed by Germans and not Poles. The Institute's findings presaged the emergence of the League of Polish Families, which immediately sought to revise the historical record in favor of one in which Poles were victims not victimizers. Similarly, in 1991, then presidential candidate Václav Havel suggested that Czechs should apologize for the expulsion of Sudeten Germans in 1945–1947. The radical Czech Republicans soon emerged to challenge the charge and successfully tapped into anti-German fears, garnering 6 percent of the vote and fourteen seats in the parliament. Radical parties, in these instances, offered a flattering historical narrative and a combative defense of national pride. This is, however, a strategy for a short-term success since, in order to gain a wider appeal, radical right parties have to appeal to the sentiments against accommodation of politically organized minorities, not historical grievances.

[20] Svoboda's regional success in Ternopil has been attributed mostly to its ability to exploit battles over nationalist policies between the Party of Regions and the parties of the Orange bloc (Kudelia 2011; Olszański 2011; Shekhovtsov 2013; Umland and Shekhovtsov 2010). Svoboda also benefited due to support from V. Yushchenko and hostility toward Y. Tymoshenko/BYuT.

As a testament to the importance of this "regional breakthrough" (Kitschelt and McGann 1995: 99–100), the second wave of Svoboda's success occurred in the national election in October 2012. In 2012, Svoboda was the first radical right party to independently win seats in the parliament. Svoboda won 10.4 percent of the popular vote and thirty-six out of 450 seats. Its regional breakthrough in western Ukraine and its success in national elections set the stage for its third success in the interim government (immediately preceded by Svoboda's activism during the Maidan protests in Kyiv).[21] In addition to holding 8 percent of the seats in the parliament in the 2012–2014 electoral cycle, Svoboda held four of the twenty posts in the interim government, which was established after the ouster of President Yanukovych.

After the Euromaidan events in 2013, Svoboda backed the abolition of the 2012 language law in the parliament in February 2014 and advocated for banning all Russian-language media in Ukraine. Since February 2014, the language law issue has come into the spotlight yet again. The Rada voted to abolish the 2012 law that allowed for the use of regional languages, and the law was a sticking point in negotiations between the Ukrainian government and eastern separatists.[22]

In March 2014, the regional administration of the Luhansk Oblast demanded that the Russian language be given official status (Gazeta 2014), and in April 2014, the Kharkiv Regional Council followed suit (Interfax 2014). President Poroshenko proposed a peace plan on June 20, 2014, that included the protection of the Russian language within Ukraine. Even though the Rada abolished the law in February 2014, the repeal of the law was not signed by the acting President Turchynov nor by President Petro Poroshenko. Public opinion from that time period suggests the deepening geographic polarization of Ukraine over the status of the Russian language.[23]

---

[21] Although active in the Euromaidan events, other groups such as Pravyi Sector gained prominence as well. Svoboda organized busing of volunteers from Lviv to Kyiv during the protests. (Source: interviews of the author with Svoboda activists, summer 2014, Lviv). Pravyi Sektor and the Social National Assembly have surpassed Svoboda's activism by forming more prominent volunteer battalions to fight in the East.

[22] February 26, 2014: Russia Demands OSCE Condemn Ukraine Language Law Plans.

[23] See Figure A5.3 in the Appendix, on attitudes toward the language situation in May 2014.

In October 2014, Svoboda was not perceived as a political force sufficiently competent to address the danger of the military threat from Russia, and its electoral support was halved.[24] Svoboda was also embroiled in corruption scandals at the local level (especially in Lviv), and numerous Svoboda members were investigated after a grenade was thrown in front of the Verkhovna Rada in early 2015.[25] The serious security crisis drew the Ukrainian electorate toward more hawkish characters, such as Oleh Lyashko and his Radical Party. Although voters concerned with sovereignty threats are sympathetic to Svoboda, the party does not have the required military muscle nor the political competence to deal with issues of national safety.

The evidence that voters flock to mainstream, radicalized parties in dangerous times comes from a survey conducted by the author in May 2016. Table 5.2 shows that those who "strongly agree" with the statement that Ukrainian sovereignty is threatened by Russia vote for the parties of the patriotic right: the party of the President (Poroshenko), the party of the former Orange revolution leader Tymoshenko (Batkivshchyna), the party with links to voluntary battalions in Donbas (Oleh Lyashko Radical Party), and the party with links to Lviv and Western Ukraine (Samopomich). In sum, the severe security threat in Ukraine did not strengthen the radical right in Ukraine; quite the contrary.[26]

Due to security fears after the annexation of Crimea in March 2014 and the outbreak of a separatist violence in the Donbas region fueled by Russia, Svoboda was no longer viewed as credible enough to avert threats. I visited Lviv in the summer of 2014 and it was clear that Svoboda had fallen asleep at the wheel. While stands in the public square of the more militant Right Sector mushroomed near the Taras Shevchenko statue in the center of the city and activists were recruiting young volunteers for the conflict in Eastern Ukraine that had just erupted, Svoboda had limited physical presence in the city and, more importantly, was committed to its pre-war ideological platform. I discussed the electoral strategy for the upcoming 2014 election with

---

[24] The party failed to cross the threshold to obtain nationwide seats and obtained only six constituency seats in the Rada.

[25] The party performed well in the regional and city elections in 2015, not only in the Western regions but also in the Kyiv region as well.

[26] It also led to the surge in support of candidates, across many parties that had direct combat experience in Donbas.

Table 5.2 *Distribution of respondents who "strongly agreed" with the statement that "Russia threatens Ukrainian sovereignty" by parties (May 2016)*

| | |
|---|---|
| All-Ukrainian Union–Batkivshchyna party (large mainstream party, Orange revolution party successor) | 23.13% |
| Oleh Lyashko Radical Party (radicalized mainstream party) | 12.93% |
| Union–Samopomich party (mainstream party with links to Lviv and Western Ukraine) | 12.24% |
| Petro Poroshenko bloc party (large mainstream party of the president) | 11.56% |
| All-Ukrainian Union–Svoboda party (radical right) | 11.56% |
| *Other Parties* | 6.80% |
| "Civil Position" party | 4.76% |
| "Opposition's bloc" party (large mainstream opposition party) | 4.08% |
| "Movement for Cleaning" party | 4.08% |
| "People's Front" party (A. Yatseniuk) | 4.08% |
| "National Movement of Dmytro Yarosh" party (radical right) | 2.72% |
| "People's Control" party | 2.04% |
| | 100% |

*Note*: The question reads: "These days, I am afraid that Ukrainian sovereignty is threatened by Russia."
*Source*: Bustikova 2016a.

Svoboda activists and a Svoboda ideologue. The platform that the party was planning on putting forward was focused on strengthening the Ukrainian culture, lustration laws, decentralization, media quotas for publishing books in Russian and tightening quotas for radio and TV broadcasts in the Russian language. We discussed issues of volunteering in the military conflict in Donbas at the personal level, but an aggressive creation of a volunteer battalion in Donbas was not a prominent party strategy.

In the fall of 2014, voters rallied behind President Poroshenko's party and other parties, which embraced many of the policies that Svoboda had advocated in its campaign during the summer of 2014 – the Communist Party was banned in 2015; the Rada passed a lustration bill in 2014; the language law of 2012 was put in a stalemate; and decentralization became a mainstream issue debated by all parties and international bodies. Svoboda was weakened, but it remained an active part of the Ukrainian radical right scene with a strong voter base. The radicalized mainstream adopted the agenda of the Svoboda party and, very importantly, was able to respond to a looming security crisis in Ukraine.[27]

When the distinction between minority accommodation and status reversal in majority–minority relations becomes blurred, radical right parties do poorly. However, when a segment of the electorate, in this case western Galicia, views minority accommodation with indignation, the radical right is well positioned to succeed, particularly when parties that could avert status reversal were not available, as was the case in Ukraine, due to the changes in the electoral law and criminal prosecution of the leadership of the Orange Revolution. The next section explores the determinants of the backlash dynamic in peaceful times.

## 5.2 Empirical Analysis

To test the propositions outlined in this book, the analysis considers three major types of threats to the dominant group: policy threats, group hostility threats related to identity and economic threats. *Policy threats* are defined as an objection to more governmental spending on different ethnic groups in Ukraine, including Ukrainians. I hypothesized that Svoboda voters and sympathizers would oppose government spending on Russians.[28] The second group of threats, *group hostility*, relate to identity. Given the history of anti-Semitic and anti-Russian statements that Tyahnybok, the leader of the Svoboda party, has made in public, one might assume that voters who express more group hostility against minorities (Jews and Russians) would be more likely to support Svoboda.[29] I expect that policy hostility, not group hostility,

---

[27] On the comparison of the Orange Revolution and Euromaidan, see Popova 2014.

[28] Russians are considered a national minority but a linguistic majority in some regions. According to the Ukrainian census of 2001, over 17 percent of Ukrainians self-identified as ethnic Russians and almost 30 percent as Russian speakers. The number of Russians and Russian speakers geographically varies. In the eastern regions of Luhansk and Donetsk, the percentage of ethnic Russians was close to 40 percent and Russian speakers were in a majority (70%). In Crimea, Russians and Russian speakers were also a majority (source: Ukrainian census 2001).

[29] Anti-Semitism is associated with Svoboda ideology (Cantorovich 2013; Kersten and Hankel 2013).

explains radical right voting. Finally, *economic threats* are defined as economic uncertainties and insecurities.

Using an original and nationally representative survey conducted in 2010 across all regions of Ukraine, the analysis shows that political sympathy toward Svoboda is rooted in policy hostility. Contrary to the perception that actual and potential Svoboda voters are exceptionally anti-Russian and xenophobic, the analysis finds that the distinctive feature of Svoboda voters and sympathizers is not their hostility toward Russians, but rather their attitudes toward government support for politicized ethnic groups.[30] Support for Svoboda stems from perceived threats and anxieties about the character of the Ukrainian state rather than inter-group ethnic hostilities (Bustikova 2014; Cantorovich 2013; Olszański 2011; Rudling 2013).[31] The survey sheds light on the period after the regional breakthrough of Svoboda in 2009 and right before Svoboda took seats in the parliament in the electoral cycle of 2012–2014. It offers a unique window into the mindset of voters who declared that they were willing to vote for Svoboda, or harbored a sympathetic view of the Svoboda party, *before* the seminal election of 2012.[32]

---

[30] Furthermore, the analysis uncovers a great degree of polarization related to economic insecurity and fears about the direction of the Ukrainian economy four years before Euromaidan. A more holistic study of Svoboda would also include supply-side factors determining Svoboda's success, such as party finances and corruption of some Svoboda representatives in public office. For example, Svoboda has been accused of obtaining funds both from the organized crime in Lviv and from oligarchs who have used Svoboda as a scarecrow to ramp up support for the Party of Regions, controlled by V. Yanukovych.

[31] The survey was conducted in twenty-six regions, including Crimea and the city of Kyiv: Ivano-Frankivs'ka, Volyns'ka, L'vivs'ka, Rivnens'ka, Ternopil's'ka, Chernigivs'ka, Kyivs'ka, c. Kyiv, Cherkas'ka, Chernivets'ka, Zakarpats'ka, Lugans'ka, Vinnyts'ka, Dnipropetrovs'ka, Donets'ka, Zhytomyrs'ka, Zaporiz'ka, Kirovograds'ka, Mykolayivs'ka, Odes'ka, Poltavs'ka, Sums'ka, Kharkivs'ka, Khersons'ka, Khmel'nyts'ka oblasts and AR Crimea.

[32] The scope of the survey is focused on demand-side factors, such as the ideational and socio-demographic determinants of Svoboda support. Although Ukrainian party system is highly volatile and programmatic structuration is weaker than in the West, the Ukrainian electorate is ideationally polarized on issues of ethnicity, poverty and the process of nation building. Regional polarization between East and West has historical and cultural roots (Arel 1995; Darden 2014; Darden and Grzymala-Busse 2006; Fournier 2002; Peisakhin 2013; Shevel 2002; but cf. Frye 2015).

### 5.2.1 Data Description

To examine who votes for the Svoboda party and who sympathizes with it, I designed a survey instrument, which was implemented by the Kiev International Institute of Sociology (KIIS) in June 2010 and employed a stratified, multistage area probability sample (KIIS 2010).[33] The sample was representative of the entire adult population of Ukraine, and included more than two thousand respondents. Since the purpose of the survey was to determine the appeal of the Svoboda party among a broad electorate, I also included a question about a hypothetical vote to identify potential Svoboda sympathizers. This question was asked only if the respondent did not intend to vote for Svoboda. The purpose of the question was to identify a pool of potential Svoboda voters.

"Hypothetically, if you had a chance to cast a second ballot in the elections to the Verkhovna Rada of Ukraine on the nearest Sunday, would you ever consider voting for: All-Ukrainian community Svoboda (O. Tyahnybok)?" (Svoboda *sympathizer*: Yes; Svoboda *opponent*: No)

Most respondents (1,634) declared that they would not consider voting for Svoboda if they had an additional vote. I refer to these respondents as Svoboda opponents. More than 200 respondents declared that they would vote for Svoboda or consider casting a second, hypothetical vote for Svoboda. Some 177 respondents did not answer or were undecided. Table 5.3 shows the distribution of voters, sympathizers and opponents by party affiliation.

---

[33] Funding for the survey was provided by Duke University. The target population was defined as the resident adult population age eighteen and older. The sample of households from which sample persons were selected was based on randomly sampled postal districts within proportionally sampled settlements. In the first stage, 110 primary sampling units were selected with probability proportional to size from cities, villages and rural counties. Urban and rural populations in this sample were represented proportionally of all twenty-four oblasts and Crimea. In the second stage, a sample of postal districts was chosen randomly from the list of residential postal districts within 110 primary sampling units. In the third stage, a randomized-number rule was used to select the street, household and apartment that the interviewer was to visit. Source: KIIS 2010. The 2016 survey was funded by Arizona State University.

Table 5.3 *Voters and sympathizers of Svoboda party*

| | Voters | | Would cast second ballot for Svoboda | | |
| | | | (Svoboda sympathizers) | | |
| | | | | Yes | No |
| | % | N | % Yes | N | N |
| All-Ukrainian community Svoboda (O. Tyagnybock) | 2.56 | 52 | | | |
| Anatoliy Hrytsenko's bloc "Gromadjans'ka pozicija" | 0.99 | 20 | 33.33 | 6 | 12 |
| Arseniy Yatseniuk's bloc "Front zmin" | 3.75 | 76 | 22.06 | 15 | 53 |
| Vitali Klitschko's bloc | 1.33 | 27 | 23.81 | 5 | 16 |
| Volodimir Litvin's bloc | 1.18 | 24 | 14.29 | 3 | 18 |
| "Narodna samooborona" bloc (Y. Lutcenko) | 0.20 | 4 | 66.67 | 2 | 1 |
| Juliya Timoshenko's bloc | 11.09 | 225 | 30.95 | 65 | 145 |
| Communist Party of Ukraine (P. Simonenko) | 2.71 | 55 | 1.96 | 1 | 50 |
| Narodniy Ruh of Ukraine (B. Tarasyuk) | 0.10 | 2 | 0 | 0 | 2 |
| Party of Regions (V. Yanukovych) | 38.91 | 789 | 1.50 | 11 | 720 |
| "Our Ukraine" party (V. Yuschenko) | 0.69 | 14 | 53.85 | 7 | 6 |
| "Strong Ukraine" party (S. Tigipko) | 7.10 | 144 | 5.43 | 7 | 122 |
| Progressive Socialist Party of Ukraine (N. Vitrenko) | 0.10 | 2 | 0 | 0 | 2 |
| Socialist Party of Ukraine (O. Moroz) | 0.20 | 4 | 25 | 1 | 3 |
| Ukrainian People's Party (Y. Kostenko) | 0.10 | 2 | 100 | 2 | 0 |
| Another party/bloc | 0.10 | 2 | 0 | 0 | 2 |
| I would vote against them all | 7.64 | 155 | 3.57 | 5 | 135 |
| I would abstain from voting | 9.27 | 188 | 4.12 | 7 | 163 |
| Difficult to say | 11.98 | 243 | 8.06 | 17 | 194 |
| Total | 100 | 2,028 | | 154 | 1,644 |

*Note*: The question reads: "If elections to the Verkhovna Rada of Ukraine were to take place on the nearest Sunday, would you vote? What choice would you make?"

Whereas about 2.5 percent of voters in the survey declared that they would have casted their vote for Svoboda, the number of "Svoboda sympathizers" was roughly three times larger. Jointly, voters and sympathizers constituted roughly 9 percent of the sample. This is approximately consistent with the electoral results from the national elections of 2012, in which the Svoboda party received 10 percent of the vote and subsequently obtained 8 percent of the seats in the parliament. According to the survey, Svoboda sympathizers are concentrated in Tymoshenko's bloc (Svoboda's ideological "cousin") since about one-third of Tymoshenko's voters would be willing to cast a second vote for Svoboda.

Ideologically, Svoboda's position on the status of the Ukrainian and Russian languages is closest to the former political allies of the Orange bloc, represented by leaders Tymoshenko and Yushchenko. Conversely, voters of the Yanukovych's Party of Regions, the Orange bloc's ideological opposite, constitute the least likely pool for potential Svoboda voters (Table 5.3). Although we might expect that Svoboda sympathizers would be located exclusively in ideologically affiliated parties, the second largest pool of sympathizers is found among ideologically footloose voters, followed by Vitali Klitschko bloc voters. Nineteen percent of sympathizers come from those who either would vote against all parties, abstain from voting or are undecided about their party affiliation.

Consistent with the results of local and national elections, Svoboda's support is regionally concentrated. The survey shows a strong regional pattern with support concentrated in Western Ukraine (Table 5.4). According to the survey, Svoboda attracted almost 19 percent of all respondents in its regional stronghold: Lviv. Fifteen percent of Svoboda's voters came from the neighboring Ternopilska and Ivano-Frankivska regions. The vast majority of Svoboda's support comes from regions in western Ukraine that became part of the Soviet Union after the onset of World War II.[34] In three Svoboda strongholds in western Ukraine – Ivano-Frankivska, Volynska and Lvivska oblast – the proportion of Svoboda sympathizers ranged between 30 and 45 percent of all respondents (Table 5.4). The region continues to be Svoboda's stronghold, as demonstrated in the October 2015 local

---

[34] According to Polyakova, Svoboda's success in Lviv can be explained by its ability to recruit students and infiltrate or create civic groups (Polyakova 2014). The number of Svoboda party members is estimated to be between 15,000 and 20,000 but can be as high as 40,000 (Polyakova 2014; Shekhovtsov 2011: 224).

Table 5.4 *Regional distribution of Svoboda voters and sympathizers*

| Svoboda Voters | | | Svoboda Sympathizers | | |
|---|---|---|---|---|---|
| Region (oblast) | N | % out of all respondents from the region | Region (oblast) | N | % out of all respondents from the region |
| L'vivs'ka | 19 | 18.81 | Ivano-Frankivs'ka | 25 | 45.45 |
| Ternopil's'ka | 7 | 15.22 | Volyns'ka | 16 | 37.21 |
| Ivano-Frankivs'ka | 8 | 14.55 | L'vivs'ka | 28 | 27.72 |
| Rivnens'ka | 3 | 6.67 | Rivnens'ka | 9 | 20.00 |
| Volyns'ka | 2 | 4.65 | Ternopil's'ka | 9 | 19.57 |
| Khersons'ka | 2 | 4.17 | Chernigivs'ka | 8 | 14.81 |
| Cherkas'ka | 2 | 3.33 | Kyivs'ka | 11 | 14.47 |
| Vinnyts'ka | 2 | 2.70 | c. Kyiv[a] | 11 | 9.48 |
| Chernivets'ka | 1 | 2.70 | Cherkas'ka | 5 | 8.33 |
| c. Kyiv | 3 | 2.59 | Chernivets'ka | 3 | 8.11 |
| Kirovograds'ka | 1 | 2.08 | Zakarpats'ka | 3 | 6.52 |
| Zaporiz'ka | 1 | 1.19 | Lugans'ka | 6 | 5.45 |
| Dnipropetrovs'ka | 1 | 0.66 | Vinnyts'ka | 4 | 5.41 |
| | | | All other regions[b] | 16 | |
| Total | 52 | | Total | 154 | |

[a] Middle-class voters from Kyiv and the Kyiv region do not fit the electoral profile of a typical Svoboda supporter, who is poorer and resides in a smaller town. Svoboda sympathizers from Kyiv and Kyiv oblast switched to Samopomich, led by a mayor of Lviv, in 2014.

[b] All other regions include all Svoboda sympathizers from one of the following regions: Dnipropetrovs'ka, Donets'ka, Zhytomyrs'ka, Zaporiz'ka, Kirovograds'ka, Mykolayivs'ka, Odes'ka, Poltavs'ka, Sums'ka, Kharkivs'ka, Khersons'ka, Khmel'-nyts'ka oblasts and AR Crimea.

elections in which Svoboda won in the Ternopil city elections and came in third in Lviv.

Identity cleavages in Ukraine are defined both by nationality and language.[35] Ninety percent of Russian nationals in the survey speak

[35] On the role of cross-cutting cleavages in civil and class wars, see Siroky and Hechter 2016.

Table 5.5 *Respondents by nationality and language in Ukraine*

| | Language spoken by respondent | | | |
|---|---|---|---|---|
| Nationality | Ukrainian | Ukrainian and Russian | Russian | Total |
| Ukrainian | 685 | 224 | 652 | 1,561 |
| Russian | 19 | 12 | 274 | 305 |
| Ukrainian and Russian | 7 | 10 | 44 | 61 |
| All other nationalities | 7 | 3 | 72 | 82 |
| Total | 718 | 249 | 1,042 | 2,009 |

Table 5.6 *Svoboda sympathizers and opponents by nationality*

| | Nationality | | | | |
|---|---|---|---|---|---|
| | Ukrainian | Ukrainian andRussian | Russian | All other* | Total |
| Would cast a second ballot for Svoboda | 144 93.51% | 2 1.30% | 5 3.25% | 3 1.95% | 154 100% |
| Would not cast a second ballot for Svoboda | 1,236 75.18% | 59 3.59% | 274 16.67% | 75 4.56% | 1,644 100% |

*Note*: All other nationalities are all non-Ukrainian and no-Russian nationalities combined

Russian. Respondents of Ukrainian nationality, in the survey, are split roughly in half, and the rest speak a mix of the two languages (Table 5.5). Not surprisingly, Ukrainian nationals were the only ones to support the Svoboda party, and 94 percent of Svoboda sympathizers are Ukrainian, yet most Ukrainians do not sympathize with Svoboda (Table 5.6).[36]

The polarizing effect of the linguistic divide is even more evident when we look at the distribution of Svoboda sympathizers and opponents by language (Table 5.7). Whereas 78 percent of Svoboda

[36] Seventy-five percent of those who would never cast a second ballot for Svoboda are of Ukrainian nationality and 17 percent are Russian. Ninety percent of respondents who identified themselves as Russian also answered that they would never vote for Svoboda had they had the chance (Table 5.7).

Table 5.7 *Svoboda sympathizers and opponents by language*

| | Language | | | |
|---|---|---|---|---|
| | Ukrainian | Mix[a] | Russian | Total |
| Would cast a second ballot for Svoboda | 117 | 8 | 25 | 150 |
| (percentage of Svoboda sympathizers by language) | (78.00%) | (5.33%) | (16.67%) | (100%) |
| Would not cast a second ballot for Svoboda | 485 | 221 | 926 | 1,632 |
| (percentage of Svoboda opponents by language) | (29.72% | (13.54%) | (56.74%) | (100%) |

[a] Mix refers to the mix of Ukrainian and Russian languages.

sympathizers speak Ukrainian, only 30 percent of Svoboda opponents speak Ukrainian, and 57 percent of Svoboda opponents speak Russian (Table 5.7). When Svoboda sympathizers and voters are combined, 95 percent are of Ukrainian nationality and 79 percent of them speak Ukrainian. In sum, Svoboda sympathizers reflect the ethnic and linguistic divisions in Ukraine, but support for Svoboda, both open and covert, is rather limited in the broader population.

## 5.2.2 Policy Hostility

Having identified major ethnic and language underpinnings of support for Svoboda, the analysis turns to the role of threats in driving support for the Svoboda party. Policy threats reflect dissatisfaction with governmental spending on minorities, whereas identity threats echo group hostility. Economic threats are tied to economic insecurities. Language laws and language policies have distributive consequences. After the Orange Revolution, President Viktor Yushchenko initiated a state program for the development and functioning of the Ukrainian language in 2004–2010 (Moser 2013: 118). The subsequent (first) Azarov government removed funding for the support of the Ukrainian language, and earmarked 1.6 million hryvnias for the regional minority languages to support the realization of the European Charter for Languages (Zachid.net 2010). This implied a transfer of governmental resources from funding the Ukrainian to the Russian language. In

2011 President Yanukovych signed the budget, even though it did not include a separate expenditure category for the development of the Ukrainian language (Moser 2013: 117).[37]

Policy hostility is defined as the degree of opposition to spending on ethnic minorities. It reflects opposition to governmental fiscal support. Since opposition to governmental spending on minorities is not related to the degree of group hostility, it is possible to independently evaluate the effect of policy threats and identity threats on support for the Svoboda party. The survey asked about governmental spending on four ethnic groups, the majority group (Ukrainians) and three minorities. Respondents voiced support for more or less spending on Ukrainians, Russians, Crimean Tatars and Roma on a four-point scale:

Do you think that government should spend much more, more, less or much less on Ukrainians?

Do you think that government should spend much more, more, less or much less on Russians?

Do you think that government should spend much more, more, less or much less on Roma?

Do you think that government should spend much more, more, less or much less on Crimean Tatars?

Overall, respondents were enthusiastic spenders, leaning toward more government spending on everybody.[38] They strongly supported an increase in government spending across all groups and political

[37] Yanukovych's polarizing Minister of Education, Tabachnyk, proposed to revise higher education so that only universities with more than 10,000 students should be recognized as universities. This was an attack on smaller, patriotic Ukrainian universities. He also aimed to decrease Ukrainian in preschools and introduced a bill that would allow the Ministry to centralize curricula at universities. His proposals were de facto striving to defund education that benefited primarily Ukrainian speakers.

[38] The Spearman rank correlation between questions on support for government spending on Ukrainians, Russians, Crimean Tatars and Roma ($N = 1,883$) is as follows:

|  | Ukrainians | Russians | Crimean Tatars |
|---|---|---|---|
| Russians | 0.42 | | |
| Crimean Tatars | 0.04 | 0.50 | |
| Roma | −.01 | 0.46 | 0.84 |

affiliations, but mostly on the titular group: most respondents would have preferred more spending on Ukrainians. Only 4 percent of non-Ukrainians, almost all of whom declared that they would never vote for Svoboda, supported spending less on Ukrainians. Svoboda voters, in particular, leaned toward more government spending on Ukrainians. The proportion of Svoboda voters that supported "spending a lot more" on Ukrainians was 63 percent, compared with 50 percent among voters of all other parties and blocs, which represents a statistically significant difference. However, when we combine respondents that support "more" and "a lot more" spending on Ukrainians, the distinction between voters, sympathizers and opponents disappears, since all respondents favor more spending.

As opposed to the relatively consistent support for spending on Ukrainians among all respondents, support for government spending on minorities, and especially on Russians, is different among respondents. The major difference between Svoboda voters, sympathizers and opponents comes from support for less government spending on Russians. The most distinctive feature of radical right voters in Ukraine is their opposition toward spending on a politically organized minority (i.e., Russians), rather than support for more spending on Ukrainians (Figure 5.3).

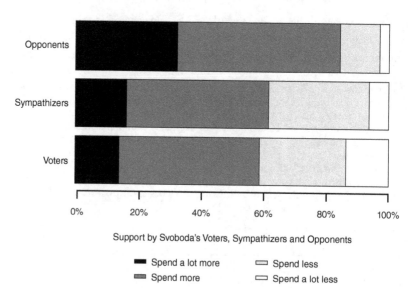

**Figure 5.3** Policy hostility: support for government spending on Russians by Svoboda's voters, sympathizers and opponents.

Fourteen percent of Svoboda voters and 6 percent of Svoboda sympathizers want the government to spend a lot less on Russians. Twenty-seven percent of Svoboda voters and 32 percent of Svoboda sympathizers want to spend less on Russians (Figure 5.3). This stands in complete contrast to the Svoboda opponents, of whom only 3 percent want to spend less on Russians. Strong opposition toward governmental spending on Russians, as opposed to generic support for more spending on Ukrainians, unites Svoboda voters with its sympathizers and distinguishes them from Svoboda opponents.[39]

In order to be electorally successful at the national level, radical right parties have to attract voters who oppose the accommodation of a politically organized minority, and not just any minority. The survey allows us to test this conjecture by examining responses to questions on government spending toward Roma and Crimean Tatars. Consistent with the theory, attitudes toward government spending on Roma and Crimean Tatars do not systematically polarize voters of different parties and blocs to the extent that attitudes toward the Russian minority do (Figure 5.4).

Attitudes toward spending on the Russian minority significantly polarize the political system. When compared with the voters of the mainstream Regions bloc and the Communists, Svoboda voters and mainstream Orange bloc voters support appreciably less government spending on Russians (Figure 5.4). However, in general, most voters are very sympathetic to more government spending on the Russian minority; only Svoboda voters and voters of the (rather marginal) Hrytsenko's bloc overwhelmingly opposed it (Figure 5.4). The general level of policy hostility toward Russians was low, but polarization on this issue was high. At the descriptive level, policy hostility is a unique, defining feature of the Svoboda voters that separates them from voters of other parties, and especially their right-wing ideological "cousins."

## 5.2.3 Group Hostility

What role do identity threats play in radical right mobilization in Ukraine? Ukrainian politics has been polarized between the

---

[39] At least half of Svoboda's voters, sympathizers and opponents support a lot more spending on Ukrainians by the government (Figure 5.3). Overall, support for governmental spending on Ukrainians is high. Only 4 percent of non-Ukrainians support spending less or a lot less on Ukrainians.

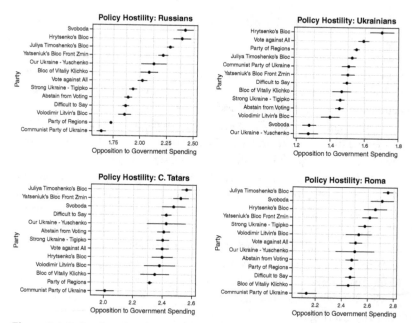

Figure 5.4 Policy hostility by parties in Ukraine.
*Note*: Means with weighted bootstrapped standard errors. Scale: 1: support for spending; 4: opposition to spending.

eastward-oriented "Party of the Regions" led by Viktor Yanukovych and the westward-oriented parties of "the Orange revolution," co-led by Yulia Tymoshenko and Viktor Yushchenko.[40] The Russian minority was backed mainly by the most powerful party in Ukraine – the Party of Regions, led by Viktor Yanukovych – but was also supported strongly by the smaller "Communist Party of Ukraine," led by Pyotr Symonenko (Kuzio 2010). When Yushchenko gained power in 2005, he engaged in the so-called war of languages (KUN 2009).[41] According

[40] In October 2011, current President Yanukovych imprisoned the major political rival to the Party of Regions, former Prime Minister Yulia Tymoshenko. The sentence was originally for seven years. She was released in 2004 but failed to resonate with Euromaidan supporters.

[41] The political forces associated with the Orange bloc have attempted to curb the rights of Russian-speaking minorities, and to ensure that the Russian language does not obtain the status of a second official language. When the Russian-speaking authorities realized that the restriction of language rights contradicted the European Charter for Minority and Regional Languages, the policy was revoked, following pressure from the European Union (Medvedev 2007: 205). Also Vasovic 2005.

to Serhiy Kudelia (2011), the primary reason for the rise of Svoboda was radicalization of the Russophile "Party of Regions," the non-proximate competitor to Svoboda:

Viktor Yanukovych has become a blessing in disguise for Ukraine's extreme right, particularly for the political fortunes of its leading flag-bearer party "Svoboda." During his first year as president, Yanukovych reversed most of the nationalist policies inherited from Yushchenko and moved much closer to Moscow than even Kuchma ever dared to. At the same time, his actions radicalized the nationalist core in the Western Ukraine, giving Svoboda the most seats in all of the region following the recent local election.

In March 2009, less than a month later, Svoboda made its first major inroads into Ukrainian politics in the Ternopil regional election.[42] Leaders from the "Orange bloc" catered to the "nationalist" base of Western Ukraine. Parties of the "Orange bloc," a nearby competitor to the radical right, had the potential to drain the pool of potential radical right voters by performing patriotic acts. For example, on October 12, 2007, President Yushchenko awarded the Hero of Ukraine title and the Order of State posthumously to the chief commander of the Ukrainian Insurgent Army (UPA) of 1942–1950, Brig. Gen. Roman Shukhevych, in a highly symbolic ceremony, courting the radical right elements.

In western Ukraine, the UPA soldiers are viewed as freedom fighters who opposed both the Nazis and the Red Army, but the left and the pro-Russian parties have accused the UPA of war crimes against civilians (*Kyiv Weekly* 2007). Even more offensive to ethnic Russians was when President Yushchenko bestowed the national award ("the Hero of Ukraine") to Stepan Bandera, who is a historically divisive figure accused of anti-Semitism, massacring of Poles during World War II and other heinous crimes.[43]

"Svoboda regards itself as the ideological successor of the Organization of Ukrainian Nationalists (OUN) led by Bandera and Stetsko" (Katchanovski 2014, 2015). Figure 5.5 displays attitudes toward the legacy of Bandera and Stalin from a survey conducted by the author in

---

[42] The extremist Congress of Ukrainian Nationalists (KUN) provided security forces to Yulia Tymoshenko during the Orange Revolution (Kuzio 1997). Similarly, the paramilitary units of UNA (another fringe radical right party in Ukraine) provided security for pro-Yushchenko and pro-Tymoshenko forces in 2004 as well.

[43] President Yanukovych revoked Bandera's posthumous award in 2011 (Levy 2011).

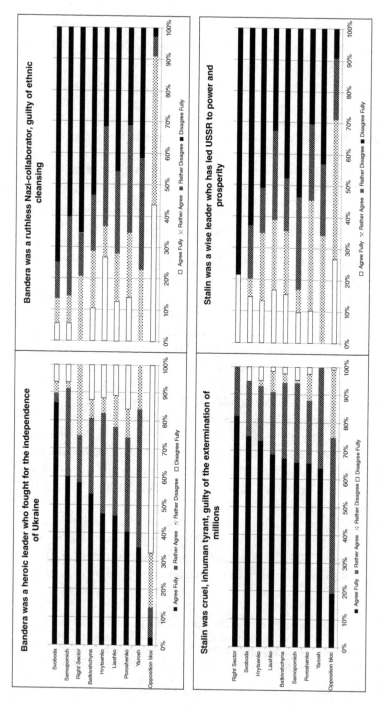

**Figure 5.5** Attitudes toward Bandera and Stalin legacy by parties (May 2016).

*Data source:* Bustikova 2016a

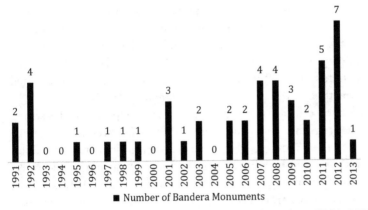

**Figure 5.6** Number of Bandera monuments erected per year (1991–2013).
*Source*: Liebich and Myshlovska 2014: 752

May 2016. Svoboda voters view Bandera in an exceptionally positive light and judge Stalin's legacy harshly. But supporters of other parties are enamored by Bandera's legacy as well (Figure 5.5). Svoboda supporters associate Bandera's legacy not with anti-Semitism but with sovereignty, which allows the leadership of Svoboda to strategically shift their rhetoric away from anti-Jewish appeals.

The resurgence of the far-right political scene in Ukraine was facilitated in part by the resonance of the Social-National Party of Ukraine. Founded in 1991, the SNPU had a platform of "classic right-wing themes," such as "anti-Semitism, national monolingualism, militarism, ethnocentrism, cryptoracism, homophobia, [and] opposition to abortion" (Shekhovtsov and Umland 2014: 59). These were combined with economically left-wing doctrines: partial nationalization, limits on land sales, and a wider social safety net (Shekhovtsov and Umland 2014: 59). Around 2004, the SNPU renamed itself as the All-Ukrainian Union "Svoboda" ("Freedom") and dropped the neo-Nazi imagery and fascist overtones in lieu of a more understated invocation of OUN-style Ukrainian nationalism.

The leadership also distanced itself from anti-Semitism and became wary of making xenophobic remarks in the public.[44] Svoboda's electoral success from 2009 to 2012 coincided with the broad resonance of its ideological platform. The increase in overall Ukrainian ultranationalism can be seen in Figure 5.6, which shows the number of

---

[44] Interviews in Lviv, July 2014. Also, discussions with Ivan Katchanovski.

Bandera monuments and statues that were erected per year. Svoboda itself has a history of holding commemorations and vigils for the OUN-B, and specifically for Stepan Bandera. The increase in monument building coincided with the first clashes and polarization over the regional status of the Russian language law in 2006 and accelerated around the time of the conflict over the language law.[45]

Support for radical right parties is typically expected to be strong among voters with highly xenophobic attitudes (Eatwell 2003; Mudde 2007). However, a strategy that exclusively attracts voters who exhibit high levels of group hostility against any minority group is not always a winning formula for national-level success (Art 2011, Rydgren 2008). Since I have argued that support for the radical right parties is rooted in policy hostility, I expect that group hostility will not uniquely distinguish Svoboda supporters. It is often assumed that Svoboda voters are hard-core xenophobes. Given the contentious role of anti-Semitism in past and current Ukrainian nation building, I measured group hostility toward Russians and Jews.[46] Similarly to Chapter 4, I created a composite index of hostility as an additive index based on two questions:

Interethnic group hostility index: Group hostility toward Russians/
   [Ukrainians]
To have a Russian/[Ukrainian] as a neighbor seems to me very attractive/
   somewhat attractive/somewhat unattractive/very unattractive.
To have a Russian/[Ukrainian] as a life partner seems to me very
   attractive/somewhat attractive/somewhat unattractive/very
   unattractive.
Group hostility index: Jews

---

[45] Lviv erected a prominent statue of Bandera in 2007.

[46] The composition of the inter-group hostility index is explained in Chapter 4, Section 4.3.2. The measure of social distance is an eight-item additive index: "To have [group name] as neighbor seems to me very attractive, somewhat attractive, somewhat unattractive, very unattractive." "To have [group name] as a life partner seems to me very attractive, somewhat attractive, somewhat unattractive, very unattractive." Value of 2 = 1 + 1. This value of two suggests that the respondent selected answers: neighbor [from group] very attractive + life partner [from group] very attractive. Value of 8 = 4 + 4 suggests that the respondent selected answers: neighbor [from group] very unattractive + life partner [from group] very unattractive. The span of the index is six.

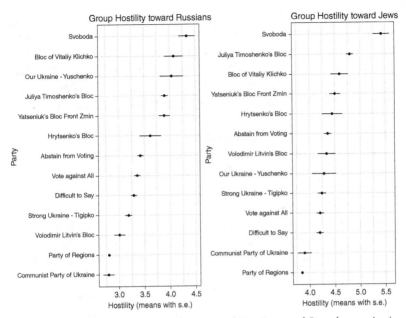

**Figure 5.7** Group hostility: prejudice toward Russians and Jews by parties in Ukraine.

*Note*: Means with weighted bootstrapped standard errors. Inter-group hostility scale: 2: low hostility; 5: medium hostility; 8: high hostility.

To have a Jew as a neighbor seems to me very attractive/somewhat attractive/somewhat unattractive/very unattractive.
To have a Jew as a life partner seems to me very attractive/somewhat attractive/somewhat unattractive/very unattractive.

Figure 5.7 shows inter-group hostility between Ukrainians and Russians and toward Jews by political parties. The most striking finding is that Svoboda voters do *not* display higher levels of group hostility toward Russians than the voters of the former Orange bloc, their "cousins."[47] Svoboda voters do not stand out as uniquely Russo-phobic or as extremely Russo-phobic. Svoboda voters exhibit similar levels of group hostility toward Russians as do the voters of the following parties: Tymoshenko's bloc, the "Our Ukraine" party (Yuschenko), Vitali Klitschko's bloc and Yatseniuk's bloc "Front

---

[47] However, the data show that group hostility toward Jews is a distinct feature of Svoboda voters.

zmin" (Figure 5.7). When considered together, voters of these parties display higher levels of group hostility toward Russians than the more Russophile parties (the "Strong Ukraine" party (Tigipko), the Party of Regions (Yanukovych) and the Communist Party of Ukraine (Symonenko)). Although the general level of group hostility toward Russians was low in 2010, it had the potential to polarize the voting public.[48]

Based on the group hostility index, which measures social distance toward Jews, Svoboda voters show higher levels of group hostility toward Jews than all other respondents. Svoboda politicians have used anti-Jewish statements in the past to mobilize voters. Since Galicia has been, historically, a home to large Jewish communities, anti-Semitism needs to be considered as a possible factor in political mobilization. Svoboda's emphasis on historical grievances in western Ukraine – such as opposition toward Ukrainian-Polish reconciliation, defense of interwar anti-Semitic Ukrainian nationalists and the revival of issues from the 1920s between Ukrainians and Russians – suggests that an ideological message of anti-Semitism should resonate with Svoboda voters.[49] However, once we control for other factors, such as economic insecurities, the predictive impact of group hostility toward Jews on support for Svoboda disappears in a multivariate analysis.[50]

In order to succeed at the national level, a party has to broaden its appeal and cannot exclusively rely on voters with high levels of

---

[48] This finding suggests that the general level of hostility toward Russians and Russian speakers was low, which explains why many fighters in the East who support Ukrainian sovereignty are Russian speakers and Russians. Similarly, Ukrainians blame the current crisis on Putin and not on the Russian minority.

[49] Using the survey data, I found that Svoboda voters are slightly younger, anxious about their economic well-being and fear security threats facing Ukraine. I found no evidence that voting for Svoboda is driven by attitudes toward corruption, satisfaction with the health care or the educational system (cf. Shekhovtsov 2011).

[50] According to the Euro-Asian Jewish Congress that monitors anti-Semitism in the former Soviet Union, physical attacks on Jews and anti-Semitic vandalism are at very low levels in Ukraine when compared with both Russia and Western Europe (Likhachev 2015). Since its independence, Ukraine's roughly 100,000 Jews have never witnessed attacks comparable to shootings in the Jewish museum in Belgium or attacks on a kosher supermarket in France, both perpetrated by criminals of Muslim faith. Source: Likhachev and Bezruk 2014: 5. Statistics of the news about victims of ethnic and racial hate crimes in Ukraine, 2006–2014, are based on the analysis of news reports about crimes.

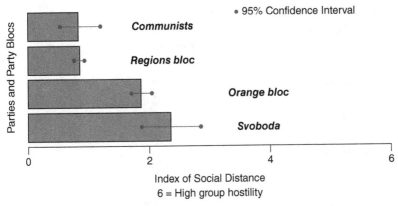

**Figure 5.8** Group hostility: prejudice toward Russians by party blocs in Ukraine. *Note*: Means with weighted bootstrapped standard errors. The index of group hostility was rescaled; on the inter-group hostility scale: 0: low hostility; 3: medium hostility; 6: high hostility.

xenophobia. Not surprisingly, the mainstream Regions bloc and the Communists are more positively inclined toward Russians than the voters of the Orange bloc and Svoboda. In order to compare voters' positions on group hostility by blocs, I divided voters into four groups using the logic of bilateral opposites: (1) voters for the radical right party: Svoboda, (2) mainstream voters for the Orange bloc,[51] (3) mainstream voters for the Party of Regions bloc and (4) voters for the Communist Party of Ukraine (Symonenko).[52] The analysis confirms that Svoboda voters are not unique in their degree of group hostility toward Russians. They are just as hostile to Russians as their ideological "cousins" (the voters of the Orange bloc, Figure 5.8).

Group hostility against Russians remains stable even after the annexation of Crimea by Russia in 2014 and the escalation of conflict in Eastern Ukraine. Civil conflict did not lead to rising xenophobia. Data from a survey conducted in 2016, after the outbreak of conflict in

[51] Parties that were included in the Orange bloc were three political allies: Yuliya Tymoshenko's bloc, Party "Our Ukraine" (Yushchenko) and Arseniy Yatseniuk's bloc "Front zmin."

[52] Parties that were included in the Party of the Regions bloc are two allied mainstream Russophile parties: Party "Strong Ukraine" (Tihipko) and Party of Regions (Yanukovych). Voters of all other parties, non-decided and non-voters serve as a baseline for comparison in a multivariate setting.

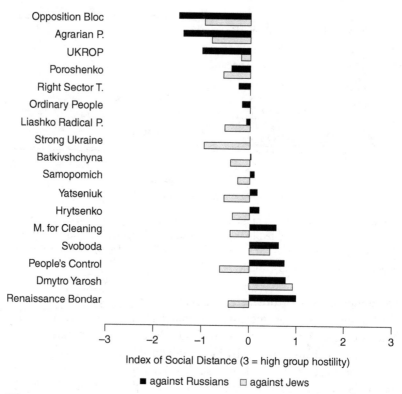

**Figure 5.9** Group hostility: prejudice toward Russians and Jews by parties in May 2016. Inter-group hostility scale: −3: low hostility; 0: medium hostility; 3: high hostility.
*Source*: Bustikova 2016a

Donbas, show that, despite the elevated sense of threat, hostility toward the Russian minority among Ukrainians is quite low (Busti-kova 2016b). Even in 2016, Svoboda voters still exhibit high(er) levels of anti-Jewish sentiments, but their views of Russians are not excep-tionally hostile and not exceptionally different from four other parties (Figure 5.9).

Radical right parties have to attract voters who oppose the accom-modation of a politically organized minority (not any minority) in order to be electorally successful at the national level. Consistent with the expectation, attitudes toward government spending on Roma and Crimean Tatars do *not* differentiate voters of different parties and blocs (Figure 5.4).[53] Svoboda voters are distinct in their views on spending on Russians, but not on spending toward these other nationalities. Group hostility toward Russians, however, is not a distinct feature of the Ukrainian radical right.

## 5.2.4 Economic Threats

Exposure to economic threats – an alternative explanation for the Svoboda support – is the last account considered here (Shekhovtsov 2011). The survey included four questions about economic insecurities related to pocketbook, sociotropic, prospective and retrospective evaluations of economic insecurity. The questions were as follows:[54]

In general, do you think that you and your family are better off, worse off, or about the same financially compared with two years ago?

Looking ahead, do you think that two years from now, you will be better off financially, worse off, or just about the same as now?

Looking ahead, do you expect that the economy will get better, get worse, or stay about the same in the next two years?

Now let's talk about the country as a whole. Would you say that most families in Ukraine are better off, worse off, or about the same financially compared with two years ago?

The results show that Svoboda voters fear economic threats, and stand out in two aspects: they agree that their family is worse off than two years ago, and that all Ukrainian families are worse off than two years ago (which voters from the Hrytsenko bloc also think). Together with voters from the Yushchenko, Hrytsenko and Tymoshenko blocs/parties, they also expect that the economy will get worse over the next two years and expect to be personally worse off in the future (Figure 5.10). Fifty-six percent of Svoboda voters think that their family is worse off financially compared with two years ago and 46 percent think that their family financial situation is the same.

[53] The level of ethnic intolerance in Ukraine is highest toward Roma and support for spending on Roma is low across voters for all parties. The voters of the Communist Party supported distinctly more spending on Crimean Tatars than the Party of Regions bloc. The Autonomous Crimea Republic had the most pro-Russian electorate in Ukraine. On the relationship between Crimean Tatars and the Ukrainian nationalists, see Shevel 2001.

[54] For analysis, the scale was recoded from better off, the same and worse off to render it ordinal.

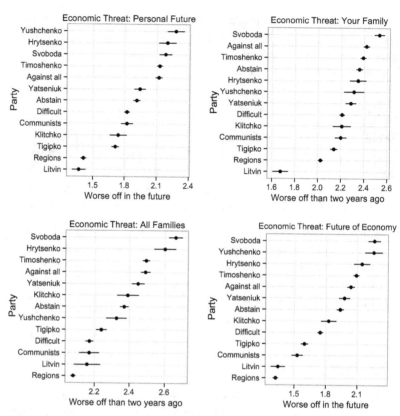

**Figure 5.10** Economic threat perception by parties in Ukraine.
*Note*: Means with weighted bootstrapped standard errors. Scale: 1: better; 3: worse off.

Among Svoboda sympathizers, the degree of economic anxiety is much lower. Thirty percent think that their family is worse off and 50 percent think that their family is financially the same as two years ago. The financial anxiety of Svoboda supporters is also considerably higher than among other voters. Thirty-six percent think that their family is worse off and the almost half (46 percent) feel that their family is financially about the same. The sense of economic deprivation among the Svoboda voters is profound: there is a 20 percent gap between Svoboda voters and all other respondents in their perception that their family's financial situation has recently deteriorated.

Support for Svoboda is thus driven by policy threats and fears of collective economic threats. Responses to questions about economic threats indicate that Svoboda voters come from a pool of voters who acutely fear exposure to economic insecurity at the personal, familial and societal level. Economic anxiety among the radical right voters was not expected by the theory. There are three factors to consider. First, western Ukraine, as opposed to the capital, large cities and industrially developed regions in the east, is relatively poor and historically relies on agriculture. Given the high degree of regional concentration of Svoboda voters, it is therefore not surprising to find higher economic anxiety among voters in economically deprived regions. But support for Svoboda is not driven by regional economic appeals associated with western Ukraine. Western Ukrainian identity evolves around Ukrainian nation building, not class-based deprivation. Furthermore, Svoboda does not campaign on issues of economic redistribution.

Another factor to consider is that Svoboda voters are as anxious as the voters of a large mainstream post–Orange bloc party when we examine two out of four types of economic threats, both associated with future expectations. In retrospective evaluations, however, Svoboda stands out but is not particularly far off from "cousins," voters of the nearest parties. In general, all Ukrainians report very high levels of economic anxieties. Svoboda therefore fits the mood.

Finally, if support for Svoboda is driven in part by economic anxieties, a deteriorating Ukrainian economy should have expanded the voting base of the radical right, which stands in contrast to the Slovak case, in which economic anxieties play no role in explaining support for the Slovak National Party. But despite the turbulences of the Ukrainian economy, widespread poverty, massive corruption and further economic anxiety induced by the conflict in Donbas and with Russia, the voting for the radical right in Ukraine is anemic. This fact also highlights limitations of purely economic explanations.

## 5.3 Radical Right Voters in Ukraine

Having considered three sources of threats at the descriptive level, the analysis now moves to the determinants of voter support for Svoboda in a multivariate setting. It models party choice using a multinomial logistic regression approach with bootstrapped errors.[55] Table 5.8

---

[55] The descriptive statistics are in Tables 5.3 and 5.4. There are 52 Svoboda voters and 154 Svoboda sympathizers in the sample.

**Table 5.8** *Determinants of support for Svoboda among voters, sympathizers and opponents in Ukraine: policy hostility*

| Parties | Variable names | Model 1 | Model 2 | Model 3 |
|---|---|---|---|---|
| Svoboda | Government spending: Russians | 1.187*** | 1.173*** | 0.770** |
| | (1= spend much more) | (0.251) | (0.323) | (0.342) |
| | Government spending: Ukrainians | −0.882** | −0.496 | −0.313 |
| | (1= spend much more) | (0.395) | (0.391) | (0.414) |
| | Government spending: Crimean Tatar | −0.891** | −0.774** | −0.076** |
| | (1= spend much more) | (0.238) | (0.321) | (0.321) |
| | Nation | 0.212 | 0.209 | −1.808*** |
| | (0 = Russian, 1 = else) | (0.434) | (0.497) | (0.407) |
| | National pride | | −2.185*** | −2.223*** |
| | (1 = very proud) | | (0.645) | (0.694) |
| | Language | 1.181*** | 1.110* | 0.784 |
| | (0 = Russian, 1 = Ukrainian) | (0.332) | (0.592) | (0.604) |
| | Income | −0.267** | −0.231** | −0.185** |
| | (1 = low) | (0.116) | (0.098) | (0.091) |
| | Education level | 0.139 | 0.282* | 0.320 |
| | (1 = low) | (0.160) | (0.166) | (0.206) |
| | Age | 0.0007 | 0.0099 | 0.0112 |
| | (years) | (0.011) | (0.010) | (0.011) |
| | Gender | | 1.640*** | 1.674*** |
| | (0 = female) | | (0.430) | (0.428) |
| | Settlement size | | 0.135 | 0.156 |
| | (1 = village) | | (0.135) | (0.115) |
| | Hostility toward Russians (index) | | | 0.651*** |
| | (8 = high hostility) | | | (0.175) |
| Svoboda Sympathizers | Government spending: Russians | 0.072*** | 0.851*** | 0.409 |
| | (1 = spend much more) | (0.251) | (0.266) | (0.262) |
| | Government spending: Ukrainians | −0.506** | −0.447* | −0.324 |
| | (1 = spend much more) | (0.218) | (0.237) | (0.297) |
| | Government spending: Crimean Tatar | −0.455*** | −0.0396* | −0.324 |
| | (1 = spend much more) | (0.171) | (0.218) | (0.213) |
| | Nation | 0.332 | 0.255 | −1.102*** |
| | (0 = Russian, 1 = else) | (0.309) | (0.408) | (0.359) |
| | National pride | | −0.702*** | −0.895*** |
| | (1 = very proud) | | (0.189) | (0.225) |
| | Language | 1.131*** | 0.676* | 0.468* |
| | (0 = Russian, 1 = Ukrainian) | (0.251) | (0.349) | (0.284) |

**Table 5.8 (*cont.*)**

| Parties | Variable names | Model 1 | Model 2 | Model 3 |
|---|---|---|---|---|
| | Income | −0.0409 | 0.0948 | 0.123* |
| | (1 = low) | (0.068) | (0.071) | (0.075) |
| | Education level | −0.00424 | 0.0657 | 0.0774 |
| | (1 = low) | (0.115) | (0.130) | (0.108) |
| | Age | 0.00937 | −0.00307 | −0.00244 |
| | (years) | (0.0063) | (0.0074) | (0.0072) |
| | Gender | | 0.708*** | 0.841** |
| | (0 = female) | | (0.269) | (0.428) |
| | Settlement size | | −0.202*** | −0.187*** |
| | (1 = village) | | (0.070) | (0.072) |
| | Hostility toward Russians (index) | | | 0.579*** |
| | (8 = high hostility) | | | (0.124) |
| Svoboda | Government spending: Russians | 0.093 | 0.183 | 0.085 |
| Opponents | (1 = spend much more) | (0.179) | (0.174) | (0.171) |
| | Government spending: Ukrainians | 0.200 | 0.163 | 0.178 |
| | (1 = spend much more) | (0.148) | (0.165) | (0.207) |
| | Government spending: Crimean Tatar | 0.082 | 0.086 | 0.053 |
| | (1 = spend much more) | (0.110) | (0.114) | (0.132) |
| | Nation | 0.303 | 0.306 | −0.026 |
| | (0 = Russian, 1 = else) | (0.215) | (0.274) | (0.337) |
| | National pride | | −0.076 | −0.130 |
| | (1 = very proud) | | (0.119) | (0.104) |
| | Language | −0.180 | −0.435** | −0.523** |
| | (0 = Russian, 1 = Ukrainian) | (0.198) | (0.194) | (0.212) |
| | Income | 0.040 | 0.085 | 0.101* |
| | (1 = low) | (0.046) | (0.053) | (0.053) |
| | Education level | 0.099 | 0.109 | 0.119 |
| | (1 = low) | (0.079) | (0.079) | (0.092) |
| | Age | 0.015*** | 0.018*** | 0.015*** |
| | (years) | (0.005) | (0.005) | (0.006) |
| | Gender | | 0.666*** | 0.784** |
| | (0 = female) | | (0.233) | (0.314) |
| | Settlement size | | −0.147*** | −0.168*** |
| | (1 = village) | | (0.052) | (0.064) |

Table 5.8 (*cont.*)

| Parties | Variable names | Model 1 | Model 2 | Model 3 |
|---------|---------------|---------|---------|---------|
| | Interethnic group hostility (index) | | | 0.261*** |
| | (8 = high hostility) | | | (0.087) |
| | N | 1416 | 1414 | 1208 |
| | Log-likelihood | −915.2 | −868.6 | −747.7 |
| | AIC | 1878.4 | 1803.3 | 1567.4 |

*Note*: Policy hostility is opposition to spending. Cell entries are multinomial logit coefficients with bootstrapped standard errors in parentheses (100 replications). The base outcome is respondents who did not answer if they would cast a second vote for Svoboda. Constants are omitted from the table.
*** $p < 0.001$; ** $p < 0.01$; * $p < 0.05$.

focuses on policy hostility as an explanatory variable and presents results for three groups: Svoboda voters, a group of Svoboda sympathizers and a group of Svoboda opponents. The baseline in the model is based on answers of respondents who were neither voters/sympathizers nor opponents.[56]

In the policy hostility model, the probability of being a voter for Svoboda and a Svoboda sympathizer increases as the respondents want to spend less on the Russian minority and as the level of inter-group hostility increases (Table 5.8). An increase in opposition to spending on Russians increases the probability that a respondent is a Svoboda sympathizer and a Svoboda voter. However, the effect of policy hostility on being a Svoboda sympathizer disappears once we control for inter-ethnic group hostility. It is crucial to note that the opposition to government spending on Russians remains a robustly significant predictor of who is likely to vote for Svoboda, even when inter-ethnic group hostility is taken into account.[57]

[56] I included a measure of national pride as a control variable in all models. National pride, which can be used as a proxy for patriotism, is a parsimonious distinctive feature of radical right voters. The respondents were asked if they were "very proud, fairly proud, not very proud, not at all proud to be a citizen of Ukraine."

[57] As one might expect, Svoboda voters and sympathizers are not recruited from Russian language speakers, while the language affiliation is irrelevant for the opponents. The noticeable feature of the Svoboda opponents is age: the older the respondent is, the more likely they oppose even a hypothetical vote for Svoboda.

The second important distinction between Svoboda voters and sympathizers is the role of economic vulnerability (Table 5.8).[58] As
the respondent's vulnerability increases, the probability of voting for
Svoboda increases. Although more vulnerable voters are more likely
to vote for Svoboda, they are not more likely to sympathize with Svoboda. Svoboda voter attitudes can be described as a unique combination
of policy hostility toward Russians, group hostility against Russians and
a high degree of economic anxiety. Policy favoritism toward Ukrainians
increases the probability of voting for Svoboda and sympathizing for
Svoboda, but it is a considerably weaker predictor. Inter-group hostility
is a strong predictor of Svoboda support, yet it increases the probability
of voting for Svoboda as well as the probability of sympathizing with
Svoboda, and thus is not unique to actual Svoboda voters.[59]

Svoboda benefited from the imprisonment of one of the leaders of
the Orange Revolution, and the former Prime Minister, Yulia
Tymoshenko. Her party was the closest nearby ideological competitor
to the Svoboda party, the ideological "cousin." We should expect
voters to rally behind a mainstream party with a tested leader who
can address and avert the danger of the status reversal, which
was already lurking as a distinct possibility in 2006. Therefore, both
Svoboda and the parties of the Orange bloc attracted voters that were
driven by policy hostility toward Russians.

Disappointment with Tymoshenko, who was viewed as both politically and economically corrupt and the inability of her party bloc to
file in certain districts, diverted some of her voters to Svoboda.
The analysis previously indicated that her party was one of the largest
reservoirs of Svoboda sympathizers, which suggests that (counterfac-
tually) Svoboda's electoral success in 2012 would have been much
smaller had Tymoshenko been able to compete on an even footing.

In sum, when compared with Svoboda sympathizers, Svoboda
voters are distinct in only two respects. First, they oppose more spending on Russians, which significantly increases the probability of
actually voting for Svoboda, after controlling for xenophobia.[60]

---

[58] Economic vulnerability is measured using income levels.
[59] In other words, the pool of voters available to be mobilized exclusively on group
hostility is deeper than the pool of Svoboda voters.
[60] Group hostility against Jews is not a predictor of whether the respondent will
vote for Svoboda in a multivariate analysis. This finding is contradictory, since
we presented evidence in the earlier sections of the chapter that Svoboda voters

Second, they are poorer than sympathizers, and economic anxiety strongly increases probability of voting for Svoboda.

Previous analysis (Table 5.8) was driven by distinctions between Svoboda voters and those who declared to be sympathetic to the party, but shied away from the direct electoral support. Now I move to the analysis of all parties. The following section looks at segments of voters determined by electoral support. It differentiates between Svoboda, parties of the Orange bloc, parties of the Party of Regions bloc and the Russophile Communist Party.

Table 5.9 presents the determinants of voter support for Svoboda by parties and by party blocs. The analysis shows that group hostility toward Russians is not a significant predictor of vote choice for either Svoboda or the Orange bloc parties in models presented in Table 5.9.[61] Furthermore, voters who preferred less spending on Russians frequently chose the Orange bloc and to a lesser extent Svoboda (Models 2–5 in Table 5.9). In stark contrast to voters of the Orange bloc, Svoboda voters also wanted the government to spend significantly *more* on Ukrainians.[62]

The survey data suggest that Svoboda's appeal is limited to a very narrow segment of Ukrainian-speaking Ukrainians. Despite its anti-Russian rhetoric, Svoboda has been unable to successfully appeal to those concerned with the threat posed by accommodative policies toward Russians, who were more inclined to vote for the Orange bloc parties. Voters who opposed more spending on *Ukrainians* were attracted to the Regions bloc. Voters who supported more spending on *Russians* and much less on Ukrainians were attracted to the

---

exhibit high levels of anti-Jewish sentiment and that those high levels were distinct when compared with supporters of other parties and respondents without political allegiances. Since the multivariate analysis controls for basic socio-demographic factors as well as economic anxieties, this finding suggests that the effect of anti-Semitism is mediated by these factors. A separate study would be required to tap into the sources of anti-Jewish attitudes in Ukraine. These findings suggest that the relationship between anti-Semitism and support for Svoboda is not a direct one. For similar results that incorporate security threats and anti-Semitism, see Bustikova 2015b.

[61] The effect of nationality on voting for Svoboda and the Orange bloc was so weak that I did not display its effect in Table 5.9.

[62] Compared with Orange bloc voters, Svoboda voters are also driven by economic concerns (M5 and M6 in Table 5.9).

Table 5.9 *Determinants of party vote in Ukraine (support for Svoboda by parties and party blocs: policy hostility)*

| Parties | | M1 | M2 | M3 | M4 | M5 | M6 |
|---|---|---|---|---|---|---|---|
| Radical right party (Svoboda) | Governmental spending: Russians (1 = spend much more) | 0.562*** (0.155) | 0.211 (0.231) | 0.211 (0.231) | 0.36 (0.234) | 0.413** (0.159) | 0.397* (0.165) |
| | Government spending: Ukrainians (1 = spend much more) | −0.887*** (0.332) | −0.854* (0.341) | −0.863* (0.349) | −0.849** (0.324) | −1.087** (0.373) | −1.136** (0.360) |
| | National pride (1 = very proud) | −2.050*** (0.434) | −1.903*** (0.497) | −1.787*** (0.407) | −1.995*** (0.359) | −2.380*** (0.593) | −2.372*** (0.554) |
| | Language (0 = Russian, 1 = Ukrainian) | 0.621 (0.332) | | | | | 0.268 (0.315) |
| | Region (0 = non-West, 1 = West) | | 1.993*** (0.380) | 1.976*** (0.380) | | | |
| | Hostility toward Russians (index) (8 = high hostility) | | | −0.019 (0.116) | 0.21 (0.110) | | |
| | Economic anxiety (index) (12 = high anxiety) | | | | | 0.157** (0.058) | 0.146* (0.058) |
| Parties of the Orange bloc | Government spending: Russians (1 = spend much more) | 0.342** (0.106) | 0.272** (0.090) | 0.222* (0.093) | 0.264** (0.100) | 0.357*** (0.085) | 0.331** (0.097) |
| | Government spending: Ukrainians (1 = spend much more) | −0.201 (0.128) | −0.121 (0.129) | −0.089 (0.127) | −0.143 (0.139) | −0.245 (0.134) | −0.257 (0.135) |
| | National pride (1 = very proud) | −0.770*** (0.100) | −0.721*** (0.091) | −0.731*** (0.117) | −0.802*** (0.104) | −0.842*** (0.091) | −0.813*** (0.107) |
| | Language (0 = Russian, 1 = Ukrainian) | 0.325* (0.129) | | | | | 0.304* (0.148) |

Table 5.9 (cont.)

| Parties | | M1 | M2 | M3 | M4 | M5 | M6 |
|---|---|---|---|---|---|---|---|
| | Region | | | | | | |
| | (0 = non-West, 1 = West) | | 0.616** | 0.572** | | | |
| | | | (0.188) | (0.188) | | | |
| | Interethnic hostility (index) | | | 0.028 | 0.097 | | |
| | (8 = high hostility) | | | (0.056) | (0.052) | | |
| | Economic anxiety (index) | | | | | 0.045 | 0.024 |
| | (12 = high anxiety) | | | | | (0.024) | (0.028) |
| Party of the Regions bloc | Government spending: Russians | -0.058 | -0.12 | -0.048 | -0.126 | -0.14 | -0.01 |
| | (1 = spend much more) | (0.081) | (0.084) | (0.084) | (0.088) | (0.088) | (0.083) |
| | Government spending: Ukrainians | 0.517*** | 0.419*** | 0.339*** | 0.436*** | 0.629*** | 0.581*** |
| | (1 = spend much more) | (0.095) | (0.095) | (0.085) | (0.101) | (0.096) | (0.107) |
| | National pride | -0.034 | -0.032 | -0.023 | 0.033 | 0.141* | 0.049 |
| | (1 = very proud) | (0.052) | (0.047) | (0.056) | (0.057) | (0.064) | (0.055) |
| | Language | -0.939*** | | | | | -0.849*** |
| | (0 = Russian, 1 = Ukrainian) | (0.109) | | | | | (0.122) |
| | Region | | -1.346*** | -1.213*** | | | |
| | (0 = non-West, 1 = West) | | (0.217) | (0.227) | | | |
| | Interethnic hostility (index) | | | -0.048 | -0.124** | | |
| | (8 = high hostility) | | | (0.047) | (0.038) | | |
| | Economic anxiety (index) | | | | | -0.101*** | -0.053* |

| (12 = high anxiety) | | | | | | (0.022) | (0.021) |
|---|---|---|---|---|---|---|---|
| Communist Party (Symonenko) | Government spending: Russians (1 = spend much more) | −0.976*** (0.255) | −0.973*** (0.256) | −0.728 (0.380) | −0.823* (0.410) | −0.865*** (0.246) | −0.798** (0.246) |
| | Government spending: Ukrainians (1 = spend much more) | 0.141 (0.384) | −0.039 (0.351) | −0.168 (0.437) | −0.069 (0.455) | 0.338 (0.370) | 0.367 (0.296) |
| | National pride (1 = very proud) | −0.332* (0.144) | −0.339* (0.150) | −0.046 (0.192) | 0.024 (0.224) | 0.004 (0.159) | −0.082 (0.179) |
| | Language (0 = Russian, 1 = Ukrainian) | −1.104*** (0.310) | | | | | −0.780* (0.332) |
| | Region (0 = non-West, 1 = West) | | −15.208*** (0.649) | −13.453*** (0.649) | | | |
| | Inter-ethnic hostility (index) (8 = high hostility) | | | −0.372 (0.191) | −0.460* (0.224) | | |
| | Economic anxiety (index) (12 = high anxiety) | | | | | −0.204*** (0.052) | −0.163* (0.066) |
| | Log-likelihood | −2107.97 | −2111.36 | −1812.79 | −1869.37 | −2106.32 | −2044.42 |
| | N | 1866 | 1883 | 1597 | 1597 | 1845 | 1828 |

*Note*: Policy hostility is opposition to spending. Cell entries are multinomial logit coefficients with bootstrapped standard errors in parentheses (100 replications). The base outcome is voters for all other parties combined and non-voters. Constants are omitted from the table. Results are robust to a series of controls, such as education, community size, household size, age, income, group hostility toward Jews and attitudes on corruption, health care and education.

\*\*\* $p < 0.001$; \*\* $p < 0.01$; \* $p < 0.05$.

Communist Party of Symonenko, the bilateral opposite party, and the most extreme force advocating more accommodation and spending on the ethnic Russian minority (Table 5.9).

These results highlight the lack of ideological differentiation between the mainstream parties and their more radical cousins and a vast polarization between two major mainstream blocs – parties associated with the Orange Revolution and the Party of Regions, which almost acts as a bilateral opposite in itself. Similarly, the boundaries of anti-minority mobilization are extremely blurred among the patriotic camp.

Since governmental support both for the titular nationality (Ukrainians) and politically organized minority (Russians) is a salient issue in Ukraine, the prospects for a successful radical right party are limited. Voters who want to counterbalance the efforts of Russophile parties to elevate the status of the Russian language unequivocally gathered behind the Orange bloc (rather than Svoboda). The mainstream Orange parties possessed the political capacity to stem the threat of status reversal that would likely result if the status of the Russian language was elevated from a minority language to an official language (see Table 5.2).[63] Svoboda views Ukrainian speakers as a minority that deserves special privileges and support from the state in order to avert the subjugation and humiliation of the Ukrainian language by the adoption of the Russian language.

To examine the substantive effects, Figure 5.11 displays the predicted probabilities of voting for Svoboda for different degrees of support for government spending on Russians, holding all else constant.[64] The results indicate that a "very proud" Ukrainian speaker who supports "much more government spending" on Russians has a 3 percent predicted probability of voting for Svoboda, whereas the same voter who wants the government to "spend much less" on

---

[63] The Orange bloc parties have strongly supported language "Ukrainization" since the Orange Revolution by maximizing the number of schools of higher education with instruction in Ukrainian, promoting the Ukrainian language in governmental bodies and encouraging the usage of Ukrainian in mass media. For example, the Regions Party and the Communists unsuccessfully introduced a bill in 2011 that would allow parents to choose between Russian speaking and Ukrainian speaking kindergartens (ZIK 2011).

[64] The simulation is based on Model 1 from Table 5.9 and the scenario is set as a situation where the respondent prefers more spending on Ukrainians, is very proud to be a citizen of Ukraine and speaks Ukrainian. The model was chosen due to its large absolute value of the log likelihood and its parsimony.

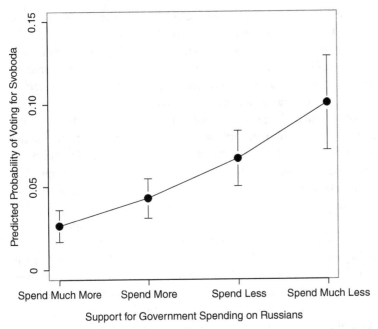

**Figure 5.11** Predicted probability of voting for the radical right party in Ukraine. *Note*: Simulations are based on Model 1 (M1) in Table 5.9. The values were set at: support for spending on Ukrainians = more, national pride = very proud, language = Ukrainian.

Russians has a 10 percent predicted probability of voting for Svoboda. This represents a large substantive effect, and suggests that if Svoboda could attract voters who strongly oppose accommodation of Russians, then they could comfortably cross the 5 percent threshold in the national election, as they did in 2012. Svoboda is the most credible party to attract those who are passionate about the Ukrainian identity, but not the most credible party to fight the Russophiles, which needs to be done by a large party. As long as those harboring policy hostilities toward Russians are split between Svoboda and the mainstream party, Svoboda's support will remain weak.

Identity threats are not a uniquely defining characteristic of Svoboda voters. Svoboda voters are driven by a mix of attitudes – opposition to state support for the Russian minority, desire to protect the dominant (titular) nationality and economic anxiety – but not by group hostility.

These are the factors that uniquely distinguish actual Svoboda voters from potential Svoboda voters as well as from voters of other parties.

This chapter shed light on Svoboda voters. It showed who was swayed to support the Svoboda party, during a critical moment in Svoboda's trajectory after its success in the 2009 regional elections and before its electoral breakthrough in 2012. The results demonstrate that uniquely high levels of xenophobia vis-à-vis Russians did not drive support for Svoboda. Opposition to government support for the Russian minority and support for the Ukrainian cause did. Although greater hostility against Russians raised the probability of supporting Svoboda, levels of hostility were very moderate both among voters and sympathizers. Economic insecurity was much more strongly predictive of voting for Svoboda after other factors were taken into account.

These findings should provide pause to claims that a disproportionately high level of xenophobia against the ethnic Russians lies at the core of Svoboda support. While levels of inter-group hostility were modest, the fact that they polarized the political system contributed to the escalation of perceived identity threats. Svoboda voters are driven by a combination of fears but not by hatred of other ethnic groups.

In the parliamentary elections of 2014, Svoboda's vote share dropped by half and it failed to cross the 5 percent electoral threshold by a narrow margin. Although this was not the result that the Svoboda leadership was hoping for, the loss of votes need not signal the party's political obscurity. Even the most successful radical right parties, such as the Slovak National Party or the Freedom Party in Austria, occasionally fall out of favor, and then bounce back after one or two electoral cycles. Most radical right parties do not secure two-digit vote shares on a regular basis and their marginal presence in the parliament is an accomplishment in itself.

Svoboda's 2014 defeat can be attributed to many factors: the party split votes with more militant Pravyi Sektor. Performance of Svoboda representatives in the interim government after Euromaidan was embarrassing; the party lost their monopoly on fervent patriotism; and Svoboda's political adversary, Viktor Yanukovych, was defeated (Shekhovtsov 2015). Furthermore, after Euromaidan and the annexation of Crimea by Russia, many of the policies to strengthen Ukrainian identity on Svoboda's wish list were implemented. In 2014, the parliamentary faction of the Communist Party, the archenemy of Svoboda, was dissolved in the Verkhovna Rada. Security issues forced the electorate to coalesce behind strong-armed leaders, and to abandon parties with a niche appeal (Table 5.2). In turbulent times, parties that demonstrate military competence, the ability to preserve territorial integrity and forestall status reversal have the upper hand, and these factors also contributed to the siphoning off of Svoboda's supporters in 2014.

## 5.4 Conclusion

This chapter explains the puzzling electoral failure of radical right parties in countries with large minorities such as Ukraine. The analysis of party dynamics in Slovakia suggested that the radical right can be successful in the presence of a small but politically organized ethnic minority, when the radical right party and its bilateral opposite compete on the issue of minority accommodation and over the "status elevation" of a minority group. In Ukraine and in other countries with large minorities, a large and politically organized ethnic "minority" threatens the titular nationality with its own "status reversal" and not just "status elevation."

At the micro-level, the major difference between the results from Slovakia and Ukraine is the ideological differentiation of the bilateral opposite from its proximate competitor in Slovakia, and the lack of such differentiation in Ukraine. In both countries, the voters for mainstream parties are polarized on the issue of government support toward minorities – the Hungarians (in the Slovak case) and Russians (in the Ukrainian case). What differentiated the configuration of the two cases? It was the *divergence* of ethnic party voter positions from the voter positions of the mainstream ally (in Slovakia), and the *convergence* of voter positions of a quasi-ethnic party (Communist Party) with the voter positions of its mainstream ally in Ukraine (the Party of Regions). The bilateral opposite of the radical right party in Ukraine was less extreme, vis-à-vis the mainstream, and therefore less polarizing. The political alliance of the Communist Party and the mainstream Party of Regions posed a substantial political threat to nationalists in Western Ukraine. Faced with the shift in language policies, voters flocked to the radical right party, when the Orange bloc was divided and fragile.

This is consistent with the theoretical expectation that increased salience of identity issues originates with the non-proximate bilateral opposite party, which leads to the backlash by the radical right party. Micro-level evidence from Slovakia and Ukraine is also consistent with the cross-national level evidence: whereas mainstream party convergence is indeterminate, the divergence between the bilateral opposite party and its mainstream competitor on identity issues is essential for the radical right party's success.

In countries with large and politically vocal minorities, radical right parties are faced with the challenge of attracting voters who oppose the status elevation of a politically salient minority, yet they must at the same time persuade voters that they can address the threat to the status of the dominant nationality. Niche parties cannot fight wars and contain civil conflicts. If the majority faces the threat of status reversal combined with serious security threats, as it is in Ukraine, voters will rally behind a radicalized mainstream party that controls the state security apparatus and the army.

Radical right parties tend to fail in countries with large minorities. Voters faced with the threat of status reversal opt for a larger mainstream party that has the political power to block it. In sum, the success of radical right parties in countries with small minorities originates in irritation and indignation at status elevation, whereas the failure of radical right parties in countries with large minorities originates in threat to ethnic dominance through status reversal.

# 6 | *Conclusion*

Ahmen Dogan should be investigated for crimes against the state. The MRF has turned Bulgaria into a network of Islamist nests.

—Volen Siderov, (leader of the radical right party Ataka in Bulgaria), attacking Ahmen Dogan, leader of the Turkish ethnic party Movement of Rights and Freedoms (MRF), May 21, 2011

The book argues that radical right mobilization follows the political ascendance of minorities. When aspirational minorities erode the status quo, the fringes of the established group mobilize in an effort to shift the status quo back and block further advancement of minorities. Nothing less than the ownership of the state by the dominant group, usually a titular ethnic group, is at stake. Minorities want to have a say in state-building efforts and in restructuring majority–minority relations, but their aspirations alarm fringe groups. When the demands of minorities are accommodated by a collaborative effort of mainstream and niche minority parties, it polarizes party systems and engenders a political backlash, which benefits radical right parties.

Pluralistic democracies across the world are sometimes able to reconcile tensions associated with the participation of candidates from religious, ethnic, regional and sexual minorities in politics. But this book suggests that there is a price to be paid, at least initially, for allowing minorities to rise and to voice their desires. In some instances, it locks party systems into a cycle of contention and recoil. In other instances, mobilization arises as new demands are born, new minorities step into the spotlight and new boundaries between the majority and minority are crafted or reinvented. Over long periods of time, some demands might become less salient when different groups mobilize at different times and demand accommodation, which implies a shift in the targets of hostility.

Minorities need political backing to achieve their goals. The most direct channel is to form ethnic parties, but they can also seek allies and patrons among mainstream parties willing to embrace pluralism and advance minority causes. In most post-communist democracies, it is almost impossible to form governing coalitions without a junior partner, due to the proportional electoral systems. Mainstream parties therefore invite niche parties into cabinets and/or rely on their support in parliaments in exchange for concessions. In so doing, however, they lose credibility as defenders of the dominant group and invite the wrath of radical right voters and parties

I test this new theory of radical right politics using a new panel dataset covering all post-communist democracies and with three original surveys that I designed, one in Slovakia and two in Ukraine. The book demonstrates that radical right parties succeed to a much greater extent *after* ethnic parties have participated in governing coalitions and mainstream parties have accommodated their demands.[1] It also shows that voters rally behind radical right parties not due to xenophobia, but because accommodation diverts resources and tilts the balance of power away from the titular nationality. Mainstream parties are willing to grant concessions to minorities because they need niche parties, minority parties and socially liberal parties in order to create majorities in parliaments. Some accommodative mainstream parties are willing to entertain the demands of ethnic and socially liberal parties because they are truly ideologically committed to diversity, whereas others do so to satisfy compliance with the country's international commitments to minority rights. The expansion of rights is rarely just symbolic, however. It elevates the status of minorities because it typically entails granting political power to them and conferring access to resources that can be used to improve their standing in society. It is this process that ignites radical right voters. The analysis focuses on three indicators of politically driven status elevation: (1) the electoral strength of bilateral opposite parties,[2] (2) the impact of the

---

[1] Opposition to corruption raises the question of whether radical right parties are merely a form of "anti-establishment parties" that arise due to the dissatisfaction with current and past practices of parties (Pop-Eleches 2010). There is a weak correlation between corruption levels and support for radical right parties over time at the country level (Bustikova 2009b). According to the survey, Svoboda voters in Ukraine were not different in their position on corruption when compared with other voters, even though the party leaders often criticize corruption of leading Ukrainian politicians.

[2] The electoral strength of the "bilateral opposite" can be viewed as a form of an ethnic "head count" (Chandra 2004), yet bilateral opposite parties (e.g., ethnic or socially liberal parties) are not present in all political systems. In Eastern Europe,

bilateral opposite parties on policy-making and (3) the access of minority groups to state transfers and state resources.[3]

While xenophobic attitudes are quite widespread and stable across populations over time, irritation with minorities fluctuates in concert with policy accommodation toward minorities. Group hostility in Eastern Europe is prevalent,[4] but if xenophobia was at the core of radical right voting in Eastern Europe, radical right parties would have already wiped the mainstream off the electoral map. Yet Eastern European radical right parties are rather anemic. They rarely gain over 10 percent in elections and struggle to obtain parliamentary representation. Compared with Western Europe, radical right parties in the East are electorally weaker, but more vitriolic and caustic (cf. Mudde 2017). By mimicking the successful strategies of their Western cousins (Art 2011), radical right parties in the East have started to professionalize their party apparatus, to shift their appeals to the center by distancing themselves from violence and to limit xenophobic rhetoric in public (Minkenberg 2015; Pirro 2015; Pytlas 2016).

Economically speaking, Eastern European radical right parties are left leaning (Bustikova and Kitschelt 2009). Their designation as "right-wing" parties therefore refers to their stance on identity issues, and not their position on redistribution. If economic conditions predicted radical right mobilization, then we would have observed spikes in radical right voting immediately after the collapse of communism, when all post-communist countries underwent a period of severe economic contraction. However, the erratic rise and fall of radical right parties does not follow the trajectory of unemployment or economic booms and busts. Instead, radical right parties in the East have followed the trajectory of Western radical right parties – their overall support is increasing over time, sometimes following an economic bust,

ethnic parties are surprisingly missing (or are fragmented) in states with large minorities.

[3] Access to governmental portfolios gives bilateral opposites the ability to change policies and access to state resources. My theory therefore is focused on the bilateral opposite party and minority status elevation, rather than on the polarization or convergence of the mainstream parties. Policy shifts represent only one of several causal mechanisms that can increase the salience of identity issues. Indeed, distributing pork to an ethnic constituency in the context of coalition politics need not generate any substantive policy shifts.

[4] The Policy Capital Institute has published multiple studies on the prevalence of xenophobia and intolerance and their studies have shown that the relationship between the degree of group hostility and the strength of radical right parties in Eastern Europe is weak.

as in Hungary and Greece, but sometimes unaffected by it, as in Albania and Ireland.[5] The economic platform is of secondary importance because the effect of economic grievances is mediated by identity concerns. Economic anxieties resonate with radical right voters if economic decay is viewed as diminishing the power of the dominant group and limiting national sovereignty.

Nationalistic mobilization has been an important ingredient that dissolved the communist regimes and spilled over into the post-1989 period, especially in disintegrating federations (USSR, Czechoslovakia and Yugoslavia). Nationalism enabled self-rule and celebrated sovereignty after 1989/1991, but then receded after independence. Focusing on cycles of democratic contestation after the founding elections, this book seeks to explain volatile spikes of radical right mobilization over time. If sovereignty was achieved, what sustains appeals based on national pride? The answer is that democratization empowered minorities, who realized that pluralistic democracy allows them to have a seat at the table and participate in the state-building process. Minority groups seized on the opportunity: they formed parties and sought political patrons. The pressure to accommodate came both from within and from abroad. At home, the pro-democratic political actors embraced minority rights to signal their commitment to pluralistic democracy and often formed governing coalitions with representatives of ethnic and minority groups. Such alliances enabled minorities with political backing to ascend.[6] However, if mainstream liberal parties mismanage the economy, economic conflict can be framed in identity terms. While lecturing the public about the need to embrace an open, cosmopolitan society, mainstream liberal parties shower ethnic and socially liberal parties with resources and concessions, which fundamentally diminish the dominant group. Conflict over sovereignty ensues.

In the same way, the logic of identity clashes can infiltrate other domains such as corruption and trust in institutions. Corruption can create powerful grievances and a desire to punish incumbents. It

---

[5] The radical right party family is the fastest growing party family in Europe (Mudde 2007). In Western Europe, radical right parties emerged in the late 1980s and have grown in importance ever since (Arzheimer 2009; Kitschelt 2007; van der Brug and Fennema 2007), whereas most East European radical right parties emerged after 1989.

[6] The Copenhagen criteria that govern the European Union accession process require protection of human rights, including the rights of minorities. External sponsors, such as Russia, Hungary and Turkey, keep an eye on ethnic kin minorities in neighboring or nearby states as well.

undermines trust in established political parties and increases volatility because voters migrate to new parties. The newcomers elected to punish the incumbents might come from radical right parties, but only if the anti-corruption ethos is intertwined with identity grievances. New parties can be formed on a purely anti-corruption and populist platform unrelated to policy and group hostility. In volatile party systems, however, new parties sometimes need to be more ideologically extreme in order to overcome information noise and to credibly signal their ideological distance from established parties (Ezrow et al. 2014). Yet these need not assume the form of radical right parties. Although economic grievances, frustration with the loss of sovereignty in the European Union and resentment of political corruption are all compatible with radical right mobilization, this book argues that indignation with minority accommodation and policy hostility lies at the core of radical right mobilization.

This book has suggested that radical right parties are chiefly reactive in nature. Their agenda is focused on counteracting the political inroads, cultural concessions and economic gains of politically organized minorities. The causal logic is rooted in a political backlash against minority accommodation and status elevation, which polarizes the electorate and enhances the salience of identity issues in party competition. Radical right parties mobilize to offset and roll back the advantages that have been afforded to minorities, and succeed when they actively promote policies that seek to reverse prior accommodation or to create new policies (e.g., language laws) that make future accommodation more difficult. This theory explains the erratic nature of their support – when accommodation increases, radical right parties gain strength. Conversely, when the status quo is preserved or accommodation is reversed, their electoral support is lackluster. The success of radical right policies is, paradoxically, a cause of their future failure.

The book has also drawn attention to different structural propensities for radical right party success across countries, and has shown how radical right parties – somewhat counterintuitively – can be successful in countries with smaller minorities. The size of minorities modifies the threat of the ascending group. If minorities have the numerical strength to form parties and compete in elections, the dominant group has reasons to worry. But threat does not rise in proportion to the size of the groups because even small groups can find patrons willing to push for their demands. Large groups can be internally divided or satisfied with the status quo. Large groups can also pose serious sovereignty risks and can threaten the dominant group with status reversal, which requires the mainstream parties to act. It is the hunger of the minority group to get "more" from the dominant group – not the mere existence of the minority – that mobilizes the opposition from the radical right.

At the individual level, the book has shown that when the bilateral opposite's position is far from the position of the proximate mainstream competitor party (the "cousin") – and is accommodated – then radical right parties tend to succeed. In Ukraine, the political system became polarized on language rights, but the bilateral opposite (the Russophile Communist Party) and the nearby large mainstream party converged on the issue. In unison, they aggressively pursued language policies that could have led to status reversal for the Ukrainian speakers, which mobilized the Ukrainian radical right. The electoral potential of Svoboda, as a niche party, was limited, however, because the party lacks the capacity and credibility to address security risks and large-scale threats.

The micro-level evidence illustrates that group hostility is not an exclusive characteristic of radical right voters, but is widespread among the electorate. Policy hostility, defined as opposition to governmental transfers toward politically organized minority groups, cannot be derived from group hostility. It would be inaccurate to conflate opposition to transfers with hostility toward minorities. In all the surveys examined in this book, group hostility was *not* correlated with opposition to transfers. The literature on redistribution and ethnic diversity (Alesina et al. 1999; Habyarimana et al. 2007; Soroka et al. 2006) links welfare chauvinism with group hostility. Rather than being a function of group hostility, opposition to governmental transfers for minorities is driven by the logic of political competition (Dancygier 2010). State favoritism, such as the opposition to government spending on minorities primarily, motivates voting for radical right parties.

An important issue for future research to determine is the generalizability of the theory advanced and tested in this book. Can the theory travel to Western Europe, or to multiethnic democracies with proportional representation in other parts of the world? A major difference between the radical right in Western and Eastern Europe is that it targets immigrants in the West, whereas native ethnic groups serve as the foil in the East. While immigrants can vote in some local elections in Western Europe, most native ethnic groups in Eastern Europe can contest national elections. The refugee crisis has shown the adaptability of the radical right to seize on new issues and new contexts in Eastern Europe. The pressure from the European Union to adapt refugee quotas ignited passions. The threat of accommodation involving non-European migrants of Muslim faith associated with severe security threats inflamed a counter-mobilization and expanded the radical right's portfolio of targets. In this sense, it "Westernized" some of the grievances of the radical right parties in Eastern Europe and increased convergence between the East and the West.

The wave of refugees from the Middle East to Europe coincided with the aftermath of the economic crisis and the illiberal inklings of radicalized mainstream parties, spearheaded in Eastern Europe by Hungary and Poland. It has often been assumed that threats to experiments in democratic pluralism originate from (left or right) extremist parties. In Eastern Europe, niche parties do not have the muscle to subvert the institutions of democratic oversight. But mainstream parties do. Redistributive radicalized mainstream parties threaten the liberal trajectory of past decades. They either adapt or strategically use the rhetoric of (ethnic) minority exclusion to achieve political power and to roll back liberal democratic institutions. The threat originates from the mainstream and is exacerbated by the fact that liberal democracy never "locked in" in Eastern Europe.[7]

Although many West European mainstream parties embrace tough policies on immigration and home-grown terrorist networks, comparatively speaking, East European mainstream parties are much more comfortable with their radical right cousins. Radical right parties thus operate in a much more permissive environment and are often incorporated into governing coalitions. Radical right parties have been successful in steadily attracting some voter support since the early 1990s in Croatia, Estonia, Latvia, Romania, Serbia, Slovakia, and Slovenia. In these countries, the radical right was able to attract between 5 and 40 percent of the popular vote at various points in time. Furthermore, in Croatia, Estonia, Latvia, Poland, Serbia, Slovakia and Ukraine, radical right parties have been present in governing coalitions since the founding elections and have significantly shaped minority policies. Because radical right parties have been in power, their anti-establishment credentials are dubious. Radical right parties are not necessarily anti-elitist (cf. Mudde 2007), since they

---

[7] On chronic instability that undermines institutional lock-in and limits path dependence, see Bernhard (2015).

often work in tandem with mainstream nationalistic parties on legislation to curb the right of minorities.

In the East, the boundaries between the "radicalized right" and "radical right" are especially blurry. It has becoming increasingly difficult to determine whether prominent mainstream parties, such as Fidesz (led by Victor Orbán) in Hungary, PiS (unofficially led by Jarosław Kaczyński) in Poland and Smer (led by Robert Fico) in Slovakia, should be considered mainstream. In the Czech case, Andrej Babiš's populist political party ANO won in a landslide with almost 30 percent of the vote in October 2017. Babiš views politics in technocratic terms and sees the "state as a firm" in which the business of government is not impeded by democratic deliberation in the parliament. He envisions a polity where executive power is highly centralized, preferably in his hands (Bustikova and Guasti 2019).

This book offers a very strict definition of radical right parties as niche, single-issue, programmatic parties that advocate for exclusion and obedience. The main distinction between the radical right and radicalized mainstream right lies in the complexity of portfolios that mainstream parties possess. Although radicalized mainstream parties embrace nationalism, they also supply complex economic platforms to their voters. Furthermore, mainstream parties at times combine programmatic politics with investments in vast clientelistic machines at the ground level. Radical right parties can be corrupt, but rarely build durable clientelistic networks. Their economic platforms, if any, are not enforceable. Mainstream parties govern and are therefore more accountable for their policy agenda. They also benefit the most if electoral rules are tilted and institutions of oversight are weakened.

Left-leaning economic interventionists lead nationalistic, radicalized, mainstream parties. It is important to note that all the above-mentioned parties that currently pose a danger to liberal democracy (Fidesz, PiS, ANO) did *not* start out as radical right parties but only later radicalized. At some point, they were more centrist-leaning mainstream parties and only later used xenophobic appeals to win votes. Redistributive radicalized mainstream parties are not single-issue niche parties. As they radicalize over time, they maintain broad economic, state-building and institutional agendas and use identity strategically to maintain power and to justify executive overreach (Bermeo 2016; Bustikova and Guasti 2017).

Higher aggregate levels of xenophobia in the East (Kopecký and Mudde 2003), which contribute to the permissiveness of radical rhetoric, indicate weak liberal democratic consolidation. Paradoxically, historical legacies of authoritarian fascist interwar regimes are more relevant after almost thirty years of democratic consolidation than they were in 1989, for radicalized mainstream politicians are now looking for new ways to organize political systems. The nostalgic association with past glory ultimately benefits both the radical right and the radicalized mainstream right, since both claim to be the political successors of earlier nationalistic movements that are frequently associated with state independence and territorial unity. If there is a reversal in liberal democratic governance in Eastern Europe, it will most likely be initiated not by a small radical right niche party but by a large radicalized mainstream party that will move the country into new and uncharted territory. Whether the presence of a radical right party will facilitate such a turn, by introducing new issues and ideas into the mainstream, or will block democratic sidelining, by offering an alternative channel for discontent, requires further investigation.

To test the propositions advanced in this book in new contexts, it would be important to examine how niche political parties that advocate accommodative policies toward immigrants and asylum seekers interact with mainstream parties, and whether their successes – particularly in the form of significant pro-minority legislation – are related to the electoral success of radical right parties in subsequent electoral cycles. Only further analysis will show the extent to which the theory travels smoothly or requires adjustments, but part of the answer may lie in reassessing consociational theory (Lijphart 1984), since the political impact of power-sharing institutions is mitigated by the size of the quarreling groups.

Netherlands initially avoided a large-scale conflict between its large pillars due to accommodation, yet it built in mechanisms to placate minorities that have arguably later fueled radical right parties in the Netherlands. Similar mechanisms might have been in place in Austria, Bosnia, Lebanon and Switzerland, where discontent has been generated by disproportionate accommodation afforded to small minorities. Power-sharing, such as the Dayton agreement that governs Bosnia and Herzegovina, can "freeze" political alliances and violent conflicts (Guss and Siroky 2012), but the primary focus of the analysis presented here is contestation between groups that refrain from violence. The implications of this book for consociational arrangements is that power-sharing institutions ultimately create grievances and incite backlash.

Immigrants might one day become natives and then perhaps form ethnic parties. Some have already attracted the attention of political parties that advocate their demands. Accommodation may be limited to relatively minor economic goods – such as access to subsidized housing, educational and health care infrastructure – or might encompass larger issues, such as religious practice, language rights and the protection of relatives from deportations. The theory developed in this book predicts that a similar backlash, mediated by the electoral institutions, would likely ensue if there was a rapid expansion of Turkish rights in Germany or Latino rights in the United States. However, the raw demographic size of the minority does not have a linear effect on the success of radical right parties, since assertive policies that would elevate the status of minority languages, such as Turkish or Spanish, would lead to radical right success only if the minority did not pose an existential threat to the dominant group. When minorities are at near parity and pose a more serious security threat, I have argued that niche radical right parties typically lose out to mainstream competitors that are better positioned to protect the state.

The election of the first black president in the United States was followed by the era of Donald Trump. When a minority candidate, Barack Obama, ascended to the highest position of power, backlash ensued.[8] Recent evidence suggests that the status anxiety of wealthy whites, not economic hardship, played an important role in Trump's political success. As Mutz writes: "The 2016 election [of Donald Trump] ... was an effort by members of already dominant groups to assure their continued dominance and by those in an already powerful and wealthy country to assure its continued dominance" (Mutz 2018: 4339). Similarly, Womick et al. (2019) find that Trump supporters scored consistently higher in group-based dominance and authoritarian aggression when compared with their "cousins" (mainstream Republican supporters).

Social dominance theory offers a useful analytic tool to separate the radical right voters in the United States from more moderate voters of the (now radicalized) mainstream right. It also helps us to understand the sources of status anxiety, but social dominance theory also reifies group boundaries. By contrast, this book suggests that politicized group boundaries are fluid and that status anxiety can be triggered by both symbolic and material threats. An African American or Latino American minority in a position of power represents a consequential

---

[8] On backlash in US politics, see Abrajano and Hajnal 2015.

material threat because of group size, but threats can be fabricated and effervescent. Jews can be enemies of the radical right, but when the attention shifts to Muslims, radical right parties can cozy up to Jews and to Israel. Transgender bathrooms are symbolic and the issue is marginal in the big picture of electoral competition but, of course, important to those who are affected. Yet if powerful political players back claims, polarization is likely to ensue. Refugees might be a fleeting threat or many miles away, but if they find political advocates, anxieties associated with refugee accommodation trigger radical right mobilization. However, without political advocates, one could equally expect that the refugee issue might recede or turn into a non-political technocratic task for the government to solve.

This book explains volatility.[9] The ebb and flow of the status quo shifts associated with minority accommodation explain why radical right mobilization can accelerate, and also why it loses steam. We should be equally interested in the rise as well as in the inevitable fall of white supremacists in mainstream politics. As long as minorities and their advocates seek and secure concessions from the majority, radical right parties are here to stay. If radical right parties are already vocal, mainstream parties should consider how best to fine-tune policies that grant concessions to minorities, while being careful not to engage in outbidding with the radical right. This iterated dynamic of minority demands and majority pushback over several electoral cycles can create an equilibrium that eventually satisfies both the dominant and the minority group, and can gradually expand minority rights in the long run. If mainstream parties are prepared to accommodate the demands of a politically mobilized minority, they ought to be prepared for the ensuing backlash. In Eastern Europe, parties quarrel over language policies. Elsewhere, politicians argue over head-coverings and housing subsidies for ethnic minorities. The vehicles of accommodation change with the context. Yet the argument that the accommodation of minorities polarizes the electorate and creates a political backlash is universal.

---

[9] On the cyclical nature of liberal and illiberal democracy from a historical perspective, see Berman (2017).

# Appendix

## Appendix to Chapter 3

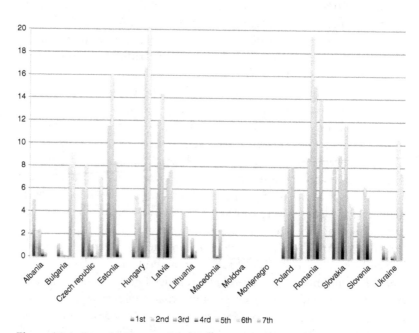

**Figure A3.1** Cumulative vote shares of radical right parties by electoral cycles.

### List of Election Sources

The vote shares for the electoral results are culled from multiple sources. When there was a discrepancy between multiple sources, I checked the official results from the country's statistical or electoral offices. Adam Carr's election source often provides direct links to country-specific official documents.

List of major databases consulted to determine vote shares:

1. Psephos, Adam Carr's Election Archive; http://psephos.adam-carr.net
2. Project on Political Transformation and the Electoral Process in Post-Communist Europe, University of Essex; www.essex.ac.uk/elections/

3. Political Data Yearbook, European Journal of Political Research Political Data Yearbook; www.politicaldatayearbook.com
4. Election Results Archive; Binghamton University; http://cdp .binghamton.edu/era/index.html
5. Baltic Voices, Centre for the Study of Public Policy, University of Strathclyde; www.balticvoices.org
6. European Election Database; www.nsd.uib.no/european_election_ database/
7. Election Resources; http://electionresources.org/eastern.europe.html

## Classification of Radical Right Parties

### Grid Group Theory

The party classification system used in the book is derived from the grid-group theoretical framework developed by anthropologist Mary Douglas (Douglas and Wildavsky 1982). Two ideological dimensions define this typology – radical nationalism and radical socio-cultural conservatism – and these dimensions correspond to two modes of social control, *grid* and *group*. Radical right parties are classified as being high on grid and high on group, or high on one of these two dimensions and "neutral" on the second dimension. Using this logic of party classification, radical right parties are either highly nationalistic or highly socially conservative.

If a party scores high on one dimension and low on the other dimension, however, it is not defined as a radical right party. This framework is particularly helpful in deciding whether some of the former unreformed communist parties (red-brown parties) should qualify as radical right parties. For example, the Czech communist party is not coded as a radical right party because it scores very low on the grid dimension as a result of its advocacy for gender equality and access to abortion.

*Grid*: The policy positions of radical right parties are captured by authoritarian social and cultural conservatism. In its pure form, it has no ethnic basis. A political party scoring high on social authoritarianism dimension might campaign against accommodating gay and lesbian couples or against abortion. Similarly, a party that promotes law and order, along with obedience to authority, religious or secular, would be classified as high on the grid dimension.

*Group*: The second dimension captures nationalism and is therefore associated with exclusionary appeals based on ethnicity. It conceptualizes identity in terms of "the ethnic other" and is grounded in a distinction between the in-group and the out-group. A party that propagates nationalism on behalf of the titular nationality would score high on the group dimension.

The classification of ethno-liberal parties mirrors this topology. Ethno-liberal parties are those that score low on both grid and group or low on one of these two dimensions and "neutral" on the second dimension. Small East European socially liberal parties embrace multiculturalism and the protection of minorities, and are often advocates of Roma rights. Even though multiculturalism is a universal position, it implies that social-liberal parties support policies that would elevate the Roma from poverty and reduce their social exclusion. Small socially liberal parties in Eastern Europe are both rare and recent.

A party that propagates nationalism on behalf of the titular nationality would qualify as a radical right party, whereas a party making cross-ethnic appeals and demanding minority rights would be coded as an ethno-liberal party. Small economically and socially liberal parties generally support policies of minority accommodation, as do ethnic and some green parties. Some of the policies that ethno-liberal parties promote include minority autonomy in schooling, elevation of the minority language to the status of the official language, quotas for ethnic minorities in parliament, positive discrimination, preferential treatment of minorities in civil service hiring practices, state resources channeled to address minority grievances and preferential economic policies that disproportionately benefit minorities.

## Grid Group Measurement

In defining radical right parties, I have relied on three sources of information: (1) expert surveys, (2) ideology communicated through web pages of radical right parties and (3) comparison with classification in the scholarly literature on radical right parties.

The position of the parties on group and grid was determined using three expert surveys: *Party Policy in Modern Democracies* (PPMD; Benoit and Laver 2006), the Chapel Hill Expert Survey (CH-H; Bakker et al. 2013) and the Democratic Accountability and Linkages Project (DALP; Kitschelt 2011). The group dimension is defined as a policy position of the party on "nationalism" (PPMD), "ethnic minorities" (CH-H) and "national identity" (DALP). The grid dimension is defined as a policy position of the party on "social" issues (PPMD), "social lifestyle" (CH-H) and "traditional authority, institutions and customs" (DALP). The expert estimates of party positions are in listed in Table A3.1.

Table A3.1 Classification of radical right parties based on expert surveys

| Country | Parties | 2003–2004 PPMD | | 2008–2009 DALP | | 2002, 2006 and 2010 CH-H | | |
| --- | --- | --- | --- | --- | --- | --- | --- | --- |
| | | Group | Grid | Group | Grid | Group | Grid | Galtan |
| Albania | PBK - BK | | | | | | | |
| | PBKD | | | | | | | |
| Bulgaria | BNRP | | | | | | | |
| | NSA | | | 8.77 | 8.00 | NA & 8.17 & 9.55 | NA & 9.40 & 9.30 | |
| Croatia | HDZ | 19.00 | 15.00 | | | | | |
| | HSP | | | 8.25 | 8.31 | | | |
| | HSP-ZDS | | | | | | | |
| | HSP-HKDU | | | | | | | |
| Czech Republic | SPR-RSČ | 19.20 | 15.90 | | | | | |
| | RMS | | | | | | | |
| | NS | | | | | | | |
| | NDS | | | | | | | |
| | DSS / DS | | | | | | | |
| Estonia | ERSP | | | | | | | |
| | EK | | | | | | | |
| | ERKL | | | | | | | |
| | PE | | | | | | | |
| | EIP | | | | | | | |
| | Isamaa | 19.10 | 14.60 | 8.67 | 7.89 | NA & 7.60 & NA | NA & 6.50 & NA | |

Table A3.1 (*cont.*)

| Country | Parties | 2003–2004 PPMD | | 2008–2009 DALP | | 2002, 2006 and 2010 CH-H | | Galtan |
|---|---|---|---|---|---|---|---|---|
| | | Group | Grid | Group | Grid | Group | Grid | |
| Hungary | MIÉP | 19.80 | 19.00 | | | NA | NA | 9.69 |
| | MIÉP-Jobbik | | | | | | | |
| | Jobbik | | | | | NA & NA & 9.00 | NA & NA & 8.94 | |
| Latvia | TB | | | | | | | |
| | TB/LNNK | 19.30 | 14.50 | 8.69 | 7.23 | NA & 9.75 & 9.22 | NA & 7.50 & 8.13 | |
| | LKDS/LTJS | | | | | | | |
| Lithuania | LNP-JL | | | | | NA | NA | |
| | LlaS | | | | | NA | NA | 8.60 |
| | LNDP | | | | | | | 8.75 |
| Macedonia | VMRO-DPMNE | 17.50 | 17.30 | 6.27 | 7.33 | | | |
| | VMRO-DP | | | | | | | |

| Country | Party | | | | | | |
|---|---|---|---|---|---|---|---|
| Poland | SN | | | | | | |
| | Party X | | | | | | |
| | PWN-PSN | | | | | | |
| | ROP | | | | | | |
| | LPR | 19.00 | 19.10 | 7.36 | 8.50 | NA & 9.00 & 8.09 | NA & 10.00 & 9.58 |
| | LPR (Prawica) | | | | | | |
| Romania | PUNR | | | | | | |
| | PRM | 19.60 | 18.70 | 9.21 | 8.93 | NA & 9.63 & 8.71 | NA & 9.75 & 8.9 |
| | PNG | | | | | | |
| | PP-DD | | | | | | |
| Serbia | SRS | 18.70 | 16.80 | 9.00 | 8.80 | | |
| | NS | | | 8.40 | 8.50 | | |
| | SPO | 13.50 | 13.80 | | | | |
| Slovakia | PSNS | | | | | NA | 8.62 |
| | SNS | 19.40 | 16.10 | 9.85 | 8.46 | NA & 9.83 & 9.93 | NA & 9.08 & 8.93 |
| Slovenia | SNS | 17.10 | 11.70 | 9.80 | 5.54 | NA & NA & 8.91 | NA & NA & 9.25 |
| Ukraine | KUN | | | | | | |
| | Rukh | | | | | | |
| | Svoboda | | | | | | |

*Note*: Empty cells mean that data are not available in the expert surveys (parties were not included in the survey).
*Sources*: PPMD – *Party Policy in Modern Democracies*; DALP – Democratic Accountability and Linkages Project; CH-H – Chapel Hill Expert Survey.

227

The full description of the questions from each of the three expert surveys and their respective scales is listed below.

The position of each party is relative to the position of other parties, since the experts evaluate all parties in a given party system. Radical right parties are those with the highest grid/group scores relative to other parties in the same country.

## PPMD – Party Policy in Modern Democracies

Source: Kenneth Benoit and Michael Laver, *Party Policy in Modern Democracies*. Expert survey scores of policy positions of political parties in forty-seven countries. Data collected in 2004–2005.

Group: Nationalism

> Strongly promotes a cosmopolitan rather than a ___ national consciousness, history and culture. (1)
>
> Strongly promotes a ___ national rather than a cosmopolitan consciousness, history and culture. (20)

Grid: Social

> Favors liberal policies on matters such as abortion, homosexuality and euthanasia. (1)
>
> Opposes liberal policies on matters such as abortion, homosexuality and euthanasia. (20)

Scale: 1–20, where 20 = high group/grid

## DALP – Democratic Accountability and Linkages Project

Source: Herbert Kitschelt, Democratic Accountability and Linkages Project, July 20, 2011 (dataset). Data collected in 2008–2009.

Group: National identity

Party advocates toleration and social and political equality for minority ethnic, linguistic, religious and racial groups and opposes state policies that require the assimilation of such groups to the majority national culture. (1)

Party believes that the defense and promotion of the majority national identity and culture at the expense of minority representation are important goals. (10)

Grid: Traditional authority, institutions, customs

Party advocates full individual freedom from state interference into any issues related to religion, marriage, sexuality, occupation, family life and social conduct in general. (1)

Party advocates state-enforced compliance of individuals with traditional authorities and values on issues related to religion, marriage,
sexuality, occupation, family life and social conduct in general. (10)
Scale: 1–10, where 10 = high group/grid

### CH-H – Chapel Hill Expert Survey

Source: Ryan Bakker, Catherine De Vries, Erica Edwards, Liesbet
Hooghe, Seth Jolly, Gary Marks, Jonathan Polk, Jan Rovny, Marco
Steenbergen and Milada Anna Vachudova, "Measuring Party Pos-
itions in Europe: The Chapel Hill Expert Survey Trend File,
1999–2010." Data collected in 2002–2010.
Group: Ethnic minorities
Position toward ethnic minorities: strongly supports more rights for
ethnic minorities. (0)
Position toward ethnic minorities: strongly opposes more rights for
ethnic minorities. (10)
Grid: Social lifestyle
Position on social lifestyle (e.g., homosexuality): strongly supports
liberal policies (0)
Position on social lifestyle (e.g., homosexuality): strongly opposes
liberal policies (10)
Galtan: This policy position was added when grid or group is not
available in the survey.
Position of the party [in year] in terms of their views on democratic
freedoms and rights. "Libertarian" or "post-materialist" parties favor
expanded personal freedoms, for example, access to abortion, active
euthanasia, same-sex marriage or greater democratic participation. (0)
"Traditional" or "authoritarian" parties often reject these ideas; they
value order, tradition and stability, and believe that the government
should be a firm moral authority on social and cultural issues. (10)
Scale: 0–10, where 10 = high group/grid

### Grid Group Measurement: Ideology on the Internet

I have consulted the web pages and Facebook profiles of parties in
order to determine whether the grid/group classification appears compatible with party ideology as communicated through media. Table
A3.2 provides a list of party web pages and indicates if the party or its
leader has a Facebook presence.

Table A3.2 *Web page and Facebook presence of radical right parties*

| Country | Parties | Party web page | Facebook page |
|---------|---------|----------------|---------------|
| Albania | PBK-BK | www.ballikombit.org/ | Yes |
|  | PBKD |  | Yes |
| Bulgaria | BNRP |  |  |
|  | NSA | www.ataka.bg | No |
| Croatia | HDZ | www.hdz.hr | Yes |
|  | HSP | www.hsp.hr | Yes |
|  | HSP-ZDS |  |  |
|  | HSP-HKDU |  |  |
| Czech Republic | SPR-RSČ | http://republikani.webnode.cz | No |
|  | RMS |  |  |
|  | NS |  |  |
|  | NDS |  |  |
|  | DSS/DS | http://delnicka.strana.sweb.cz | No |
| Estonia | ERSP |  |  |
|  | EK |  |  |
|  | ERKL |  |  |
|  | PE |  | Yes |
|  | EIP | www.iseseisvuspartei.ee | Yes |
|  | Isamaa | www.irl.ee/ | Yes |
| Hungary | MIÉP |  |  |
|  | MIÉP-Jobbik |  |  |
|  | Jobbik | www.jobbik.com | Yes |
| Latvia | TB |  |  |
|  | TB/LNNK | www.tb.lv | Yes |
| Lithuania | LKDS/LTJS |  |  |
|  | LNP-JL | www.jaunalietuviai.lt | Yes (leader) |
|  | LlaS |  |  |
|  | LNDP | www.lndp.lt | No |
| Macedonia | VMRO-DPMNE | http://vmro-dpmne.org.mk | Yes |
|  | VMRO-DP | www.vmro-dp.org.mk/ | Yes |
| Poland | SN | www.polskapartianarodowa.org | No |
|  | Party X |  |  |
|  | PWN-PSN | www.pwn.waw.pl | No |
|  | ROP |  |  |
|  | LPR | www.lpr.pl | No |

Table A3.2 (*cont.*)

| Country | Parties | Party web page | Facebook page |
|---|---|---|---|
| | LPR (Prawica) | | |
| | Ruch Narodowy | | |
| Romania | PUNR | | |
| | PRM | http://prm-central.ro | No |
| | PNG | www.png.ro | No |
| | PP-DD | www.partidul.poporului.ro | Yes (leader) |
| Serbia | SRS | www.srpskaradikalnastranka.org.rs | Yes |
| | NS | www.nova-srbija.org/ | Yes |
| | (regional) | | SPO |
| | www.spo.rs/ index.php | Yes | |
| Slovakia | PSNS | | Yes |
| | SNS | www.sns.sk | Yes |
| Slovenia | SNS | www.sns.si | Yes (leader) |
| Ukraine | KUN | http://cun.org.ua | Yes |
| | Rukh | www.nru.org.ua | Yes |
| | Svoboda | www.svoboda.org.ua | Yes |

This source was particularly useful in classifying recently emerged parties or parties that might be considered borderline cases. For example, the new Romanian party Partidul Poporului–Dan Diaconescu (PP-DD) lists its policy goals and ideological preferences on its website (www.partidul.poporului.ro). The website states: "Romania's ethnic parties will not be able to participate in elections." This speaks directly to the group dimension and is a clear attack on the Hungarian ethnic party whose voters are Romanian citizens with full rights. The party is coded as high on the group dimension. Another doctrinal statement of the party relates to the grid dimension: "Emergency rejuvenation of the population and increasing the number of inhabitants of Romania." This statement relates to state's role in regulating sexual behavior of its citizens, and indicates a high degree of intrusion into social issues. The party is thus coded as high on the grid dimension.

**Grid Group Measurement: Comparison with Other Classifications**
I have also compared my classification of parties to five prominent classifications of radical right parties in the scholarly literature: Minkenberg (2002), Mudde (2007, 2000), Pop-Eleches (2007) and Ramet (1999). Table A3.3 summarizes these comparisons. The authors use different labels for radical right parties and focus on different policies. Ramet (1999) classifies highly nationalistic parties as "radical right" parties and movements. Mudde (2000, 2007) uses "extremist right" and "populist radical right" to underscore the anti-establishment appeal of the parties. Minkenberg (2002) differentiates between three different types of parties and social organizations/movements in the radical-right family: racist-ethnocentrist, fascist-authoritarian and religious-fundamentalist. Finally, Pop-Eleches (2010) uses the label "extreme-nationalist" to denote parties that promulgate ethnic appeals and are non-ideological/personality driven parties.

A closer examination of these party classifications revealed seven borderline cases, listed below. These borderline cases were classified by only some of the other authors as "extreme." If there was any doubt about whether the party ideology was sufficiently high on "group" issues, it was excluded from the radical right category. If the movement/social organization was not a party, it was also excluded from the radical right party family.

Latvia: Popular Movement for Latvia (TKL-ZP, Siegerist party). Classified as an extreme nationalist party by Pop-Eleches (2010). Classified as a "bizarre" extreme right party and borderline Latvian extreme right party by Mudde (2000). The leader Siegerist was in favor of selling land to foreigners and was not strongly anti-Russian (Jeffries 2004).

Poland: Christian National Union (ZChN). Classified as a religious-fundamentalist party/organization by Minkenberg (2002). Classified as a national-populist party by Pop-Eleches (2010). Classified as a mainstream radical right organization by Ramet (1999).

Poland: Confederation of Independent Poland (KPN). Classified as a radical right party by Ramet (1999), as racist-ethnocentrist by Minkenberg (2002) and extreme nationalist by Pop-Eleches (2010). Patriotic party formed in 1979. KPN displayed moderation and inclusiveness not typical for extremist parties (Hockenos 1993; Pankowski 2010).

Table A3.3 *Comparative classification of radical right parties*

| Country | Parties | Ramet 1999 | Mudde 2000 | Minkenberg 2002 | Mudde 2007 | Pop-Eleches 2010 |
|---|---|---|---|---|---|---|
| Albania | PBK-BK | | | | | National populist (PBK) |
| | PBKD | | | | | |
| Bulgaria | BNRP | RR | ER | | | Extreme nationalist |
| | NSA | | | | | National populist |
| Croatia | HDZ | RR (fraction) | ER (fraction) | | | |
| | HSP | RR | ER | | P-RR | Extreme nationalist |
| | HSP-ZDS | | | | | |
| | HSP-HKDU | | | | | |
| Czech Republic | SPR-RSČ | | ER | Racist–ethnocentrist | | Extreme nationalist |
| | RMS | | | | | |
| | NS | | | | | |
| | NDS | | | | | |
| | DSS/DS | | | | | |
| Estonia | ERSP | | ER | | | National populist |
| | EK | | | | | |
| | ERKL | | ER | | | |
| | PE | | | | | |
| | EIP | | | | | |
| | Isamaa | | NC | | | |

Table A3.3 (*cont.*)

| Country | Parties | Ramet 1999 | Mudde 2000 | Minkenberg 2002 | Mudde 2007 | Pop-Eleches 2010 |
|---|---|---|---|---|---|---|
| Hungary | MIÉP | RR | ER | Racist-ethnocentrist | P-RR | Extreme nationalist |
| | MIÉP-Jobbik | | | | | |
| | Jobbik | | | | | |
| Latvia | TB | | | | | National populist |
| | TB/LNNK | | | | | National populist (LNNK) |
| Lithuania | LKDS/LTJS | | | | | Extreme nationalist |
| | LNP-JL | | | | | |
| | LlaS | | | | | |
| | LNDP | | | | | |
| Macedonia | VMRO-DPMNE | | | | | National populist (VMRO) |
| | VMRO-DP | | | | | |
| Poland | SN | | | | | |
| | Party X | | ER (fraction) | Racist-ethnocentrist | | |
| | PWN-PSN | | ER | Fascist-authoritarian | | |
| | ROP | M-RR | | Religious-fundamentalist | | |
| | LPR | | | | P-RR | National populist |
| | LPR (Prawica) | | | | | National populist |

234

| Country | Party | | | Racist-ethnocentrist / Fascist-authoritarian | P-RR | |
|---|---|---|---|---|---|---|
| Romania | PUNR | RR | ER | | | National populist |
| | PRM | RR | ER | | P-RR | Extreme nationalist |
| | PNG | | | | | New/centrist populist |
| | PP-DD | | | | | |
| Serbia | SRS | RR | ER | | | |
| | NS | | | | | |
| | SPO | | | | | |
| Slovakia | PSNS | RR | ER | | | Extreme nationalist |
| | SNS | | | | P-RR | Extreme nationalist |
| Slovenia | SNS | RR | ER | | | Extreme nationalist |
| Ukraine | KUN | RR | ER | | | |
| | Rukh | | | | | |
| | Svoboda | | | | | |

*Note*: ER: extreme right party; M-RR: mainstream radical right party; NC: national conservative party; P-RR: populist radical right party; RR: radical right party.

235

Table A3.4 Vote shares for the radical right parties (over time and by party since the first foundational elections)

| | 1st | 2nd | 3rd | 4th | 5th | 6th | 7th |
|---|---|---|---|---|---|---|---|
| Albania | 4.97 1996 PBK | 2.30 1997 PBK | 2.40 2001 PBK | 0.60 2005 PBKD | 0.34 2009 PBK | | |
| Bulgaria | 1.13 1991 BNRP | 0.54 1994 BNRP | 0.18 1997 BNRP | 0.07 2001 BNRP | 8.14 2005 Ataka | 9.36 2009 Ataka | |
| Croatia | 50.00 1992 HDZ & HSP | 47.51 1995 HDZ & HSP | 31.85 2000 HDZ & HSP-HKDU | 6.37 2003 HSP - ZDS | 3.50 2007 HSP | 3.00 2011 HSP | |
| Czech Republic | 5.98 1992 SPR-RSC | 8.01 1996 SPR-RSC | 3.09 1998 SPR-RSC | 1.08 2002 RMS | 0.17 2006 NS | 1.14 2010 DSS | |
| Estonia | 11.50 1995 Isamaa & EK | 16.10 1999 Isamaa | 8.40 2003 Isamaa & EKRP | 1.70 2007 IRL & EKRP | 0.40 2011 EIP | | |
| Hungary | 1.59 1994 MIEP | 5.47 1998 MIEP | 4.37 2002 MIEP | 2.20 2006 MIEP-Jobbik | 16.67 2010 Jobbik | | |

|  | | | | | |
|---|---|---|---|---|---|
| Latvia | 11.99 1995 TB | 14.37 1998 TB-LNNK | 5.39 2002 TB-LNNK | 6.94 2006 TB | 7.67 2010 NA +TB-LNNK |
| Lithuania | 4.01 1996 LNP-JL | 2.77 2000 LNP-JL | 0.28 2004 LNP-JL | 1.75 2008 JL | 0.63 2012 JL |
| Macedonia | 0.00 1998 | 0.00 2002 | 6.10 2006 VMRO-NP | 0.24 2008 VMRO-NP | 2.51 2011 VMRO-NP |
| Moldova | 0.00 1994 | 0.00 1998 | 0.00 2001 | 0.00 2005 | 0.00 2009 | 0.00 2010 |
| Montenegro | 0.00 2001 | 0.00 2002 | 0.00 2006 | 0.00 2009 | 0.00 2012 |
| Poland | 2.85 1993 PARTY X & PWN-PSN | 5.63 1997 ROP & PWN-PSN | 7.87 2001 LPRodz | 8.00 2005 LPRodz | 1.30 2007 LPR | 0.07 2011 NDP-Samoobrona-AL |
| Romania | 8.82 1996 PRM & PUNR | 19.48 2000 PRM | 15.12 2004 PRM & PNG | 5.42 2008 PRM & PNG | 13.98 2012 PP-DD |

Table A3.4 (*cont.*)

| | 1st | 2nd | 3rd | 4th | 5th | 6th | 7th |
|---|---|---|---|---|---|---|---|
| Serbia Montenegro, FRY | 8.60 2000 SRS | 35.27 2003 SRS & SPO-NS | 28.59 2007 SRS | 29.46 2008 SRS | 4.63 2012 SRS | | |
| Slovakia | 7.93 1992 SNS | 5.40 1994 SNS | 9.07 1998 SNS | 6.98 2002 SNS-PSNS | 11.73 2006 SNS | 5.07 2010 SNS | 4.55 2012 SNS |
| Slovenia | 3.22 1996 SNS | 4.39 2000 SNS | 6.27 2004 SNS | 5.40 2008 SNS | 1.80 2011 SNS | | |
| Ukraine | 1.25 1994 KUN | 1.00 1998 KUN | 0.00 2002 | 0.36 2006 Svoboda | 0.76 2007 Svoboda | 10.45 2012 Svoboda | |

Poland: National Rebirth of Poland. Classified as a radical right organization by Ramet (1999). Classified as a fascist-authoritarian right social movement organization by Minkenberg (2002). Marginal movement. Crossover between a social movement and a political party (www.nop.org.pl).

Poland: Realpolitik Union. Classified as an extreme nationalist party by Pop-Eleches (2010). Marginal political party. Its main political platform is mostly focused on economic issues (UPR program: www.upr.org.pl/main/index.php?strid=1&katid=79).

Romania: Socialist Workers Party (PSM). Classified as a party of radical continuity by Ramet (1999). Classified as a racist-ethnocentrist party by Minkenberg (2002). Classified as a radical left party by Pop-Eleches (2010). Neo-socialist nationalistic party.

Ukraine: UNA-UNSO. Classified as a radical right movement by Ramet (1999). Pan-Slavic political/social movement.

### Ethno-liberal Parties

Table A3.5 lists ethno-liberal (ethnic and social liberal parties). The vast majority of parties are ethnic parties. Four socially liberal parties are/were present in ethnically homogeneous countries: Czech Republic, Hungary, Poland and Slovenia. However, even in these three cases, socially liberal parties advocated minority protection and accommodation under the umbrella of cosmopolitism.

Table A3.5 *List of ethno-liberal (ethnic and socially liberal) parties*

| Country | Primary appeal | Minority |
|---|---|---|
| **Albania** | | |
| PMDN – Human Rights Party | Ethnic | Greeks |
| UHRP – United for Human Rights Party | Ethnic | Greeks |
| PBDNJ – United Human Rights Party | Ethnic | Greeks |
| HRPP – Human Rights Protection Party | Ethnic | Greeks |
| **Bulgaria** | | |
| DPS – Movement for Rights and Freedoms | Ethnic | Turks |

**Table A3.5 (*cont.*)**

| Country | Primary appeal | Minority |
|---|---|---|
| **Croatia** | | |
| SDS – Serb Democratic Party | Ethnic | Serbs |
| SNS – Serb People Party | Ethnic | Serbs |
| I – Independent Democratic Serb Party | Ethnic | Serbs |
| **Czech Republic** | | |
| ODA (only 1992–1996) – Civic Democratic Alliance | Socially liberal and ethnic | Cosmopolitan, Sudeten Germans |
| **Estonia** | | |
| EUPR – Estonian United People's Party | Ethnic | Russians |
| Constitution – Constitution Party | Ethnic | Russians |
| VEE – Russian Party in Estonia | Ethnic | Russians |
| **Hungary** | | |
| SZDSZ – Alliance of Free Democrats | Socially liberal and ethnic | Cosmopolitan, Roma, Jews |
| **Latvia** | | |
| TSP – National Harmony Party | Ethnic | Russians |
| PCTVL – For Human Rights in United Latvia | Ethnic | Russians |
| **Lithuania** | | |
| AWPL – Electoral Action of Poles | Ethnic | Poles |
| **Macedonia** | | |
| DPA – Democratic Party of Albanians | Ethnic | Albanians |
| BDI (DUI) – Democratic Union for Integration | Ethnic | Albanians |
| **Moldova** | | |
| None | | |
| **Montenegro** | | |
| HGI – Croatian Civic Initiative | Ethnic | Croats |

**Table A3.5 (*cont.*)**

| Country | Primary appeal | Minority |
|---|---|---|
| HGI-BS – Croatian Civic Initiative– Bosniak Party | Ethnic | Croats, Bosniaks |
| **Poland** | | |
| UW – Freedom Union | Socially liberal | Cosmopolitan |
| MN – German Minority | Ethnic | Germans |
| **Romania** | | |
| UDMR – Democratic Union of Hungarians | Ethnic | Hungarian |
| **Serbia** | | |
| SVM – Alliance of Vojvodina Hungarians | Ethnic | Hungarians |
| MK – Hungarian Coalition | Ethnic | Hungarians |
| **Slovakia** | | |
| MK – Hungarian Coalition | Ethnic | Hungarians |
| SMK – Party of the Hungarian Coalition | Ethnic | Hungarians |
| Most-Hid – Bridge | Ethnic | Hungarians |
| **Slovenia** | | |
| LDS – Liberal Democracy of Slovenia | Socially liberal | Cosmopolitan |
| **Ukraine** | | |
| SDPU – Social Democratic Party of Ukraine (since 2002) | Ethnic | Russians |
| KPU – Communist Party (since 2006) | Ethnic | Russians |

# Appendix to Chapter 4

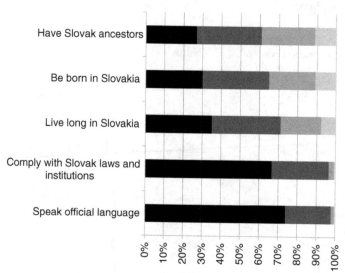

**Figure A4.1** Importance of being a true Slovak.
*Source*: N = 1,487; Slovak Data Archive, SASD, 2008.

**Table A4.1** *Determinants of vote choice by group hostility toward Hungarians*

|  |  | SE |
|---|---|---|
| HZD (Hnutie za demokraciu) | −0.73 | 1.65 |
| KDH (Kresťansko-demokratické hnutie) | 0.93 | 0.56 |
| KDS (Konzervatívni demokrati Slovenska) | 0.27 | 1.21 |
| KSS (Komunistická strana Slovenska) | 1.07 | 0.65 |
| LIGA, občiansko-liberálna strana | 0.27 | 1.21 |
| ĽS-HZDS (Ľudová strana–HZDS) | 0.27 | 0.56 |
| MOST-Híd (Hungarian party) | −1.628** | 0.55 |
| SaS (Sloboda a Solidarita) | 0.39 | 0.7 |

**Table A4.1 (*cont.*)**

|  |  | SE |
|---|---|---|
| SDKÚ-DS (Slov.dem. a kresťan.únia -Demokr.str.) | 0.4 | 0.5 |
| SDĽ (Strana demokratickej ľavice) | −2.73 | 1.65 |
| SF (Slobodné fórum) | 1.77 | 0.9 |
| SMER-SD (Smer–sociálna demokracia) | 0.1 | 0.45 |
| SMK (Strana maďarskej koalície) (Hungarian party) | −1.876*** | 0.54 |
| SNS (Slovenská národná strana) (radical right party) | 0.91 | 0.52 |
| SZ (Strana zelených) | −0.73 | 1.65 |
| Will not vote | −0.4 | 0.46 |
| Constant | 4.733*** | 0.41 |
| N | 324 | |
| Adj. R^2 | 0.171 | |

*Note*: Linear regression (OLS). Dependent variable: group hostility toward Hungarians.
Independent variables (as factor): vote choice (parties).
Baseline (0): no answer.
* $p < 0.05$, ** $p < 0.01$, *** $p < 0.001$.

**Table A4.2 *Group hostility toward Hungarians in Slovakia (expansion of Table 4.6)***

|  | M1 | M2 | M3 |
|---|---|---|---|
| Individual economic threats (Hungarians) | −0.692*** (0.137) |  | −0.588*** (0.141) |
| Collective sovereignty threat (Hungarians) |  | −0.542*** (0.144) | −0.399** (0.148) |
| Collective sovereignty threat (Hungary) | −0.222 (0.124) | −0.156 (0.149) | 0.021 (0.152) |
| Collective sovereignty threat (EU) | 0.0104 (0.121) | −0.0593 (0.118) | 0.0288 (0.12) |
| HZD (Hnutie za demokraciu) | −2.167 (1.527) | −1.481 (1.546) | −1.826 (1.515) |

Table A4.2 (*cont.*)

| | M1 | M2 | M3 |
|---|---|---|---|
| KDH (Kresťansko-demokratické hnutie) | 0.653 | 0.706 | 0.768 |
| | (0.587) | (0.528) | (0.582) |
| KDS (Konzervatívni demokrati Slovenska) | 0.514 | −0.945 | 0.335 |
| | (1.536) | (1.127) | (1.52) |
| KSS (Komunistická strana Slovenska) | −0.0355 | 0.478 | 0.067 |
| | (0.693) | (0.643) | (0.686) |
| LIGA, občiansko-liberálna strana | 0.419 | 0.752 | 0.588 |
| | (1.113) | (1.117) | (1.102) |
| ĽS-HZDS (Ľudová strana–HZDS) | −0.298 | 0.0415 | −0.148 |
| | (0.561) | (0.525) | (0.557) |
| MOST-Híd | −1.213* | −0.904 | −1.01 |
| | (0.551) | (0.522) | (0.55) |
| SaS (Sloboda a Solidarita) | 0.734 | 1.023 | 0.839 |
| | (0.735) | (0.681) | (0.728) |
| SDKÚ-DS (Slov.dem. a kresťan.únia -Demokr.str.) | 0.341 | 0.453 | 0.45 |
| | (0.52) | (0.476) | (0.515) |
| SDĽ (Strana demokratickej ľavice) | −2.13 | −1.869 | −1.944 |
| | (1.513 | (1.533) | (1.498) |
| SF (Slobodné fórum) | 1.128 | 1.214 | 1.089 |
| | (0.851 | (0.837) | (0.842) |
| SMER-SD (Smer–sociálna demokracia) | −0.0275 | 0.0762 | 0.0666 |
| | (0.471) | (0.421) | (0.467) |
| SMK (Strana maďarskej koalície) | −1.588** | −1.394** | −1.453** |
| | (0.545) | (0.511) | (0.541) |

Table A4.2 (*cont.*)

|  | M1 | M2 | M3 |
|---|---|---|---|
| SNS (Slovenská národná strana) (radical right party) | 0.517 (0.532) | 0.853 (0.492) | 0.641 (0.528) |
| SZ (Strana zelených) | −1.265 (1.519) | −0.723 (1.543) | −0.889 (1.509) |
| Will not vote | −0.627 (0.477) | −0.363 (0.43) | −0.506 (0.474) |
| Constant | 7.741*** (0.628) | 6.899*** (0.556) | 7.692*** (0.621) |
| N | 296 | 310 | 296 |
| Adj. R^2 | 0.333 | 0.299 | 0.348 |

*Note*: Dependent variable: group hostility toward Hungarians.
Baseline (0): no answer.
* $p < 0.05$, ** $p < 0.01$, *** $p < 0.001$.

## List of Parties in Slovakia and Ideologically Aligned Political Blocs

### List of Parties in Slovakia

KDH – Krestansko-demokraticke hnutie
ĽS-HZDS – Ludova strana–HZDS
MOST-HID
SDKU-DS – Slovenska demokraticka a krestanska unia–Demokraticka strana
SMER-SD – Smer-socialna demokracia
SMK – Strana madarskej koalicie
SNS – Slovenska narodna strana

### Ethnic Hungarian Parties

MOST-HID
SMK

### Coalition Partners of the Hungarian Ethnic Party

KDH

SDKU-DS

### Coalition Partners of the SNS, Radical Right Party

ĽS-HZDS

SMER-SD

### Radical Right Party

SNS

## Questionnaire for Slovakia (in English)

*Question about Governmental Spending*

Respondents were asked the following questions about governmental spending on the majority and two minorities (Hungarians and Roma):

"In the current economic situation, it may be difficult for the government to cover all its expenses. When the resources are limited, and the government cannot raise taxes, some groups get more and some groups get less. In your view, as a citizen of the Slovak Republic, how should this situation affect Slovaks, Hungarians and Roma?"

1. Do you think that the government should spend much more, more, less or much less on Slovaks?
2. Do you think that the government should spend much more, more, less or much less on Hungarians?
3. Do you think that the government should spend much more, more, less or much less on Roma?

## Question Wording for Key Concepts
### Economic Perceptions

"In general, do you think that you and your family are better off, worse off, or about the same financially compared with two years ago?" (coded as: 1 = better, 2 = same, 3 = worse)

"Looking ahead, do you think that two years from now you will be better off financially, worse off, or just about the same as now?"

"Looking ahead, do you expect that the economy will get better, get worse, or stay about the same in the next two years?"

"Now let's talk about the country as a whole. Would you say that most families in Slovakia are better off, worse off, or about the same financially compared with two years ago?

## Social Distance (Eight-Item Additive Index: Two Items Repeated for Each of Two Groups: Hungarians and Roma)

"To have [group name] as neighbor seems to me very attractive/somewhat attractive/somewhat unattractive/very unattractive."

"To have [group name] as a life partner seems to me very attractive/somewhat attractive/somewhat unattractive/very unattractive."

## Threat Items

"Now I am going to read you some statements and I want to know whether you agree or disagree with each."

"Do you agree strongly, agree somewhat, disagree somewhat, or disagree strongly?"

Individual economic threat: "I am afraid that my economic prospects will get worse [because of Hungarians]."

Collective sovereignty threat: "These days, I am afraid that the sovereignty of Slovakia is threatened [because of Hungarians/Hungary/the EU]."

## Redistribution toward the Majority and Redistribution toward the Minorities (Hungarians and Roma)

"Do you think that the government should spend a lot more, more, less or a lot less on Slovaks?"

"Do you think that the government should spend a lot more, more, less or a lot less on Hungarians?"

"Do you think that the government should spend a lot more, more, less or a lot less on Roma?"

## National Pride

"Please tell me if you feel very proud, rather proud, rather not proud, not at all proud that you are a citizen of Slovakia?" (2 = rather proud)

## Self Esteem and Authoritarian Values

"I am going to make a few statements about people's mentality in general and yourself. Please tell me whether you think they are true or false." "I certainly feel useless at times." "It is better to live in orderly society in which the laws are vigorously enforced than to give people too much freedom."

## Coding of the Occupational Profile Based on the FOCUSbus Categories

Creative, independent occupational profile (low grid job prescription): coded as 0

Creative worker (university educated), such as physician, teacher, lawyer, scientist, analyst, artist, IT person, etc.

CEO of a firm, deputy CEO, highly trained bureaucrat, highly trained governmental official, politician, and army officers (director, vice-manager, politician)

Self-employed entrepreneur without employees (independent gainfully active [entrepreneur, businessman, private doctor, private lawyer, etc.] with no employees)

Self-employed entrepreneur with employees (independent gainfully active [entrepreneur, businessman] with employees)

Student (above high school)

Non-creative, dependent occupational profile (high grid job prescription), coded as 1

Unqualified worker, manual worker in agriculture, industry or service sector

Qualified manual worker (craftsmen, repairman, machine service operator, farmer)

Administrative clerk, lower administrative worker, entry-level administrative worker, secretary, and bookkeeper, clerk at post office or bank (service worker [shop assistant, hairdresser, driver, cook])

Technical worker, medic, nurse/medical assistant, guidance counselor, tutor, technician, desk clerk, customs officer, executive worker

Pensioner

Housewife or on maternity/parental leave

Unemployed

# Appendix to Chapter 5

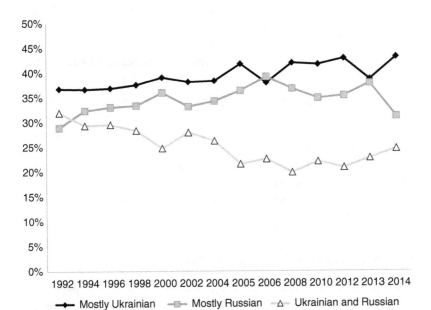

**Figure A5.1** What language do you speak mostly in your family (at home)?

*Source*: Representative surveys by the Institute of Sociology, National Academy of Sciences, Ukraine; "Results of National Surveys 1992–2014. Ukrainian Society: Monitoring Social Change," p. 65

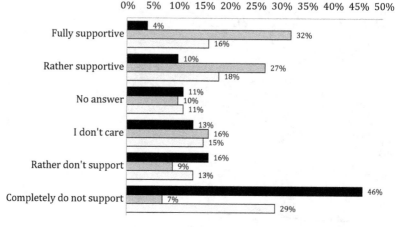

**Figure A5.2** Attitudes toward the use of regional languages in the 2012 language law in Ukraine.
*Note*: On July 3, 2012, parliament passed a law on the basic principles of the politics of languages, according to which the official use of regional languages is possible with local authorities if at least 10 percent of the population speaks it (July 27, 2012).
*Source*: Guttke and Rank 2012: 16

## Questionnaire for Ukraine (in English)

If elections to the Verkhovna Rada of Ukraine were to take place on the nearest Sunday, would you vote? What choice would you make?

Hypothetically, if you had a chance to cast a second ballot in the elections to the Verkhovna Rada of Ukraine on the nearest Sunday, would you ever consider voting for: All-Ukrainian community "Svoboda" (O. Tyahnybock)?

What is your nationality?

These days, I am afraid that Ukrainian sovereignty is threatened.

I am afraid that my economic prospects will get worse.

Do you think that government should spend much more, more, less or much less on Ukrainians?

Do you think that government should spend much more, more, less or much less on Russians?

Do you think that government should spend much more, more, less or much less on Roma?

Do you think that government should spend much more, more, less or
   much less on Crimean Tatars?
   (a) These days, I am afraid that Ukrainian sovereignty is threatened
       by Russians (in Ukraine).
   (b) These days, I am afraid that Ukrainian sovereignty is threatened
       by Russia.
   (c) These days, I am afraid that Ukrainian sovereignty is threatened
       by the European Union.


I am afraid that my economic prospects will get worse because of
   Russians/Ukrainians.
In general, do you think that you and your family are better off,
   worse off or about the same financially compared with two
   years ago?
Looking ahead, do you think that two years from now, you will be
   better off financially, worse off or just about the same as now?
Looking ahead, do you expect that the economy will get better, get
   worse or stay about the same in the next two years?
Now let's talk about the country as a whole. Would you say that most
   families in Ukraine are better off, worse off or about the same
   financially compared with two years ago?
To have a Russian [Ukrainian] as a neighbor seems to me very attract
   ive/somewhat attractive/somewhat unattractive/very unattractive.
To have a Russian [Ukrainian] as a life partner seems to me
   very attractive/somewhat attractive/somewhat unattractive/very
   unattractive.
To have a Jew as a neighbor seems to me very attractive/somewhat
   attractive/somewhat unattractive/very unattractive.
To have a Jew as a life partner seems to me very attractive/somewhat
   attractive/somewhat unattractive/very unattractive.
Would you say you are very proud, fairly proud, not very proud, not at
   all proud to be a citizen of Ukraine?
It is better to live in an orderly society in which the laws are vigorously
   enforced than to give people too much freedom.
I certainly feel useless at times
Providing health care for the sick?
Providing education for children and youth?
Fighting corruption of public officials?

Gender
Age
What is your education?
What is your MAIN occupation?
Religious confession (religion)
Marital status
Look at this card. Including all incomes of all the members of your
    family per 1 month, what income group does your family belong to?
How many people, including you, live with you?
What language respondent speaks
Region of the respondent (place of residence), oblast
Type and size of settlement

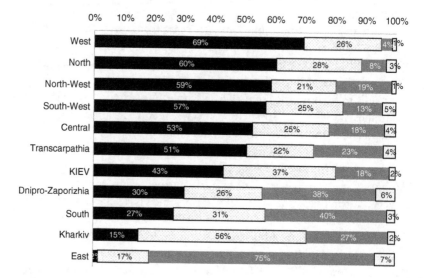

**Figure A5.3** Attitudes toward the language situation in May 2014. Question:
Currently, the language situation in the Ukraine is heavenly debated. How
should Ukrainians and Russians coexist in Ukraine in your opinion?
(May 2014).

*Source*: Center for Social and Marketing Research 2014

**Table A5.1** *Regional distribution of Svoboda voters*
Imperial legacies (rulers)

| Region (oblast) | N | Percentage out of all respondents from the region | 18th century–1918 | 1918–1939 |
|---|---|---|---|---|
| L'vivs'ka | 19 | 18.81 | Austria-Hungary | Poland |
| Ternopil's'ka | 7 | 15.22 | Austria-Hungary | Poland |
| Ivano-Frankivs'ka | 8 | 14.55 | Austria-Hungary | Poland |
| Rivnens'ka | 3 | 6.67 | Russian Empire | Poland |
| Volyns'ka | 2 | 4.65 | Russian Empire | Poland |
| Khersons'ka | 2 | 4.17 | Russian Empire | Soviet Union |
| Cherkas'ka | 2 | 3.33 | Russian Empire | Soviet Union |
| Vinnyts'ka | 2 | 2.70 | Russian Empire | Soviet Union |
| Chernivets'ka | 1 | 2.70 | Austria-Hungary | Romania |
| c. Kyiv | 3 | 2.59 | Russian Empire | Soviet Union |
| Kirovograds'ka | 1 | 2.08 | Russian Empire | Soviet Union |
| Zaporiz'ka | 1 | 1.19 | Russian Empire | Soviet Union |
| Dnipropetrovs'ka | 1 | 0.66 | Russian Empire | Soviet Union |
| Total | 52 | | | |

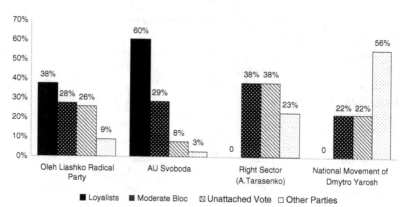

**Figure A5.4** Radical right voter party loyalty in Ukraine (2012–2014).
*Note*: Declared radical right voter loyalty in Ukraine (2012–2014). Survey responses: Vote in 2014 is compared with the vote in 2012. Sixty percent of Svoboda voters who reported that they voted for Svoboda in 2014 also reported that they voted for Svoboda in 2012 (loyalists). Twenty-nine percent of voters who voted for Svoboda in 2014 did not vote for Svoboda in 2012 and voted for their ideological "cousin" in 2012 (moderate bloc). Fifty-six percent of voters of a new party National Movement of D. Yarosh voted for "other parties" in 2012 and those parties were not the parties of the moderate bloc. Radical right parties: AU Svoboda, Oleh Liashko Radical Party, Right Sector, and National Movement of Dmytro Yarosh. Right Sector and National Movement did not exist in 2012. The moderate bloc (ideological "cousin," mainstream right): P. Poroshenko bloc, People's Front, and AU Batkivshchyna. Unattached vote: The following responses are merged: "I crossed all parties, spoiled the ballot," "I did not participate in the elections," "Difficult to say," and "Refused." Loyalists: voters voted for the same party in 2012 and in 2014; moderate bloc: mainstream right (ideological "cousins"); unattached vote: unaffiliated voters; other parties: voters from other parties (not radical right parties, not mainstream right parties).
*Data source*: Bustikova 2016a

# Bibliography

Abdelal, Rawi, Yoshiko Herrera, Alastair Johnson and Rose McDermott. 2006. "Identity as a Variable." *Perspectives on Politics* 4 (4): 695–711.

Abrajano, Marisa, and Zoltan Hajnal. 2015. *White Backlash: Immigration, Race and American Politics.* Princeton: Princeton University Press.

Abramson, Paul, John Aldrich, André Blais, Matthew Diamond, Abraham Diskin, Indridi Indridason, Daniel Lee and Renan Levine. 2010. "Comparing Strategic Voting under FPTP and PR." *Comparative Political Studies* 43 (1): 61–90.

Adams, James, and Samuel Merrill III. 2009. "Policy-Seeking Parties in a Parliamentary Democracy with Proportional Representation: A Valence-Uncertainty Model." *British Journal of Political Science* 39 (3): 539–558.

Adams, James, Michael Clark, Lawrence Ezrow and Garrett Glasgow. 2006. "Are Niche Parties Fundamentally Different from Mainstream Parties? The Causes and the Electoral Consequences of Western European Parties' Policy Shifts, 1976–1998." *American Journal of Political Science* 50 (3): 513–529.

Adams, James, Samuel Merrill III and Bernard Grofman. 2005. *A Unified Theory of Party Competition.* Cambridge: Cambridge University Press.

Adams, James, and Zeynep Somer-Topcu. 2009. "Do Parties Adjust Their Policies in Response to Rival Parties' Policy Shifts? Spatial Theory and the Dynamics of Party Competition in Twenty-Five Democracies." *British Journal of Political Science* 39 (4): 825–846.

Agarin, Timofey. 2016. "Extending the Concept of Ethnocracy: Exploring the Debate in the Baltic Context." *Cosmopolitan Civil Societies Journal* 8 (3): 81–99.

Aktuality. 2012. "Foto: Spišiak Mickey Mouse, Matovič šašo," aktuality.sk, February 6. Available at: www.aktuality.sk/clanok/201107/foto-spi siak-mickey-mouse-matovic-saso/.

2009. "Billboardy SMK, Porušili autorské práva?" Aktuality.sk, September 18. Available at: www.aktuality.sk/clanok/145644/billboardy-smk-porusili-autorske-prava/.

Aktualne. 2009. "Poslanci schválili jazykový zákon. Aj s pokutami." June 30. Available at: http://aktualne.atlas.sk/poslanci-schvalili-jazykovy-zakon-aj-s-pokutami/slovensko/politika/.

Alashri, Saud, Sultan Alzahrani, Lenka Bustikova, David Siroky and Hasan Davulcu. 2015. "What Animates Political Debates? Analyzing Ideological Perspectives in Online Debates between Opposing Parties." Proceedings of the ASE/IEEE International Conference on Social Computing (SocialCom-15), Stanford, CA.

Aldrich, John. 1995. *Why Parties?* Chicago: University of Chicago Press.

Alesina, Alberto, Reza Baqir and William Easterly. 1999. "Public Goods and Ethnic Divisions." *The Quarterly Journal of Economics* 114 (4): 1243–1284.

Alexseev, Mikhail. 2006. "Ballot-Box Vigilantism? Ethnic Population Shifts and Xenophobic Voting in Post-Soviet Russia." *Political Behavior* 28 (3): 211.

Allen, Trevor. 2015. "All in the Party Family? Comparing Far Right Voters in Western and Post-Communist Europe." *Party Politics*. doi: 10.1177/1354068815593457.

Alonso, Sonia, and Rubén Ruiz-Rufino. 2007. "Political Representation and Ethnic Conflict in New Democracies." *European Journal of Political Research* 46 (2): 237–267.

Anastasakis, Othon. 2002. "Political Extremism in Eastern Europe: A Reaction to Transition." *Papeles del Este: Transiciones poscomunistas* 3: 1–16.

Arel, Dominique. 1995. "Language Politics in Independent Ukraine: Towards One of Two State Languages." *Nationalities Papers* 23 (3): 597–622.

Art, David. 2011. *Inside the Radical Right: The Development of Anti-Immigrant Parties in Western Europe.* Cambridge: Cambridge University Press.

Art, David, and Dana Brown. 2007. "Making and Breaking the Radical Right in Central Eastern Europe." Manuscript.

Arzheimer, Kai. 2018. "Explaining Electoral Support for the Radical Right." In: *The Oxford Handbook of the Radical Right*, ed. Jens Rydgren. Oxford University Press, pp. 143–165.

   2010. "A Matter of Timing? The Dynamics of Radical Right Party Support and Mainstream Parties' Programmatic Change in France." University of Mainz/University of Essex, Working Paper; ECPR General Conference.

   2009. "Contextual Factors and the Extreme Right Vote in Western Europe, 1980–2002." *American Journal of Political Science* 53 (2): 259–275.

Arzheimer, Kai, and Elisabeth Carter. 2006. "Political Opportunity Structures and Right-Wing Extremist Party Success." *European Journal of Political Research* 45 (3): 419–443.

Auers, Daunis, and Andreas Kasekamp. 2015. "The Impact of Radical Right Parties in the Baltic States." In: *Transforming the Transformation: The East European Radical Right in the Political Process*, ed. Michael Minkenberg. Abingdon: Routledge, pp. 137–153.

Bakker, Ryan, Catherine De Vries, Erica Edwards, Liesbet Hooghe, Seth Jolly, Gary Marks, Jonathan Polk, Jan Rovny, Marco Steenbergen and Milada Anna Vachudova. 2015. "Measuring Party Positions in Europe: The Chapel Hill Expert Survey Trend File, 1999–2010." *Party Politics* 21 (1): 143–152.

Bakker, Ryan, Seth Jolly and Jon Polk. 2013. "Complexity in the European Party Space: Exploring Dimensionality with Experts." *European Union Politics* 13 (2): 219–245.

Balcerowicz, Leszek. 1995. "Understanding Postcommunist Transitions." In: *Economic Reform and Democracy*, ed. Larry Diamond and Mark Plattner. Baltimore: Johns Hopkins University Press, pp. 86–100.

Bale, Tim. 2003. "Cinderella and Her Ugly Sisters: The Mainstream and Extreme Right in Europe's Bipolarising Party Systems." *West European Politics* 26 (3): 67–90.

Bale, Tim, Christoffer Green-Pedersen, André Krouwel, Kurt Richard Luther and Nick Sitter. 2010. "If You Can't Beat Them, Join Them? Explaining Social Democratic Responses to the Challenge from the Populist Radical Right in Western Europe." *Political Studies* 58 (3): 410–426.

Banting, Keith, and Will Kymlicka, eds. 2006. *Multiculturalism and the Welfare State: Recognition and Redistribution in Contemporary Democracies*. Oxford: Oxford University Press.

Bárdy, Peter. 2015. "Kotlebovo? Ako vládne župan Marian Kotleba v Banskej Bystrici." Aktuality.sk, February 24. Available at: www.aktuality.sk/cla nok/271100/kotlebovo-ako-vladne-zupan-marian-kotlebu-v-banskej-bystrici/.

Barlett, Jamie, Jonathan Birdwell, Peter Krekó, Jack Benfield and Gabor Gyori. 2012. *Populism in Europe: Hungary*. London: Demos.

Bauman, Zygmunt. 2000. *Liquid Modernity*. Cambridge: Polity Press.

BBC. 2009. "Protests over Slovak Language Law." September 2. Available at: http://news.bbc.co.uk/2/hi/8232878.stm.

Beichelt, Tim. 2003. "Nationalism and Anti-EU Mobilization in Postsocialist Europe." Paper presented at the Eighth Biennial International Conference of the European Union Studies Association, March 27–29, Nashville, TN.

Beissinger, Mark. 2013. "The Semblance of Democratic Revolution: Coalitions in Ukraine's Orange Revolution." *American Political Science Review* 107 (3): 574–592.

2002. *Nationalist Mobilization and the Collapse of the Soviet State*. New York: Cambridge University Press.

Belanger, Eric, and Bonnie Meguid. 2008. "Issue Salience, Issue Ownership, and Issue-Based Vote Choice." *Electoral Studies* 27 (3): 477–491.

Benoit, Kenneth, and Michael Laver. 2006. *Party Policy in Modern Democracies*. London: Routledge.

Berman, Sheri. 2017. "The Pipe Dream of Undemocratic Liberalism." *Journal of Democracy* 28 (3): 29–38.

1997. "Civil Society and the Collapse of the Weimar Republic." *World Politics* 49 (3): 401–429.

Bermeo, Nancy. 2016. "On Democratic Backsliding." *Journal of Democracy* 27 (1): 5–19.

Bernauer, Julian, and Daniel Bochsler. 2011. "Electoral Entry and Success of Ethnic Minority Parties in Central and Eastern Europe: A Hierarchical Selection Model." *Electoral Studies* 30: 738–755.

Bernhard, Michael. 2015. "Chronic Instability and the Limits of Path Dependence." *Perspectives on Politics* 13 (4): 976–991.

Berwick, Andrew. 2011. "A European Declaration of Independence." London. Facebook account of Breivik. Video posted before the shooting: www.telegraph.co.uk/news/worldnews/europe/norway/8657669/Norway-shootings-Anders-Behring-Breiviks-YouTube-video-posted-hours-before-killings.html, in *The Telegraph*, August 29, 2011, "Norway Shootings: Anders Behring Breivik's YouTube Video Posted Hours before Killing."

Betz, Hans-Georg. 1994. *Radical Right-Wing Populism in Western Europe*. Basingstoke: Macmillan.

1993. "The New Politics of Resentment: Radical Right-Wing Populist Parties in Western Europe." *Comparative Politics* 25 (4): 413–427.

Bilaniuk, Laada, and Svitlana Melnyk. 2008. "A Tense and Shifting Balance: Bilingualism and Education in Ukraine." *International Journal of Bilingual Education and Bilingualism* 11 (3–4): 340–372.

Birch, Sarah. 2000. *Elections and Democratization in Ukraine*. Basingstoke: Macmillan.

Bornschier, Simon. 2011. "Why a Right-Wing Populist Party Emerged in France but Not in Germany: Cleavages and Actors in the Formation of a New Cultural Divide." *European Political Science Review* 4 (1): 1–25.

2010. *Cleavage Politics and the Populist Right: The New Cultural Conflict in Western Europe*. Philadelphia: Temple University Press.

Bowyer, Benjamin. 2008. "The Trouble with Tobit: A District-Level Sample Selection Model of Voting for Extreme Right Parties in Europe, 1989–2004." Paper presented at the 2008 Annual Meeting of the Society for Political Methodology, University of Michigan, Ann Arbor.

Bozoki, Andras, and John Ishiyama, eds. 2002. *The Communist Successor Parties of Central and Eastern Europe*. New York: M. E. Sharpe.

Brewer, Marilynn, and Wendi Gardner. 1996. "Who Is This 'We'?: Levels of Collective Identity and Self Representations." *Journal of Personality and Social Psychology* 71 (1): 83–93.

Brubaker, Rogers. 1997. *Nationalism Reframed: Nationhood and the National Question in the New Europe*. Cambridge: Cambridge University Press.

Bruckner, Markus, and Hans Peter Gruner. 2010. "Economic Growth and the Rise of Political Extremism: Theory and Evidence." Public Policy Papers, Discussion Paper No. 7723, Centre for Economic Policy Research, UK, March.

Bruno, Giuseppe. 2004. "Limited Dependent Panel Data Models: A Comparative Analysis of Classical and Bayesian Inference among Econometric Packages." *Computing in Economics and Finance*. 41. Society for Computational Economics. Available at: http://editorialexpress.com/cgi-bin/confer ence/download.cgi?db_name=SCE2004&paper_id=41.

Budge, Ian, and Dennis Farlie. 1983. *Explaining and Predicting Elections*. London: Allen & Unwin.

Bunce, Valerie. 1999. *Subversive Institutions: The Design and the Destruction of Socialism and the State*. Cambridge: Cambridge University Press.

Bunce, Valerie, and Sharon Wolchik. 2010. "Defeating Dictators: Electoral Change and Stability in Competitive Authoritarian Regimes." *World Politics* 62: 43–86.

Bustikova, Lenka. 2018. "The Radical Right in Eastern Europe." In: *The Oxford Handbook of the Radical Right*, ed. Jens Rydgren. New York: Oxford University Press, 565–581.

2016a. Dataset. Survey in Ukraine. May. Survey Administered by KIIS.

2016b. "Populism in Eastern Europe." In: Symposium: Populism in Comparative Politics, ed. Matt Golder and Sona Golder. *CP: Newsletter of the Comparative Politics Organized Section of the American Political Science Association* 26 (1): 15–19.

2015a. "The Democratization of Hostility: Minorities and Radical Right Actors after the Fall of Communism." In: *Transforming the Transformation*, ed. Michael Minkenberg. Abingdon: Routledge, pp. 58–79.

2015b. "Voting, Identity and Security Threats in Ukraine: Who Supports the Ukrainian 'Svoboda' Party?" *Communist and Post-Communist Studies*, 48 (2–3): 239–256.

2014. "Revenge of the Radical Right." *Comparative Political Studies* 47 (12): 1738–1765.

2013. "Welfare Chauvinism, Ethnic Heterogeneity and Conditions for the Electoral Breakthrough of Radical Right Parties: Evidence from Eastern Europe." In: *Right-Wing Radicalism Today: Perspectives from Europe and the US*, ed. Sabine von Mering and Timothy Wyman McCarty. New York: Routledge, pp. 106–123.

2010. Dataset. Survey administered by Kiev International Institute of Sociology. Omnibus 2010. Kiev.

2009a. Dataset. Survey administered by FOCUS. Bratislava 2009. Kyiv.

2009b. "The Extreme Right in Eastern Europe: EU Accession and the Quality of Governance." *Journal of Contemporary European Studies* 17 (2): 223–239.

Bustikova, Lenka, and Elizabeth Zechmeister. 2016. "Voting in New Democracies." In: *SAGE Handbook of Electoral Behaviour*, ed. Kai Arzheimer, Jocelyn Evans and Michael Lewis-Beck. London: Sage, pp. 92–133.

Bustikova, Lenka, and Herbert Kitschelt. 2011. "The Radical Right and Its Nearby Competitors: Evidence from Eastern Europe." In: *Europeanising Party Politics: Comparative Perspectives on Central and Eastern Europe*, ed. Paul Lewis and Radoslaw Markowski. Manchester: Manchester University Press, pp. 143–178.

2009. "The Radical Right in Post-Communist Europe: Comparative Perspectives on Legacies and Party Competition." *Communist and Post-Communist Studies* 42 (4): 459–483.

Bustikova, Lenka, and Petra Guasti. 2019. "The State as a Firm: Understanding the Autocratic Roots of Technocratic Populism." *East European Politics and Societies: and Cultures*. 33 (2): 302–330.

2017. "The Illiberal Turn or Swerve in Central Europe?" *Politics and Governance* 5 (4): 166–176.

2012. "Hate Thy Imaginary Neighbor: An Analysis of Antisemitism in Slovakia." *Journal for the Study of Antisemitism* 4 (2): 469–493.

Bútora, Martin. 2007. "Nightmares from the Past, Dreams of the Future." *Journal of Democracy* 18 (4): 47–55.

Cantorovich, Irena. 2013. "Defending the Interests of the Ukrainians: The Empowerment of the Svoboda Party." *Israel Journal of Foreign Affairs* 7 (1): 95–104.

Capoccia, Giovanni. 2001. "Defending Democracy: Reactions to Political Extremism in Inter-War Europe." *European Journal of Political Research* 39: 431–460.

Carpenter, Michael. 1997. "Slovakia and the Triumph of Nationalist Populism." *Communist and Postcommunist Studies* 30 (2): 205–220.

Carter, David, and Kurt Signorino. 2010. "Back to the Future: Modeling *Time* Dependence in Binary Data." *Political Analysis* 18 (3) (Summer): 271–292.

Carter, Elisabeth. 2005. *The Extreme Right in Western Europe: Success or Failure?* Manchester: Manchester University Press.

2002. "Proportional Representation and the Fortunes of Right-Wing Extremist Parties." *West European Politics* 25 (3): 124–146.

Carter, Jeff, Michael Berhnard and Timothy Nordstrom. 2016. "Communist Legacies and Democratic Survival in a Comparative Perspective: Liability or Advantage." *East European Politics & Societies* 30 (4): 830–854.

Casal Bértoa, Fernando, and Dane Taleski. 2015. "Regulating Party Politics in the Western Balkans: The Legal Sources of Party System Development in Macedonia." *Democratization* 23 (3): 545–567.

Cederman, Lars-Erik, Andreas Wimmer and Brian Min. 2010. "Why Do Ethnic Groups Rebel? New Data and Analysis." *World Politics* 62: 87–119.

Ceka, Besir. 2013. "The Perils of Political Competition Explaining Participation and Trust in Political Parties in Eastern Europe." *Comparative Political Studies* 46 (12): 1610–1635.

Center for Social and Marketing Research. 2014. Kiyv Institute of Sociology and Center for Social and Marketing Research. Rating May 8–13, May. Representative Survey. UA 133. Available at: http://socis.kiev.ua/ua/press/rezultaty-sotsiolohichnoho-doslidzhennja-reytyn hy-kandydativ.html.

Central Election Commission of Ukraine. 2015. Кандидати, яких обрано депутатами рад. Available at: www.cvk.gov.ua/pls/vm2015/PVM002?PT001F01=100&pt00_t001f01=100.

Chai, Sun-Ki, Kyle Hampton, Dolgorsuren Dorj and Ming Liu. 2009. "Grid/Group Cultural Theory and Behavior in Voluntary Contributions Public Goods Experiments." Working Paper.

Chambers, Simone, and Jeffrey Kopstein. 2001. "Bad Civil Society." *Political Theory* 29 (6): 837–865.

Chandra, Kanchan. 2005. "Ethnic Parties and Democratic Stability." *Perspectives on Politics* 3 (2): 235–252.

2004. *Why Ethnic Parties Succeed.* Cambridge: Cambridge University Press.

Charnysh, Volha. 2013. "Analysis of Current Events: Identity Mobilization in Hybrid Regimes: Language in Ukrainian Politics." *Nationalities Papers* 41 (1): 1–14.

Christensen, Robert, Edward Rakhimkulov and Charles Wise. 2005. "The Ukrainian Orange Revolution Brought More than a New President: What Kind of Democracy Will the Institutional Changes Bring?" *Communist and Post-Communist Studies* 38: 207–230.

Clasen, Dennis, and Thomas Dormody. 1994. "Analyzing Data Measured by Individual Likert-Type Items." *Journal of Agricultural Education* 35 (4): 31–35.

Colomer, Josep, and Riccardo Puglisi. 2005. "Cleavages, Issues and Parties: A Critical Overview of the Literature." *European Political Science* 4: 502–520.

Conrad, Courtenay, and Sona Golder. 2010. "Measuring Government Duration and Stability in Central Eastern European Democracies." *European Journal of Political Research* 49 (1): 119–150.

Cordell, Karl, ed. 2000. *The Politics of Ethnicity in Central Europe*. New York: St. Martin's Press.

Coughlin, Richard, and Charles Lockhart. 1998. "Grid-Group Theory and Political Ideology." *Journal of Theoretical Politics* 10 (1): 33–58.

Council of Europe. 2007. "Roma and Travelers." European Roma and Travelers Forum. Strasbourg. Council of Europe.

Council of the European Union. 2015. Council Decision Establishing Provisional Measures in the Area of International Protection for the Benefit of Italy and Greece. 12098/15. Brussels, September 22.

Crepaz, Markus, and Regan Damron. 2009. "Constructing Tolerance." *Comparative Political Studies* 42 (3): 437–463.

CSES/ISSP. 2016. CSES/The International Social Survey Program: Role of Government Module.

Cunningham, Kathleen. 2014. *Inside the Politics of Self-Determination*. Oxford University Press.

Curini, Luigi, and Paolo Martelli. 2010. "Ideological Proximity and Valence Competition: Negative Campaigning through Allegation of Corruption in the Italian Legislative Arena from 1946 to 1994." *Electoral Studies* 29 (4): 636–647.

CVVM. 2017. Uprchlická krize. Centrum pro výzkum veřejného mínění, Sociologický ústav AV ČR, October 19.

Daftary, Farimah, and Kinga Gal. 2000. "The New Slovak Language Law: Internal or External Politics?" ECMI Working Paper #8. September.

Dancygier, Rafaela. 2010. *Immigration and Conflict in Europe*. Cambridge: Cambridge University Press.

D'Anieri, Paul, and Taras Kuzio, eds. 2007. *Aspects of the Orange Revolution I: Democratization and Elections in Post-Communist Ukraine*. Stuttgart: ibidem Verlag.

Darden, Keith. 2014. *Resisting Occupation: Mass Literacy and the Creation of Durable National Loyalties*. New York: Cambridge University Press.

Darden, Keith, and Anna Grzymala-Busse. 2006. "The Great Divide: Pre-Communist Schooling and Post-Communist Trajectories." *World Politics* 59 (1): 83–115.

Deegan-Krause, Kevin. 2006. *Elected Affinities: Democracy and Party Competition in Slovakia and the Czech Republic.* Stanford: Stanford University Press.

Deegan-Krause, Kevin, and Tim Haughton. 2009. "Toward a More Useful Conceptualization of Populism: Types and Degrees of Populist Appeals in the Case of Slovakia." *Politics & Policy* 37 (4): 821–841.

de Lange, Sarah. 2012. "New Alliances: Why Mainstream Parties Govern with Radical Right-Wing Populist Parties." *Political Studies* 60 (4): 899–918.

2008. "From Pariah to Power: The Government Participation of Radical Right-Wing Populist Parties in West European Democracies." PhD dissertation, University of Antwerp.

de Lange, Sarah, and Simona Guerra. 2009. "The League of Polish Families between East and West, Past and Present." *Communist and Post-Communist Studies* 42 (4): 527–549.

Deutsche Presse-Agentur. July 20, 2001. Cited in Minorities at Risk Project, Chronology for Turks in Bulgaria, 2004. Available at: www.unhcr.org/refworld/docid/469f38702.html.

Deutsche Welle. 2007. "Ultra-Right Gaining Ground in Bulgaria." *DW.* September 1. Available at: www.dw-world.de/dw/article/0,,2758993,00.html.

de Varennes, Fernand. 1999. "Non-Citizens and Minorities in Estonia and Their Economic and Social Opportunities." In: *Minorities in Europe: Croatia, Estonia and Slovakia*, ed. Snežana Trifunovska. The Hague: T. M. C. Asser Press, pp. 123–142.

Dolezalova, Jitka, Vlastimil Havlík, Antonín Slaný and Petra Vejvodová. 2017. "Economic Factors and the Electoral Success of Far-Right and Far-Left Parties in the EU Countries." *Society and Economy* 39 (1): 27–48.

Douglas, Mary, and Aaron Wildavsky. 1982. *Risk and Culture: An Essay on the Selection of Technological and Environmental Dangers.* Berkeley: University of California Press.

Downs, William. 2002. "How Effective Is the Cordon Sanitaire? Lessons from Efforts to Contain the Far Right in Belgium, France, Denmark, and Norway." *Journal für Konflikt und Gewaltforschung* 4 (1): 32–51.

2001. "Pariahs in Their Midst: Belgian and Norwegian Parties React to Extremist Threats." *West European Politics* 24 (3): 23–42.

Dubovyk, Volodymur. 2015. "Making Sense of Ukraine's Local Elections." PONARS Eurasia, November 4.

Dziewanowski, Marian. 1996. *A History of Soviet Russia and Its Aftermath.* Englewood Cliffs, NJ: Prentice Hall.

Eatwell, Roger. 2003. "Ten Theories of the Extreme Right." In: *Right-Wing Extremism in the Twenty-First Century*, ed. Peter Merkl and Leonard Weinberg. Portland, OR: Frank Cass, pp. 45–70.

Eberhardt, Piotr. 1994. *Przemiany Narodowościowe na Ukrainie XX wieku*. Warsaw: Biblioteka Obozu.

EBRD. 2013. Transition Report 2012. Available at: www.ebrd.com/publica tions/transition-report-2012.pdf.

Efron, Bradley, and Robert Tibshirani. 1993. *An Introduction to the Boot-strap*. Boca Raton, FL: Chapman & Hall/CRC.

Eger, Maureen. 2010. "Even in Sweden: The Effect of Immigration on Support for Welfare State Spending." *European Sociological Review* 26 (2): 203–221.

Ekiert, Grzegorz. 2006. "L'instabilité du Système Partisan. Le Maillon Faible de la Consolidation Démocratique en Pologne." *Pouvoirs* 118: 37–58.

1996. *The State against Society*. Princeton: Princeton University Press.

Ekiert, Grzegorz, and Jan Kubik. 1999. *Rebellious Civil Society*. Ann Arbor: University of Michigan Press.

Elias, Norbert, and John Scotson. 1965. *The Established and the Outsiders*. London: SAGE Publications.

Enyedi, Zsolt, with Ferenc Erős. 1999. *Authoritarianism and Prejudice: Central European Perspectives*. Budapest: Osiris.

EUA. 2012. The Situation of Roma in 11 Member States – Survey Results at a Glance. European Agency for Fundamental Rights. UNDP. Available at: https://fra.europa.eu/en/publication/2012/situation-roma-11-eu-member-states-survey-results-glance.

EURACTIV. 2018. "MEPs Trigger Article 7 against Hungary." EURACTIV. com, September 12. Available at: www.euractiv.com/section/justice-home-affairs/news/meps-trigger-article-7-against-hungary-after-evasive-juncker-speech/.

European Commission. 2016. "Financial Services: Commission Requests Bulgaria, Hungary, Latvia, Lithuania and Slovakia to Comply with EU Rules on the Acquisition of Agricultural Land." Press release. Brussels, May 26. Available at: http://europa.eu/rapid/press-release_IP-16-1827_en.htm.

Ezrow, Lawrence, Margit Tavits and Jonathan Homola. 2014. "Voter Polarization, Strength of Partisanship, and Support for Extreme Parties." *Comparative Political Studies* 47 (11): 1558–1583.

Fearon, James, and David Laitin. 2000. "Violence and the Social Construction of Ethnic Identities." *International Organization* 54 (4): 845–877.

Fedotov, Egor. 2015. "Weak Language Norm(s) versus Domestic Interests: Why Ukraine Behaves the Way It Does." *Review of International Studies* 41 (4): 739–755.

Fish, Steven. 1998. "The Determinants of Economic Reform in the Post-Communist World." *East European Politics and Societies* 12 (1): 31–77.

Fish, Steven, and Robin Brooks. 2004. "Does Diversity Hurt Democracy?" *Journal of Democracy* 15 (1): 154–166.

Flesnic, Florin. 2007. "Does Romania Have One Extreme Right or Two?" Paper presented at the Annual Convention of the American Political Science Association.

Fournier, Anna. 2002. "Mapping Identities: Russian Resistance to Linguistic Ukrainisation in Central and Eastern Ukraine." *Europe-Asia Studies* 54 (3): 415–433.

Fredheim, Rolf. 2014. "The Memory of Katyn in Polish Political Discourse: A Quantitative Study." *Europe-Asia Studies* 66 (7): 1165–1187.

Frye, Timothy. 2015. "What Do Voters in Ukraine Want? A Survey Experiment on Candidate Ethnicity, Language, and Policy Orientation." *Problems of Post-Communism.* 62 (5): 247–257.

2010. *Incredible Transformation: Building States and Markets after Communism.* Cambridge: Cambridge University Press.

2002. "Capture or Exchange? Business Lobbying in Russia." *Europe-Asia Studies* 54 (7): 1017–1036.

Galbreath, David. 2005. *Nation-Building and Minority Politics in Post-Socialist States: Interests, Influences and Identities in Estonia and Latvia.* Stuttgart: ibidem-Verlag.

Gallagher, Michael. 2013. Election Indices Dataset. Available at: www.tcd.ie/Political_Science/staff/michael_gallagher/ElSystems/index.php.

Ganev, Venelin. 2017. "'Neoliberalism Is Fascism and Should Be Criminalized': Bulgarian Populism as Left-Wing Radicalism." *Slavic Review* 76 (S1): S9–S18.

1995. "The Mysterious Politics of Bulgaria's Movement for Rights and Freedoms." *East European Constitutional Review* 4: 1–49.

Gavriliu, Andrea. 2010. "Ethno-business: The Unexpected Consequence of National Minority Policies in Romania." Changing Europe V; Informal Networks, Clientelism and Corruption in Politics, State Administration, Business and Society. Central and Eastern Europe; Prague, Institute of Sociology of Czech Academy of Sciences; August 1–7.

Gazeta. 2014. Облсовет Луганска угрожает разоружить Майдан руками "братской" России. March 2. Available at: http://gazeta.ua/ru/articles/politics/_oblsovet-luganska-ugrozhaet-razoruzhit-majdan-rukami-bratskoj-rossii/545140.

Gellner, Ernest. 1983. *Nations and Nationalism.* Ithaca: Cornell University Press.

Gibson, James, and Marc Howard. 2004. "Russian Anti-Semitism and the Scapegoating of Jews." Studies in Public Policy No. 397. Centre for the Study of Public Policy, University of Strathclyde.

Gidron, Noam, and Bart Bonikowski. 2013. "Varieties of Populism: Literature Review and Research Agenda." Working Paper Series 13-0004. Weatherhead Center for International Affairs, Harvard University.

Giuliano, Elise. 2015. "The Origins of Separatism: Popular Grievances in Donetsk and Luhansk." October, Memo #396. Ponars Policy Memo.

Givens, Terri. 2005. *Voting Radical Right in Western Europe*. Cambridge: Cambridge University Press.

Givens, Terri, and Rhonda Evans Case. 2014. *Legislating Equality: The Politics of Antidiscriminatory Policy in Europe*. Oxford: Oxford University Press.

Goffman, Irwin W. 1957. "Status Consistency and Preference for Change in Power Distribution." *American Sociological Review* 22 (3): 275–281.

Golder, Matt. 2016. "Far Right Parties in Europe." *Annual Review of Political Science* 19: 477–497.

2003. "Explaining Variation in the Success of Extreme Right Parties in Western Europe." *Comparative Political Studies* 36 (4): 432–466.

Golder, Matt, and Sona N. Golder, eds. 2016. "Symposium: Populism in Comparative Politics." *CP: Newsletter of the Comparative Politics Organized Section of the American Political Science Association* 26 (1). APSA Comparative Section, Newsletter on Populism, Fall.

Gow, James, and Cathie Carmichael. 2000. *Slovenia and the Slovenes*. Bloomington: Indiana University Press.

Greene, William. 2008. *Econometric Analysis*, 6th edition. New York: Prentice Hall.

2004. "Fixed Effects and Bias Due to the Incidental Parameters Problem in the Tobit Model." *Econometric Reviews* 23 (2): 125–147.

Greskovits, Béla. 2007. "Economic Woes and Political Disaffection." *Journal of Democracy* 18 (4): 40–46.

Grina, Jana, Robin Bergh, Nazar Akami and Jim Sidanius. 2016. "Political Orientation and Dominance: Are People on the Political Right More Dominant?" *Personality and Individual Differences* 94: 113–117.

Grittersova, Jana, Indridi Indridason, Christina Gregory and Ricardo Crespo. 2016. "Austerity and Niche Parties: The Electoral Consequences of Fiscal Reforms." *Electoral Studies* 42: 276–289.

Grün, Michala. 2002. "Rechtsradikale Massenmobilisierung und 'Radikale Kontinuität' in Rumänien." *Osteuropa* 52 (3): 293–304.

Grzymala-Busse, Anna. 2007. *Rebuilding Leviathan*. Cambridge: Cambridge University Press.

2002. *Redeeming the Communist Past*. Cambridge: Cambridge University Press.

2001. "Coalition Formation and the Regime Divide in New Democracies: East Central Europe." *Comparative Politics* 34 (1): 85–104.

Guasti, Petra, and Zdenka Mansfeldová, eds. 2018. *Democracy under Stress: Changing Perspectives on Democracy, Governance and Their Measurement*. Prague: Institute of Sociology of the Czech Academy of Sciences.

Guasti, Petra, David Siroky and Daniel Stockemer. 2017. "Judgment without Justice: On the Efficacy of the European Human Rights Regime." *Democratization* 24 (2): 226–243.

Gurr, Ted, and Will Moore. 1997. "Ethnopolitical Rebellion: A Cross-Sectional Analysis of the 1980s with Risk Assessments for the 1990s." *American Journal of Political Science* 41 (4): 1079–1103.

Guss, Jason, and David S. Siroky. 2012. "Living with Heterogeneity: Bridging the Ethnic Divide in Bosnia and Beyond." *Comparative Sociology*, 11 (3): 304–324.

Guttke, Matthias, and Hartmut Rank. 2012. "Mit der Sprachenfrage auf Stimmenfang. Zur aktuellen Sprachgesetzgebung in der Ukraine." *Ukraine-Analysen* 106 (11.09): 11–16. Available at: www.laender-analysen.de/ukraine/pdf/UkraineAnalysen106.pdf.

Gyárfášová, Olga. 2018. The Fourth Generation: From Anti-establishment to Anti-system Parties in Slovakia." *New Perspectives* 26 (1): 109–133.

Gyárfášová, Olga, and Grigorij Mesežnikov. 2015. "Actors, Agenda, and Appeal of the Radical Nationalist Right in Slovakia." In: *Transforming the Transformation*, ed. Michael Minkenberg. New York: Routledge, pp. 224–248.

Habyarimana, James, Macartan Humphreys, Daniel Posner and Jeremy Weinstein. 2007. "Why Does Ethnic Diversity Undermine Public Goods Provision?" *American Political Science Review* 101 (4): 709–725.

Hainmueller, Jens, and Michael J. Hiscox. 2007. "Educated Preferences: Explaining Attitudes toward Immigration in Europe." *International Organization* 61 (2): 399–442.

Hanley, Sean. 2015. "All Fall Down? The Prospects for Established Parties in Europe and Beyond." *Government and Opposition* 50 (2): 1–24.

Hanley, Sean, and Allan Sikk. 2014. "Economy, Corruption or Floating Voters? Explaining the Breakthroughs of Anti-establishment Reform in Eastern Europe." *Party Politics* 22 (4): 522–533.

Haughton, Tim, and Kevin Deegan-Krause. 2015. "Hurricane Season Systems of Instability in Central and East European Party Politics." *East European Politics and Societies* 29 (1): 61–80.

Haughton, Tim, and Marek Rybář. 2008. "A Change in Direction: The 2006 Parliamentary Elections and Party Politics in Slovakia." *Journal of Communist Studies and Transition Politics* 24 (2): 232–255.

Hechter, Michael. 2013. *Alien Rule*. Cambridge: Cambridge University Press. 2000. *Containing Nationalism*. Oxford: Oxford University Press.

1987. *Principles of Group Solidarity*. Berkeley: University of. California Press.

Hegel, Georg Wilhelm Friedrich. 1807. *Hegel's Phenomenology of Spirit*. Trans. A. V. Miller. Oxford: Oxford University Press.

Held, Joseph, ed. 1996. *Populism in Eastern Europe: Racism, Nationalism, and Society*. Boulder: East European Monographs.

Henningsen, Arne. 2011. "Estimating Censored Regression Models in R Using the censReg Package," CRAN. Available at: cran.r-project. org/web/packages/censReg/vignettes/censReg.pdf.

Herszenhorn, David. 2012. "Latvians Reject Russian as a Second Language." *New York Times*. February 19. Available at: www.nytimes.com/2012/02/20/world/europe/latvia-rejects-bid-to-adopt-russian-as-second-language.html?_r=1.

Hintze, Jerry, and Ray Nelson. 1998. "Violin Plots: A Box Plot–Density Trace Synergism." *The American Statistician* 52 (2): 181–184.

Hobolt, Sara, and Catherine de Vries. 2016. "Public Support for European Integration." *Annual Review of Political Science* 19: 413–432.

Hockenos, Paul. 1993. *Free to Hate: The Rise of the Right in Post-Communist Eastern Europe*. New York: Routledge.

Holyoke, Thomas. 2009. "Interest Group Competition and Coalition Formation." *American Journal of Political Science* 53 (2): 360–375.

Honaker, James, and Drew Linzer. 2006. "Analysis of Vote Shares across Party Systems." Paper presented at the Annual Convention of the American Political Science Association, Philadelphia, August 31–September 2.

Hood, M. V. (Trey) III, Quentin Kidd and Irwin Morris. 2012. *The Rational Southerner*. New York: Oxford University Press.

Horowitz, Donald. 1993. "Democracy in Divided Societies." *Journal of Democracy* 4 (October): 18–38.

1985. *Ethnic Groups in Conflict*. Berkeley: University of California Press.

Hospodárske noviny. 2012. Známe výroky Jána Slotu. October 10. Available at: https://slovensko.hnonline.sk/486126-zname-vyroky-jana-slotu.

Hughes, James. 2005. "'Exit' in Deeply Divided Societies: Regimes of Discrimination in Estonia and Latvia and the Potential for Russophone Migration." *Journal of Common Market Studies* 43 (4): 739–762.

*Huffington Post*. 2011. "Anna Grodzka Becomes Poland's First Openly Transgender Member of Parliament." *Huffington Post*, October 11. Available at: www.huffingtonpost.com/2011/10/11/anna-grodzka-transgender-politician_n_1004840.html.

Human Rights Watch. 1996. *Rights Denied: The Roma in Hungary*. New York: Human Rights Watch/Helsinki.

Huntington, Samuel. 1968. *Political Order in Changing Societies*. New Haven: Yale University Press.

iDnes. 2016. "Kotleba posílá do vlaků své hlídky. Vyhodím je, varuje Jančura." April 13. Available at: http://zpravy.idnes.cz/kotlebovci-si-tvori-vlakove-hlidky-slovensko-fos-/zahranicni.aspx?c=A160413_172737_zahranicni_jkk.

Ignazi, Piero. 1992. "The Silent Counter-Revolution. Hypotheses on the Emergence of Extreme Right-Wing Parties in Europe." *European Journal of Political Research* 22 (1): 3–34.

Ilievski, Zoran, and Dane Taleski. 2009. "Was the EU's Role in Conflict Management in Macedonia a Success?" *Ethnopolitics* 8 (3–4): 355–367.

Immerzeel, Tim, Hilde Coffé and Tanja van der Lippe. 2015. "Explaining the Gender Gap in Radical Right Voting: A Cross-National Investigation in 12 Western European Countries." *Comparative European Politics* 13 (2): 263–228.

Inglehart, Ronald, and Christian Welzel. 2005. *Modernization, Cultural Change, and Democracy*. New York: Cambridge University Press.

Inglehart, Ronald, and Norris Pippa. 2016. "Trump, Brexit, and the Rise of Populism: Economic Have-Nots and Cultural Backlash." Faculty Research Working Paper Series, Harvard Kennedy School.

Interfax. 2014. "Kharkiv Regional Council Demands Official Status for Russian Language." Available at: http://en.interfax.com.ua/news/general/202138.html.

International Crisis Group. 2001. "Report on Macedonia." Available at: http://eastofcenter.tol.org/2011/09/ten-years-after-ohrid-a-stalled-macedonia/.

Ishiyama, John. 2009. "Historical Legacies and the Size of the Red Brown Vote in Post Communist Politics." *Communist and Post-Communist Studies* 42 (4): 485–504.

———. 2001. "Ethnopolitical Parties and Democratic Consolidation in Postcommunist Eastern Europe." *Nationalism & Ethnic Politics* 7 (3): 25–45.

———. 1997. "The Sickle or the Rose?" *Comparative Political Studies* 30 (3): 299–330.

Jackman, Robert, and Karin Volpert. 1996. "Conditions Favouring Parties of the Extreme Right in Western Europe." *British Journal of Political Science* 26 (4): 22.

Jeffries, Ian. 2004. *The Countries of the Former Soviet Union at the Turn of the Twenty-First Century*. London: Routledge.

Jenne, Erin. 2007. *Ethnic Bargaining: The Paradox of Minority Empowerment*. Ithaca: Cornell University Press.

———. 2004. "A Bargaining Theory of Minority Demands: Explaining the Dog That Didn't Bite in 1990s Yugoslavia." *International Studies Quarterly* 48 (4): 729–754.

Jobbik. 2011. "The Truth about Gyöngyöspata and Ethnic Violence in Hungary. Statement by Márton Gyöngyösi." May 30. Available at: www.jobbik.com/hungary/3201.html.

Jobbik Media Service. 2015. "Jobbik Criticizes Corruption of Roma Self-Governments." August. Available at: www.jobbik.com/vona_the_prime_minister_was_afraid_of_questions.

Jowitt, Ken. 1992. *New World Disorder: The Leninist Extinction*. Berkeley: University of California Press.

Kasekamp, Andres. 2015a. "Estonia." In: *Central and South-Eastern Europe 2016*. Abingdon: Taylor & Francis/CRC Press, pp. 252–258.

2015b. "Latvia." In: *Central and South-Eastern Europe 2016*. Abingdon: Taylor & Francis/CRC Press, pp. 391–396.

2003. "Extreme-Right Parties in Contemporary Estonia." *Patterns of Prejudice* 37 (4): 401–414.

Katchanovski, Ivan. 2015. "Terrorists or National Heroes? Politics and Perceptions of the OUN and the UPA in Ukraine." *Communist and Postcommunist Studies* 48 (2–3): 217–228.

2014. An Interview with Reuters Concerning Svoboda, the OUN-B, and Other Far Right Organizations in Ukraine. March 4. Available at: www.academia.edu/6327298/Interview_with_Reuters_re_Svoboda_the_OUN-B_and_other_Far_Right_Organizations_in_Ukraine_March_4_2014_FullText.

Katz, Richard, and Peter Mair. 2009. "The Cartel Party Thesis: A Restatement." *Perspectives on Politics* 7 (4): 753–766.

Katz, Richard S., and Peter Mair. 1995. "Changing Models of Party Organization and Party Democracy: The Emergence of the Cartel Party." *Party Politics* 1 (1): 5–28.

Kedar, Orit. 2005. "When Moderate Voters Prefer Extreme Parties: Policy Balancing in Parliamentary Elections." *American Political Science Review* 99: 185–199.

Kelemen, R. Daniel, and Mitchell A. Ornstein. 2016. "Polish Democracy's Final Days?" *Foreign Affairs*. Available at: www.foreignaffairs.com/articles/poland/2016-01-07/europes-autocracy-problem.

Kelley, Judith. 2004a. *Ethnic Politics in Europe: The Power of Norms and Incentives*. Princeton: Princeton University Press.

2004b. "International Actors on the Domestic Scene: Membership Conditionality and Socialization by International Institutions." *International Organization* 58 (3): 425–457.

Kersten, Joachim, and Natalia Hankel, 2013. "A Comparative Look at Right-Wing Extremism, Anti-Semitism, and Xenophobic Hate Crimes in Poland, Ukraine, and Russia." In: *Right-Wing Radicalism Today:*

*Perspectives from Europe and the US*, ed. Sabine von Mering and Timothy McCarty. Abingdon: Routledge, pp. 85–105.

KIIS [Kiev International Institute of Sociology]. 2010. *Methodological Report: Opinions and Views of Ukrainian People*. Kiev.

Kitschelt, Herbert. 2018. "Party Systems and Radical Right Parties." In: *The Oxford Handbook of the Radical Right*, ed. Jens Rydgren. New York: Oxford University Press, pp. 166–199.

——— 2011. "Clientelistic Linkage Strategies. A Descriptive Exploration." Paper prepared for the Workshop on Democratic Accountability Strategies, Duke University, May 18–19.

——— 2007. "Growth and Persistence of the Radical Right in Postindustrial Democracies: Advances and Challenges in Comparative Research." *West European Politics* 30 (5): 1176–1206.

——— 1995. "The Formation of Party Cleavages in Post-Communist Democracies: Theoretical Propositions." *Party Politics* 1: 447–472.

——— 1994. *The Transformation of European Social Democracy*. Cambridge: Cambridge University Press.

Kitschelt, Herbert, and Anthony McGann. 1995. *The Radical Right in Western Europe: A Comparative Analysis*. Ann Arbor: University of Michigan Press.

Kitschelt, Herbert, and Steven Wilkinson. 2007. *Patrons, Clients and Policies*. Cambridge: Cambridge University Press.

Kitschelt, Herbert, Kent Freeze, Kiril Kolev and Yi-Ting Wang. 2009. "Measuring Democratic Accountability: An Initial Report on an Emerging Data Set." *Revista de Ciencia Politica* 29 (3): 741–773.

——— et al. 2008. Democratic Accountability and Linkages Project. Duke University. Available at: www.duke.edu/web/democracy/.

Kitschelt, Herbert, Zdenka Mansfeldova, Radoslaw Markowski and Gabor Toka. 1999. *Post-communist Party Systems: Competition, Representation, and Inter-party Cooperation*. Cambridge: Cambridge University Press.

Klašnja, Marko, Joshua Tucker and Kevin Deegan-Krause. 2014. "Pocketbook vs. Sociotropic Corruption Voting." *British Journal of Political Science* 46 (1): 67–94.

Klimša, Karel. 2010. "Maďarsko: Volby vypsány, vítěz je znám!" Britské listy. January 27. Available at: www.blisty.cz/art/50949.html.

Kluknavská, Alena, and Josef Smolík. 2016. "We Hate the All? Issue Adaptation of Extreme Right Parties in Slovakia 1993–2016." *Communist and Postcommunist Studies* 49: 335–344.

Kohut, Andrew, Richard Wike, Juliana Horowitz, Kathleen Sprehe and Jacob Poushter. 2009. "Two Decades after the Wall's Fall: End of Communism Cheered but Now with More Reservations." In *The Pew*

*Global Project Attitudes*. Pew Research Center. Available at: www.pewglobal.org/2009/11/02/end-of-communism-cheered-but-now-with-more-reservations/.

Kolesnichenko, Vadym, and Ruslan Bortnik. 2012. "The Second Periodical Public Report on Implementation of the Provisions of the European Charter for Regional or Minority Languages by Ukraine." Council of the Human Rights Public Movement "Russian-Speaking Ukraine" and Ukrainian Public Organization "The Human Rights organization 'Common Goal.'" Available at: http://r-u.org.ua/en/announ/427-news.html.

Kolev, Kiril, and Yi-ting Wang. 2019. "Ethnic Group Inequality, Partisan Networks, and Political Clientelism" *Political Research Quarterly* 72 (2): 329–341.

Koopmans, Ruud, ed. 2005. *Contested Citizenship: Immigration and Cultural Diversity in Europe*. Minneapolis: University of Minnesota Press.

Kopanic, Michael. 1999. "The New Minority Language Law in Slovakia." *Central Europe Review* 1 (2) July. Available at: www.ce-review.org/99/2/kopanic2.html.

Kopecky, Petr, and Cas Mudde, eds. 2003. *Uncivil Society? Contentious Politics in Post-Communist Europe*. London: Routledge.

2002. "The Two Sides of Euroscepticism: Party Positions on European Integration in East Central Europe." *European Union Politics* 3 (3): 297–326.

Kopstein, Jeffrey. 2003. "Post-Communist Democracy: Legacies and Outcomes." *Comparative Politics* 35 (1): 231–250.

Kopstein, Jeffrey, and David Reilly. 2000. "Geographic Diffusion and the Transformation of the Postcommunist World." *World Politics* 53 (1): 1–37.

Kopstein, Jeffrey, and Jason Wittenberg. 2018. *Intimate Violence*. Ithaca: Cornell University Press.

2011. "Deadly Communities: Local Political Milieus and the Persecution of Jews in Occupied Poland." *Comparative Political Studies* 44 (3): 259–283.

2010. "Beyond Dictatorship and Democracy: Rethinking Minority Inclusion and Regime Type in Interwar Eastern Europe." *Comparative Political Studies* 43 (8): 1089–1118.

2009. "Does Familiarity Breed Contempt? Inter-ethnic Contact and Support for Illiberal Parties." *Journal of Politics* 43 (1): 61–90.

Krastev, Ivan. 2007. "The Strange Death of the Liberal Consensus." *Journal of Democracy* 18 (4): 56–63.

Kreidl, Martin, and Klara Vlachova. 1999. "Rise and Decline of Right-Wing Extremism in the Czech Republic in the 1990s." *Prague: Academy of Sciences Working Papers* 99: 10.

Krekó, Péter, and Gregor Mayer. 2015. "Transforming Hungary – Together? An Analysis of the Fidesz-Jobbik Relationship." In: *Transforming the Transformation: The East European Radical Right in the Political Process*, ed. Michael Minkenberg. Abingdon: Routledge, pp. 183–205.

Krekó, Peter, Krisztian Szabados, Csaba Molnar, Attila Juhasz and Alexander Kuli. 2010. "Back by Popular Demand, DEREX: Demand for Right-Wing Extremism," 2009. Political Capital Institute. February 11.

Krekó, Péter, Marie Macaulay, Csaba Molnár and Lóránt Győri. 2015. "Europe's New Pro-Putin Coalition: The Parties of 'No.'" August 3, Political Capital Institute (Hungary). Institute of Modern Russia.

Kriesi, Hanspeter. 1998. "The Transformation of Cleavage Politics: The 1997 Stein Rokkan Lecture." *European Journal of Political Research* 33 (2): 165–185.

Kubicek, Paul. 1999. "What Happened to the Nationalists in Ukraine?" *Nationalism and Ethnic Politics* 5 (1): 29–30.

Kudelia, Serhiy. 2011. "The Dilemma of Ukraine's Extreme Right." Ukraine Watch. February 1. Available at: http://ukrainewatch.wordpress.com/2011/02/01/the-dilemma-of-ukraine%E2%80%99s-extreme-right/.

Kukiz'15. Kukiz'15 web page. Available at: http://ruchkukiza.pl/klub-poselski/strategia-zmiany/.

KUN. 2009. Available at: http://cun.org.ua/ukr/content/view/1364/66/.

Kuzio, Taras. 2010. "Russophile Agenda Rising once Again." *Kyiv Post*, August 12. Available at: www.kyivpost.com/news/opinion/op_ed/detail/78132/.

2007. "Radical Nationalist Parties and Movements in Contemporary Ukraine before and after Independence: The Right and Its Politics, 1989–1994." *Nationalities Papers* 25 (2): 211–242.

2002. "Nationalism in Ukraine: Towards a New Theoretical and Comparative Framework." *Journal of Political Ideologies* 7 (2): 133–161.

1997. "Radical Right Parties and Civic Groups in Belarus and the Ukraine." In: *The Revival of Right-Wing Extremism in the Nineties*, ed. Peter Merkel and Leonard Weinberg. London: Frank Cass, pp. 203–230.

*Kyiv Post*. 2012a. "Lviv Regional Council Declares Language Law Invalid on Region's Territory." October 10. Available at: www.kyivpost.com/content/ukraine/lviv-regional-council-declares-language-law-invalid-on-regions-territory-314198.html.

2012b. "Regional State Council: Language Law Has No Effect in Ivano-Frankivsk Region." October 10. Available at: www.kyivpost.com/content/ukraine/regional-state-counci-language-law-has-no-effect-in-ivano-frankivsk-region-314191.html.

2009 "Poll: More than Half of Ukrainians Do Not Consider Language Issue Pressing." November 25.

Kyiv Weekly. 2007. "President Yushchenko Awarded the Hero of Ukraine Title." October 15. Available at: www.kyivweekly.com/.

Kymlicka, Will, ed. 2006. Multiculturalism and the Welfare State: Recognition and Redistribution in Contemporary Democracies. Oxford: Oxford University Press.

Laitin, David. 1998. Identity in Formation: The Russian-Speaking Populations in the Near Abroad. Ithaca: Cornell University Press.

Lajčáková, Jarmila. 2013. "Správa občianskej spoločnosti o implementácii stratégie Slovenskej republiky pre integráciu Rómov do roku 2020 a revidovaného akčného plánu dekády na Slovensku." Available at: www.romadecade.org/cms/upload/file/9270_file22_sk_civil-society-moni toring-report_sk.pdf.

Land, Thomas. 2001. "Frustrated Hungary Flirts with Far-Right Politics." Contemporary Review (January): 1–5.

Lang, Kai-Olaf. 2005. "Populism in Central and Eastern Europe – A Threat to Democracy or Just Political Folklore?" Slovak Foreign Policy Affairs (Spring): 6–16.

Laver, Michael. 1998. "Models of Government Formation." Annual Review of Political Science 1 (1): 1–25.

Laver, Michael, and Norman Schofield. 1990. Multiparty Government: The Politics of Coalition in Europe. Ann Arbor: University of Michigan Press.

Levy, Clifford. 2011. "'Hero of Ukraine' Prize to Wartime Partisan Leader Is Revoked." New York Times. January 12. Available at: www.nytimes.com/2011/01/13/world/europe/13ukraine.html.

Lewis, Paul. 2009. "Party System Stabilisation in Central Europe: Records and Prospects in a Changing Socio-Economic Context." ECPR General Conference, Potsdam, September 10–12.

Liebich, Andre, and Oksana Myshlovska. 2014. "Bandera Memorialization and Commemoration." Nationalities Papers 42 (5), 750–770.

Lijphart, Arend. 1984. Democracies: Patterns of Majoritarian and Consensus Democracies in Twenty-One Countries. New Haven: Yale University Press.

1968. The Politics of Accommodation: Pluralism and Democracy in the Netherlands. Berkeley: University of California Press.

Likert, Rensis. 1932. "A Technique for the Measurement of Attitudes." Archives of Psychology 22 (140): 1–55.

Likhachev, Viacheslav, ed. 2015. "Antisemitism in FSU-2014." Issue #12. Euro-Asian Jewish Congress. Available at: www.eajc.org/data//file/ AntisemitismReport2014engl.pdf.

Likhachev, Viacheslav. 2013. "Right-Wing Extremism on the Rise in Ukraine." *Russian Politics & Law* 51 (5): 59–74.

Likhachev, Viacheslav, and Tatiana Bezruk. 2014. "Ksenofobiia v Ukraine v 2014." Association of Jewish Organizations and Communities of Ukraine. Available at: http://vaadua.org/sites/default/files/files/Xenopho bia_in_Ukraine_2014_rus.pdf.

Lipset, Seymour Martin. 1960. *Political Man. The Social Bases of Politics.* Garden City, New York: Doubleday.

Lipset, Seymour, and Stein Rokkan, eds. 1967. *Party Systems and Voter Alignments: Cross-National Perspectives.* London: Collier–Macmillan– Free Press.

Liu, Amy. 2017a. "The Isolation of Chinese Migrants in Eastern Europe." *Journal of Chinese Overseas* 13 (1): 31–47.

2017b. "Democracy and Minority Language Recognition: Tyranny of the Majority and the Conditional Effects of Group Size." *Democratization* 24 (3): 544–565.

2014. *Standardizing Diversity. The Political Economy of Language Regimes.* University of Pennsylvania Press.

Lovatt, Catherine. 1999. "Iron Guard Revival." *Central European Review* 1 (3). Available at: www.ce-review.org/99/3/lovatt3.html.

Loxbo, Karl. 2010. "The Impact of the Radical Right: Lessons from the Local Level in Sweden, 2002–2006." *Scandinavian Political Studies* 33 (3): 295–315.

Luna, Juan, and Elizabeth Zechmeister. 2005. "Political Representation in Latin America." *Comparative Political Studies* 38 (4): 388–416.

Luttmer, Erzo. 2001. "Group Loyalty and the Taste for Redistribution." *Journal of Political Economy* 109 (3): 500–528.

ĽS – Naše Slovensko 2018. "Naše návrhy zákonov." Available at: www.naseslovensko.net/kategoria/ls-nase-slovensko-v-nr-sr/nase-navrhy-zakonov/.

Malinkovich, Vladimir. 2005. "The Degree of Ukrainization of Education in Ukraine." Institute of Humanities-Political Research, March 10. Уровень украинизации школьного образования в различных регионах Украины. Available at: www.igpi.ru/info/people/malink/1111152776.html.

MAR. 2008. "Minorities at Risk." Available at: www.cidcm.umd.edu/mar/assessment.asp?groupId=31001.

Maravall, Jose. 2010. "Accountability in Coalition Governments." *Annual Review of Political Science* 13: 81–100.

Mareš, Miroslav. 2011. "Czech Extreme Right Parties an Unsuccessful Story." *Communist and Post-Communist Studies* 44 (4): 283–298.

2009. "The Extreme Right in Eastern Europe and Territorial Issues." *Central European Political Studies Review* 11 (2–3): 82–106.

2007. "Národní garda zaregistrována!" *Hospodářské noviny*, December 15. Available at: http://domaci.ihned.cz/komentare-rozhov ory/c1–22623220-miroslav-mares-narodni-garda-zaregistrovana.

2006. "Transnational Networks of Extreme Right Parties in East Central Europe: Stimuli and Limits of Cross-Border Cooperation." Manuscript.

2003. *Pravicový extremismus a radikalismus v ČR*. Brno: Barrister & Principal.

Mareš, Miroslav, and Vratislav Havlík. 2016. "Jobbik's Successes: An Analysis of Its Success in the Comparative Context of the (V4) countries." *Communist and Post-Communist Studies* 49: 323–333.

Markowski, Radosław. 2018. "Backsliding into Authoritarian Clientelism: The Case of Poland." In: *Democracy under Stress*, ed. Petra Guasti and Zdenka Mansfeldová. Sociologický ústav AV ČR, pp. 75–96.

Markowski, Radosław, Clare McManus-Czubinska and William Miller. 2003. "The New Polish 'Right'?" *The Journal of Communist Studies and Transition Politics* 19 (2): 1–23.

Masalkova, Olga. 2010. "Yanukovich Denies Russian the Status of Second Official Language." *RT*. March 11. Available at: http://rt.com/politics/ yanukovich-denies-russian-status/.

Maškarinec, Pavel, and Petr Bláha. 2016. "Křivda jako příležitost pro nové politické strany? Kotleba – Lidová strana Naše Slovensko na cestě do parlamentu." *Politics in Central Europe* 12 (2): 45–66.

McFaul, Michael. 2002. "The Fourth Wave of Democracy and Dictatorship: Noncooperative Transitions in the Postcommunist World." *World Politics* 54 (January): 212–244.

McPhedran, Charles. 2012. "Official Terror for Hungary's Roma." *Global Mail*, February 7. Available at: www.theglobalmail.org/feature/official-terror-for-hungarys-roma/35/.

Medvedev, Roy. 2007. "A Splinted Ukraine." *Russia in Global Affairs* 5 (3): 194–213.

Meguid, Bonnie. 2008. *Party Competition between Unequals*. Cambridge: Cambridge University Press.

2005. "Competition between Unequals: The Role of Mainstream Party Strategy in Niche Party Success." *American Political Science Review* 99 (3): 347–359.

Merkl, Peter, and Leonard Weinberg, eds. 2003. *Right-Wing Extremism in the Twenty-First Century*. Portland: Frank Cass.

eds. 1997. *The Revival of Right-Wing Extremism in the 90s*. London: Frank Cass.

Merton, Robert. 1938. "Social Structure and Anomie." *American Sociological Review* 3 (5): 672–682.

Mesežnikov, Grigorij, Olga Gyarfášová and Daniel Smilov, eds. 2008. "Populist Politics and Liberal Democracy in Central and Eastern Europe." IVO (IPA) working paper series, Bratislava.

Michnik, Adam. 2007. "The Polish Witch-Hunt." *New York Review of Books*, June 28.

Milazzo, Caitlin, Ethan Scheiner and Robert Moser. 2018. "Social Diversity Affects the Number of Parties Even under First-Past-the-Post Rules." *Comparative Political Studies* 51 (7): 938–974.

Ministerstvo kultúry Slovenskej republiky. (2009). Jazykový zákon a práva menšín na Slovensku. Available at: www.culture.gov.sk/aktuality/jazy kovy-zakon-a-prava-mensin-na-slovensku.

Minkenberg, Michael. 2017. *The Radical Right in Eastern Europe: Democracy under Siege?* New York: Palgrave Macmillan.

Minkenberg, Michael, ed. 2015. *Transforming the Transformation: The East European Radical Right in the Political Process*. Abingdon: Routledge.

———. 2009. "Leninist Beneficiaries? Pre-1989 Legacies and the Radical Right in Post-1989 Central and Eastern Europe. Some Introductory Observations." *Communist and Post-Communist Studies* 42 (4): 445–458.

———. 2007. "Between Tradition and Transition: The Central European Radical Right and the New European Order." In: *Europe for the Europeans: The Foreign and Security Policy of the Populist Radical Right*, ed. Christina Schori Liang. Aldershot: Ashgate, pp. 261–281.

———. 2002. "The Radical Right in Postsocialist Central and Eastern Europe: Comparative Observations and Interpretations." *East European Politics and Society* 16 (2): 335–362.

Minkenberg, Michael, and Pascal Perrineau. 2007. "The Radical Right in the European Elections 2004." *International Political Science Review/ Revue internationale de science politique* 28 (1): 29–55.

Minkenberg, Michael, and Timm Beichelt. 2001. "Explaining the Radical Right in Transition, Theories of Right-Wing Radicalism and Opportunity Structures in Post-Socialist Europe." Paper presented at 2001 Annual Meeting of the American Political Science Association, San Francisco.

Mols, Frank, and Jolanda Jetten. 2016. "Explaining the Appeal of Populist Right-Wing Parties in Times of Economic Prosperity." *Political Psychology* 37: 275–292.

Moser, Michael. 2013. *Language Policy and the Discourse of Languages in Ukraine under President Viktor Yanukovych*. Stuttgart: ibidem-Verlag.

Mudde, Cas. 2017. "Politics at the Fringes? Eastern Europe's Populists, Racists, and Extremists." In: *The Routledge Handbook of East European Politics*, ed. Adam Fagan and Petr Kopecký. Abingdon: Routledge, pp. 254–264.

———. 2016. "The Study of Populist Radical Right Parties: Towards a Fourth Wave." C-REX Working Paper Series, No 1.

2007. *Populist Radical Right Parties in Europe*. Cambridge: Cambridge University Press.

2005a. *Racist Extremism in Central and Eastern Europe*. London: Routledge.

2005b. "Racist Extremism in Central and Eastern Europe." *Eastern European Politics and Societies* 19 (2): 161–184.

2004. "The Populist Zeitgeist." *Government & Opposition* 39 (3): 541–563.

2003. "EU Accession and a New Populist Center–Periphery Cleavage in Central and Eastern Europe." Available at: http://works.bepress.com/cas_mudde/10/.

2001. "In the Name of the Peasantry, the Proletariat, and the People: Populisms in Eastern Europe." *East European Politics and Societies* 14 (2): 33–53.

2000. "Extreme Right Parties in Eastern Europe." *Patterns of Prejudice* 34 (1): 5–27.

1996. "The War of Words: Defining the Extreme Party Family." *West European Politics* 19 (2): 225–248.

Mudde, Cas, and Cristobal Rovira Kaltwasser. 2018. "Studying Populism in Comparative Perspective: Reflections on the Contemporary and Future Research Agenda." *Comparative Political Studies*. First online. Doi: 10.1177/0010414018789490.

2013. "Exclusionary vs. Inclusionary Populism: Comparing Contemporary Europe and Latin America." *Government and Opposition* 48 (2): 147–174.

2011. "Voices of the Peoples: Populism in Europe and Latin America Compared." Working Paper 378, Kellogg Institute. Available at: https://kellogg.nd.edu/publications/workingpapers/WPS/378.pdf.

2010. "Voices of the Peoples: Populism in Europe and Latin America Compared." Paper presented at the Latin American Studies Association (LASA) International Congress, Toronto, ON, October 6–9.

Mungiu-Pippidi, Alina. 2007. "EU Accession Is No End of History." *Journal of Democracy* 18 (4): 8–16.

Mutz, Diana. 2018. "Status Threat, Not Economic Hardship, Explains the 2016 Presidential Vote." *PNAS* 115 (19): 4330–4339.

Národná rada. 2018. Parlamentná tlač 1125. Available at: www.nrsr.sk/web/Default.aspx?sid=zakony/cpt&ZakZborID=13&CisObdobia=7&ID=1125.

National Academy of Sciences. 2014. Representative surveys by the Institute of Sociology, National Academy of Sciences, Ukraine; Results of national surveys 1992–2014. NB. Ukrainian society: Monitoring Social Change, 65.

National Democratic Institute. 2012. "Slovakia Elects First Roma Representative to Parliament." April 23. Available at: https://mail.google.com/mail/u/0/#inbox/15b79f68fb7c3180?projector=1.

NDI/OSCE. 2006. "The Hungarian Minority Self-Government System as a Means of Increasing Romani Political Participation." National Democratic Institute Assessment Report (September/October). OSCE/ODIHR.

NewsNow. 2016. "Government Proxy for Roma Pollak Wants PG to Ban ĽSNS." *NewsNow.sk*, March 15. Available at: http://newsnow.tasr.sk/policy/government-proxy-for-roma-pollak-wants-pg-to-ban-lsns/.

Nissen, Scott. 2004. "An Explanation of Electoral Popularity for Far Right Reactionary Parties in Eastern Europe and the Former Soviet Union." Paper presented at the annual meeting of the Midwest Political Science Association, Chicago, Illinois, April 15.

Norris, Pippa. 2005. *Radical Right: Voters and Parties in the Electoral Market*. Cambridge: Cambridge University Press.

Nunnally, Jum. 1978. *Psychometric Theory*. New York: McGraw Hill.

O'Dwyer, Conor. 2018. *Coming Out of Communism: The Emergence of LGBT Activism in Eastern Europe*. New York: New York University Press.

——— 2014. "What Accounts for Party System Stability? Comparing the Dimensions of Party Competition in Postcommunist Europe." *Europe-Asia Studies* 66 (4): 511–535.

——— 2012. "Does the EU Help or Hinder Gay-Rights Movements in Postcommunist Europe? The Case of Poland." *East European Politics* 28 (4): 332–352.

O'Dwyer, Conor, and Katrina Schwartz. 2010. "Minority Rights after EU Enlargement: A Comparison of Antigay Politics in Poland and Latvia." *Comparative European Politics* 8 (2): 220–243.

Oesch, Daniel. 2009. "Explaining Workers' Support for Right-Wing Populist Parties in Western Europe: Evidence from Austria, Belgium, France, Norway, and Switzerland." *International Political Science Review* 29 (3): 349–373.

Olson, Mancur. 1965. *The Logic of Collective Action*. Cambridge: Cambridge University Press.

Olszański, Tadeusz. 2012. "The Language Issue in Ukraine: An Attempt at a New Perspective." No. 40, May, OSW/Center for Eastern Studies, Waszaw.

Olszański, Tadeusz A. 2011. "Svoboda Party – The New Phenomenon on the Ukrainian Right-Wing Scene." Available at: www.osw.waw.pl/en/publikacje/osw-commentary/2011-07-05/svoboda-party-new-phenomenon-ukrainian-rightwing-scene.

Olzak, Susan. 1992. *The Dynamic of Ethnic Competition and Conflict.* Palo Alto: Stanford University Press.

Ost, David. 2005. *The Defeat of Solidarity: Anger and Politics in Postcommunist Europe.* Ithaca: Cornell University Press.

Pankowski, Rafal. 2010. *The Populist Radical Right in Poland: The Patriots.* New York: Routledge.

Peisakhin, Leonid. 2013. "In History's Shadow: Do Formal Institutions Leave a Cultural Legacy?" Paper presented at the annual general conference of the European Political Science Association, Barcelona, June 20–22.

Petai, Vello. 2006. "Explaining Ethnic Politics in the Baltic States: Reviewing the Triadic Nexus Model." *Journal of Baltic Studies* 37 (1): 124–136.

Petersen, Roger. 2002. *Understanding Ethnic Violence.* Cambridge: Cambridge University Press.

2001. *Resistance and Rebellion: Lessons from Eastern Europe.* Cambridge: Cambridge University Press.

Peterson, Britt. 2014. "The Long War over the Ukrainian Language." *Boston Globe.* March 16.

Petkova, Lilia. 2002. "The Ethnic Turks in Bulgaria: Social Integration and Impact on Bulgarian–Turkish Relations, 1947–2000." *The Global Review of Ethnopolitics* 1 (4): 42–59.

Petrocik, John. 1996. "Issue Ownership in Presidential Elections, with a 1980 Case Study." *American Journal of Political Science* 40 (3): 825–850.

Petrocik, John, William Benoit and Glenn Hansen. 2002. "Issue Ownership and Presidential Campaigning, 1952–2000." *Political Science Quarterly* 118 (4): 599–626.

Petsinis, Vassilis. 2015. "The 'New' Far Right in Hungary: A Political Psychologist's Perspective." *Journal of Contemporary European Studies* 23 (2): 272–287.

Pirro, Andrea. 2016. "Hardly Ever Relevant? An Appraisal of Nativist Economics through the Hungarian Case." *Acta Politica* 1–22.

2015. *The Populist Radical Right in Central and Eastern Europe: Ideology, Impact, and Electoral Performance.* Abingdon: Routledge.

2014. "Digging into the Breeding Ground: Insights into the Electoral Performance of Populist Radical Right Parties in Central and Eastern Europe." *East European Politics* 30 (2): 246–270.

Pluska. 2016. "Brutálna dráma na trati Nové Zámky: Pre 1 euro surovo škrtil mladé dievča!" April 9. Available at: www.pluska.sk/krimi/krimi/brutalna-drama-trati-nove-zamky-1-euro-surovo-skrtil-mlade-dievca.html.

2015. Pollák sľubuje Rómom: Útok policajtov prešetrí generálna prokur-atúra. *Pluska.sk*, April 4. Available at: www.pluska.sk/krimi/domace-krimi/pollak-slubuje-romom-utok-policajtov-presetri-generalna-prokuratura.html.

Poláčková, Karolína. 2018. "The White Dream of Marian Kotleba." *Political Critique*, August 25.

Polgár Foundation for Equal Opportunities. 2008. "The Movement for Desegregation Foundation." Available at: www.polgaralapitvany.hu/dokumentumok/socialreport2008.pdf.

Poliglotti4.eu. 2012. "Azarov: New Language Law Is the Reaction to the Russian Language Oppression." June 26. Available at: http://poliglotti4.eu/php/media-centre/index.php?doc_id=1908&lg=en.

Political Capital. 2012. "Attitude Radicals in Hungary – In International Context." February 29. Available at: www.politicalcapital.hu/.

Polyakova, Alina. 2015. *The Dark Side of European Integration: Social Foundations and Cultural Determinants of the Rise of Radical Right Movements in Contemporary Europe.* Stuttgart: Ibidem-Verlag; New York: Columbia University Press.

2014. "From the Provinces to the Parliament: Nationalism in the Galician Heartland." *Communist and Post-Communist Studies* 47 (2): 211–225.

2012. "Organizing Nationalism: How the Radical Right Succeeds and Fails in Ukraine." IREX Scholarly Research Brief. Available at: www.irex.org.

Pop-Eleches, Grigore. 2010. "Throwing Out the Bums: Protest Voting and Unorthodox Parties after Communism." *World Politics* 62 (2): 221–260.

2007. "Historical Legacies and Post-Communist Regime Change." *Journal of Politics* 69 (4): 908–926.

Popova, Maria. 2016. "Who Brought Ataka to the Political Scene?" In: *Beyond Mosque, Church and State*, ed. Theodora Dragostinova and Yana Hashamova. Budapest: Central European University Press, pp. 259–286.

2014. "Why the Orange Revolution Was Short and Peaceful and Euro-maidan Long and Violent." *Problems of Post-Communism* 61 (6): 64–70.

Powell, Eleanor, and Joshua Tucker. 2014. "Revisiting Electoral Volatility in Post-Communist Countries: New Data, New Results, and New Approaches." *British Journal of Political Science* 44 (1): 123–147.

Pratto, Felicia, Jim Sidanius and Shana Levin. 2006. "Social Dominance Theory and the Dynamics of Intergroup Relations: Taking Stock and Looking Forward." *European Review of Social Psychology* 17 (1): 271–320.

Pravda. 2012. "Pollák: Streľba v Hurbanove je neospravedlniteľná a nepo-chopiteľná." *Pravda.sk*, June 18. Available at: http://spravy.pravda .sk/domace/clanok/247019-pollak-strelba-v-hurbanove-je-neospravedl nitelna-a-nepochopitelna/.

Prokop, David. 2010. "Maďarský fašizmus má i teroristické složky." iDNES, February 27. Available at: http://prokop.blog.idnes.cz/c/ 125964/Madarsky-fasizmus-ma-i-teroristicke-slozky.html.

Pupovac, David. 2015. "The Radical Right in Policy Space: A Comparative Analysis of Radical Right Parties in Eastern and Western Europe." PhD dissertation, Central European University.

———. 2010. "Classifying European Radical Right Parties: A Comparative Analysis of Clustering Methods." Paper presented at the 3rd European Consotrium for Political Research Graduate Conference, August 30–September 1, Dublin, Ireland.

Pytlas, Bartek. 2018. "Radical Right Politics in East and West: Distinctive yet Equivalent." *Sociology Compass*. Early view, doi: 10.1111/ soc4.12632.

———. 2016. *Radical Right Parties in Central and Eastern Europe*. Abingdon: Routledge.

Rabinowitz, George, and Stuart Macdonald. 1989. "A Directional Theory of Issue Voting." *American Political Science Review* 83 (1): 93–121.

Rafaj, Rafael. 2011. "Pomaďarčovací zákon o používaní jazykov menšín smeruje k deslovakizácii južného Slovenska." April 7. Available at: www.sns.sk/aktuality/rafael-rafaj-pomadarcovaci-zakon-o-pouzivani-jazykov-mensin-smeruje-k-deslovakizacii-juzneho-slovenska/.

Ramet, Sabrina. 2007. *The Liberal Project and the Transformation of Democracy: The Case of East Central Europe*. College Station: Texas A&M University Press.

Ramet, Sabrina, ed. 1999. *The Radical Right in Central and Eastern Europe since 1989*. University Park: Pennsylvania State University Press.

Razumkov Center. 2012. Opinion Poll: How the Russian and the Ukrainian Languages Should Co-exist. Available at: www.razumkov.org.ua/ukr/ poll.php?poll_id=289.

Rechel, Bernd, ed. 2009. *Minority Rights in Central and Eastern Europe*. Abingdon: Routledge.

Reif, Karlheinz, and Hermann Schmitt. 1980. "Nine Second-Order National Elections – A Conceptual Framework for the Analysis of European Election Results." *European Journal of Political Research* 8 (1): 3–44.

Reflex. 2018. "Koncentrační tábor v Letech: Základní fakta o údajně neex-istujícím pseudokoncentráku." February 7. Available at: www.reflex.cz/ koncentracni-tabor-lety.

Reuters. 2013. "Hungary Loosens Farm Ownership Rules, Far-Right Cries Treason." June 21. Available at: www.reuters.com/article/hungary-farmland/hungary-loosens-farm-ownership-rules-far-right-cries-treason-idUSL5N0EX11X20130621.

Rev, Istvan. 1994. "The Postmortem Victory of Communism." *Daedalus*, Summer: 159–171.

RFE. 2005. "Macedonia: Did Nationalist Leaders Plan to Divide Country along Ethnic Lines?" Radio Free Europe, June 7.

Riker, William. 1986. *The Art of Political Manipulation.* New Haven: Yale University Press.

1962. *The Theory of Political Coalitions.* New Haven: Yale University Press.

Ringold, Dena. 2000. *Roma and the Transition in Central and Eastern Europe: Trends and Challenges.* Washington, DC: World Bank. Available at: http://siteresources.worldbank.org/ECAEXT/Resources/publications/Roma-and-the-Transition/coverTOC.pdf.

Robotin, Monica-Emilia. 2002. "The Electorate of the Extreme-Right: The Case of Greater Romania Party." Master's thesis, Central European University.

Roemer, John, Woojin Lee and Karine Van der Straeten. 2007. *Racism, Xenophobia, and Distribution: Multi-issue Politics in Advanced Democracies.* Cambridge, MA: Harvard University Press.

Rohrschneider, Robert, and Stephen Whitefield. 2009. "Understanding Cleavages in Party Systems: Issue Position and Issue Salience in 13 Post-Communist Democracies." *Comparative Political Studies* 42 (2): 280–313.

Roland, Gerard. 2000. *Politics, Markets and Firms: Transition and Economics.* Cambridge, MA: MIT Press.

Roma Decade. 2005. "Decade of Roma Inclusion 2005–2015." Available at: www.romadecade.org/itentcms/www/roma/index.php.

Rosenberg, Tina. 1996. *The Haunted Land: Facing Europe's Ghosts after Communism.* New York: Random House.

Rothschild, Joseph, and Nancy Wingfield. 2000. *Return to Diversity: A Political History of East Central Europe since World War II,* 3rd edition. Oxford: Oxford University Press.

Rovny, Jan. 2013. "Where Do Radical Right Parties Stand? Position Blurring in Multidimensional Competition." *European Political Science Review* 5 (1): 1–26.

Rovny, Jan, and Erica Edwards. 2012. "Struggle over Dimensionality: Party Competition in Western and Eastern Europe." *East European Politics and Societies* 26 (1): 56–74.

Rudakov, Alexander. 2006. "A Totalitarian Scenario for Kiev." *Globoscope*, September 6. Available at: www.globoscope.ru/eng/content/articles/1/?bxajaxid=24e07ae585d703e04905b619ec6f9d97.

Rudling, Per Anders. 2013. "The Return of the Ukrainian Far Right: The Case of VO Svoboda." In: *Analyzing Fascist Discourse: European Fascism in Talk and Text*, ed. Ruth Wodak and John Richardson. London: Routledge, pp. 228–255.

   2012. "Anti-Semitism and the Extreme Right in Contemporary Ukraine." In *Mapping the Extreme Right in Contemporary Europe: From Local to Transnational*, ed. Andrea Mammone, Emmanuel Godin and Brian Jenkins. London: Routledge, pp. 189–205.

Rupnik, Jacques. 2007. "From Democracy Fatigue to Populist Backlash." *Journal of Democracy* 18 (4): 17–25.

Rustow, Dankwart A. 1970. "Transition towards Democracy." *Comparative Politics* 2 (3): 337–363.

Rydgren, Jens, ed. 2018. *The Oxford Handbook of the Radical Right*. New York: Oxford University Press.

Rydgren, Jens. 2008. "Immigration Sceptics, Xenophobes or Racists? Radical Right-Wing Voting in Six West European Countries." *European Journal of Political Research* 47 (6): 737–765.

   2002. "Radical Right Populism in Sweden: Still a Failure, but for How Long?" *Scandinavian Political Studies* 25 (1): 27–56.

Saideman, Stephen. 2001. *The Ties That Divide: Ethnic Politics, Foreign Policy, and International Conflict*. New York: Columbia University Press.

Sartori, Giovanni. 1976. *Parties and Party Systems*. Cambridge: Cambridge University Press.

Schmitt, Carl. 1976 [1932]. *The Concept of the Political*. New Brunswick, NJ: Rutgers University Press.

Schopflin, Gyorgy. 2007. "Democracy, Populism, and the Political Crisis in Hungary. A Reply to Thomas von Ahn." *Eurozine*, September 18.

Scrutton, Alistair and Andrius Sytas. 2015. "Lithuania Stages 'Little Green Man' War Games with an Eye on Moscow." Available at: businessinsider.com/r-lithuania-stages-little-green-man-war-games-with-eye-on-moscow-2015-5.

Shafir, Michael. 2008. "Rotten Apples, Bitter Pears: An Updated Motivational Typology of Romania's Radical Right's Anti-Semitic Postures in Post-communism." *Journal for the Study of Religions and Ideologies* 7 (21): 149–187.

   2007. "Vox Populi, Vox Dei and the [Head-]Master's Voice: Mass and Intellectual Neo-Populism in Contemporary Romania." In *Populism in Central Europe*, ed. Václav Nekvapil and Maria Staszkiewucz. Prague: Association for International Affairs, pp. 81–109.

   2002. "Between Denial and 'Comparative Trivialization': Holocaust Negotiations in Post-Communist East Central Europe." *Analysis of Current Trends in Antisemitism* 19: 1–77.

2000. "Marginalization of Mainstream? The Extreme Right in Post-Communist Romania." In: *The Politics of the Extreme Right: From the Margins to the Mainstream*, ed. Paul Hainsworth. London: Pinter, pp. 247–267.

1997. "Romania's Road to 'Normalcy.'" *Journal of Democracy* 8 (2): 144–158.

Shekhovtsov, Anton. 2015. "Whither the Ukrainian Far Right?" Anton Shekhovtsov's blog. January 30. Available at: http://anton-shekhovtsov .blogspot.com/2015/01/whither-ukrainian-far-right.html.

2013. "From Para-Militarism to Radical Right-Wing Populism: The Rise of the Ukrainian Far-Right Party Svoboda." In: *Right-Wing Populism in Europe: Politics and Discourse*, ed. Ruth Wodak, Majid Khosravinik and Brigitte Mral. London: Bloomsbury, pp. 249–263.

2011. "The Creeping Resurgence of the Ukrainian Radical Right? The Case of the Freedom Party." *Europe-Asia Studies* 63 (2): 203–228.

Shekhovtsov, Anton, and Andreas Umland. 2014. "Ukraine's Radical Right." *Journal of Democracy* 25 (3): 58–63.

Shevel, Oxana. 2002. "Nationality in Ukraine: Some Rules of Engagement." *East European Politics and Society* 16 (2): 386–413.

2001. "Crimean Tatars and the Ukrainian State: The Challenge of Politics, the Use of Law, and the Meaning of Rhetoric." *Krimski Studii* 1 (7): 109–129.

Shulman, Stephen. 2005. "Ukrainian Nation-building under Kuchma." *Problems of Post-Communism* 52 (5): 32–47.

Sidanius, Jim, and Felicia Pratto. 2001. *Social Dominance: An Intergroup Theory of Social Hierarchy and Oppression*. New York: Cambridge University Press.

Siroky, David, and Christopher Hale. 2017. "Inside Irredentism: A Global Empirical Analysis." *American Journal of Political Science* 61 (1): 117–128.

Siroky, David, and John Cuffe. 2015. "Lost Autonomy, Nationalism and Separatism." *Comparative Political Studies* 48 (1): 3–34.

Siroky, David, and Michael Hechter. 2016. "Ethnicity, Class and Civil War: The Role of Hierarchy, Segmentation and Crosscutting Cleavages." *Civil Wars* 18 (1): 91–107.

SITA. 2010. "Slota: Maďarská armáda cvičí prechod cez Dunaj." *Aktualne. sk*, January 10. Available at: http://aktualne.centrum.sk/domov/poli tika/clanek.phtml?id=1199397.

*Slovak Spectator*. 2012. "Three Dead and Two Wounded after Police Shooting in Hurbanovo." *Slovak Spectator*, June 17. Available at: http:// spectator.sme.sk/c/20043753/three-dead-and-two-wounded-after-police-shooting-in-hurbanovo.html.

SME. 2018. "Domov. Dankov návrh o antisemitizme ohrozuje slobodu slova, upozornili aktivisti October 23." Available at: https://domov .sme.sk/c/20944788/dankov-navrh-definicie-antisemitizmu-ohrozuje-slo bodu-slova.html.

2010. "Švantner: SNS hrozí rozpad. Belousovová to poprela." September 21, Available at: www.sme.sk/c/5558286/svantner-sns-hrozi-rozpad-belousovova-to-poprela.html.

2006. "Ján Slota Attacked Hungarians before the Elections." Available at: www.sme.sk/c/3124289/Petransky-Jozefa-Tisa-si-pre-nieco-vazim.html.

Smetanková, Daša. 2012. "Menšinová politika v období rokov 1993 až 1998 na Slovensku. Komparácia rómskej a maďarskej menšiny." *Acta Politologica* 4 (2): 154–166.

Smith, Jason. 2010. "Does Crime Pay? Issue Ownership, Political Opportunity, and the Populist Right in Western Europe." *Comparative Political Studies* 43 (11): 1471–1498.

Smolar, Aleksander. 2007. "Poland: Radicals in Power." *Eurozine*, September 18.

Smooha, Sammy, and Priit Jarve. 2005. *The Fate of Ethnic Democracy in Europe*. Budapest: Open Society Institute: ECMI.

Sniderman, Paul, Louk Hagendoorn and Markus Prior. 2004. "Predisposing Factors and Situational Triggers: Exclusionary Reactions to Immigrant Minorities." *American Political Science Review* 98 (1): 35–49.

SNS. 2013. "A.Danko pre TASR: Lacné divadlo SMK." SNS news, February 15. Available at: www.sns.sk/aktuality/a-danko-pre-tasr-lacne-divadlo-smk/.

Snyder, Timothy. 2009. "The Historical Reality of Eastern Europe." *East European Politics and Societies* 23 (1): 7–12.

Solchanyk, Roman. 2011. Україні 20 років: мова. Ukraini 20 rokiv: mova; 19.06. Available at: http://zgroup.com.ua/article.php?articleid=4844.

1999. "The Radical Right in Ukraine." In: *The Radical Right in Central and Eastern Europe since 1989*, ed. Sabrina Ramet. University Park: Pennsylvania State University Press.

Soroka, Stuart, Keith Banting and Richard Johnson. 2006. "Immigration and Redistribution in a Global Era." In: *Globalization and Egalitarian Redistribution*, ed. Pranab Bardhan, Samuel Bowles and Michael Wallerstein. Princeton: Princeton University Press, pp. 261–288.

Spies, Dennis, and Simon Franzmann. 2011. "A Two-Dimensional Approach to the Political Opportunity Structure of Extreme Right Parties in Western Europe." *West European Politics* 34 (5): 1044–1069.

Spirova, Maria. 2008. "The Bulgarian Socialist Party: The Long Road to Europe." *Communist and Post-Communist Studies* 41: 481–495.

Spravy Pravda. 2012. "Pollák: Streľba v Hurbanove je neospravedlniteľná a nepochopiteľná." Available at: https://spravy.pravda.sk/domace/cla nok/247019-pollak-strelba-v-hurbanove-je-neospravedlnitelna-a-nepo chopitelna/.

State Department. 2014. "Slovakia 2013 Human Rights Report." Available at: www.state.gov/documents/organization/220542.pdf.

Stefanova, Boyka. 2009. "Ethnic Nationalism, Social Structure, and Political Agency: Explaining Electoral Support for the Radical Right in Bulgaria." *Ethnic and Racial Studies* 32 (9): 1534–1556.

——— 2007. "Testing Theories of Radical Right Voting: Social Structure versus Political Agency and Electoral Support for the Attack Party in Bulgaria." Paper presented at the Annual Meeting of the American Political Science Association, Chicago, August 30–September 2.

Stockemer, Daniel. 2017. "The Economic Crisis (2009–2013) and Electoral Support for the Radical Right in Western Europe – Some New and Unexpected Findings." *Social Science Quarterly* 98 (5): 1536–1553.

——— 2015a. "Immigration or Immigration Perceptions? What Accounts for the Electoral Success of the Radical Right in Europe?" *Journal of Common Market Studies*. First published online: 10.1111/jcms.12341.

——— 2015b. "Introduction to the Special Issue: Explaining the Spike in Electoral Support for the Front National in France." *French Politics* 13 (4): 319–323.

Stojarová, Věra. 2012. "The Extreme Right in Croatia, Bosnia-Herzegovina and Serbia." In: *Mapping the Extreme Right in Contemporary Europe: From Local to Transnational*, ed. Andrea Mammone, Emmanuel Godin and Brian Jenkins. London: Routledge, pp. 143–158.

Stojarova, Vera, and Peter Emerson, ed. 2013. *Party Politics in the Western Balkans*. London: Routledge.

Stokes, Donald. 1963. "Spatial Models of Party Competition." *American Political Science Review* 57 (2): 368–377.

Stolz, Joelle. 2011. "Roma Hunting Season Set to Continue." *Presseurop*, April 6. Available at: www.presseurop.eu/en/content/article/586961-roma-hunting-season-set-continue.

Stuttaford, Andrew. 2015. "A Hybrid Defense for the Baltic States." *National Review*. Available at: www.nationalreview.com/corner/421840/hybrid-defense-baltic-states-andrew-stuttaford.

Svoboda. 2012. "Свобода" впевнено долає 5% бар'єр на шляху до Верховної Ради. March 6. Official Svoboa party site. Available at: www.tyahnybok.info/diyalnist/novyny/028299/.

Swank, Duane, and Hans-Georg Betz. 2003. "Globalization, the Welfare State and Right-Wing Populism in Western Europe." *Socio-Economic Review* 1 (2): 215–245.

Symonenko, Petro. 2012. Симоненко договорився: комуністи навчили українців писати, Вівторок, 29.5., *Pravda*. Available at: www.pravda.com.ua/news/2012/05/29/6965496/.

Szczerbiak, Aleks. 2017. "An Anti-establishment Backlash That Shook Up the Party System? The October 2015 Polish Parliamentary Election." *European Politics and Society* 18 (4): 404–427.

    2015. "What Does Paweł Kukiz's Election Success Mean for Polish Politics?" *EUROPP* blog, May 15. Available at: http://blogs.lse.ac.uk/euro ppblog/2015/05/15/whatdoes-pawel-kukizs-election-success-mean-for-polish-politics/.

    2007. "'Social Poland' Defeats 'Liberal Poland'? The September–October 2005 Polish Parliamentary and Presidential Elections." *Journal of Communist Studies and Transition Politics* 23 (2): 203–232.

Szelényi, Iván, and Szonja Szelényi. 1995. "Circulation or Reproduction of Elites during the Postcommunist Transformation of Eastern Europe." *Theory and Society* 24: 615–638.

Szocs, Laszlo. 1998. "A Tale of the Unexpected: The Extreme Right *vis-à-vis* Democracy in Post-Communist Hungary." *Ethnic and Racial Studies* 21 (6): 1096–1115.

Taggart, Paul, and Aleks Szczerbiak. 2004. "Contemporary Euroscepticism in the Party Systems of the European Union Candidate States of Central and Eastern Europe." *European Journal of Political Research* 43: 1–27.

Tamas, Miklós. 2007. "Counter-Revolution against a Counter-Revolution." *Eurozine*, September 18. Available at: www.eurozine.com/articles/2007-09-18-tamas-en.html.

TASR. 2016. "Government Proxy for Roma Pollak Wants PG to Ban LSNS." *NewsNow.sk*, March 15. Available at: https://newsnow.tasr .sk/policy/government-proxy-for-roma-pollak-wants-pg-to-ban-lsns/.

Tavits, Margit. 2007. "Party Systems in the Making: The Emergence and Success of New Parties in New Democracies." *British Journal of Political Science* 38: 113–133.

    2005. "The Development of Stable Party Support: Electoral Dynamics in Post-Communist Europe." *American Journal of Political Science* 49 (2): 283–298.

Temple, Mark. 1996. "The Politicization of History: Marshal Antonescu and Romania." *East European Politics and Societies* 10 (3): 457–503.

Thompson, Michael, Richard Ellis and Aaron Wildavsky. 1990. *Cultural Theory*. Boulder: Westview Press.

Tismaneau, Vladimir. 2007. "Leninist Legacies, Pluralist Dilemmas." *Journal of Democracy* 18 (4): 34–39.

Topky. 2018. "Katolícki kňazi podporujú Kotlebu! Vo výzve zverejnili dôvody, je medzi nimi aj kontroverzný Kuffa." Available at: www.topky.sk/cl/100535/1711385/Katolicki-knazi-podporuju-Kotlebu–Vo-vyzve-zverejnili-dovody–je-medzi-nimi-aj-kontroverzny-Kuffa.

Tucker, Joshua. 2006. *Regional Economic Voting: Russia, Poland, Hungary, Slovakia, and the Czech Republic, 1990–1999.* New York: Cambridge University Press.

Tworzecki, Hubert. 2003. *Learning to Choose: Electoral Politics in East-Central Europe.* Palo Alto: Stanford University Press.

Ucen, Peter. 2007. "Parties, Populism, and Anti-establishment Politics in East Central Europe." *SAIS Review* 27 (1): 49–62.

Ukrainian News. 2011. Львовский облсовет пожаловался Януковичу на нежелание министров общаться на украинском. Українські Новини (Ukranews.com). http://ukranews.com/news/48963.—.ru07.25.

Umland, Andreas. 2014. "Is Tiahnybok a Patriot? How the Spread of Banderite Slogans and Symbols Undermines Ukrainian Nation-building." *Foreign Policy*, January.

2013. "Starting Post-Soviet Ukrainian Right-Wing Extremism Studies from Scratch." *Russian Politics and Law* 51 (5): 3–10.

2010. "The Rise of the Radical Right in Ukraine." *Kyiv Post*, October 21. Available at: www.kyivpost.com/news/opinion/op_ed/detail/87119/print/

Umland, Andreas, and Anton Shekhovtsov. 2013. "Ultraright Party Politics in Post-Soviet Ukraine and the Puzzle of the Electoral Marginalism of Ukrainian Ultranationalists in 1994–2009." *Russian Politics and Law* 51 (5): 33–58.

2010. Праворадикальная партийная политика в постсоветской Украине и загадка электоральной маргинальности украинских ультранационалистов в 1994–2009 гг. Ab *Imperio*, 2.

UNA-UNSO. 2009. "Andrew Shkil Joined Yulia Tymoshenko Faction." Available at: www.unaunso.org/av/mainview.asp?TT_id=16&TX_id=118.

Urbinati, Nadia. 2014. *Democracy Disfigured.* Cambridge, MA: Harvard University Press.

Vachudova, Milada. 2008a. "Tempered by the EU? Political Parties and Party Systems before and after Accession." *Journal of European Public Policy* 15 (6): 861–879.

2008b. "Centre-Right Parties and Political Outcomes in East Central Europe." *Party Politics* 14 (4): 387–405.

2006. "The Foreign Policy of EU Enlargement in the Western Balkans and Beyond: Does It Lessen a North–South Divide?" Paper presented at the annual meeting of the International Studies Association, San Diego, California, March 22.

2005. *Europe Undivided: Democracy, Leverage, and Integration after Communism.* Oxford: Oxford University Press.

Vachudova, Milada, and Liesbet Hooghe. 2009. "Postcommunist Politics in a Magnetic Field: How Transition and EU Accession Structure Party Competition on European Integration." *Comparative European Politics* 7 (2): 179–212.

2006. "Euroscepticism after Communism." Paper presented at the conference on "Causes and Consequences of Euroskepticism," July 1–2, Vrije Universiteit Amsterdam.

Van der Brug, Wouter. 2004. "Issue Ownership and Party Choice." *Electoral Studies* 23 (2): 209–233.

Van der Brug, Wouter, and Meindert Fennema. 2007. "What Causes People to Vote for a Radical Right Party? A Review of Recent Work." *International Journal of Public Opinion Research* 19 (4): 474–487.

Van der Brug, Wouter, Meindert Fennema and Jean Tillie. 2005. "Why Some Anti-immigrant Parties Fail and Others Succeed: A Two-Step Model of Aggregate Electoral Support." *Comparative Political Studies* 38 (5): 537–573.

Van Spanje, Joost, and Wouter van der Brug. 2009. "The Exclusion of Western European Anti-immigration Parties and Its Consequences for Party Choice." *Acta Politica* 44 (4): 353–384.

Vangeli, Anastas. 2011. "Nation-Building Ancient Macedonian Style: The Origins and the Effects of the So-Called Antiquization in Macedonia." *Nationalities Papers: The Journal of Nationalism and Ethnicity* 39 (1): 13–32.

Vanhuysse, Pieter. 2006. *Divide and Pacify: Strategic Social Policies and Political Protests in Post-Communist Democracies.* Budapest: Central European University Press.

Vano, Boris. 2001. "Demografická charakteristika romskej populácie v SR." Infostat – Institut Informatiky a Statistiky. Výskumné demografické centrum. Bratislava: Akty. Available at: www.infostat.sk/vdc/pdf/rom.pdf.

Varga, Mihai. 2014. "Hungary's 'Anti-capitalist' Far-Right: Jobbik and the Hungarian Guard." *Nationalities Papers: The Journal of Nationalism and Ethnicity* 42 (5): 791–807.

Vasovic, Aleksandar. 2005. "Far-Right Group Flexes during Ukraine 'Revolution.'" National Coalition Supporting Eurasian Jewry/AP, January 1. Available at: www.ncsj.org/AuxPages/010105AP_Ukraine.shtml.

Vassilev, Rossen. 2001. "Post-Communist Bulgaria's Ethnopolitics." *The Global Review of Ethnopolitics* 1 (2): 37–53.

Verchovnaya, Rada. 2009. "Andriy Shkil Elected to Verkhovna Rada for the Lviv District." Available at: http://gska2.rada.gov.ua/pls/site/p_exdepu tat?d_id=5412&skl=5.

Vermeersch, Peter. 2006. *The Romani Movement: Minority Politics and Ethnic Mobilization in Contemporary Central Europe.* Oxford: Berghahn Books.

Vigderhous, Gideon. 1977. "The Level of Measurement and 'Permissible' Statistical Analysis in Social Research." *Pacific Sociological Review* 20 (1): 61–72.

Volden, Craig, and Clifford Carruba. 2004. "The Formation of Oversized Coalitions in Parliamentary Democracies." *American Journal of Political Science* 48 (3): 521–537.

Volkens, Andrea, Onawa Lacewell, Sven Regel, Henrike Schultze and Annika Werner. 2010. The Manifesto Data Collection. Manifesto Project (MRG/CMP/MARPOR). Berlin: Wissenschaftszentrum Berlin für Sozialforschung (WZB).

Volovici, Leon. 1994. "Antisemitism in Post-Communist Eastern Europe: A Marginal or Central Issue?" *Analysis of Current Trends in Antisemitism* 5: 1–13.

von Beyme, Klaus. 1988. "Right-Wing Extremism in Post-War Europe." *West European Politics* 11 (2): 1–18.

Vona, Gábor. 2009. "What Do We Mean by Radicalism?" *Jobbik*, November 28. Available at: www.jobbik.com/hungary-news/3138.html.

Votruba, Martin. 1998. "Linguistic Minorities in Slovakia." In: *Linguistic Minorities in Central and Eastern Europe*, ed. Christina Paulston and Donald Peckham. Clevedon: Cromwell Press, pp. 255–278.

Vowles, Jack, and Georgios Xezonakis. 2010. "From Positional to Valence Issues? Ideology, Leadership, Globalization, and Electoral Choice." Paper presented at the Elections, Public Opinion, and Parties Conference, University of Essex, September 10–12; working paper.

Waldron-Moore, Pamela. 1999. "Eastern Europe at the Crossroads of Democratic Transition." *Comparative Political Studies* 32 (1): 36–62.

Warner, Carolyn. 2007. *The Best System Money Can Buy.* Ithaca: Cornell University Press.

Way, Lucan, and Steven Levitsky 2007. "Linkage, Leverage, and the Post-Communist Divide." *East European Politics and Societies* 21 (1): 48–66.

Weaver, Eric. 2007. "The Communist Legacy? Populist but Not Popular – The Foreign Policies of the Hungarian Radical Right." In: *Europe for the Europeans: The Foreign and Security Policy of the Populist Radical Right*, ed. Christina Schori Liang. Aldershot: Ashgate, pp. 177–185.

2006. *National Narcissism: The Intersection of the Nationalist Cult and Gender in Hungary*. Oxford: Lang.

Wilkinson, Steven. 2004. *Votes and Violence: Electoral Competition and Ethnic Riots in India*. Cambridge: Cambridge University Press.

Wilson, Andrew. 1997. *Ukrainian Nationalism in the 1990s: A Minority Faith*. Cambridge: Cambridge University Press.

Wimmer, Andreas. 2017. "National Identity and Ethnopolitical Inequality around the World." *World Politics* 69 (4): 605–639.

Wintrobe, Ronald. 2006. *Rational Extremis: The Political Economy of Radicalism*. Cambridge: Cambridge University Press.

Wittenberg, Jason. 2006. *Crucibles of Political Loyalty*. New York: Cambridge University Press.

Womick, Jake, Tobias Rothmund, Flavio Azevedo, Laura King and John Jost. 2019. "Group-Based Dominance and Authoritarian Aggression Predict Support for Donald Trump in the 2016 U.S. Presidential Election." *Social Psychological and Personality Science* 10 (5): 643–652.

Wood, Dan. 2011. "Maximum Likelihood and Limited Dependent Variables." 2011 Essex Summer School in Social Science Data Analysis and Collection.

World Bank, Foundation S.P.A.C.E., INEKO and the Open Society Institute. 2002. *Poverty and Welfare of Roma in the Slovak Republic*. Bratislava. Available at: http://siteresources.worldbank.org/EXTROMA/Resources/povertyinslovak.pdf.

Zachid.net. 2010. Україна витратить 1,6 млн гривень на регіональні мови. 18 червня. Available at: http://zaxid.net/news/showNews.do?ukrayina_vitratit_16_mln_griven_na_regionalni_movi&objectId=1104882.

Zákon. 1995. Jazykový zákon – Zákon č. 270/1995 Z. z. o štátnom jazyku Slovenskej republiky. Available at: www.vyvlastnenie.sk/predpisy/jazy kovy-zakon/.

2009. Zákon Národnej rady Slovenskej republiky #184/1999. Available at: www.ucps.sk/Zakon_184_1999_o_pouzivani_jazykov_narodnostnych_mensin/.

Zeman, Václav. 2008. "Kam míří česká ultrapravice." MF DNES, May 23. Available at: http://peopleinneed.cz/index2.php?id=143&idArt=815.

ZIK. 2011. Колесніченко став на захист звільненого за «телячу мову» працівника ДАІ. January 28. Available at: http://zik.ua/ua/news/2011/01/28/269368.

Zuber, Christina, and Edina Szöcsik. 2015. "Ethnic Outbidding and Nested Competition: Explaining the Extremism of Ethnonational Minority Parties in Europe." *European Journal for Political Research* 54 (4): 784–801.

# Index

Abdelal, Rawi, 3
abortion, 66, 72–3, 156, 189
Abramson, Paul, 51, 107
accountability, 30, 97
Adams, James, 107
Albania, 54, 60, 74, 79, 214. *See also*
    Eastern Europe
Aldrich, John, 51, 107, 137
Alesina, Alberto, 216
anti-elitism. *See* anti-establishment
anti-establishment, 6, 50, 69, 75, 154,
    160, 217, 232
anti-globalism, 6
anti-Semitism, 55, 65, 154, 156, 187,
    190, 192
Art, David, 6, 11, 23, 107
Arzheimer, Kai, 23, 25, 34, 50
authoritarian values, 123, 139. *See also*
    grid-group
Azarov government, 162

Bale, Tim, 107
Bandera, Stepan, 187, 189
Beissinger, Mark, 20, 63
Berényi, József, 109
Bermeo, Nancy, 218
Bernhard, Michael, 217
Biedroń, Robert, 39
Bilaniuk, Laada, 166
Bochsler, Daniel, 55
Bosnia and Herzegovina, 60, 63, 75,
    219. *See also* Eastern Europe
Bratislava, 156
Brubaker, Rogers, 20
Bulgaria, 48, 57, 60, 74, 76, 105.
    *See also* Eastern Europe
Bustikova, Lenka, 30, 55, 218

Capoccia, Giovanni, 107
Carter, Elisabeth, 34

Catholic Church, 75, 156
censored models, 86–7
census, 59–60
Central European University, 65
Chandra, Kanchan, 53
civil society, 69
cleavage, 46–7, 53, 65–6, 77, 97, 156,
    162, 164, 180. *See also* cross-
    cutting cleavages
coalitions, 37, 47, 85, 110, 127, 152
    bilateral opposite and, 88, 115
communism, 115
    fall of, 4, 20, 213
conflict
    native-immigrant, 59
    violent, 59, 79, 108, 160, 173, 193,
        197, 210, 219
conservative, 1, 5, 9, 12, 22, 38–40, 72,
    74–6, 223. *See also* authoritarian
    values; grid-group
consociational theory, 219
Constitution, 38, 65, 157, 162, 168
contact theory, 58
corruption, 6–7, 10, 75, 105, 159, 173,
    197, 214
Crimea, 160, 164, 167–8, 208
Croatia, 63, 74, 79, 121, 217. *See also*
    Eastern Europe
cross-cutting cleavages, 53
Czech Republic, 57, 60, 74, 79, 105,
    110, 239. *See also* Eastern
    Europe
Czechoslovakia, 55, 63, 109, 114, 143,
    214. *See also* Eastern Europe

Dancygier, Rafaela, 59
D'Anieri, Paul, 170
Danko, Andrej, 156
Darden, Keith, 163
de Lange, Sarah, 6

Decade of Roma Inclusion: 2005–2015, 102
Demand for Extremism Index, (DEREX), 27–30
democracy, 9, 12, 154, 214
  backsliding, 75
  democratization, 8–14
  liberal, 12–13, 217–18
dominant group, 8, 20–1, 27, 35–9, 42–4, 54–7, 63, 77, 113, 121–2, 136, 152, 175, 212, 220; *see also* group hierarchy
  titular group, 56, 184
Donbas, 160, 168, 173, 194, 197
Donetsk, 164, 166–7
double-barreled question, 137
Douglas, Mary, 72

Eastern Europe, 2, 4, 6, 11–12, 19, 25, 31, 38, 44, 55–6, 70, 72, 74–5, 77, 102, 108, 213, 216–17, 219, 221. *See also names of specific countries*
Eatwell, Roger, 22, 46
EBRD transition scores, 94
economic threats, 30, 122, 133–4, 175, 182, 195–7; *see also* explanations, demand side, economic
  liberalization, 41, 57, 76, 94
  welfare state, 31
effective number of parties, 97
elections
  founding, 5, 214, 217
  Hungary (2010), 35, 106
  Hungary (2010 and 2014), 75
  Macedonia (2002), 79
  Macedonia (2016), 154
  Poland (2001 and 2005), 75
  Poland (2015), 34
  Romania (2000 and 2004), 75
  Slovakia (1994 and 2012), 110
  Slovakia (1998), 115, 117
  Slovakia (2002), 118
  Slovakia (2012), 47, 69, 119
  Ukraine (2009), 208
  Ukraine (2012), 160–1, 172, 179
  Ukraine (2014), 160, 208
  Ukraine (2015), 179
electoral threshold, 97
elites, 8. *See also* anti-establishment
Estonia, 15, 27, 29, 54, 60, 74, 79, 217. *See also* Eastern Europe

Euromaidan, 160, 172, 208
European Court of Human Rights, 69
European Union, 6, 38, 40, 56, 94, 117, 137, 153, 215
  enlargement, 6, 38, 41, 49, 94
  European Charter for Minority Languages, 162, 164, 169
expert surveys, 73
  Chapel Hill Expert Survey, 78
  Democratic Accountability and Linkages Project, 78
  Party Policy in Modern Democracies, 78
explanations, demand side, 25, 36
  economic, 2, 4, 7, 9, 16, 22, 24–5, 31, 34, 41–2, 49, 53, 75, 77, 94, 97, 104, 111, 122, 126, 130, 134, 139, 161, 182, 189, 195, 197, 201, 208, 213–14
explanations, supply side, 23, 35
extreme right, 18, 187, 232, 235. *See also* niche parties

far right, 1, 5, 22, 34, 40, 70, 77, 102, 105. *See also* niche parties
Fico, Robert, 118, 218
Fish, Steven, 20
Frye, Timothy, 42

Galicia, 163, 169, 175, 192
Ganev, Venelin, 48
Gelner, Ernest, 63
Georgia, 64. *See also* Eastern Europe
Golder, Matt, 86
Golder, Sona, 18, 45
grid-group, 71–6, 78–9, 223–32
Grittersova, Jana, 2
Grodzka, Anna, 39
group hierarchy, 33, 44, 158; *see also* dominant group; group hostility
  demoted groups, 43–5
  status reversal, 22, 35, 45, 65–6, 159, 161, 175, 206, 209, 216
  welfare chauvinism, 33
group hostility, 20, 23, 29, 32, 43, 111–12, 120, 128–30, 152, 154, 175, 183, 185–95, 201–2, 208, 213, 216; *see also* group hierarchy
  homophobia, 4, 39, 189
  prejudice, 21, 27, 29, 119–20, 122, 130

racism, 29, 104
xenophobia, 4, 7, 23, 25, 27, 130,
    193, 201, 208, 218
Grzymała-Busse, Anna, 19
Guasti, Petra, 218
Guiliano, Elise, 164
Gyarfášová, Olga, 110
Gyurcsány, Ferenc, 103

Hagendoorn, Louk, 137
Hanley, Sean, 110
Haughton, Tim, 110
Hechter, Michael, 44, 63
Herrera, Yoshiko, 3
Hódmezővásárhely, 65
Horowitz, Donald, 34, 50, 63
human rights, 57, 118. *See also*
    European Court of Human Rights
Hungary, 9, 29, 35, 38, 41, 65, 74–5,
    77, 101–7, 109, 120, 136, 139,
    142, 214, 217–18. *See also* Eastern
    Europe
Huta Pieniacka, 171

identity priming, 112, 148–9
Ignazi, Piero, 23, 107
immigration, 46, 51, 66, 77, 217
independence, 1, 5, 17, 55, 74, 76, 110,
    114, 160, 162, 169, 219. *See also*
    sovereignty threats
inter-war period, 11, 13, 30, 97, 192.
    *See also* legacies
Ishiyama, John, 72
Israel, 156, 221
Ivano-Frankivska, region, 169, 179

Jenne, Erin, 107

Kaczyński, Jarosław, 218
Kaczyński, Lech, 40, 171
Kasekamp, Andres, 54
Katchanovski, Ivan, 187
Katz, Richard, 34
Kelley, Judith, 107
Kharkiv, 172
Kitschelt, Herbert, 12, 23, 34
Klaus, Václav, 114
Klitschko, Vitali, 179
Kolev, Kiril, 60
Kopecky, Petr, 4
Kopstein, Jeffrey, 60

Kotleba, Marian, 153–7
Krekó, Peter, 30
Kuchma, Leonid, 187
Kudelia, Serhiy, 187
Kukiz, Paweł, 39
KUN, 166, 170
Kuzio, Taras, 170

Laitin, David, 63
language law, 2, 47, 113, 167–8, 172
language rights, 7, 47, 110, 115, 168,
    182
Latvia, 1–2, 30, 54, 60, 74, 79, 217.
    *See also* Eastern Europe
legacies, 11–13, 97, 114, 187
Lety, 55
Lijphart, Arend, 219
Lithuania, 74. *See also* Eastern Europe
Liu, Amy, 48
Luhansk, 164, 166–7, 172
lustration, 174
Lviv, 163–4, 169, 171

Macedonia, 54, 60, 74, 79. *See also*
    Eastern Europe
mainstream parties, 34–5, 39, 41, 50,
    53, 59–60, 77, 97, 101, 106, 111,
    127, 129, 142, 153, 158, 160, 206,
    209, 212, 216–21
convergence, 34, 49, 93, 101, 210,
    217
non-proximate, 35, 51, 101, 107,
    187, 209; *see also* niche parties
proximate, 23, 34–5, 50–1, 53, 73,
    98, 106–7, 127, 147, 158, 209,
    216
radicalized, 10, 24, 78, 217–18
Mair, Peter, 34
Matica Slovenská, 118
Mečiar, Vladimír, 114
Medgyessy, Peter, 103
media, 117, 172, 174
Meguid, Bonnie, 23, 34–5
Mesežnikov, Grigorij, 110
Minkenberg, Michael, 24, 34
minority accommodation, 1, 21, 45–53
minority groups, 8, 11–12, 33, 40, 56,
    59, 110, 120, 190, 216; *see also*
    census
Albanians, 79
Crimean Tatars, 168, 183, 194

minority groups (cont.)
  gays and lesbians, 45, 48, 55
  Germans, 14, 63, 74
  Hungarians, 44, 58, 114–19
  Jews, 9, 55, 154, 190, 192
  Muslims, 55–6, 66, 154, 217, 221
  Roma, 9, 45, 55, 68–72, 102–6, 122,
    129
  Russians, 44, 54, 63, 182–93
  Turks, 14, 49, 57
Miskolc, 104
Moldova, 44, 60, 63, 79. *See also*
  Eastern Europe
Montenegro, 60, 79. *See also* Eastern
  Europe
monuments,
  Bandera, 190
Mudde, Cas, 25, 30

National Roma Minority Self-
  Government, 103
nationalism, 20, 72, 74, 152, 167, 189,
  214; *see also* dominant group;
  grid-group
nation building, 159, 190, 197
NATO, 136, 142
niche parties, 5, 9, 12, 24, 36, 41, 44,
  50, 110, 210, 212, 217–18
  bilateral opposite, 35, 45, 49–53, 58,
    72–3, 84, 88, 101, 103, 105–7,
    115, 142, 159, 168–9, 193, 206,
    209, 213, 216
  ethnic parties, 12, 17, 35, 45, 47, 52,
    54, 57, 60, 66, 74, 97, 110, 126,
    142, 152, 157, 209, 211, 220
  socially liberal parties, 12, 24–5, 39,
    47, 52–3, 72, 101, 212, 214, 239

Obama, Barack, 220
O'Dwyer, Conor, 55
Ohrid Agreement, 79
Okoč (Ekecs), 109
Olszański, Tadeusz, 167
Olzak, Susan, 63
Orange revolution, 173, 175, 182, 186,
  201, 206
Orbán, Viktor, 34, 65, 143
other, the, 9
OUN, 170, 187
OUN-B, 190

outbidding, ethnic, 34, 65, 107. *See also*
  polarization

panel data, 86, 212
paramilitary, 68, 154
  home guards, 65, 68, 106
party manifesto, 69, 76, 85
Pasztor, Albert, 104
people, the, 8–9, 21
Petersen, Roger, 63
Pirro, Andrea, 25, 34
pluralism, 5, 8–9, 23, 42, 58, 212, 217
Poland, 29–30, 34, 38–41, 55, 59, 75,
  77, 217–18. *See also* Eastern
  Europe
polarization, 34, 42–3, 52, 93, 101,
  103, 148, 161, 164, 172, 185, 190,
  206, 221
policy hostility, 7, 23, 33, 43, 59, 111,
  119–28, 143, 147, 176, 182–5,
  190, 201, 206, 215
  governmental support, 110, 112,
    116, 119, 123, 143, 152, 206
  welfare chauvinism, 27, 31, 33, 77,
    122, 216
political parties
  Alliance of Free Democrats (SzDSz),
    102
  Ataka, 48, 76
  Batkivshchyna, 173
  Bridge (Most-Híd), 126
  Civic Platform (PO), 40
  Communist Party of Ukraine, 167,
    186, 192
  Direction – Social Democracy
    (SMER), 40, 77, 126, 218
  Fidesz, 34, 38, 65, 75, 105, 143, 218
  Greater Romanian Party, 75
  Hungarian Life and Justice Party
    (MIÉP), 76, 105, 110
  Jobbik, 9, 35, 38, 65, 75–6, 102,
    105–6
  Kukiz'15, 38
  Law and Justice Party (PiS), 34, 40,
    77, 218
  League of Polish Families (LPR), 75
  left, 2, 4–5, 19, 24, 51, 53, 65, 76–8,
    103–5, 126, 187, 213, 218
  Movement for Rights and Freedoms
    Party (DPS), 48

Orange bloc, 179, 185, 187, 193, 202
Ordinary People, Independent Personalities (OL'aNO), 69
Palikot Movement, 39
Party of the Hungarian Coalition (SMK), 117, 119, 126
Party of Regions, 167, 169–70, 179, 186, 206
People's Party – Movement for a Democratic Slovakia (HZDS), 118, 126
People's Party – Our Slovakia party (ĽSNS), 153, 156
Right Sector, 173, 208
Slovak Democratic and Christian Union – Democratic Party (SDKU), 126, 142, 152–3
Slovak National Party (SNS), 29, 47, 74, 110
Svoboda, 160–1, 173, 176, 179, 187, 195, 201
VMRO-DPMNE, 79
Pollák, Peter, 69
Pop-Eleches, Grigore, 50
Popova, Maria, 48
populism, 6, 18. *See also* niche parties
Prior, Markus, 137
protest, 2, 31, 49, 156, 160, 167, 169, 171–2
Pytlas, Bartek, 25, 34

radical right, 2, 18–43, 66. *See also* niche parties
backlash, 13, 23, 43, 56, 58, 107, 158
definition, 5, 71, 76, 218
mobilization, 18–38
parties, 2, 5, 7, 25, 64, 71, 73, 79
resentment, 6, 8, 20, 22, 36–7, 47, 49, 54, 58, 79, 215
voters, 2, 6, 21–2, 32, 37, 45, 52, 57, 112, 120, 126–36, 141–53, 173, 177, 197–209
voting, 24, 57, 64, 77, 79, 94, 126, 129, 147, 176, 201, 206, 222
referendum, 1, 9, 47, 118, 156
refugees, 75, 119, 155, 217, 221. *See also* immigration
religion, 51. *See also* Catholic Church; grid-group

Romania, 44, 60, 74–5, 79, 101, 106, 217. *See also* Eastern Europe
Russia, 40, 160, 163, 173, 193, 208
Rydgren, Jens, 25, 30, 120

salience, 8–9, 36, 43–53, 83, 151
Sartori, Giovanni, 35, 58
Schmitt, Carl, 58
schooling, 47, 73, 88, 101, 162, 164, 166, 224. *See also* language law; language rights
Serbia, 74, 79, 217. *See also* Eastern Europe
Shekhovtsov, Anton, 161, 208
Shevel, Oksana, 176
Shukhevych, Roman, 187
Siroky, David, 137, 219
Slota, Ján, 114, 118
Slovakia, 29, 44, 47, 57, 60, 66, 68–9, 74, 77, 88, 109–58, 209, 217. *See also* Eastern Europe
Slovenia, 30, 60, 74, 79, 217. *See also* Eastern Europe
Sniderman, Paul, 137
social dominance theory, 3, 220
Solchanyk, Roman, 164
Somer-Topcu, Zeynep, 107
Soros, George, 65
sovereignty threats, 111, 130–42, 173. *See also* dominant group
Stalin, Joseph, 187
state, 10, 14, 20, 22, 27, 31–2, 36, 38–9, 41, 46, 57–8, 64, 71, 73, 76, 78, 104, 112, 114, 117, 136, 143, 158–9, 162, 169, 176, 207, 211, 214. *See also* dominant group; sovereignty threats
state building, 5, 10, 41, 211, 218
Stockemer, Daniel, 2
survey, 16
European Social, 27
expert, 73, 78. *See also* expert surveys
in Slovakia, 111, 113
in Ukraine, 180, 183
in Ukraine (2016), 187
World Value, 26
Symonenko, Petro, 167, 169, 186
Szczerbiak, Aleks, 39
Szöcsik, Edina, 54

Tavits, Margit, 97
Ternopil, 164, 169–71, 180
Tetovo, 79
Tiso, Jozef, 113
Trianon Treaty, 106, 136, 142
Trump, Donald, 220
Tucker, Joshua, 53
Tudor, Corneliu Vadim, 75
Tyahnybok, Oleh, 171
Tymoshenko, Yulia, 161, 167, 179, 201

Ukraine, 27, 57, 60, 63, 74, 159–210, 212, 216. *See also* Eastern Europe
Umland, Andreas, 172
UNA, 170
UPA, 187

Vachudova, Milada, 12, 94
vigilantes, 71. *See also* paramilitary
volatility, 2, 24–5, 31, 47, 50, 66, 75, 215, 221
  economic, 94
Vona, Gábor, 65, 105

Wang, Yi-ting, 60
waves, political mobilization, 5
Wildavsky, Aaron, 72
Wittenberg, Jason, 60

Yanukovych, Viktor, 160, 162, 168, 170, 179
Yushchenko, Viktor, 167, 171, 179, 182

Zuber, Christina, 54